Also in the Variorum Collected Studies Series

CHRISTOPHER PAGE
Music and Instruments of the Middle Ages: Studies on Texts and Performance

DAVID FALLOWS
Songs and Musicians in the Fifteenth Century

RICHARD L. CROCKER
Studies in Medieval Music Theory and the Early Sequence

RUTH STEINER
Studies in Gregorian Chant

ROGER BOWERS
English Church Polyphony: Singers and Sources from the 14th to the 17th Century

ERNEST H. SANDERS
French and English Polyphony of the 13th and 14th Centuries: Style and Notation

JAMES McKINNON
The Temple, the Church Fathers and Early Western Chant

Also by **Ashgate**

LIONEL PIKE
Hexachords in Late-Renaissance Music

RICHARD RASTALL and JULIE RAYNER
William Byrd: Six Part Fantasias in G Minor

JOHN HARLEY
William Byrd: Gentleman of the Chapel Royal

ANDREW ASHBEE
William Lawes (1602–1645): Essyas on his Life, Times and Music

TIMOTHY J. McGEE
Medieval and Renaissance Music: A Performers Guide

JOHNATHAN P. WAINWRIGHT
Musical Patronage in Seventeenth-Century England: Christopher, First Baron Hatton (1605–1670)

VARIORUM COLLECTED STUDIES SERIES

Music and Musicians
in Renaissance Rome
and Other Courts

DEDICATION

To the memory of Jean Lionnet, indefatigable student of the papal chapel, and true lover of music.

Richard Sherr

Music and Musicians
in Renaissance Rome
and Other Courts

VARIORUM

Aldershot · Brookfield USA · Singapore · Sydney

This edition copyright © 1999 by Richard Sherr.

Published in the Variorum Collected Studies Series by

Ashgate Publishing Limited
Gower House, Croft Road,
Aldershot, Hampshire GU11 3HR
Great Britain

Ashgate Publishing Company
Old Post Road,
Brookfield, Vermont 05036–9704
USA

ISBN 0–86078–768–0

British Library Cataloguing-in-Publication Data
Sherr, Richard
    Music and Musicians in Renaissance Rome and Other Courts. –
    (Variorum Collected Studies Series: CS641)
    1. Choral Music – Italy – Rome – History – 16th Century. 2. Choirs (Music) –
    Italy – Rome – History – 16th Century. 3. Music – Italy – Rome – 15th
    Century. 4. Music – Italy – Rome – 16th Century. 5. Papal Courts. 6. Music –
    Italy – 16th Century. I. Title
    782.5'0945'632'09031

US Library of Congress Cataloging-in-Publication Data
Sherr, Richard
    Music and Musicians in Rome and Other Courts / Richard Sherr.
        p.   cm. – (Variorum Collected Studies Series: CS 641)
    1. Church Music – Italy – Rome – 15th Century. 2. Church Music – Italy –
    Rome – 16th Century 3. Capella Sistina (Vatican Palace, Vatican City).
    I. Title. II. Series: Variorum Collected Studies Series: CS641.
    ML3033.8.R66S5   1999   99–11126
    781.71'2'00945634–dc21   CIP

The paper used in this publication meets the minimum requirements of the
American National Standard for Information Sciences – Permanence of
Paper for Printed Library Materials, ANSI Z39.48–1984. ♾ ™

Printed in Great Britain by Galliards, Great Yarmouth

VARIORUM COLLECTED STUDIES SERIES CS641

CONTENTS

Acknowledgements   viii

Preface   ix

MUSICIANS, MUSIC, AND PERFORMANCE PRACTICE AT THE PAPAL COURT

Musicians: Archival Studies

I	Notes on Some Papal Documents in Paris *Studi Musicali 12. Florence, 1983*	5–16
II	A Note on the Biography of Juan del Encina *Bulletin of the Comediantes 34. Los Angeles, 1982*	159–172
III	New Archival Data Concerning the Chapel of Clement VII *Journal of the American Musicological Society 29. Philadelphia, 1976*	472–478
IV	From the Diary of a 16th-Century Papal Singer *Current Musicology 25. New York, 1978*	83–98
V	A Letter from Paolo Animuccia: A Composer's Response to the Council of Trent *Early Music 12. Oxford, 1984*	74–78

Music

VI	Notes on the Biography and Music of Bertrandus Vaqueras (ca. 1450–1507) *Studien zur Musikgeschichte: Eine Festschrift für Ludwig Finscher, ed. Annegrit Laubenthal. Kassel, 1995*	111–122
VII	The Relationship between a Vatican Source of the Gloria of Josquin's Missa de Beata Virgine and Petrucci's Print *Atti del XIV Congresso della Società Internazionale di Musicologia, ed. Angelo Pompilio et al. Bologna, 1990*	266–271

VIII	*Illibata dei virgo nutrix* and Josquin's Roman Style *Journal of American Musicological Society 41.* *Philadelphia, 1987*	434–464
IX	The Medici Coat of Arms in a Motet for Leo X *Early Music 15. Oxford 1987*	31–35
X	Ceremonies for Holy Week, Papal Commissions, and Madness (?) in Early Sixteenth-Century Rome *Music in Renaissance Cities and Courts: Studies in Honor of Lewis Lockwood, ed. Jesse Ann Owens and Anthony M. Cummings, Detroit Monographs in Musicology/Studies in Music 18. Warren, 1997*	391–403

Performance Practice

XI	The Singers of the Papal Chapel and Liturgical Ceremonies in the Early Sixteenth Century: Some Documentary Evidence *Rome in the Renaissance, the City and the Myth, ed. P.A. Ramsey. Binghamton, 1982*	249–264
XII	Speculations on Repertory, Performance Practice, and Ceremony in the Papal Chapel in the Early Sixteenth Century *Studien zur Geschichte der päpstlichen Kapelle: Tagungsbericht Heidelberg 1989, Cappellae Apostolicae Sixtinaeque Collectanea Acta Monumenta, Collectanea II, ed. Bernhard Janz. Vatican City, 1994*	103–122
XIII	Performance Practice in the Papal Chapel during the 16th Century *Early Music 15. Oxford, 1987*	453–462
XIV	Competence and Incompetence in the Papal Choir in the Age of Palestrina *Early Music 22. Oxford, 1994*	606–629

ARCHIVAL STUDIES: OTHER RENAISSANCE COURTS AND CITIES

Mantua

XV	Mecenatismo Musicale a Mantova: Le Nozze di Vincenzo Gonzaga e Margherita Farnese *Rivista Italiana di Musicologia 19.* *Florence, 1984*	3–20
XVI	Guglielmo Gonzaga and the Castrati *Renaissance Quarterly 33. New York, 1980*	33–56

CONTENTS

XVII	The Publications of Guglielmo Gonzaga *Journal of the American Musicological Society 31. Philadelphia, 1978*	118–125

Florence

XVIII	Lorenzo de' Medici, Duke of Urbino, as a Patron of Music *Renaissance Studies in Honour of Craig Hugh Smyth, ed. Piero Morselli et al. Florence, 1985*	627–638
XIX	Verdelot in Florence, Coppini in Rome, and the Singer 'La Fiore' *Journal of the American Musicological Society 37. Philadelphia, 1984*	402–411

France

XX	The Membership of the Chapels of Louis XII and Anne de Bretagne in the Years Preceding their Deaths *The Journal of Musicology 6. Los Angeles, 1988*	60–82

Loreto

XXI	A Canon, A Choirboy, and Homosexuality in Late Sixteenth-Century Italy: A Case Study *Journal of Homosexuality 21. Binghamton, 1991*	1–22

Addenda and Corrigenda	1–6
Index of Names and Works	1–9
Index of Music Manuscripts	1

This volume consists of xii + 326 pages

ACKNOWLEDGMENTS

For permission to reprint these essays, I am grateful to The University of Chicago Press (for essays III, VIII XVII, XIX); Oxford University Press (for essays V, IX, XIII, XIV); Leo S. Olschki Publisher (for essays I, XV); Arizona State University (for essay XI); The Haworth Press (for essay XXI); *Current Musicology* (for essay IV); Bärenreiter Music Corporation (for essay VI); The Regents of the University of California (for essay XX); Giunti Gruppo Editoriale (for essay XVIII); Harmonie Park Press (for essay X); the Biblioteca Apostolica Vaticana (for essay XII); The Renaissance Society of America (for essay XVI); *The Bulletin of the Comediantes* (for essay II); and E.D.T. Edizioni di Torino (for essay VII).

PREFACE

The essays that follow have been chosen to reflect that part of my scholarly interests (for the moment, the greater part) that has been directed towards the study of musical institutions in 15th and 16th century Italy. Chief among these has been the papal choir in all its aspects, institutional history, membership, repertory, performance practice, but I have also had things to say about Mantua, Florence, and even France. Many of the essays in this volume have appeared in standard musicological journals, but some are extant only in Festschriften and Conference Reports or have appeared in journals not always consulted by the musicological community.

The material that stands behind these essays was drawn largely from archives. Archival research is not fashionable these days, but it was quite fashionable when I began my scholarly career, and I have never lost my interest in it. Most of my time has been spent in the archives of the enormous bureaucracy that was the Roman Curia, going through hundreds of thousands of stultifying legal documents that resulted from the never-ending quest for benefices that occupied the clerics of 15th- and 16th-century Europe and particularly the singers in the papal chapel my focus was on the reign of Pope Julius II (1503–1513). These documents can lead in fruitful directions, as anyone who has read the research of Alejandro Planchart on the early 15th century or the work of Pamela F. Starr on the middle 15th century, or has followed the recent revolution in Josquin's biography can attest. In the over 20 years in which I have made regular visits to the Archivio Segreto Vaticano, I have amassed a large fund of material, very little of which actually has made it into any of my articles, since in general I feel that articles are not the proper venue for the very long calendar of documents and lists that really should be consulted as the *pièces justicatives* of a monographic study or as part of a much larger documentary study of the papal chapel (both projects are in fact underway at the moment). I have made one exception to this in essay XX, but that was because the calendar of documents serves to establish the membership of two French royal chapels in the early 16th century. This seemed worth doing since there is almost no information about the French royal chapel and the study actually resulted in 'discovering' the chapel of Anne of Brittany, Queen of France. Results of work in the beneficial records will also be found in essays II and VI where it has been used in the service of establishing the details of biography of specific individuals. I have made much greater use of other types of documents, particularly the pay records of the papal chapel now housed in the Archivio di Stato of Rome, the archive of documents relating to the College of Singers in the Biblioteca Apostolica Vaticana, and even some non-beneficial documents in the Archivio Segreto. These have provided information that led to the studies of the institutional history of the papal singers and of their performance practices in essays II, III, and XI–XIV.

I have also worked in a very different kind of archive, the type that houses the diplomatic correspondence of an Italian court. These documents are individually always much more interesting than those in the Vatican, and I suppose it was a desire for a little relief from supplications and papal bulls, that I undertook a 'fishing expedition' to the Archivio di Stato of Mantua. There turned out to be many fish that could be caught, and the Archivio Gonzaga provided the documents that form the basis of essays XV–XVII. In 1982–83, I received a fellowship at the Villa i Tatti in Florence on the basis of a proposal that stated that I wished to spend most of my time writing about Rome. After a while, I figured that as long as I was there, I might pay at least one visit to the Archivio di Stato. Six months later, I emerged, having discovered somewhat to my shock that this most poured over of all archives still contained undiscovered material about music and musicians that was relevant not only to Florence, but to Rome as well. The result of this work may be seen in essays V, XVIII, XIX, and XXI. Finally, I have included in essays VI–X studies inspired not by archives but by music.

Studies concerned with the papal chapel in the 15th and 16th centuries form the bulk of the material presented in this volume. Essays in the first group provide some information about the membership of the chapel in periods for which there has been little documentation, relate some details from the private diary of a papal singer, and provide some information regarding two individuals who stood outside the chapel itself, even though one of them, Paolo Animuccia, tried hard but unsuccessfully to get in. The second group of essays deal with individual works that can be connected in some way with the repertory of the papal singers. Essay VIII in particular puts forth what I thought was a neat idea about the effect that local taste might have had on a great composer when he joined the papal chapel. This neat idea has met with little acceptance, but I still like it. The third group of papal chapel essays contains various thoughts on what the papal singers actually did and what they actually may have sounded like, one of them suggesting that perhaps we might not even want to try to to recreate that sound. The essays that follow collect various studies on Italian courts, Mantua in the reign of Guglielmo Gonzaga, Florence in the early 16th century, and the French chapels of the early 16th century. Finally, the volume ends with a story of illicit passion in the pilgrimage town of Loreto in which music played a small but not insignificant part, and which ends in an execution.

RICHARD SHERR

Northampton, MA
October, 1998

I

NOTES ON SOME PAPAL DOCUMENTS IN PARIS

Students of the history of the Vatican Archive have long known of its removal to Paris by Napoleon, and of its subsequent relocation (not without major losses).[1] Less widely known, perhaps, is that a certain number of volumes have remained in Paris, where they now form part of the series L of the Archives Nationales. In a recent article, Msgr. Martino Giusti has drawn attention to the Paris volumes by describing the detailed inventory made by Eugène Martin-Chabot, and now in the microfilm collection of the Archives Nationales with the call number 246 Mi.[2] Recent consultation of the inventory and some of the documents has further shown that they contain information of interest to musicologists concerned with the papal chapel in Rome in the 15th and early 16th centuries.

First, a word about the documents themselves. Most of them are bound volumes of registers, each of which is given a separate signature (A10, A11, etc.). They are now in the boxes making up the series L 24-52, with about three volumes per box, and they will be cited by L number and signature of the volume itself (ie. L 26, A10). Martin-Chabot, in his inventory, gave each of the volumes new signatures, and provided a concordance between his numbers and the older numbers (not, however, indicating the L number). Appendix I is a list of the documents consulted for this study, giving the present call numbers, Martin-Chabot's numbers, and some comments. For further information, the reader is directed to Giusti's article and to the inventory itself. The documents are in very bad condition – in many there has been so much water damage that they are totally illegible, in others only parts of pages are legible, and in others pages have been hopelessly stuck together – so that the information presented here cannot be said to be the result of a

---

[1] For an overview, see M. Giusti, *Studi sui registri di bolle papali*, Vatican City, Archivio Segreto Vaticano 1968 (« Collectanea Archivi Vaticani », 1).

[2] M. Giusti, *Materiale documentario degli archivi papali rimasti nell'archivio nazionale di Parigi dopo il loro ritorno a Roma negli anni 1814-1817*, in *Römische Kurie. Kirchliche Finanzen. Vatikanisches Archiv. Studien zu Ehren von Hermann Hoberg*, I, Rome, Università Gregoriana 1979 (« Miscellaneae Historiae Pontificiae », 45), pp. 263-274. The inventory on microfilm is entitled: *Epaves des Archives Vaticanes laissées à Paris en 1817 en L'Hotel de Soubise: Inventaire et extraits par Eugène Martin-Chabot, conservateur honoraire des Archives de France, ancien membre de l'Ecole française de Rome*.

complete reading of each volume. The inventory, however, is an invaluable guide because of the many extracts it contains, and I have relied on it occasionally to check readings. I have also restricted myself to documents of the later 15th and first two decades of the 16th centuries, with the exception of one important document of 1400.[3]

1. *The Earliest Extant Lists of the Papal Chapel in Rome.*

L 166 of the Archives Nationales is a box containing miscellaneous packets of documents, no. 6 of which preserves a fragment of a book of the *mandati camerali* of the 11th year of the reign of Boniface IX (1400), prepared in Rome, as indicated by the introductory statement on fol. 1*r*:

Quaternus exitus camere apostolice, inceptus Rome, sub anno domini millesimo quadringentesimo, indictione octava, die primo mensis februarii, pontificatus sanctissimi in Christo patris et domini nostri domini Bonifatii divina providentia pape noni anno undecimo.

Ever since Haberl's pioneering study, the musicological world has been cognizant of the books of the *mandati camerali* (records of the « orders to pay » sent from the Chamberlain of the Apostolic Chamber to the papal Treasurer, now mostly in the Archivio di Stato of Rome) as a major source of the lists of the papal chapel.[4] The significance of the *mandati* and the problems of Haberl's use of them have been discussed elsewhere; suffice it to say here that his work was not thorough, and that he had no knowledge of the fragment of *mandati* extant in Paris.[5] In fact, the fragment preserves three chapel lists (one not complete) for three months in the year 1400, thus providing the first specific information about the personnel of the chapel during the reign of Boniface IX.[6] The first list, found on fol. 1*v*, reads as follows:

---

[3] It should be mentioned that the inventory lists a number of documents from the early 15th century.

[4] F. X. HABERL, *Die Römische « schola cantorum » und die päpstlichen Kapellsänger bis zur Mitte des 16. Jahrhunderts*, Leipzig, Breitkopf und Härtel 1888 (« Bausteine für Musikgeschichte », III).

[5] See R. SHERR, *The Papal Chapel ca. 1492-1513 and its Polyphonic Sources*, diss., Princeton University 1975; and J. NOBLE, *New Light on Josquin's Benefices*, in *Josquin des Prez: Proceedings of the International Josquin Festival-Conference*, London, Oxford University Press 1976, pp. 76-102.

[6] Discussed and transcribed in the Inventory on p. 463 and 472.

Abbas Angelus, magister capelle   fl. iiii ca.[7]
Jacobus de Aquila   fl. ii ca.
+ Johannes Ortega   fl. ii ca.
Zacchara   fl. ii ca.
Michael   fl. iiii ca.
Cicchus   fl. iii ca.
+ Paulus de Frosolona   fl. iii ca.
Antonius de Reate   fl. [illegible]
Antonius de Aquila   fl. [illegible]
Paulus de Aversa [illegible]
Johannellus, clericus capelle

Indictione viii, die vi mensis februarii, Lande, solvas predictis cantoribus capelle domini nostri pape [rest, illegible].

This, then, is a list of the papal chapel for the month of February or January, 1400.[8] It shows a Master of the Chapel, who seems not to have been a singer (as was to be the custom in the papal chapel), 9 singers (labeled « cantores » in another list), and a clerk of the chapel. On fol. 7v, basically the same list appears with certain changes: Zacchara becomes Zacharias, Cicchus is called presbyter, Paulus de Frosolona becomes Paulus de Frisinona (the entry for Johannellus is not visible). The date is illegible, but it seems perfectly logical to assume that this is a list of the next month, February or March, 1400. On fol. 13v, only the name of the Master of the Chapel appears, but it could be supposed that the list, had it been completed, would have been the same, and would have represented the chapel in April or May, 1400.

It should be noted, first of all, that only two of the singers in the lists correspond to any singers of Boniface's chapel known from the researches of Haberl and Agostino Ziino.[9] One is Zacchara, who must be identical with the composer Antonius Zacharias da Teramo, shown by Ziino to have been a papal singer in 1391, and present in Rome as a *scriptor apostolicus* at least until 1407; the present lists show further that he combined the two jobs.[10] The other is Michael, who may be

---

[7] Four cameral florins.

[8] In the later 15th century, payments were always for the month previous to the month of the entry. This is what Martin-Chabot suggests in his reading of the final paragraph, where he adds: « pro provisione eorum men[sis januarii proximi preteriti] ». However, I can find no trace of this in the actual document.

[9] F. X. HABERL, *op. cit.*; and A. ZIINO, '*Magister Antonius dictus Zacharias de Teramo*': *alcune date e molte ipotesi*, « Rivista Italiana di Musicologia », XIV, 1979, pp. 311-348.

[10] A. ZIINO, *op. cit.*, pp. 311-324.

Michael de Wettere, cleric of Tournai, who was a papal singer in 1394.[11] I have not been able to identify the other singers, but the lists are remarkable in showing a clear majority of Italians, as opposed to one Fleming (Michael) and one possible Spaniard (Johannes Ortega), especially when compared to the nationalities in the chapel from 1417 on (dominated by northerners). But, in 1400, the Great Schism was not yet over, and northern singers might have been prevented from going to Rome for this reason. The meaning of the crosses before Ortega's and Frosolona's names in the first list (not repeated in the second) is not clear; sometimes that meant that the singer had died (which does not appear to be the case) or that he was on a leave of absence (which does not seem to be the case either), and for the moment, I have nothing to offer by way of explanation. Nor is there an immediately apparent reason for the differences in the salaries of the singers, but it probably was not based on musical merit, and may reflect extra duties in the chapel or in the papal *familia*.[12] Further research may throw light on this, as well as on the singers themselves.

2. *A Document Concerning Josquin des Prez.*

Most of the documents remaining in Paris are not fragments, but are complete books from the series of *Annate* and *Obligationes Particulares* (now mostly in the Archivio Segreto Vaticano), books which recorded the promises of individuals to pay taxes on benefices and privileges received from the pope.[13] One of these volumes (L 27, A13) contains annates for the year 1490-1491 (reign of Innocent VIII). One of the entries for March 30, 1491 (the volume has no foliation) reads as follows:

Dicta die [March 30, 1491] d. Judocus de Pratis, clericus Cameracensis diocesis, in capella sacri palatii cantor, principalis obligavit se camere apostolice pro facultate resignandi et ex causa permutationis [*sic*] omnia bene-

---

[11] A. ZIINO, *op. cit.*, p. 322.

[12] For evidence of this practice, see N. PIRROTTA, *Musical and Cultural Tendencies in 15th-Century Italy*, «Journal of the American Musicological Society (hereafter, 'JAMS')», XIX, 1966, pp. 127-161.

[13] Short descriptions of these and other Vatican documents can be found in R. SHERR, *op. cit.*, and in the standard guides to the Archivio Segreto Vaticano. See L. BOYLE O. P., *A Survey of the Vatican Archives and of its Medieval Holdings*, Toronto, Pontifical Institute of Medieval Studies 1972.

ficia ecclesiastica que obtinet [given to him by a bull] sub datum Rome quindecimo kalendas septembris, anno quinto [August 18, 1489].

The main interest of this document (apart from it as yet another addition to the small amount of information about Josquin) is its reference to a bull of an earlier date. The copy of the actual bull, previously unknown, is preserved in Vatican City, Archivio Segreto Vaticano, Registri Vaticani 753, fols. 157*r*-161*r*, and contains more faculties (such as the faculty of holding a benefice in an area with a language different from one's own) than those mentioned in the Paris document.[14] These appear to be the earliest known privileges Josquin received after joining the papal chapel – the first bull published by Noble is dated September 9, 1489 – and their blanket nature suggests that the composer had decided seriously to begin the process of collecting benefices through his position as a singer in the chapel, linked probably to a decision to remain in Rome for an extended period (he stayed in the chapel until 1494 at least).

3. *A Document Concerning Johannes Tinctoris.*

Volume A14 in box L 27, *Annate* for the year 1502 (reign of Alexander VI), contains an entry on fol. 28*r* at once more complicated and more interesting than the one discussed above.

Dicta die [July 12, 1502] Raphael de Bartholis de Florentia, institutor societate de Gaddis de Romana Curia, ut principalis et nomine d. Johanni Andree de Gatta, clerici Neapolitani, obligavit se camere apostolice pro annate parrocchialis ecclesie Sancti Georgi ad Mercatum Veterem Neapolitane, vacantis apud sedem per liberam cessionem d. Johannes Tinctoris, cujus fructus etc. centum ducatorum auri de camera non excedunt. Et promisit solvere dictam annatam infra quatuor menses proximi sequentes, prout de illa solvendo d. Depositarius etiam promisit per cedulam suam, ex quo dicto Johanni Andree commendatur sub datum Rome, tertio idus junii, anno decimo [June 11, 1502].[15]

The gist of this is that the representative of a Roman bank has obligated himself to pay an annate for Johannes Andree de Gatta (Gaeta?) – bankers and merchants often paid annates for other people –

---

[14] I am grateful to Adalbert Roth for bringing this document to my attention, and for showing me a facsimile and transcription of it.

[15] Quoted in full in the Inventory, p. 262.

on a benefice in Naples worth about 100 ducats, resigned by Johannes Tinctoris « in Rome » (« apud sedem ») on June 11, 1502.[16] It represents the first definite proof that the theorist did spend some time in Rome; this has always been surmised because of a motet he wrote in honor of Alexander VI (although that in itself does not constitute proof that he went to Rome), and also, I suppose, because of the closeness of Naples to the city, but no documents until now have been produced to support the thesis. More importantly, the present document comes from a period in Tinctoris's life about which we know absolutely nothing.[17] It probably is not a coincidence that Tinctoris is in Rome in 1502 resigning a Neapolitan benefice. The Aragonese dynasty he had served so faithfully had been driven from the Kingdom in August, 1501, and the Paris document may well be a record of Tinctoris's last months in Italy, the result of a decision to leave Naples and return home to Flanders.

4. *Some Documents Concerning Members of the Chapel of Leo X.*

Volume A20 in box L 29 is a book of *Obligationes Particulares* for the year 1518, containing records of the obligations made by members of the papal court who received expectatives from Leo X on November 1, 1517.[18] As Frey has already pointed out, many singers in the papal chapel (in fact, probably every member of the chapel) received expectatives on that date, so this volume should contain references to them.[19]

---

[16] There might be a question raised about this, because of the use of the word « cessionem » instead of « resignationem ». I am informed by Adalbert Roth that the « ceding » of a benefice usually took place as a result of a lawsuit which could have been carried out through procurators (*ie.* the lawsuit could have been settled in Rome, but Tinctoris did not have to be there in person). But there is a kind of cross-reference to this entry in A14, fol. 139, and here the words used to describe the reason for the vacancy are « [...] ex causa resignationis apud sedem per eum [Tinctoris] facte domino Johanni Andree de Gatta, clerico Neapolitano, sub datum tertio nonas junii anno decimo ». There is a slight discrepancy in the date, but there can be no doubt that this is the same benefice – the cross-reference is to fol. 28 of A14 – and that Tinctoris is described as having « resigned it » (*ie.* in person) in Rome.

[17] For the latest discussion of Tinctoris's biography, see R. WOODLEY, *Iohannes Tinctoris: A Review of the Documentary Biographical Evidence*, « JAMS », XXXIV, 1981, pp. 217-248.

[18] An expectative required that the person named be granted the first vacant benefice in a diocese. Quite often, expectatives were coupled with outright grants of canonries and various dispensations. See C. TIHON, *Les expectatives in forma pauperum particulièrement au XIV*^{e} *siècle*, « Bulletin de l'Institut Historique Belge de Rome », V, 1925, pp. 51-118.

[19] H.-W. FREY, *Regesten zur päpstlichen Kapelle unter Leo X und zu seiner Privatkapelle*, « Die Musikforschung », VIII, 1955, pp. 58-73, 178-199, 412-437; IX, 1956, pp. 46-57, 139-156, 411-419.

In fact, it does; unfortunately, the state of preservation is such that not all entries can be read. In any case, 9 names of singers also reported by Frey can be found.

NAME	DATE OF OBLIGATION	REF. IN FREY	
Laurentius de Bergomotis	August 13, 1518 [20]	(1955):	417
Thomas de Fazanis	July 27, 1518 [21]	(1955):	195
Elzéar Genet	July 30, 1518 [22]	(1956):	413
Andreas Michot	September 5 [?], 1518 [23]	(1956):	413
Vincent Misonne	July 19, 1518 [24]	(1955):	196
Martinus de Monteaguto	September 16, 1518 [25]	(1955):	198
Bernardus Pauli [Pisano]	July 28, 1518 [26]	(1956):	413
Paulus de Trottis	August 11, 1518 [27]	(1956):	416
Petrus de Vien	July 27, 1518 [28]	(1956):	416

Also present are the scribe of the chapel, Claudius Gellandi, whose obligation dates from July 30, 1518, Johannes Hanguemar, the librarian, July 23, 1518, and Paride de Grassi, the senior master of ceremonies, July 30, 1518.[29] There are also one singer not mentioned by Frey as having received an expectative, Petrus Perez,[30] and one singer, Mutinel Sermentis, not mentioned anywhere else.[31]

Unfortunately, the state of the volume prevented me from reading every entry, and so I cannot say whether it sheds any light on a point of some controversy: the date of Costanzo Festa's entry into the papal chapel. This date rests on the interpretation of a document discovered by Frey; this document is a copy of a bull, dated November 1, 1517, calling Festa « cantor capellanus » of the papal chapel, and granting him expectatives in the diocese of Mondovì, and from those in the collation of the Abbey of San Michele della Chiusa in the diocese of Torino (Festa

---

[20] Fol. 34r.
[21] Fol. 25v.
[22] Fol. 29r.
[23] Fol. 56r.
[24] Fol. 13r. The obligation is made for him by Johannes Baylluy, cleric of Cambrai.
[25] Fol. 59r.
[26] Fol. 26v.
[27] Fol. 37v.
[28] Fol. 25r.
[29] Fol. 29v, see (1955): 64; fol. 23r; fol. 29r.
[30] Obligation dated July 17, 1518 (fol. 11r).
[31] Obligation dated July 17, 1518 (fol. 10r).

is called a cleric of that diocese).³² The date would seem to lead to the conclusion that Festa was a member of the papal chapel at least by November, 1517, and had received an expectative along with all the other singers, but this has been challenged by Edward Lowinsky, first in his introduction to the Medici Codex edition, then in his reply to an article by David Crawford; he wishes to place Festa's entry into the chapel after 1517, and has suggested that the description of the composer as « cantor capellanus » in the document of 1517 was part of a plan to lure him to Rome.³³ While I am not convinced by Lowinsky's interpretation of the document, I do believe that its date must be questioned. Expectatives were a special class of papal bull. They were issued in great numbers by popes on a specific day in their pontificates (the day for Leo clearly being November 1, 1517), to all members of the Curia and the papal *familia*. But this date was also considered to be the legal date of expectatives granted *after* the original release of graces, and such expectatives were backdated, sometimes by a statement within the document itself (as in the bull of Sept. 9, 1489 discovered by Noble), and sometimes simply by being given the older date.³⁴ There is evidence of this practice in two documents in the Archivio Segreto Vaticano concerning the composers Eustachio de Monteregalis and Antoine Bruhier.

When expectatives were granted, separate entries for each person or group of people were registered in a special volume of the *Registers of the Supplications* called an *Expectativarium*. Unfortunately, the volume for the expectatives of November 1, 1517 is lost, but the Vatican Archives do preserve one from 1519.³⁵ This volume contains entries of two kinds: in one type, a clause is added reading (with variations), « perinde valeat ac si sub datum kalendas novembris anno quinto [November 1, 1517] », and the document is dated at the end; but in the other type, the clause reads « Et sub datum kalendas novembris anno quinto », and there is no date, simply the inscription « Bal. Dat. »

---

³² (1955): 64-65.

³³ E. LOWINSKY, *The Medici Codex of 1518: Historical Introduction and Commentary*, Chicago, Chicago University Press 1968 (« Monuments of Renaissance Music », III), p. 59, n. 17; D. CRAWFORD, *A Review of Costanzo Festa's Biography*, « JAMS », XXVIII, 1975, pp. 102-111; E. LOWINSKY, *On the Presentation and Interpretation of Evidence: Another Review of Costanzo Festa's Biography*, « JAMS », XXX, 1977, pp. 106-128.

³⁴ See E. PITZ, *Supplikensignatur und Briefexpedition und die römischen Kurie im Pontifikat Calixts III*, Tübingen, Max Niemayer Verlag 1972.

³⁵ Vatican City, Archivio Segreto Vaticano, Registri delle Suppliche (hereafter, RS) 1601. See B. KATTERBACH, *Inventario dei Registri delle Suppliche*, Vatican City, Archivio Segreto Vaticano 1932.

(Baldassarius Datarius – Baldassarius Turini, the Datary from April, 1518 to the end of Leo's pontificate).³⁶ I can think of only one explanation for these different phrases: they must be instructions concerning the dating of the actual bulls. In the first type, the bull, when written, was to bear the date at the end of the supplication, and contain a clause backdating it to November 1, 1517, but in the second type, the bull, when written, was simply to be dated November 1, 1517 (this giving it greater legal force than the other). But regardless of that, there can be no doubt that the documents preserved in this volume of the *Registers of Supplications* are records of expectatives granted in 1519.³⁷

Among the documents of the second type are those concerning Monteregalis and Bruhier. Monteregalis is called a clerk of Arras, and it is said that the expectative is being granted according to privileges given to the singers of the papal chapel; it therefore seems likely that he was a member of the chapel also.³⁸ Bruhier is called a papal singer and familiar, and the same statement about the privileges of the chapel is inserted; it therefore seems likely that he had moved to the papal chapel by this time.³⁹ And the bull prepared for Bruhier from this document of 1519, discovered by Frey, is dated November 1, 1517.⁴⁰ The bull written for Monteregalis has not yet been found, but the entry in the *Registers of Supplications* now proves that he was a member of the chapel at least as early as 1519.⁴¹

The implications of all this for Festa's biography are obvious, for if the dates on bulls granting expectatives cannot be trusted, if they can

---

³⁶ On Turini, see W. VON HOFMANN, *Forschungen zur Geschichte der Kurialen Behörde vom Schisma bis zur Reformation*, II, Rome, Loescher und C. 1914, p. 102.

³⁷ The *Registers of Supplications* are the most consistently dated of all Vatican documents. Not only were supplications registered as soon as they were signed, but the scribes of the Registers regularly noted the month and day (sometimes year) they began copying each gathering. If an undated document is found among others all dating from a certain time, it is certain that it was registered at the same time. The dated documents surrounding the expectatives for Monteregalis and Bruhier in *Register of Supplications* 1601 are from April and June 1519.

³⁸ RS 1601, fols. 112r-112v. The phrase concerning the privileges reads: « iuxta privillegia sive indulta apostolica cantoribus capellanis etiam in capella nostra actu perinde concessa ». Much the same wording appears in the document concerning Festa.

³⁹ *Register of Supplications* 1601, fols. 157r-157v. Bruhier had been a *cantore segreto*. See (1955): 61-62.

⁴⁰ (1955): 61-62.

⁴¹ It has been asserted that Monteregalis was a singer in the Cappella Giulia because of a reference to an Eustachio there in April-June, 1514. This, however, is the first clear evidence placing him in Rome during the pontificate of Leo X. See H. T. DAVID, et. al., *Eustachio Romano Musica Duorum Rome, 1521*, Chicago, Chicago University Press 1975 (« Monuments of Renaissance Music », VI), p. 10. On Monteregalis's presence in Rome during the reign of Clement VII, see R. SHERR, *New Archival Data Concerning the Chapel of Clement VII*, « JAMS », XXIX, 1976, pp. 472-478.

actually be the product of a legal fiction, then it cannot immediately follow from Festa's expectative that it really was granted on November 1, 1517, and that the composer was a member of the chapel then. It is here that the Paris volume of *Obligationes* could have been of great service, for had it recorded an obligation from Festa for his expectative within a few months of November, 1517, then it would have been fair to say that he really was in Rome in that year. The reference may be there, hidden somewhere in the illegible portions of the volume, but for the moment, the question of the date of Festa's entry into the papal chapel must remain open.

Appendix I

DOCUMENTS CONSULTED IN THE ARCHIVES NATIONALES

Call. No., Vol. No.	Martin-Chabot No.	Remarks
L 26, A10	Ob. An. 8	*Annate* for 1482-83.
L 26, A12	Ob. An. 10	*Annate* for 1489-90. No foliation. Very faint.
L 27, A13	Ob. An. 11	*Annate* for 1490-91. No foliation.
L 27, A14	Ob. An. 12	*Annate* for 1502.
L 28, A16	Ob. An. 13	*Annate* for 1515-16. No foliation.
L 28, A17	Ob. An. 14	*Annate* for 1516. Mostly illegible.
L 28, A18	Ob. An. 15	*Annate* for 1518. Mostly illegible.
L 29, A19	Ob. An. 16	*Annate* for 1519.
L 29, A20	Ob. P. 2	*Obligationes Particulares* for 1518.
L 166, No. 6	None	1 + 19 unbound folios containing *mandati camerali* for Feb., March, April, June (frag.), and August (frag.), 1400. Badly damaged so that only tops of folios are legible.

Appendix II

REFERENCES TO OTHER SINGERS

Document   L 26, A12 (no foliation).
Name   Bishop of Cortona (Master of the Chapel).
Benefice   Church of St. Munetius in the diocese of Geneva, vacant on the death of Robertus Boniti in Rome.
Date   November 2, 1489.

Document   L 26, A12 (no foliation).
Name   Bertrandus Vaqueras.
Benefice   Archdeaconry in the cathedral of Vaison, granted on May 27, 1490.
Date   July 14, 1490.

Document   L 27, A13 (no foliation).
Name   Innocentius Cossee.
Benefice   Provostship of the Church of St. Géry in the diocese of Cambray, granted on October 19, 1490.
Date   October 29, 1490.

Document   L 27, A13 (no foliation).
Name   Marbrianus de Orto.
Benefice   Church of St. Carolus in the diocese of Tournai, granted on September 10, 1488.
Date   June 22, 1491.

Document   L. 27, A14, fol. 23v.
Name   Garsias de Salinas.
Benefice   Church of St. Martinus in the diocese of Toledo.
Date   July 7, 1502.

Document   L 29, A19, fol. 63v.
Name   Laurentius de Bergomotis.
Benefice   Benefices in the diocese of Modena, granted on January 13, 1519 (see (1955): 434).
Date   May 12, 1519.

Document   L 29, A19, fol. 115r.
Name   Lambertus Martini.
Benefice   Church of St. Macharius in Vlake in the diocese of Utrecht, granted on August 13, 1518 (see (1955): 186).
Date   June 21, 1519.

II

A NOTE ON THE BIOGRAPHY OF JUAN DEL ENCINA*

Many biographers of Juan del Encina have drawn attention to the difficulties he had in obtaining political and ecclesiastical appointments; indeed, the man's character and his poetry have been analyzed as reflecting a life of constant frustration in this regard.[1] A few documents survive showing that Encina attempted to obtain ecclesiatical benefices while in Salamanca (where he was thwarted by local opposition) and later in Rome through the influence of the pope, and it has been suggested plausibly that his decision to leave Spain around 1499 was triggered by a desire to seek benefices from the Spanish pope Alexander VI (Rodrigo Borgia). He was, in fact, moderately successful, the pope providing him with at least two bulls granting benefices in Salamanca and supporting him against the local officials, while also accepting him into the papal household. But from 1502 (the date of Alexander's last letter) to 1508 (the date of a bull by Julius II) there has been practically no information about Encina's ecclesiastical career, nor indeed about Encina himself. Documents recently discovered in the Vatican Archive help fill part of this lacuna (the years 1503-06). They show Encina still residing in Rome, in contact with a heretofore unknown patron, and actively pursuing his beneficial career.

The bulk of this new information comes from an enormous series of registers in the Vatican Archives known as the *Registers of the Supplications*.[2] These contain records of all requests for benefices that had been approved by the pope or by his surrogate. When a supplicant wished to obtain a benefice, he submitted a legal document (the Supplication) to an official known as a Referendary who brought it to the pope for action. If the pontiff approved the request, the document was given a date by the Datary, and at this point had the force of law. The Datary then took the approved supplications to the scribes of the *Registers of the Supplications* whose job it was to copy the supplications as they stood and as soon as possible. Once a supplication had been registered, it was sent to the Chancery or Apostolic Chamber for the preparation of the actual bull to be sent back to the supplicant. These completed bulls were also recorded, but the *Registers of the Supplications* are the most complete of any of the records of the papal benefice granting procedure. Unfortunately, this completeness is the very reason they have not been often used by scholars; for the reign of Julius II alone (1503-13), there are some 240 extant volumes, of about 300 folios each, with about 6 entries per folio (hence, hundreds of thousands of supplications), all completely unindexed.[3]

A recent search through 40 volumes of the *Registers* covering the years 1503-06 has turned up 14 documents concerning Encina, these documents giving a picture of him as he acted within the court of the successors of his original patron, Alexander VI (See Appendix). It is apparent from the first documents, for instance, that Encina stopped being a member of the papal household on the death of Alexander; this is simply because he does not describe himself as being a familiar of the next pope (Pius III) to whom the letters are addressed, as he almost certainly would have done had that been the case. He is, however, asserting privileges belonging to the familiars of Alexander, since many of the benefices requested were held by deceased members of Alexander's household.

Document 3, though, adds an intriguing bit of information: it states that Encina («dictus orator») has described himself as having been in the service of Cesare Borgia (son of Alexander VI), and as having entered the pope's household through Cesare's influence. If this is true, then the earliest it could have happened was in 1500, since in 1498 and 1499 Cesare was either in France (receiving a French duchy and a French bride after having been allowed to resign the cardinalate), or engaged in military campaigns in the Romagna. He returned to Rome in February, 1500, and stayed for several months, and it is perhaps not coincidental that the date of the first bull granted Encina is May 12, 1500. So, Encina may have arrived in Rome only at the end of 1499 or the beginning of 1500, or he may have spent a year floundering about looking for a patron.

So far, Documents 1-4 have shown Encina in Rome, busily pursuing the benefices of dead colleagues in the year 1503. Document 5, however, creates problems. This document (dated April 19, 1504) grants, by *motu proprio*, two benefices in Salamanca to Bernardinus Gutteri, one of the masters of ceremonies of the papal chapel. This is not remarkable—what is disturbing is that the benefices are said specifically to have become vacant on the death of «Johannes del Enzina» outside of Rome. One of the benefices (in the church of St. Johannes de la Zogue in the town of Medina del Campo) had been granted in Document 3 to the person I have identified as Juan del Encina, so Documents 3 and 5 seem to be talking about the same man. But we know that the poet Encina did not die in 1504, and thus are led to conclude that there were in fact two Juan del Encinas, both clerics of Salamanca, both familiars of Alexander VI, one of whom died in 1504. This is not the case, however, for it is almost certain that Document 5 is in error when it says that the benefices were vacant because of Encina's death. The proof is in Document 8 (dated September 19, 1504, four months after the date of Document 5). Here, a major new fact about Encina emerges: that he was a member of the household of the Spanish cardinal Franciscus de Loriz (Illoris, de Loris). He is so described in the document, and its very purpose is to ask that Encina be allowed to resign a large number of benefices in the cardinal's favor. Comparison of Documents 8 and 3 shows that benefices granted in 3 are resigned in 8, therefore the Encina named in 3 and 8 must be the same person. And since benefices mentioned in Document 5 were also granted in Document 3, there cannot have been two people of the same name, nor could Encina have been dead when Document 5 was written. The reason for the misstatement in 5 is not clear; maybe it was a mistake, or perhaps Gutteri had falsely claimed that Encina was dead in order to possess his benefices.

About Cardinal Franciscus Loriz not too much is known. He was considered to be the nephew of Juan Borgia, Cardinal of Monreale, and was thus a close relative of Alexander and of Cesare; in fact, he was one of Cesare's intimate friends. His ecclesiastical career was certainly advanced by his high connections; he held a number of papal offices and, when Cesare resigned his benefices, Loriz was awarded the bishopric of Elne. He is often referred to as «electus Elnensis» (bishop-designate of Elne), and when he became a cardinal in 1503, he took, along with other titles, the sobriquet «Elnensis.»

II

162

First made cardinal-deacon with the title Santa Sabina on May 31, 1503, he was translated to Santa Maria Nova on December 17, 1505, and also bore the purely honorary title of Patriarch of Constantinople. He died in Rome on July 22, 1506, and was buried in the church of Santa Maria delle Febbre (attached to old St. Peter's) in the chapel containing other Borgia tombs. According to Pastor, Loriz was not of good character, and had indeed purchased his red hat at a great price.[5] This judgment is confirmed in a way by Paris de Grassis, the master of ceremonies under Julius II, who reported the cardinal's death in his Diary by stating that it was rumored that he had died of excessive sexual intercourse. But in spite of this (or perhaps because of it) Loriz must have been popular; de Grassis was surprised by the number of people «of both sexes» who followed the body to the church, and he especially marveled at the « . . . infinite number of women of diverse nationalities . . . » who pressed forward to kiss the dead man's hand, even though the body stank so badly that de Grassis himself did not want to go near it.[6] Loriz was in his life style undoubtedly typical of many high ecclesiastics of his time. He was probably also a great patron of arts, letters, and music, for it seems unlikely that Encina would have turned to him if he had not felt that his talents would be appreciated.

Several more documents testify to the relationship between Encina and Loriz. In Document 9, the cardinal seems to have proposed Encina for a benefice under his control, Document 11 concerns a benefice in Perpignan (in his diocese of Elne), and Documents 13, 14, and 15 show an even greater favor.

Document 13 is a long Indult granted those conclavists who took part in the conclave that elected Julius II. It is dated January 28, 1505, and ends with a list of all the conclavists and substitutes who were to benefit from the bull. One name has been added in the margin, however: «Johannes del Enzina.» It is further stated that the addition was made at the order of the pope in the third year of his reign (November, 1505— November, 1506), and that the document concerning this can be found in another of the *Registers of Supplications* (the very folio is specified). This means that Encina was not on the original list (or rotulus) of the conclavists, and was inserted later by papal command. Document 14 appears in fact to be the document referred to in Document 13, and from it, it can be learned that the person behind the insertion of Encina's name was not the pope, but Cardinal Loriz. The cardinal asks specifically that Encina be added to the rotulus in the place of Johannes Perez, who had died, and that Encina be considered as having served the cardinal during the conclave. This suggests that the relationship between Encina and Loriz dates back to October, 1503 (the month Julius II was elected), but things are not that clear. The conclave that elected Julius was one of the shortest on record (lasting only for the day of October 31, 1503), and it hardly seems likely that there would have been time for substitutions. Furthermore, the year of Perez's death is not given; that, coupled with the lateness of the request (three years after the conclave), suggests that perhaps the cardinal wished to create a legal fiction by saying that Encina had served in the conclave, a fiction designed to give Encina certain rights and privileges. But it may simply be that there was not time in 1503 to insert Encina's name officially in the rotulus, and that he only called upon his patron to rectify the omission when he knew that privileges were due to be granted. In any case, the pope agreed to the cardinal's request, and Encina was added to the list of conclavists.

It is in this context that the last document in the Appendix must be viewed. Document 15 is different from the others, being not the record of a request for a benefice, but the record of an actual bull; it is preserved in a series of registers of papal bulls known as the *Vatican Registers*.[7] It is futhermore a very particular type of papal letter known as an expectative. An expectative was a papal order granting a benefice not yet vacant, and it specified that the person involved was to be given the next vacant benefice of a particular type in a particular diocese. Expectatives were a favorite way of rewarding papal servants, and popes would regularly during their reigns release thousands of these graces to members of their household and to members of the households of cardinals and other curial officials. The graces were considered to have been given on one particular day, and expectatives actually conferred after that day were often backdated, sometimes entirely without comment. In the reign of Julius II, March 1, 1506, was the date on which large numbers of expectatives were granted to members of the papal court.

Document 15 is one such expectative made to the order of Juan del Encina. It is quite extensive, for not only does it grant expectatives in the dioceses of Salamanca, Avila, and Oviedo, but it confers canonries and prebends in those dioceses as well (Encina is addressed as if he were already a canon of Salamanca). Mention is also made of Encina's having been accepted as a substitute for Johannes Perez in the conclave that elected Julius II. The first problem posed by the document concerns its date of March 1, 1506. Cardinal Loriz's request that Encina be put in the rotulus of conclavists is dated April 14, 1506, a month later than the date of Document 15, but since Document 15 could not have been written before this request had been granted, it seems fair to say that its date is wrong and that this expectative was of the type simply backdated to March 1, its actual date being unknown. The next problem concerns the conferral of a canonry in Salamanca, seeming to confirm the old notion that Encina was indeed a canon in that cathedral. It must be borne in mind in this regard, however, that the mere existence of a document in the Vatican Archives granting a benefice does not mean that possession was ever taken. The documents of Encina's beneficial career show that he resigned or was forced to resign many of the benefices granted him (including 300 ducats-worth ceded to Cardinal Loriz). Local opposition to papal bulls could be strong, and given that Encina had not entered into higher Holy Orders, I think it likely that he was prevented from taking possession of the canonries and prebends granted in Document 15. Indeed, further research in the *Registers of the Supplications* may show him resigning every one of them.

And at least once, he requested something other than an ecclesiastical benefice. As is well known, Encina was a Bachelor of Laws, having received his degree at the University of Salamanca. He was apparently not satisfied with this, however, since in Document 12 he asks the pope to grant him the degree of Doctor of Canon and Civil Law. Again, this may never have taken effect, as Encina is not addressed as Doctor of Laws in any other documents.

What conclusions can be drawn from this short report? Encina clearly was an ambitious man, frustrated in his own country, who apparently moved to Rome with the hope of getting ecclesiastical preferments from Alexander VI. As a member of the papal household, Encina did receive a number of papal bulls granting benefices, and later on asked for the benefices of dead colleagues. His direct connection with the household seems to have ceased with the death of Alexander, and in need of another patron, he established ties with another Spaniard, Cardinal Franciscus Loriz. By the way, that Loriz was the *maestro* of the papal chapel in 1501-02 provides the only link (and that a tenuous one) between Encina and that organization; Sullivan's and others' statements to the contrary, there is not yet a single shred of evidence suggesting that Encina was a member of the papal choir.[8] But he was in such close proximity, that it seems likely that he knew some of the singers, particularly the Spanish ones.[9]

While this research has only been carried up to 1506, it is almost certain that further work in the Vatican Archives will turn up more information about Encina and other notable Spaniards. Encina was an indefatigable benefice hunter, as were almost all who flocked to Rome in the late 15th century, and furthermore, was not daunted by insuccess. Were new documents discovered, they would probably illuminate additional corners of the life of this important Spanish poet, playwright, and musician.[10]

NOTES

*This article is a revised version of a paper read in the Renaissance section organized by John Lihani at the University of Kentucky Foreign Language Conference, April 1981. Research was carried out with the help of a grant from the American Philosophical Society.

1. For the most recent treatment of Encina's life, see Henry W. Sullivan, *Juan del Encina* (Boston, 1976). For a discussion of Encina's character, see J. Richard Andrews, *Juan del Encina: Prometheus in Search of Prestige* (Berkeley, 1959).
2. The *Registers of the Supplications* are described in most of the standard guides to the Vatican Archives. See: Leonard Boyle O.P., *A Survey of the Vatican Archives and of its Medieval Holdings* (Toronto, 1971); Hermann Diener, *Die Grosse Registerserien im vatikanischen Archive (1378-1523)* (Tübingen, 1972); Karl August Fink, *Das vatikanische Archiv* (Rome, 1951); also, P. Bruno Katterbach O.F.M., *Inventario dei Registri delle Suppliche* (Vatican City, 1932), and Katterbach, *Specimina Supplicationum ex registris Vaticanis* (Vatican City, 1927).
3. For more on the process and on the various offices, see: L. Célier, *Les Dataries du XVe siècle et les origines de la Datarie Apostolique*, Bibliothèque des Ecoles françaises d'Athènes et de Rome 103 (Rome, 1910); and Ernst Pitz, *Supplikensignatur und Briefexpedition an die römischen Kurie* in *Pontificat Calixts III* (Tübingen, 1972).
4. On Loriz, see: William Harrison Woodward, *Cesare Borgia* (New York, 1914), p. 390; and Conrad Eubel, *Hierarchia Catholica* (Regensburg, 1914), II and III.
5. Ludwig Pastor, *The History of the Popes*, Frederick Ignatius Antrobius, ed., V (London, 1901), pp. 170-71.
6. Here is what de Grassis has to say (taken from Vatican City, Biblioteca Apostolica Vaticana, MS Vaticanus Latinus 5635, fol. 232v-234r).

Mors Cardinalis Elnensis

Die Mercurii, 22 mensis Juli, Cardinalis Helnensis, nomine Dominus Franciscus electus patriarcha Constantinopalitanus, mortuus est ex nimis (ut dicunt) coitu; hoc audiens, ivi ad eius domum ubi inveni magistrum domus papae et auditorem camerae facientes inventarium bonorum eius cardinalis de mandato papae, qui ex quo ipse cardinalis testamentum non fecerat, voluit habere curam et onus haereditatis. Et cum petissem ab eis quid fiendum super sepulturam, et non intelligerem, ivi ad papam, cum quo inveni cardinales tres, qui dicebantur fuisse deputati executores testamenti ad ipso cardinali, et papa vocavit me, dixitque ut ipsum defunctum non ad basilicam Sanctae Mariae Maioris ubi dicebatur quod cardinalis defunctis sibi sepulturam eligerat, sed in basilica Sancti Petri in cappella de febribus apud cardinalem Montis Regalis, patruum olim istius nunc defuncti, et quod fecerem cum solemniter et honorifice sepelliri . . . (there follow descriptions of the laying out of the body, of people to be invited to the funueral, of the first rites).

Hora xxa, incepimus officium et portavimus corpus ad ecclesiam sequentibus solis praelatis et familia papae. Adruit tanta populi utriusque sexus multitudo, cum mea maxima admiratione, ut vix poterim in ecclesia populum removere donec fieret per canonicos absolutio. Infinitae mulieres diversarum nationum osculatae sunt illi manum, sed erat ita foetens ut ego non potuerim approximare me illi . . . Corpus eius positum fuit in loco qui de febribus dictus in cappella beneficatorum Sancti Petri, ubi est depictus crucifixus et beneficiati depicti etc.

7. See Note 2.

8. See Franz Xaver Haberl, «Die Römische 'Schola Cantorum' und die Päpstlichen Kapellsänger bis zur Mitte des 16. Jahrhunderts,» *Bausteine für Musikgeschichte,* 3 (Leipzig, 1888), 127, where he confuses Loriz with Franciscus Sinibaldi (a later *maestro di cappella*). I have examined all the lists of the papal chapel for the period Encina was in Rome, along with many other documents relating to the chapel. In none of them can Encina's name be found.

9. He could hardly have avoided such avid hunters of benefices in Spain as Alfonsus de Troya (singer and later subdeacon of the chapel) or Juan Escribano (a singer and fellow Salamancan).

10. In fact, after the completion of this article, two documents concerning Encina dating from the reign of Leo X were found. They are given at the end of the Appendix.

II

167

APPENDIX OF DOCUMENTS

Because of the length and formulaic nature of these documents, it does not seem advisable to provide transcriptions. Instead, I append here brief summaries of their contents. I have tried to make as much sense as I could of the spellings of names and places, but there may be mistakes owing to the vagaries of 16th-century spelling, the difficulties Italian scribes might have had with Spanish words, and general illegibility.

DOCUMENT 1: Vatican City, Archivio Segreto Vaticano, Registri delle Suppliche (hereafter, RS) 1171, fol. 129v.
DATE: 8 October, 1503

Encina (described as a cleric of Salamanca) is granted by *motu proprio* two simplex benefices: one in «Frades» in the diocese of Salamanca, the other «del Gango» in the diocese of Ciudad-Rodrigo. These had become vacant on the death of Franciscus Troche, who had been a scribe, secretary, notary, chamberlain, and familiar of Alexander VI, and who had died in Rome (actually, he was executed for treason). The income was not expected to exceed 50 ducats.

DOCUMENT 2: RS 1170, fols. 167r-167V.
DATE: 9 October, 1503.

Encina (described as a cleric of Salamanca) asks to be granted two simplex benefices: one in «Cabrillegos» in the diocese of Salamanca, the other in «Fanhilla» in the diocese of Palencia. These had become vacant on the death of Christophorus de Torres, who had been a familiar of Alexander VI, and who had died outside of Rome. The income was not expected to exceed 50 ducats.

DOCUMENT 3: RS 1171, fols. 74v-75r.
DATE: 16 October, 1503.

Encina (described as a cleric of Salamanca) asks to be confirmed in a number of benefices granted by Alexander VI:

1. The parish church of «Cavalejas» in the diocese of Cuenca, made vacant by the death of Petrus de Poyatus not far from Rome.

2. Three simplex benefices: one «de Rabe,» another in the church of St. Johannes de la Zogue in the town of Medina del Campo (both of these in the diocese of Salamanca), and another «de Ragama» in the diocese of Avila. These had become vacant on the death of Franciscus Troche.

3. A simplex benefice in the church of St. Paulus «alias de Santpolo» in the diocese of Salamanca, made vacant by the death of Franciscus de Paz.

The total income of all these benefices was not expected to exceed 300 ducats. Later on in the document, it says that Encina has described himself as having been in the service of Cesare Borgia, and as having been made a familiar of Alexander VI through Cesare's influence («... quod dictus orator in serviciis Illustrissimi duci Cesari Borgia de Francia insistendo dixit se familiaris & continuus comensalis Alexandri Sexti ... »).

DOCUMENT 4:   RS 1173, fol. 262r.
DATE: 11 December, 1503.

Encina (described as a cleric of Salamanca) asks that the union of the parish churches «Demora» in the diocese of Urgel and «Arbecha» in the diocese of Tarragona to the priory «Sancti Laurentii de Sancto Laurentio» of the Benedictine Order in the diocese of Tortosa be maintained. The union had ceased with the death of Franciscus Troche. The income was not expected to exceed 280 ducats.

DOCUMENT 5:   RS 1181, fol. 199v.
DATE: 19 April, 1504.

Bernardinus Gutteri (described as a cleric of Salamanca and master of ceremonies in the papal chapel) is granted by *motu proprio* two

169

simplex benefices: one in «Beate Marie loci de Rabe» in the diocese of Salamanca (see Document 3.2) whose income was not expected to exceed 24 ducats, and another in St. Johannes de la Zogūe in the town of Medina del Campo in the diocese of Salamanca (see Document 3.2) whose income was not expected to exceed 24 ducats. These are said to have become vacant on the death of «Johannes del Enzina» outside of Rome (but this is probably a mistake, see below). Later on, it says that they become vacant on the death of Franciscus Troche.

DOCUMENT 6:   RS 1190, fol. 277r.
DATE: 1 August, 1504.

Encina (described as a cleric of Salamanca) asks for a prorogation of six months to allow him to take possession of the parish church in the town of Huerta in the diocese of Salamanca. The benefice had become vacant on the death of Alfonsus Bramo, and Encina had claimed it by virtue of an expectative granted him by Alexander VI.

DOCUMENT 7:   RS 1192, fol. 52r.
DATE: 19 September, 1504.

Encina (described as a cleric of Salamanca) asks to be granted a simplex benefice in «Sancte Marie de la Atigua» and the parish church «Sancte Columbe de Sancta Columba» in the diocese of Astorga. These had become vacant on the death of Franciscus Troche. The income was not expected to exceed 150 ducats.

DOCUMENT 8:   RS 1192. fol 15r.
DATE: 10 November, 1504.

Encina (described as a cleric of Salamanca and familiar of the Cardinal of Elne /Franciscus Loriz/) cedes a number of benefices because letters conferring them had not been written:

> 1. The parish church of «Cavalejas» in the diocese of Cuenca made vacant on the death of Petrus de Poyatos (see Document 3.1).

II

2. Three simplex benefices: one in St. Paulus «alias de sanpolo» in the diocese of Salamanca (see Document 3.3), another in «Adea de Alve [?]» in the diocese of Ciudad-Rodrigo, and another «de Belvis» in the diocese of Palencia made vacant by the death of Franciscus de Pozoz (Paz).

3. Three simplex benefices: one, «del Gango,» in the diocese of Ciudad-Rodrigo, another «de Frades» in the diocese of Salamanca (see Document 1), and another in Sancte Marie del Antigua», and the parish church «Sancte Columbe de Sancta Columba» in the diocese of Astorga, made vacant by the death of Franciscus Troche (see Document 7).

The cardinal asks that he be granted all these benefices. The total income was not expected to exceed 300 ducats.

DOCUMENT 9:   RS 1194, fol. 92v.
DATE: 7 December, 1504.

Encina (described as a cleric of Salamanca) asks to be granted the parish church of St. Bartholomeus de Turon in the diocese of Oviedo, made vacant by the death of Bartholomeus Grundissalvi outside of Rome. The church was in the collation of a monastery in the diocese of which Cardinal Loriz was abbot *in commendam*, and the cardinal had presented Encina for the benefice. The income was not expected to exceed 24 ducats.

DOCUMENT 10:   RS 1201, fols. 137v-138r.
DATE: 17 February, 1505.

Encina (described as a cleric of Salamanca) asks permission to cede the parish church of St. Mabiri [?] in the city of «Depricatia» in the diocese of Montefeltro [?-«Feretran»] to Julianus Christophorus de Monte Cupiobo, a priest of that diocese. The income was not expected to exceed 20 ducats, and Encina is granted a pension of 6 ducats.

II

171

DOCUMENT 11:   RS 1203, fols. 191r-191v.
DATE: 2 March, 1505.

Encina (described as a cleric of Salamanca) has been unable to take possession of a canonry and prebend in the church of St. Johannes in the town of Perpignan in the diocese of Elne, and asks permission to resign it in favor of Johannes Binnerandi, cleric of Urgel. The income was not expected to exceed 24 ducats, and Encina is granted a pension of 6 ducats.

DOCUMENT 12:   RS 1229, fols. 27v-28r.
DATE: 25 February, 1506.

Encina (described as a cleric of Salamanca, Bachelor of Laws, and familiar of Cardinal Loriz) asks to be granted the degree of Doctor of Canon and Civil Law.

DOCUMENT 13:   RS 1218, fols. 211r-212v.
DATE: 28 January, 1505.

This is a long Indult granted to the conclavists at the conclave that elected Julius II (October 31, 1503), and ends with a list of the conclavists. On folio 212v, the following has been added in the margin:

> Jo. del Enzina, cassatum et descriptum de mandato S.D.N. Registro lib. tertio X, fol. ccxxv, per me, N. de Aretio, anno tertio eiusdem S.D.N.

DOCUMENT 14:   RS 1233, fol. 230v.
DATE: 14 April, 1506.

Cardinal Franciscus Loriz asks that Juan del Encina (described as a cleric of Salamanca and the cardinal's familiar) be inscribed in the rotulus of the conclavists in the conclave that elected Julius II in the place of Johannes Perez, who had died, and that he be granted all rights and privileges accorded the conclavists.

II

172

DOCUMENT 15: Vatican City, Archivio Segreto Vaticano, Registri Vaticani 1804, fols. 137r-138v.
DATE: 1 March, 1506.

Encina (described as a canon of Salamanca, Bachelor of Laws, and papal familiar) is granted canonries and prebends in the dioceses of Salamanca, Avila, and Oviedo, along with expectatives in those dioceses. Encina is also described as having been a substitute for Johannes Perez as a servant of Cardinal Loriz in the conclave that elected Julius II.

EXTRA DOCUMENTS RECENTLY DISCOVERED

DOCUMENT 16: RS 1588, fols, 261v-262r.
DATE: 29 December, 1517.

Encina (described as a cleric of Salamanca and papal familiar) cedes canonries and prebends in the churches of «St. Martinus de Arnolda» and «Marie Rotundus de lo Granno» in the dioceses of Calahorra and Calzada. Didacus de Villoslada, dean of those churches and papal familiar, asks to be given the benefices. The income was not expected to exceed 24 ducats, and Encina is granted a pension of 8 ducats. He had been given the benefices by Cardinal Jaime Serra.

DOCUMENT 17: RS 1603, fols. 157v-158r.
DATE: 29 March, 1518.

Encina (described as a cleric of Salamanca) has been in litigation in Rome with Didacus de Ortega and others concerning a canonry and prebend in the cathedral of Calahorra. It has been asserted that none of the claimants has any right to the benefice, and Encina asks that, if that be the case, he be awarded it. The income was not expected to exceed 24 ducats. Encina is also described as a familiar of Franciscus de Bobadilla, Bishop of Salamanca, but in Rome as a curial official (see Walther von Hofmann, *Forschungen zur Geschichte de Kurialen Behörden vom Schisma bis zur Reformation,* (Rome: Bibliothek des Kgl. Preuss. Historischen Instituts in Rome 12 *[*1914*]*, II, 193.)

III

New Archival Data Concerning the Chapel of Clement VII

A NY STUDENT of the history of the papal chapel is familiar with the *mandati camerali*, the documents, now in the Archivio di Stato di Roma, which transmit the names of the chapel members.[1] But the *mandati* have suffered many losses, with the result that there are no records for the years 1494-1501, most of the reigns of Leo X and Adrian VI (1513-1523), and the first years of the reign of Clement VII (d. 1534). Franz Xavier Haberl, in his pioneering study of the *Schola cantorum*, now sorely in need of revision, could cite no lists between 1509 and 1529, although he does provide information from other sources. Recent research in the Archivio, moreover, has turned up nothing to fill the lacuna.[2] The archives of the Cappella Sistina, however, now in the Cappella Sistina collection of manuscripts in the Vatican Library, contain two long-forgotten personnel lists of the chapel: one for the month of December 1526, the other undated. The lists are on separate sheets of paper, bound into C.S. MS 681 as folios 75 and 76. (See Figs. 1-3 and the transcriptions in Appendices A and B.)[3]

The documents are companions to the lists in the *mandati*, supplying the names of chapel personnel along with the salary paid each, but they clearly served a different purpose. The *mandati camerali* were part of the archives of the papal treasurer, and they record all the "orders to pay" or *mandati* as they came down from the Cardinal Chamberlain.[4] The lists in C.S. 681 would appear to have originated in the papal chapel itself. In fact, they are signed by many of the chapel members with the words "recepi ut supra," or an indication that they were picking up money for someone else. Such documents probably formed a large collection, now unfortunately destroyed.[5]

Folio 75 of C.S. 681 is dated "de mense deceb 1526" and provides an important record of the members of the chapel of Clement VII before the sack of Rome (May 6, 1527). First named are the *maestro di cappella* and the *sacrista*, both ecclesiastics;

---

[1] For information about the provenance and function of these documents, see Adolf Gottlob, *Aus der Camera Apostolica des 15. Jahrhunderts* (Innsbruck, 1889); also Richard Sherr, "The Papal Chapel ca. 1492-1513 and its Polyphonic Sources" (Ph.D. diss., Princeton Univ., 1975).

[2] Franz Xavier Haberl, "Die römische 'schola cantorum' und die päpstlichen Kapellsänger bis zur Mitte des 16. Jahrhunderts," *Bausteine für Musikgeschichte*, III (Leipzig, 1888). For a discussion of the deficiencies in this work, see Sherr, *op. cit.*

[3] These lists must have been known to Guiseppe Baini, since he included Scaliono, who is mentioned only in these documents, in his catalogue of *maestri* of the papal chapel, *Memorie storico-critiche della vita e delle opere di Giovanni Pierluigi da Palestrina*, 2 vols. (Rome, 1828), I, 267. He is probably also responsible for the copy of folio 75 (now fol. 2 of C.S. 681), and for the information about Scaliono and Gabrielli, the *sacriste*, written so that it appears upside down on folio 75—presumably to distinguish it from the document itself.

[4] See Gottlob, *Camera Apostolica*, p. 141.

[5] Two more such documents are bound into C.S. MS 678 as fols. 105 and 107. The first is dated "mense septèbre," but a modern hand (that of Baini?) has written "Settembre 1563" in the upper right hand corner of the page. In fact, the list agrees with the *mandati* list of September 1563. Thirty-nine singers are named, including Domenico Ferrabasco and Palestrina, who were receiving pensions. Fol. 107 is labeled "pro mense 8bris 1563" and contains essentially the names of the same singers listed on fol. 105. (Petro Lambert, however, does not appear, and Christiano Ameyden is added.)

© 1976 by the American Musicological Society. All rights reserved.

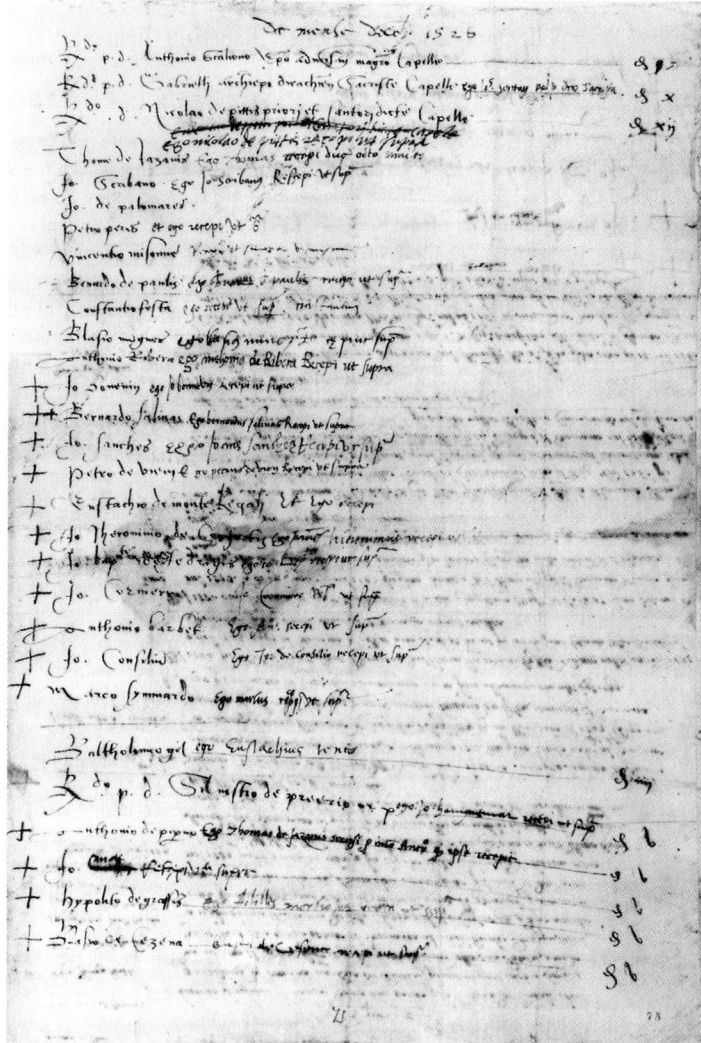

Figure 1. MS C.S. 681, folio 75ʳ

next in the list is the *prior*, Niccolo de Pictis, followed by twenty singers, recognizable by their names and salary of eight ducats. The singers are separated from the following names by a horizontal line; the positions of the latter men are not identified, but I would take them to be three chaplains, three masters of ceremonies, two clerks, two scribes, one keeper of the books, and the *mundatori capelle*.[6]

[6] The identification of the positions is based on the order of names and the salaries in the *mandati* lists. Furthermore, certain of these people can be specifically identified. Anthonio

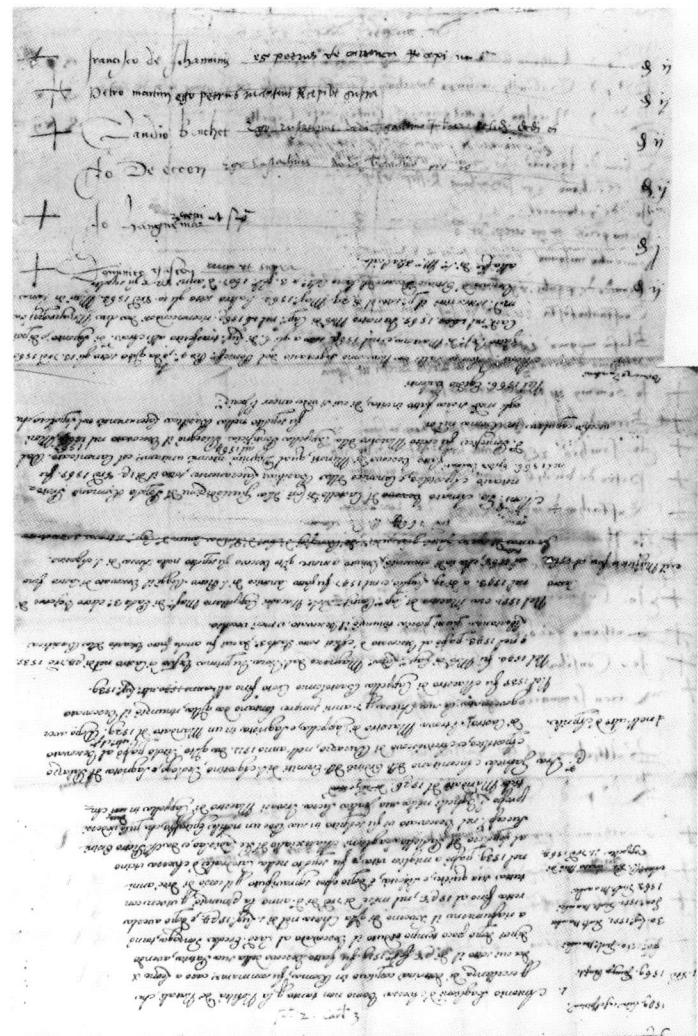

Figure 2. MS C.S. 681, folio 75ᵛ

Folio 76 contains a similar receipt list, but it is undated and in a different hand from that of folio 75. It also lists two singers not in the preceding document.[7] By drawing on known information, however, it is possible to arrive at an approximate date for this list. The *terminus ante quem* must be the sack of Rome: this is indicated

---

Piperno is listed as a chaplain in 1509; Blasio de Cesena was a long-time master of ceremonies; Johannes Occon is listed as a scribe until August 1538; and Johannes Hanguemar is called *custode librorum* in a *motu proprio* of 1513.

[7] Guillermus Gomont and Jo. Francisco Felicis.

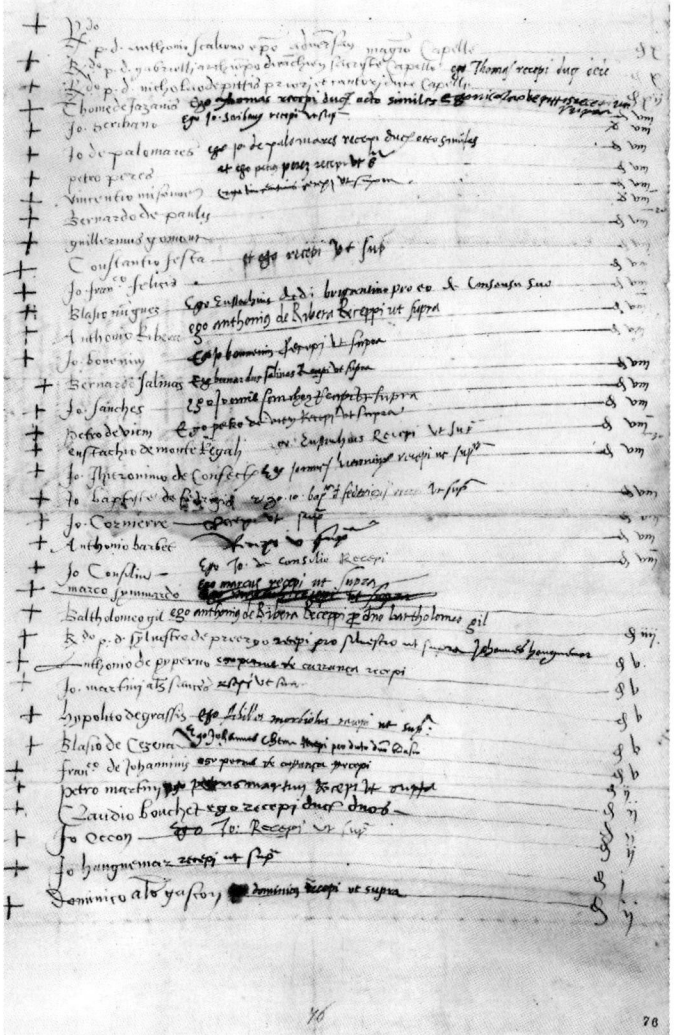

Figure 3. MS C.S. 681, folio 76ʳ

by the presence of two names on the list: Niccolo de Pictis, who left Rome shortly after the massacre, not returning until after December 1528 and Antonio Scaliono, who died on December 19, 1528.[8] Any list containing both their names would have to have been written before the sack. The *terminus post quem* is sometime in 1524, the

---

[8] See Hermann-Walther Frey, "Klemens VII und der Prior der päpstlichen Kapelle Nicholo de Pictis," *Die Musikforschung*, IV (1951), 175 ff.; and Conrad Eubel, *Hierarchia Catholica medii aevi*, III (Regensburg, 1923).

year Eustachio de Monte Regalis left Modena.[9] Beyond this, folio 76 cannot be dated with accuracy, but it is clear that, along with folio 75, it provides a picture of the chapel of Clement VII in the first few years of his reign.

Part of the interest of the documents is surely that they preserve the signatures of many singers—among them the composers Festa, Bonnevin, Missionne, Conseil, and Scribano—as well as that of the scribe Johannes Occon. Particularly intriguing is the appearance of Eustachio de Monte Regalis. In a recent publication, Howard Brown has postulated the presence of Eustachio in Rome because a Eustachio is listed in the Cappella Giulia in 1514, and because a motet by Eustachio de Monte Regalis is included in the Vatican manuscript C. S. 46.[10] This evidence is not entirely conclusive, for there could have been any number of musicians named Eustachio, and Vatican manuscripts often contain pieces by non-resident singers. Now, however, Monte Regalis can definitely be placed in Rome in December 1526. He may even be the *Eustachio cantore* recorded as living in Rome with a household of five *bocche* in a census taken at the end of 1526 or the beginning of 1527. Quite possibly, he may have died during the sack of Rome.[11] Whether he was in Rome before the beginning of the reign of Clement VII is, however, still open to question.

Smith College

[9] See Gino Roncaglia, *La cappella musicale del duomo di Modena*, Historiae musicae cultores. Biblioteca, Vol. V (Florence, 1957), p. 22.

[10] Howard Mayer Brown and Edward Lowinsky, eds., Eustachio Romano. *Musica duorum, Rome, 1521*, Monuments of Renaissance Music, VI (Chicago, 1975), p. 10.

[11] Of course, this could also be Eustachio Romano; see Domenico Gnoli, "Descriptio urbis o censimento della populazione di Roma avanti il sacco Borbonico," *Archivio della R. Società Romana di Storia Patria*, XVII (1894), 375–520, esp. 428. Also in the census are a Nicolo cantore (Niccolo de Pictis?) with a household of five (p. 439) and Vincentio Missonne, with a household of four (p. 439). I could not find the names of the other members of the chapel. Perhaps they were subsumed into the papal *familia* numbering seven hundred (p. 453).

APPENDIX A*

C.S. MS 681, folio 75–75^v
de mense dec[embris] 1526

R^{do} p. d. Anthonio scalionio E[pisco]po adversan[sis] mag[ist]ro Capelle	d x
R^{do} p. d. Gabrielli archie[pisco]po dirachien[sis] Sacriste Capelle ego Jo. sontay r[ecep]i p[ro] d[omi]no sacrista	d x
R^{do} d. Nicolao de pittis priori et Cantori dicte Capelle	d xii
E nicolao de pittis priori et cantori dicte capelle	
ego nicolao de pittis recepi ut supra	

Thome de fazanis Ego Thomas recepi duc[atos] octo similes
Jo. Scribano Ego Jo. Scriban[us] Rescepi ut sup[ra]
Jo. de palomares
Petro peres et ego recepi ut s[upra]
Vincentio misonne Recepi ut supra v. misonne

* For information about the singers, the reader is referred to Haberl, "Die römische 'schola cantorum' "; and Hermann-Walther Frey, "Regesten zur päpstlichen Kapelle unter Leo X und zu seiner Privatkapelle," *Die Musikforschung*, VIII (1955), 58–73, 178–99, 412–37; IX (1956), 46–57, 139–56, 411–19.

III

477

Bernardo de paulis ego b[er]nar[dus] d[e] paulis recepi ut sup[ra]
Constantio festa ego recepi ut sup[ra] constantius
Blasio nugnes ego blasi[us] nunez r[ecepi] ut sup[ra]
Anthonio Ribera ego anthoni[us] de Ribera Recepi ut supra
Jo Bonevin ego Jo bonnevin recepi ut supra
Bernardo salinas Ego bernardus salinas Recepi ut supra
Jo. sanches E[t] Ego Joanis Sanchez Recepi ut sup[ra]
Petro de vieni Ego petrus de vien Recepi ut supra
Eustachio de monte Regali Et Ego recepi
Jo Hieronimo de Confectus Ego Joan[n]es hieronimus recepi ut s[upra]
Jo Bap[tis]te de fedrigis ego io Bap[tis]te recepi ut sup[ra]
Jo Cornierre Jo Corniere Re[cepi] ut sup[ra]
Anthonio barbet Ego An. recepi ut sup[ra]
Jo. Consiliu[m] Ego Jo. de Consilio recepi ut sup[ra]
Marco symmardo Ego marcus re[ce]pi ut sup[ra]

Baltholomeo gil ego Eustachius tenes	d iiii
R^{do} p. d. Silvestro preeris or.[?] p^{egu}[?] Jo hanguemar recepi ut sup[ra]	d v
Anthonio de pip[er]no Ego Thomas de fazanis scripsi p[ro] d[omi]no Ant[oni]o q[ui] ipse recepit	d v
Jo sancii Resepi ut supra	d v
hypolito de grassis Ego Achilles morbiotus recepi ut sup[ra]	d v
Blasio de Cezena Blasius de Cesena recepi ut sup[ra]	d v

[folio 75^v]

francisco de Johanninis ego petrus de cazzanca Recepi ut s[upra]	d ii
Petro martini Ego petr[us] martini R[e]cepi ut supra	d ii
Claudio Bouchet Ego Eustachius dedi b[ri]gantino Futuri[?] resid[?] dedi ei**	d ii
Jo De occon Ego Eustachius dedi b[ri]gantino pro eo	d ii
Jo hanguemar recepi ut sup[ra]	d i
Dominco gascon recepi ut sup[ra]	d ii

APPENDIX B
C.S. MS 681, folio 76

R^{do} p. d. anthonio scaliono e[pisco]po adversan[sis] mag[ist]ro Capelle	d x
R^{do} p. d. gabrielli archie[pisco]po dirachien[sis] sacriste Capelle ego Thomas recepi duc[atos] dece[m]	d x
R^{do} p. d. nicholao de pittis priori et cantori dicte Capelle ego nicolao de pittis recepi ut supra	d xii
Thome de Fazanis Ego Thomas recepi duc[atos] octo similes	d viii
Jo. Scribano Ego Jo. scriban[us] recepi ut sup[ra]	d viii
Jo de palomares Ego Jo. de palomares recepi duc[atos] otto similes	d viii
petro peres Et ego petr[us] perez recepi ut s[upra]	d viii
Vincentio misonne Ego vincentius recepi ut supra	d viii
Bernardo de paulis	d viii
guillermus gomont	d viii
Constantio festa et ego recepi ut sup[ra]	d viii
Jo. tran[cis]co felicis	d viii
Blasio nugnez Ego Eustachius dedi brigantino pro eo d[e] consensu suo	d viii
Anthonio Ribera ego anthoni[us] de Ribera Receppi ut supra	d viii
Jo. bonevin Ego Jo bonnevin Recepi ut supra	d viii
Bernardo salinas Ego bernardus salinas Recepi ut supra	d viii

** This would appear to mean that Eustachio is picking up Bouchet's salary.

Jo. sanches Ego Joannis sanchez Recepi ut supra	d viii
petro de vieni Ego petro de vieni Recepi ut supra	d viii
eustachio de monte Regali Ego Eustachius Recepi ut sup[ra]	d viii
Jo. Hieronimo de Confect[us] Ego Joannes Hieronim[us] recepi ut sup[ra]	d viii
Jo. baptiste de fedrigis Ego io. bap[tiste] d[e] fedrigis recepi ut sup[ra]	d viii
Jo. Cornierre Recepi ut sup[ra]	d viii
Anthonio barbet Recepi u[t] sup[ra]	d viii
Jo Consilium Ego Jo. de consilio Recepi	d viii
marco symmardo Ego marcus recepi ut supra	
ego marcus recepi ut supra	d viii

Bartholomeo gil ego anthoni[us] de Ribera Receppi p[ro] d[omi]no bartholomeo gil	d iiii
R^{do} p. d. sylvestro de preerys recepi pro silvestro ut supra Johannes hanguemar	d v
Anthonio de pyperno ego petrus de cazzanca recepi	d v
Jo. martinii al[ia]s sances recepi ut supra	d v
hypolito de grassis Ego Achilles morbiotus recepi ut sup[ra]	d v
Blasio de Cezena Ego Johannes Chemi Recepi pro dicto d[omi]no blasio	d v
fran[cis]co de Johanninis ego petrus de cazzanca Recepi	d ii
petro martinii Ego petrus martinii Recepi ut supra	d ii
Claudio bouchet ego recepi duc[atos] duos	d ii
Jo occon Ego Jo. Recepi ut sup[ra]	d ii
Jo hanguemar recepi ut sup[ra]	d i
dominico al[ia]s gascon ego dominic[us] recepi ut supra	d ii

IV

FROM THE DIARY OF A 16TH-CENTURY PAPAL SINGER*

Among the many manuscripts in the Cappella Sistina collection of the Vatican Library not catalogued by Haberl or Llorens is one numbered 651 (hereafter CS 651).[1] This paper manuscript of thirty-six folios bound in parchment is a combination diary/account book compiled by one of the most long-lived of papal singers, Giovanni Antonio Merlo, who joined the chapel in September 1551 after having served in the Cappella Giulia, and remained until his death on 28 December 1588.[2] The manuscript contains notes and jottings made over a number of years (1559-1588) in approximately chronological order.[3] Included are drafts of correspondence and memoranda, lists of assets and debits, and mention of historical events (there is even a fragment of music), all combining to give an idea of the daily concerns of a typical papal singer in the second half of the 16th century.

The majority of entries are financial. As a member of the papal chapel, Merlo received a monthly salary of 9 ducats,[4] but such salaries had never constituted the whole remuneration given the singers. It had long been the custom, for instance, for gratuities to be given the singers by celebrants of Masses and by newly created cardinals; Merlo actually records a number of payments in the diary,[5] and is further careful to record the special payments made *sedia vacante* (the period between the death of one pope and the election of his successor).[6] He apparently had other avenues open to him also, being at various times in the employ of Cardinal Sermoneta (in 1559) and Cardinal Farnese (in 1569), and in later life (1575-1580) receiving a pension from the pope of first 40, then 50 ducats a year.[7]

But the most common way of augmenting the salaries of papal servants was by the granting of benefices. Clerical preferments in Italy, France, and Spain had long been conferred upon members of the chapel, of course with the understanding that they would not have to take up residence in order to enjoy the income.[8] In the second half of the 16th century, however, a new reforming spirit had taken over in these matters, as the following excerpt from CS 651 relates:

1567	1567
Die xxiii mense februarii D.ns Marinus Lupi occurse che m. Marino Lupi gli fu comendato da Mons.r	On 23 February D.no Marino Lupi. It happened that M. Marino Lupi was commanded by Msgr. Romanetto

IV

Romanetto per parte de Sua S.ta havendo una parrochiale in la sua patria che dovess'andar'a resider' overo resignar' detta parrochia il detto m. Marino dimando licentia alla compagnia et al m.o di cappella per andar alla patria per accomodar detto suo benefitio et gli fu dato licentia per mesi dui el detto m. Marino ritorno dalla patria et non portando cosa niuna sopra la risegnia di detta parrocia capito avanti a Mons.r Romanetto con dirgli che non haveva trovato il vescovo di Ascoli in la cita et che per questo non haveva potuto interamente far quanto era el desiderio suo ma che il vicario d'Ascoli gli haveva dato licentia per vinti giorni potessi venir in Roma per espedir le cose sue finalmente el detto Mons.r non gli volse far buona alcuna sua ragione ma volse che in termine di otto giorni devessi ritornar alla sua cura vetandogli che in modo niuno non potessi venir a servir la nostra chappella. Et questo fu tempore Pii Quinti Anno secundo pontificatus sui 1567.[9]

in the name of His Holiness that, since he had a *parrochiale* in his country, he should either go and reside there or should resign it. M. Marino asked the Chapel and the maestro di cappella for a leave of absence to go home and arrange things about his benefice, and he was given leave to go for two months. The said M. Marino returned from his home and [since] he did not have anything concerning the resignation of the benefice, he appeared before Msgr. Romanetto and told him that he had not been able to find the Bishop of Ascoli in the city, and therefore could not entirely do what he desired, but that the bishop's vicar had given him leave for twenty days to return to Rome for his affairs. But finally the said Msgr. did not accept his reasons and demanded that he return to his cure within eight days, letting him know that there was no way he could return to serve in our chapel. And this was in the time of Pius V, the second year of his pontificate, 1567.

It is probably no accident that this strict enforcement of the rules of residence comes a few years after the final sessions of the Council of Trent (the Council's decrees being quite specific on this point).[10] The singer in question appears to have attempted a bit of subterfuge (saying he could not find the bishop and therefore could not resign the benefice), but was sternly ordered away from Rome. Shortly after, he did resign the benefice, returned to Rome with proof, and was readmitted to the chapel.[11]

In spite of this, Merlo himself held for many years an absentee benefice in Bisignano (Calabria), appointing a vicar and enjoying the income without ever being called into account. The first mention of the benefice is in 1560.

1560 Santa Maria Nova
Addi quindici di ottobre hebbi li primi denari del mio benefitio quali furno scudi trentuno con il nome di iddio benedetto.[12]

1560 Santa Maria Nova
On 15 October I had the first money from my benefice which consisted of thirty-one ducats. Blessed be the name of the Lord.

In December 1560 he received 36 ducats, and continued to hold the benefice at least until 1574. However, many of his entries about it indicate that he had appointed a vicar; the clearest of these is dated 15 March 1566.

Addi quindici di Marzo de 66 hebbi da s.r scipione spinola per commissione di m. Baldessar' calamaro segretario di Mons.r de Bisignano scuti trent'uno di oro in oro et giulii duodeci quali sono per l'affitto de s.ta maria la nova dell anno 1566 Il qual'affitto incomincia il di xii de Maggio 1566. Et detto m. Baldessar e mio procurator di detto benefitio dal giorno sopradetto xii de Maggio.[13]	On 15 March 1566, I had from Sig. Scipione Spinola acting for M. Baldessar Calamaro, secretary of Msgr. of Bisignano, thirty-one gold ducats and twelve giulii which are for the rent of Santa Maria la Nova for the year 1566 which begins on 12 May 1566. And the said M. Baldessar is my vicar for that benefice from that day, 12 May.

It would appear that Merlo cleared about 40 ducats a year from his benefice in Calabria, but this may not have been the only one he had. In February 1563, for instance, he renounced a benefice in favor of one Giovanni Antonio Longobardo, and was reimbursed for his trouble, and there is even mention of a priory in Rouen granted Merlo through the good graces of Cardinal del Monte; in fact, he probably owed his Bisignano benefice to his one-time employer Cardinal Sermoneta, Bishop of Bisignano from 1558 to 1563.[14] Perhaps Merlo was never disciplined like his colleague Lupi because he had special influence or because the benefices were of a type not requiring residence.

In fact, CS 651 makes Merlo appear to be financially successful. Many entries show him employed in money transactions, and he is constantly lending funds. This occurs so frequently that it suggests a thriving moneylending business, even though he often specifies that the money is being lent *gratis* (at the same time being careful to list the collateral put up by the borrower). In any case, the extent of some of the transactions suggests a healthy amount of capital, as does Merlo's investment in 1565 of 300 ducats in the Monte della Farina at 8 per cent interest (the sum being about three times his yearly chapel salary of 108 ducats).[15]

Merlo was also a home- and landowner; a long list of payments in 1565 and 1566 concerns the construction of a "giardino" (with house) at the cost of several hundred ducats.[16] The expenses included large amounts of lime (*calcie*), rock, boards (*tavole*), roofing tile (*teicole*), and nails, the digging of a well, removing earth and building a cellar (*cantina*), and a hedge (*fratte*) to separate the property from the neighbors. But almost as soon as the house was finished, Merlo rented it out, and con-

IV

tinued to rent it for many years; indeed that may have been the reason it was built in the first place.[17] The entries concerning this make it possible to locate the property. Merlo on various occasions refers to it as being "in the new street which goes towards the Borgetto," as being "under the monte della trinita," and as the "casa di populo."[18] It is likely then that the house and garden were situated on the via del Babuino, newly completed in 1565, running from the Piazza di Spagna (then Piazza della Trinità) to the Piazza del Popolo, the last street it crosses being the viccolo del Borgetto. This area, known as the Campo di Marzo, was largely unpopulated until the second half of the 16th century, and Merlo represents one of the influx of new homeowners.[19] He received a yearly rent of 24 ducats for the house, and in 1568 himself rented another house at the cost of 38 ducats a year.[20]

That Merlo was generally trusted in money matters is indicated by entries showing him acting as an agent for members of the papal chapel who were on leave and not in Rome. From 1561 to 1564, for instance, he procured letters of credit for Giovanni Antonio Latino, a singer attending the Council of Trent; Merlo would pay money to Venturino Manelli in Rome who would then transfer the funds to his brother Antonio, *depositarius* of the Council, for payment to Latino in Trent.[21] Merlo's services for another singer, Niccolo Barrone, included picking up his salary as well as buying various items in Rome and having them shipped; needless to say, he expected to be repaid for these favors.[22] For many years, Merlo also acted as the agent for a certain Madonna Antonia de Amatis and later for her daughter Emilia in various transactions, and in 1573 received 62 ducats, 50 baiocchi from Cardinal Savello who was renting Madonna Antonia's house (of course, the relationship Merlo had with the lady that allowed him to act for her in such matters must remain in the realm of speculation).[23] All this suggests that Merlo was well off or at least comfortable; certainly the diary contains no evidence of monetary difficulties or complaints of poverty, but seems rather to be a record of profitable investments. However, only a thorough study of the economy of the time would yield a true assessment of his worth.[24]

From our point of view, the most interesting sections of CS 651 are those dealing directly with matters concerning the papal chapel. The lists of gratuities have already been mentioned; folios 9′ and 13′ record ceremonies held on important feast days in 1567, mentioning the celebrant, the number of singers attending, and the tip (usually one or two giulii) given each singer. Notices of this nature are also to be found in the *Diarii Sistini*, except that the *Diarii* record singers who were absent and fined for being so.[25] However, Merlo also wrote a number of *memorie* dealing with other matters. For instance, he describes a direct affront to the College of Singers in the year 1571.

IV

Nel 1571 al tempo de Mons.r sacrista et nostro m.o de chappella chiamato Giuseppe occurre un caso di molto consideratione et fu questo venendo occhasione de ricever'cantori per la nostra chappella el nostro m.o ne propose tre cantori uno chiamato m. Ipolito et l'altro m. Tomasso et l'altro m. Francesco venimo al scrutino el primo ebbe voti 12 el secondo 7 et l'altro nove et noi eravamo cantori decidotto al votare de maniera che niuno di questi ebbe il compimento intiero delli voti secondo i nostri statuti attal che tutti tre furno esclusi mentre di meno el sopradetto nostro m.o con l'aiuto del R.mo Char.le Morone nostro protectore con esponergli alcuna cosa contra di noi ottene di poter ammetter'li detti cantori ancora che fusse contro gli nostri statuti et un' sabbato matina detta la cotta a tutti tre senz'il voler nostro subbito ricorremo da N.S. con un memoriale narrandogli com il fatto era passato dicendogli che Sua S.ta era gabbato et che nui avendogli giurato fidelta non potevamo maneare far'il debbito nostro in fargliele intendere pero Sua S.ta era padrone facessi quello che a lei piacesse Et anco incorremo da Mons.r Carniglia come sopraintendente della casa di Sua S.ta pregandolo fussi contento farne una parola con Sua S.ta el quale Mons.re ne parlo al papa et intendendo che non erano entrati secondo l'ordini nostri dette commissione si dovessero mandar' con dio Et detti tre cantori servirno con la cotta un'mese intiero etiam in una messa papale et in capo de un'mese furno licentiati tutti dal sopradetto nostra m.o cosa che credo veramente non sia occursa in molt'anni Onesto lo dico accio che voi che verrete dopo noi vi ricordiate di mantener queste nostre constitutione et far'come avemo fatto noi altri per servitio di quelli

In 1571 in the time of Msgr. Sacrista and our maestro di cappella named Giuseppe, there occurred an event of much importance, which was this. It being the occasion for us to receive singers into our chapel, our maestro proposed three, one called M. Ippolito, another M. Tomasso, and the third M. Francesco. We voted, and the first had twelve votes, the second seven, and the third nine, and there were eighteen of us voting, so that none of them had the number of votes required by our statutes, and they were all rejected. But nonetheless, the said maestro with the help of our protector Cardinal Morone [obtained] by telling him certain things against us, managed to get them admitted even though it was against our statutes, and one Saturday morning gave them the *cotta* all without our consent. We immediately sent a memorandum to His Holiness telling him what had happened and that he had been deceived, and that we, having sworn fealty to him were only doing our duty in letting him know, although His Holiness was the master and could do anything he wished. And also we went to Msgr. Carniglia as superintendant of the papal household and asked him if he would please have a word with His Holiness, and the said Msgr. talked about it to the pope who, hearing that they (the singers) had not been admitted according to the correct manner, ordered that they be sent on their way. And the three singers served with *cotta* for a whole month including a papal Mass, and at the beginning of the next month they were fired all three by the said maestro, something which had not occurred in many years. I say this honestly so that you who will come after us will maintain our constitution and do as we did for the

87

IV

che verranno dopo noi si com'anno fatto i nostri passati per noi Di poi passati giorni 15 ritornammo a pigliar' un contralto de questi che furno espulsi chiamato m. Ipolito per causa che Mons.r m.o de chappella ne proposa che questo m. Ipolito era ricorso da Sua S.ta dolendosi che avendo auti le doi parte delli voti et non manchandonegli se non uno pregava Sua S. li volessi far' gratia insieme con la compagnia admetterlo tanto piu quanto essendo un delli nostri cantori amalato chiamato Don Paulo Biancho et per causa del'infirmita non si puotte trovar'el giorno del scrutino ma ben si trovo el giorno che detti cantori furno provati et avendolo sentito et satisfattogli gli mando el suo voto in scriptis et fu dato in mano del m.o de chappella attal' che ne parse admetterlo per tutti questi rispetti ancora che fu contrastato molto sopra questo voto che fu mandato cosi in scriptis per rispetto che chi voleva che fusse valido et chi no pero la cosa non fu decisa per non esser'occurs'altre volte ma resto impendente tempore Pii Quinti 1571 mense februarij.[26]

good of those who will come later, as our predecessors have done for us. Furthermore, after fifteen days, we reconsidered the contralto of the three named M. Ippolito because Msgr. the maestro di cappella said that this Ippolito had complained to His Holiness saying that he had had two-thirds of the vote, and since only one [more vote] was needed, asking that His Holiness have the goodness to admit him into the chapel, even more so because one of our singers named Don Paulo Biancho was sick and therefore could not attend on the day of the voting, but was there when the said singers were auditioned and, having heard him and being satisfied, gave him his vote in writing. And this was given to the maestro so it appeared that he should be admitted because of this, although there was much debate concerning this vote sent in writing; whether it was valid or not. But the thing was not decided for lack of precedent and rested impending in the time of Pius V, 1571, the month of February.

Here are chapel politics in action. Three singers are proposed to the chapel by the maestro di cappella; they are auditioned and then a vote is taken. According to the chapel constitution, a more than two-thirds majority of those present was needed for admission, and none of the singers receives the required number of votes. The matter should have ended there, but the maestro must have had a personal stake in the affair, since he enlists the help of Cardinal Morone "by telling him certain things" against the singers, and manages to have his protégés hired. The singers are not going to stand for this, and immediately address themselves directly to the pope through a memorandum and through the superintendant of the papal household. When the pope (the austere Pius V) hears that the three singers have not been correctly admitted, he orders them to be fired—a clear victory for the College of Singers. But complications arise. One of the singers had received exactly two-thirds of the vote (twelve out of eighteen), and complains to the pope that he should be admitted, especially since the singers had failed to count a deciding vote in his favor, sent in as a proxy by a singer who was ill at the time of the scrutiny, but who had heard the auditions. The matter is, however, left up in the air for lack of precedent. The point is that the singers successfully defended their rights and privileges in the face of their own maestro di cappella (who was a prelate) and in the face of Cardinal Morone, the savior of the Council of Trent.[27]

It turns out that Merlo may have had a personal reason for being so interested in this affair, for he himself had nearly been expelled from the papal chapel for opposing a similar arrangement. The *Diarii Sistini* record that in March 1558 Pope Paul IV (Gian Pietro Caraffa) had decided to bring to the chapel two singers from Naples, Ferdinando and Francesco Bustamante (the Caraffa were a Neapolitan family). In April a vote was held, and the newcomers were unanimously approved by the singers with the exception of Merlo and Nicolo Clinca, who apparently refused to vote at all (not accepting the *fabas botandum* or "voting beans") to the great annoyance of the maestro who began proceedings against them for insubordination. Now, an interpretation of Merlo's action could be that he felt that the new singers were being forced on the chapel by the pope, and, since he could not prevent their admission, he refused to have anything to do with a "sham" procedure. This must have angered the pope (who was a difficult man to get along with in any case), and he sent his nephew Cardinal Caraffa to the chapel with the order that Merlo and Clinca be expelled; it was only by special petition that the other singers managed to get this punishment reduced to a fine.[28] The memory of the affair might explain why Merlo was careful to record in great detail, and for no apparent purpose, a similar incident in which "right" prevailed (i.e. the singers refused to allow outside interference), and it might also throw some light on one of the few purely historical notations in the diary.

Addi sei de marzo 1561 fu strangolato il Char.le Charaffa in castello et tagliato il capo al s. ducha suo fratello insieme con il conte de Alife suo cognati et don Leonardo de Chardini Requiescant in pace.[29]	On 6 March 1561, Cardinal [Carlo] Caraffa was strangled in the Castello, and his brother the Duke had his head cut off along with the Count di Alife his brother-in-law and Don Leonardo de Chardini. Requiescant in pace.

Merlo was in the chapel during several of its reforms, including the "cardinals' commission" of 1565, when he was a member of the delegation of singers that met with Cardinals Borromeo and Morone.[30] The result of the reform was the reduction of the number of singers by ten, who were then designated "Second Class" and paid reduced wages (presumably they ceased singing in the chapel). It may also have been in response to a wish for information about the chapel that Merlo began a list of singers, now on folio 22 of CS 651, stating the year of entry if he knew it, and continuing the list until 1585.

Twenty years after the cardinals' commission, Merlo was involved in yet another reform.

Memoria qualmente addi 20 di giugnio 1586 la S.ta di N.S. Papa Sisto Quinto avendo ragionato piu volte con meco et il s.r Sotto cantor' di cappella sopra il nostro m.o de cappella dicendo che a lui pareva cosa giusta che avend' aver la cappella un m.o li pareva cosa giusta che piu presto fuss'un' huomo della medesma professione che un prelato il qual'non avessi intelligentia di musica gli fu da noi replicato che non era cosa solita ne vi era di bisognio per tal effetto essendo che quasi tutti quelli che erano m.i detta cappella erano huomi sufficienti da poter' reger' detta cappella In resulutione Sua S.ta si risolse di voler che a'hogni modo fussi m.o di cappella uno della professione et ci mando a dir per il s. Antonio Bocchapaduli nostro m.o di cappella et da parte del R.mo Char.le Azzolino segretario di N.S. che Sua S.ta ci proponeva questi infrascritti partiti che vedessimo se tra nui vi erano huomini a questo proposito che lui si contentava che si elegesse uno di nui in quel modo che a noi piacesse cioe o per tre mesi o per sei mesi o per un anno overo perpetuo overo se volevamo alcuno fuora del gremmio overo lui cenne averria dato un a suo modo basta che ne fece proporre tutti li sopradetti partiti cosa veramente di grandissima consideratione della sua grand' amorevolezza verso di nui.[31]	Memorandum that on 20 June 1586, His Holiness Pope Sixtus V discussed many times with me and with Sig. Sotto, singer in the chapel [the subject of] the maestro di cappella, saying that it appeared to him that it would be a good thing, considering that the chapel had to have a maestro, that he be a man of the same profession rather than a prelate who might not understand music. We replied that it was neither usual nor necessary considering that practically all who had been maestri had known enough to be able to direct the chapel. In resolution, His Holiness decided that at all costs the maestro should be one of the profession, and ordered our maestro di capella Sig. Antonio Bocchapaduli, speaking also for the Most Rev. Cardinal Azzolino, secretary to His Holiness to propose the following: that if there were people among us [who could do the job] he suggested that one of us be elected in any way we wished, for three months, or for six months, or for a year, or for life; or we could select one from outside; or he could appoint one himself. Finally he had proposed all the above suggestions, something which truly showed his great tenderness towards us.

In 1586, the energetic Pope Sixtus V suggests a major change in the hierarchy of the chapel. In the past, although the positions of *Abbas, Decano,* and *Punctatore* had been held by singers elected for a certain period of time, the job of maestro di cappella had always gone to a prelate (usually a bishop). The pope, perhaps with the examples of St.

Mark's in Venice and St. Peter's in Rome before him, has come to the conclusion that the maestro should be "one of the same profession," i.e., a singer. The idea is not greeted enthusiastically by the singers, who state that the earlier maestri had generally known enough about music to run things (but perhaps not enough to interfere). Sixtus, however, will not be thwarted, and so gives the singers a wide choice; they can elect one of their number for three, six, or twelve months, or for life, or one can come from the outside, or the pope can appoint one. Eventually the singers decided to elect one of their own number for a year, and the first recipient of the honor was none other than Giovanni Antonio Merlo himself.[32] He thus becomes the first singer since Carpentras to lead the papal chapel, and the first to be elected by the other singers. Undoubtedly his age had something to do with it; he had been in the chapel for thirty-five years in 1586.

By far the most intriguing entries concerning the chapel appear on folios 30' and 31 of CS 651, and may shed some light on the pieces actually sung by papal singers in 1568.

Avertire che il giorno della creation'de Sua S.ta e il gradual vol'esser' Beata gens et poi veni sancte spiritus cioe il giorno del'epifania 1568 tempore Pii V	Remember that on the day of the election of His Holiness the Gradual should be *Beata gens,* and then *Veni sancte spiritus,* that is the day of Epiphany 1568 in the time of Pius V.[33]
Ottobre Avertire che un mottetto di Giovanni Moton Confitebimur a un contralto sopra il tenore che va alla quarta	October Remember that a motet, *Confitebimur,* by Jean Mouton, has a contralto over the tenor at the fourth.
Un altro mottetto del medesmo auttore che dice Benedicamus domino a una parte sopra il tenore che aspetta dui tempi et si piglia una voce piu alta del tenore	Another motet by the same author called *Benedicamus Domino* has a part over the tenor which waits for two beats and begins a step higher than the tenor.
La epifania el mottetto Illumina	For Epiphany, the motet *Illumina.*
El giorno della creation'del papa e di poi de epifania el mottetto Veni sancte spiritus Infra ottava epifania cie un mottetto di Compert	For the day of the pope's election and also for Epiphany, the motet *Veni sancte spiritus.* Within the Octave of Epiphany there is a motet by Compère.
In die coronationis si canta Corona Aurea di Arcadelt	On the day of the Coronation, *Corona aurea* by Arcadelt is sung.
In die chatedra S.ti Petri Quem dicunt homines	On the Feast of St. Peter's Chair, *Quem dicunt homines.*

IV

Avertir'che la notte del natale quando Sua S.ta fa l'uffitio quando dice il suo evangelium ditto che averra Jube domini benedicere bisogna responder' Amen	Remember that on Christmas Eve when His Holiness is celebrating, when he reads the Gospel, at the point where "Jube domini benedicere" comes, it is necessary to respond "Amen."
Ricordo Avertire che il vespero del'epifania vol esser'intonato molto basso	Reminder Remember that the Vespers of Epiphany should be intoned very softly.
Avertir'che l'ultimo notturno delli morti vol esser'intonato basso	Remember that the last Nocturne of All Soul's should be intoned softly.
Per l'ottavia di homnia santi ce una messa di Comper'molto bona con il suo motetto Ave Maria la mess'e del 4 tono	For the Octave of All Saints there is a Mass by Compère which is very good, with his motet *Ave Maria*. The Mass is in the fourth mode.
Una messa vecchia di Rubret' Fevino nel libro vecchio	An old Mass by Robert Févin in the old book.
Un'altra chiamato La chastagnia	Another called *La Castagnia*.
Una missa de Pipelare super'L'om' arme ad Agnus ce un contr'alto sopr'el basso che va all decima el basso un duplichato	A Mass by Pipelare on *L'homme armé*. At the Agnus there is a contralto over the bass which duplicates the bass at the tenth.[34]
Una messa di Giovanni Monton sopr'Alma redentoris	A Mass by Jean Mouton on *Alma redemptoris*.
Domenicha 3 adventus se dice Alma redemptoris (overo Veni domine) di Constantio Festa	On the third Sunday in Advent *Alma redemptoris* (or *Veni Domine*) by Costanzo Festa is sung.
Domenicha 4 Missus est	Fourth Sunday, *Missus est*.
Natale La notte del natale il primo responsorio va cantato con il contrapunto et cosi l'ultimo el secundo non si fa contrapunto avertir'a pigliar'un poco basso el secundo noctturno	Christmas On Christmas Eve, the first responsory is sung in counterpoint as is the last.[35] The second is not sung in counterpoint. Remember to begin the second Nocturne a little softly.
El secundo giorno del natale si suol' dir'el mottetto O beata infantia di Pieton	On the second day of Christmas, the motet *O beata infantia* by Piéton is usually sung.

El vespero di pasqua rosata vol esser intonato molto basso	The Vespers of Pasqua Rosata should be intoned very softly.
El vespero della trinita vol esser intonato basso	The Vespers of Trinity should be intoned softly.
Ricordo che la domenicha delle palme si cantano li Chirie della madonna in canto fermo sono in la fine del libro	Remember that on Palm Sunday the Kyrie is that of the Madonna in chant at the end of the book.
Un mottetto per l'otttavia del epifania vechio di non so se dice In illo tempore cum battizaretur'di	An old motet for the Octave of Epiphany by I-don't-know-who called *In illo tempore cum battizaretur* by

There are two categories of entries; one deals with performance (the correct way to begin Offices, when to sing in improvised counterpoint), and one specifies a repertory of pieces sometimes ascribed to particular composers and assigned to particular feasts. Much of the polyphony can be found in extant manuscripts in the Sistine collection. Going down the list: the motet by Mouton called *Confitebimur* may be the one entitled *Confitemini Domino* in CS 38 which has a canon at the fourth;[36] the second motet by Mouton is almost certainly the *Benedicam Dominum* in the same manuscript with a canonic voice at the second entering after two semibreves; no composer is named for *Illumina,* but there is a setting of *Illumina oculos meos* by de Silva in CS 55; there are many settings of *Veni sancte spiritus;* the motet by Compère for the Octave of Epiphany has not been identified; Arcadelt's *Corona aurea* is in CS 24; there is a setting of *Quem dicunt homines* by Richafort in CS 46; Compère's *Ave Maria* is in CS 15, and his *Missa L'homme armé* which is in the fourth mode is in CS 35; there are two Masses by Robert de Févin in the collection—the *Missa Le villain jaloux* in CS 23 and the *Missa Ave Maria* in CS 26; the *Missa Castagnia* has not been found; Pipelare's *Missa L'homme armé* is in CS 41; Mouton's *Missa Alma redemptoris* is in CS 45; neither of Festa's motets could be found; there are settings of *Missus est* by Josquin in CS 63 and 19, and by Mouton in CS 42; *O beata infantia* by Pieton is in CS 24; *In illo tempore cum battizaretur* might be the motet *Factum est cum baptizaretur* by Prioris in CS 42.

A striking thing about the repertory is its age. The list was apparently written ca. 1568, yet Palestrina is not mentioned once, although he was regularly being paid to produce music for the use of the chapel, nor is there any mention of other composers living and working in Rome at the time.[37] The references to Mouton, Arcadelt, and Festa are, on the other hand, not surprising as their music was still being copied into chapel manuscripts.[38] This was not the case with some of the other names on the list, however. Merlo specifically mentions an "old Mass by Robert de Févin in the old book," and indeed the manuscripts containing Masses by that composer could have been considered old in 1568; the same holds true for Pipelare's *Missa L'homme armé*.[39] Most interesting are the references to Compère, the oldest composer in the group, one who had long since dropped out of the repertory, whose pieces were preserved in the oldest of the "old books."[40]

It seems then that these *ricordi* are the fruits of a search through the library of the chapel, including some of the oldest musical sources contained therein. They have all the markings of a selection of repertory for the papal singers (hence the connection of certain pieces with specific feasts) and are interspersed with practical performance hints. This implies that Merlo had at one time the job of picking the chapel repertory, and it is true that from 1566 to 1569 he held the administrative post of *Abbas*, although there is no indication that the functions of the position ever included the selection of works to be sung.[41]

Also, although the list is far from comprehensive, it suggests a retrospective attitude (soon to be a characteristic of the papal chapel); this is strange, however, because the music for the chapel at this time should have been selected according to the standards laid down by the Council of Trent, standards presumably not met by these pre-Tridentine pieces.[42] The list, then, may reflect nothing more than Merlo's personal antiquarian interests and his knowledge of the chapel library, although the real possibility exists that the list constitutes one of our few references to pieces actually sung by the chapel in the 16th century; as such it provides evidence that motets with texts appropriate to certain feasts were actually sung during those feasts, not, however, specifying when in the service they were performed.[43]

CS 651 also contains entries of a more personal nature. For instance, we learn that Merlo was the brother of Alessandro Merlo, the composer and famous bass, whose admission to the papal chapel is recorded with pride.

| Addi 12 de decembre 1561 Alessandro mio fratello fu votato dalli cantori de N.S. et hebbi egli a suffitientia quanti bisognavano et di piu.[44] | On 12 December 1561, my brother Alessandro was elected to membership in the papal singers, and he had more than enough votes. |

The brothers lived together, and entered the services of the same cardinals. This is true at least of Cardinals Sermoneta and Farnese, and it could be assumed that a notice that Alessandro was attached to the Cardinal of Aragon means that Giovanni was also in his employ; the entry also indicates that the brothers could afford a servant.[45] The Merlos also had a sister who was a nun living in the convent of Santa Lucia in Silice and who died on 7 September 1577, and there is mention of an aunt, named Pantasilea, who died on 11 September 1574.[46]

Finally, the diary ends with a number of miscellaneous notes; a homily to patience, information concerning indulgences, fragments of poetry, and some home remedies, two of which are given here for the benefit of those who may find themselves stranded and afflicted in Italy some day.

Recetta per oppilatione Farrete prendere oncia sei di acciaio fino che non sia ruginoso e lo farrete inforchare et poi spengerlo in accqua Et poi lo farrete limar'sottilmente lo metteret' amollo in aceto biancho e forte Et la schiuma che farra si toglia via Et cosi se gli muti l'aceto 4 volt'il giorno per spatio di tre giorni all fila Et poi mettasi asciugare sopr'un tagliero netto e asciutto e poi si metti in un fiasco di vin'biancho maturo e ben chiaro e si lasci cusi per spatio di tre giorni Et poi si comminci a prendere di quel vino sei oncie la matina a levata de sole e oncie cinque ne pigli la sera tre hore avanti cena tanto la matina quanta la sera si facci exercitio continuando a chavar'la ditta quantita di vino e agiungercelo matin'e sera quanto ne chavera cioe fino che giudichi che quello che resta nel fiasco lo possa condurre fino al termine di un mese.[47]

Prescription for constipation. Take six ounces of fine steel which is not rusty and heat it [red hot] and then plunge it in water. And then polish it finely and soak it in strong white vinegar and remove the foam that appears. And continue to change the vinegar four times a day for three days in a row. Then let [the steel] dry on a clean and dry wooden cutting block, and then put it in a flask of mature, very clear white wine, and leave it for the space of three days. And then begin to take six ounces of that wine in the morning when the sun rises and take five ounces in the evening three hours before dinner, and get used to doing this in the morning and the evening continuing to take the said amount of wine and replacing in the morning and evening the amount taken until you judge that there is enough left in the flask to last until the end of a month.

Contra il fegato
Piglia tre scudi di oro di tre cogni et piglia una scodeletta di creta biancha con accqua corrente et farrai el segnio della croce sopra di quel'accqua et voltate dond'escie il sole et piglia uno di quelli scudi et tocchari il corpo overo sopra li panni et dirrai fele torna avacca et oro torna in accqua fele torna above et accqua torna in oro Et hogni volta butter quello scudo in quel'accqua et la dirai nove volte Et si vol dire il giovedi et la domenicha prima che escha il sole et poi che glie calato il sole.[48]

For the liver
Take three gold ducats [weighing] three *cogni* and take a white clay saucer with running water [in it], and make the sign of the Cross over the water. Turn to the East and take one of the ducats and touch your body or clothes and say, "Bile return to the cow and gold return to water, bile return to the ox and water return to gold." And each time throw the ducat in the water, and do this nine times. And this should be done on Thursdays and on Sundays before the sun rises and before it sets.

NOTES
* This article is an expanded version of a paper read before the New England Chapter of the American Musicological Society in Boston on 14 May 1977. In the transcriptions of Italian, I have expanded all simple abbreviations, but not titles (m. = *messer*, m.o = *maestro*, S.ta = *Santità*, R.mo = *Reverendissimo*, etc.).

[1] See Franz Xaver Haberl, *Bibliographischer und thematischer Musikkatalog des päpstlichen Kapellarchives im Vatican zu Rom*, Bausteine für Musikgeschichte 2 (Leipzig: Breitkopf und Härtel, 1888), also in *Monatshefte für Musikgeschichte* 19 (1887) and 20 (1888) Beilagen; and Joseph Llorens, *Capellae Sixtinae Codices musices notis instructi sive manu scripti sive praelu excussi* (Vatican City, 1960). These catalogues only deal with the music sources in the collection. An index of the other manuscripts is in the Index Room of the Vatican Library. I hope to publish a complete transcription of this document elsewhere.

[2] See Ariane Ducrot, "Histoire de la Cappella Giulia au XVIe siècle depuis sa fondation par Jules II (1513) jusqu'à sa restauration par Grégoire XIII (1578)," *Mélanges d'Archéologie et d'Histoire* 75 (1963) pp. 179-240, 467-559; and E. Celani, "I cantori della Cappella Pontificia nei secoli XVI-XVIII," *Rivista Musicale Italiana* 14 (1907) p. 103, who gives his last name as "Merula."

[3] But not always. See fol. 15' with entries dated 1571, 1577, and 1585.

[4] See the records of the *mandati camerali* in the Archivio di Stato di Roma. In December 1540, the singers had gotten their first raise in about a hundred years when their monthly salary was augmented by one ducat from 8 to 9. (The ducat was the largest unit of currency at the time and was divided into 10 giulii, the giulio divided into 10 baiocchi. There was also a distinction made between a cameral ducat—"oro in oro"—and a ducat "de moneta," the cameral ducat being worth slightly more.)

[5] See folios 9', 10, 13, and 14.

[6] See folios 5, 5', and 15'.

[7] See folios 1, 6', and 15. This is, as far as I know, the first documentary evidence to come to light showing that singers were employed by cardinals at the same time that they were members of the papal chapel, and is of some interest to students of an earlier period, especially considering Edward Lowinsky's theories about Josquin and Cardinal Ascanio Sforza. See his "Ascanio Sforza's Life: a Key to Josquin's Biography and an Aid to the Chronology of his Works," Lowinsky ed., *Josquin des Prez, Proceedings of the International Josquin Festival Conference . . . June 1971* (London: Oxford University Press, 1976) pp. 31-75.

[8] For an excellent discussion of how this worked in the late 15th century, see Jeremy Noble, "New Light on Josquin's Benefices," ibid., pp. 76-102.

[9] Folio 11. Lupi is absent from the *mandati* lists from February to November 1567 (actually his name is crossed off the list of January 1567). See Archivio di Stato di Roma, *mandati camerali* 917, folios 116 ff. Interestingly, there is no mention of this case in the *Diarii Sistini* for the year 1567 (see Biblioteca Apostolica Vaticana, Cappella Sistina, ms. *Diarii Sistini*, 8).

[10] See H. J. Schroeder, O. P. ed., *Canons and Decrees of the Council of Trent* (St. Louis: B. Herder, 1960) pp. 164-166.

[11] Folio 11. Actually, Merlo says that Lupi was not readmitted until January (1568), while the *mandati* have him back in December 1567. Another reference to a singer's benefice on folio 15 shows the chapel supporting Christian Ameyden in litigation for a benefice in Douai.

[12] Folio 3.

[13] Folio 6.

[14] Folios 4, 16', and 36.

[15] Folio 3'. On the Monti, see Jean Delumeau, *Vie économique et sociale de Rome*

dans la seconde moitié du XVIe siècle, Bibliothèque des Ecoles françaises d'Athènes et de Rome, fasc. 184, pt. 2 (Paris: E. de Boccard, 1959).

[16] See particularly folios 7-9.

[17] It was first rented in November 1567 (see folios 12' and 21).

[18] Folios 21, 21', and 25; this last entry is dated 28 March 1588.

[19] See Delumeau, pt. 1 (1957) p. 307.

[20] Folio 21.

[21] See Folio 2'.

[22] See folios 6', 16, and 17. Among the things Merlo procured for Barrone were a copy of two motets and a "salve for obesity [unguente per carnosica]." He performed similar services for Giovanni Figueroa in 1568 (see folios 12 and 16').

[23] See folios 6', 18, and others.

[24] See, for example, the discussion in Delumeau.

[25] See Raffaele Casimiri, *I Diarii Sistini, i primi 25 anni (1535-1559)* (Rome: Edizioni "Psalterium," 1939); also in the journal *Note d'Archivio per la Storia Musicale* vols. 1 (1924) through 16 (1939) *passim*.

[26] Folios 27 and 27'.

[27] The *mandati* record that on 9 February 1571 Ippolito Gambocci, Thomasso Gomez, and Francesco Adriano were admitted to the papal chapel *(mandati* 923, folio 164). The three do not appear on any lists, but on 13 March 1571 there is a notice (folio 168) that Hipolito Gamboccio, priest from Gubbio, has been admitted to the chapel, and he is added to subsequent chapel lists. This means that the "matter left undecided" in Merlo's memorial was in fact decided that very month and that the proxy vote was accepted. There is no mention of this in the *Diarii* for 1571 *(Diarii Sistini* 9).

[28] Casimiri, pp. 380, 410-411. There were two cardinal nephews, Alfonso and Carlo Caraffa, but only Carlo was referred to as Cardinal Caraffa, the other being called the Cardinal of Naples. It should be remembered also that Paul IV had caused Palestrina, Leonardo Barre, and Domenico Ferrabosco to be expelled from the chapel because they were married. The other singers managed to get them put on permanent pensions amounting to about two-thirds of their regular salaries (5 ducats, 87 baiocchi).

[29] Folio 3. On the downfall of the Caraffa, see Ludwig Pastor, *History of the Popes* vol. 15, ed. Ralph Francis Kerr (London: Kegan Paul, Trench, Trubner & Co., 1928) pp. 131-178.

[30] Folio 7. See Franz Xaver Haberl, "Die Cardinalskommission von 1564 und Palestrinas Missa Papae Marcelli," *Kirchenmusikalisches Jahrbuch* 7 (1892) pp. 82-97.

[31] Folio 26'. This document is partially quoted in Giuseppe Baini, *Memorie storico-critiche della vita e delle opere di Giovanni Pierluigi da Palestrina* (Rome: Società Tipografica, 1828) vol. 1, p. 272, n. 375.

[32] See Baini, vol. 1, p. 269-923, and also a notice in the *Diarii Sistini* for 1587 to the effect that Merlo has given up the job of maestro *(Diarii* 16—there is no diary for 1586). Incidentally, Merlo was succeeded by Sotto.

[33] Michele Ghislieri was elected pope and took the name Pius V on 7 January 1566, but apparently the anniversary of his election was celebrated on 6 January.

[34] This is a mistake; the canonic voice is at the octave.

[35] *Contrapunto* or improvised counterpoint. All singers were supposed to be able to sing *contrapunto*. This remark is in keeping with chapter 64 of the Chapel Constitution of 1545 as published in Haberl, *Die römische 'schola cantorum' und die päpstlichen Kapellsänger bis zur Mitte des 16. Jahrhunderts*, Bausteine für Musikgeschichte 3 (Leipzig: Breitkopf und Härtel, 1888); also in *Vierteljahrsschrift für Musikwissenschaft* 3 (1887) pp. 284-296.

[36] Although it is at the lower fourth.

[37] Beginning in August 1565 Palestrina is paid in the *mandati* a monthly salary of

3 ducats, 13 baiocchi "ex causa diversarum compositionum musicalium quas hactemus ededit et est editurus ad comodum dicte cappelle." Since he was already receiving a pension of 5 ducats, 87 baiocchi, this brought his salary up to 9 ducats, equal to that of the other singers.

[38] See CS 38, dated 1563, and containing motets by these and other composers.

[39] The section of CS 23 containing this Mass was probably copied ca. 1507 and the entire manuscript put together before 1512; CS 26 was written during the reign of Leo X (1513-1521); the section of CS 41 containing Pipelare's Mass was probably copied ca. 1503-07 and the whole manuscript put together before 1513. See Richard Sherr, "A Note on two Roman Manuscripts of the Early Sixteenth Century," *The Musical Quarterly* 63 (1977) pp. 48-73, and "The Papal Chapel ca. 1492-1513 and its Polyphonic Sources," (Ph.D. diss., Princeton University, 1975).

[40] CS 15 was probably written ca. 1492-1501, and most of CS 35 was probably written during the reign of Innocent VIII (1484-1492). See Sherr, diss.

[41] See Chapter 38 of the Constitution. A note in the diary of 1569 states that Merlo has been *Abbas* for three years, and was just giving up the post (*Diarii* 9, folio 6').

[42] There is evidence that people in Rome took these standards seriously. See Lewis Lockwood, *The Counter-Reformation and the Masses of Vincenzo Ruffo* (Venice: Universal Edition, 1970); and Haberl, "Cardinalskommission." In 1566-68, Giovanni Animuccia is paid by the Cappella Giulia for writing pieces "secundum formam concilii." See Ducrot, pp. 514-516.

[43] For instance, *Corona aurea* is assigned in the list to commemorate the coronation of the pope, *Quem dicunt homines* to a feast of St. Peter, *Missus est* to Advent, *O beata infantia* to Christmas.

[44] Folio 2.

[45] Folio 4'.

[46] Folios 21' and 10. What appears to have happened is that on 20 November 1570 Merlo's sister left the convent since he collects (riscuotere) the dowry. On 20 May 1571 she returned, and on 7 September 1577 she died in the convent.

[47] Folio 35.

[48] Folio 35'.

V

A letter from Paolo Animuccia
A composer's response to the Council of Trent

All students of Renaissance music are familiar with the debates about sacred music during the last sessions of the Council of Trent, and with the eventual decision that 'the whole plan of singing in musical modes should be constituted not to give empty pleasure to the ear, but in such a way that the words be clearly understood by all'.[1] Although the overall effect of the council's decree on music was perhaps not great, there can be little doubt that in Rome, at least, serious attempts were made to have music written in an 'intelligible' style by commissioning pieces from composers residing elsewhere (as Cardinal Carlo Borromeo did with Vincenzo Ruffo) or by having them written by composers in Rome (as the Cappella Giulia did with Giovanni Animuccia).[2] But very few documents have come to light in which a composer, not responding to a set of instructions, addresses himself to the issues raised by the Council of Trent. Such is the letter presented below: a rare case of an autograph letter by a Renaissance composer that not only says something interesting, but also can be related to important events in the history of music.

The letter was sent from Pesaro by Paolo Animuccia, brother of Giovanni Animuccia and *maestro di cappella* to the Duke of Urbino, to Simone Fortuna, one of the Duke's secretaries, in Rome. It is dated January 1566; the day is left blank, but it must be after 7 January, the date of the election of the 'new pope' (Pius V) to whom the letter refers. Not much is known about Paolo Animuccia, except that he was for two years (1550–52) the *maestro di cappella* of St John Lateran, and then became *maestro* in the Urbino court.[3] He published two books of responsories, and other works appear in anthologies or in publications devoted to the works of other composers, and he seems to have been, in Lewis Lockwood's words, 'a moderately productive composer of motets and madrigals, although he was clearly less successful and less gifted than his brother Giovanni'.[4] Paolo, however, had a more positive view of himself, for his letter is nothing less than a bold offer to become the composer to and musical leader of the papal chapel with the specific job of arranging all the music (chant and polyphony) so that it would be 'reformed', that is, written in the way required by the Council of Trent.

Animuccia declares that he is sure that the new pope (whose reformatory zeal must have been well known) would want to have the music of the chapel redone 'so that the words can be understood and be accompanied by the devout music necessary for ecclesiastical functions'. As this would be an enormous undertaking involving much editing (of chant) as well as many newly written compositions, it would best be handled by one man in an authoritative position, and Animuccia presents himself as that man. In doing so, he shows that he is aware of the reactions in Rome to the suggestions of the Council of Trent. Indeed, he had probably been told all about it by his brother, Giovanni, at the time well ensconced in the Cappella Giulia and certainly privy to the attempts to have music written in the new style; perhaps he had told Paolo about the meeting of the papal singers in Cardinal Vitelozzi's house on 28 April 1565 'to sing some Masses and to test whether the words can be understood, as their Eminences desire',[5] and he may also have known about the masses Cardinal Borromeo commissioned from Ruffo in 1565.[6] Alternatively, Paolo could have heard about the situation in Rome from a cardinal directly connected with Urbino, Cardinal Giulio della Rovere, brother of Duke Guidobaldo II; in any case, he certainly counted on the cardinal's influence to advance his prospects, for he seemed to think that Cardinal Giulio would be heeded when he advised the pope on musical matters and about the papal chapel.

Cardinal Giulio della Rovere was certainly knowledgeable about and concerned with music. This can be demonstrated from what little has been published about him, and more importantly from information contained in the 31 volumes of correspondence making up Cl.I.Div.E of the Archivio di Urbino in the Archivio di Stato of Florence (where Animuccia's letter is found), an extremely rich source, never tapped by musicologists

V

Florence, Archivio di Stato, Archivio di Urbino, Cl.I.Div.E filza 62, ff.927r–927v: Paolo Animuccia to Simone Fortuna, January 1566

Da M. Carlo ho saputo come da Sua S.ria Ill.ma, V.S. ha havuto parte di riconoscimento delle sue fatiche, che me ne sono molto rallegrato, et di nuovo con lei me ne rallegro come di cosa che mi potesse occurrere; che Dio per sua bontà gliene dia quel contento che la desidera.

Perché io ho sempre confidato in lei più che in altr'huomo che vive, mi pare che alla nuova creatione del pontefice mi si potesse fare un grandissimo benefitio, et maggiormente essendo che il cardinale ci ha tanta parte, et quel che mi spinge a tentare questo mio pensiero si è la buona e cortese inclinatione che ha V.S. verso di me insieme con l'autorità grandissima et amorevolezza del cardinale. Però io credo certissimo che Sua Santità vorrà reformare la cappella e di compositioni musicali et di canti fermi, et ridurla a un segno che le parole fossero intese et accompagnate con modulationi devote et necessarie alle cose ecclesiastiche, et anche quando il papa non ci pensasse, mi rendo certissimo che essendogli preposto con l'autorità di Sua S.ria Ill.ma che tal carico havrei io, et mi sarebbe di grand'honore et utile et di infinita satisfactione di V.S. che per mezzo suo consegnisse tal cosa, perché benché io sia maritato, non importerebbe, perché non occurrerebbe andassi in cappella ma ne havessi il carico per ridurla a buon segno, che senza capo è tutta disordinata. Et tutto questo fatto lo potrebbe negotiare il cardinale, et ne havrebbe honore, essendo necessarissimo che le cose della musica sieno nette e governate da uno solo et reformate, e la reformatione sarebbe tale che ne sarei lodatissimo da ognuno. Però, M. Simone mio, ne lascerò la cura alla prudenza di V.S., che a lei non mancheranno modi di entrarci et con bel modo persuaderlo al cardinale che in verità starei volentieri a Roma et con occasione di farmi cognoscere al mondo per qualcosa, et più il cardinale sa quanto la cappella habbia bisogno d'aiuto; però sopra di questo non mi distenderò più, essendo lei prudentissima et piena di desiderio di vedermi exultato. Bacciandole humilmente le mani, di Pesaro alli di gennaro, 1566. D.V.S. servitore affectionatissimo,

Paolo Animuccia

Et di già un musico che sta in Roma, maritato che si chiama Gianetto, per havere composto non so che per la cappella ha provisione perpetua senza servire; ma io vorrei servire del continuo e fare ciò che bisognasse giornalmente per la cappella; però a questo particolare si potrebbe benissimo operare, essendo che senza capo la cappella va in rovina, se bene ha per superiore un vescovo, ma ha bisogno d'un musico per ordinare et reggere, et il tutto sia negotiato come da voi che ne spero benissimo, et anche quando il cardinale ne volesse ragionare meco; verr[e]i a Roma quando ci fosse intentione di Sua Santità.

I have heard from M. Carlo that you have received tokens of thanks from His Most Illustrious Lordship [Cardinal Giulio della Rovere] for Your Lordship's efforts, about which I was very happy, and I rejoice with you once again as over something that might have happened to me; may God in his goodness give you the contentment you desire.

Since I have always confided in you more than in any other man alive, it seems to me that with the creation of the new pope I might do myself a great service (especially as the cardinal had so much part in it), and the thing which prompts me to try out my idea is Your Lordship's gentle and benevolent feelings towards me along with the great authority and friendship of the cardinal. For I consider it most certain that His Holiness will want to reform the [papal] chapel's musical compositions and chant so that the words can be understood and be accompanied by the devout music necessary for ecclesiastical functions; and even if the pope does not think of these things, I am certain that, if proposed by the authority of His Most Illustrious Lordship, I will be given the job, which would be of great honour and utility to me and of infinite satisfaction to Your Lordship, who would be the means of making this happen. Even though I am married, this would not matter, because it would not be necessary for me to enter the chapel, but only that I should have the job of putting everything in good order, because without someone in charge everything is in disorder. All of this the cardinal could negotiate, and he would receive honour from it, it being most necessary that the music be cleaned up and regulated by one man alone and reformed, and the reform would be such that I would be greatly praised by everybody. However, M. Simone, I will leave it all to your Lordship's discretion, because you will be able to broach the matter and persuade the cardinal to good effect that in truth I would do very well in Rome with this opportunity to make my name in the world; and furthermore, the cardinal knows how much the chapel needs help. However, I will not go on further about this, you being full of discretion and desirous of seeing me successful. Humbly kissing your hands, from Pesaro, January 1566. Your Lordship's most affectionate servant,

Paolo Animuccia

And there is already a musician in Rome who is married and is called Gianetto and who has a perpetual provision for having composed I-don't-know-what for the chapel without having to serve; but I would want to serve continuously and do as is daily necessary for the chapel; but this detail can be easily worked out, and I believe that His Holiness would be pleased by this proposal, since without a leader the chapel will go to ruin (even though it is headed by a bishop, it has need of a musician to run things), and everything could be negotiated by you which I greatly hope, and also if the cardinal wants to talk to me about it; I would come to Rome if it be the wish of His Holiness.

and rarely consulted by anybody else. The documents in the *carteggio* include a number of letters from composers and musicians written directly to the cardinal (24 from Costanzo Porta, for instance) and also illustrate many aspects of his patronage of music, particularly in two areas where he exercised direct control: Loreto (he was the Cardinal Protector from 1566 until his death in 1578) and Ravenna (he was archbishop from 1566 to 1578).[7] A complete discussion of his patronage is not appropriate here, but the evidence does show him overseeing many aspects of music in Loreto and Ravenna; the seminary students in Ravenna (where Costanzo Porta had been brought by the cardinal as *maestro di cappella* and music teacher), for instance, sent him monthly examples of their *contrapunti* and motets, and he was regularly informed about their musical performances. And the cardinal also had some kind of relationship with the papal choir, or at least knew some of the singers in it. For instance, in 1565, when Bartholomeo Bartoli was dismissed from the chapel because of the reform carried out by a commission of cardinals, he immediately wrote to Cardinal Giulio asking to be taken back into his service, stating that he felt himself to be less unfortunate than the other members who had been dismissed because 'God has given me a patron so that I can live happily in spite of my bad fortune'.[8] The cardinal also knew, and perhaps had once employed, the singer Francesco Druda (a number of Drudas are mentioned in the cardinal's correspondence and in his *famiglia*), who on one occasion in 1566 had a mass copied and sent to the cardinal, and on another in 1567 sent some Passions 'written in the style of the chapel'.[9] Furthermore, Cardinal Giulio was one of those concerned that the musical requirements of the Council of Trent be met by composers in places under his control. In the dedication to him of Costanzo Porta's first book of masses (Venice, 1578), the composer says that he had been instructed to compose the pieces in the new style; this is confirmed by a letter of 7 October 1577 from Porta to the cardinal stating that he has finished a number of masses written 'according to the instructions given me by Your Most Illustrious Lordship that the words be understood, that they be easy for the most part, short and, if I am not wrong, melodious' and asking permission to go to Venice to oversee their publication.[10] There was reason, then, to believe that the cardinal would be interested in Animuccia's proposal and that his word might be influential with the pope.

Animuccia, however, seems to have been a little afraid of approaching the cardinal directly, writing as he did to one of the duke's secretaries (but that the letter is in the cardinal's *carteggio* indicates that he eventually saw it). Perhaps Paolo thought that the cardinal would need some persuading if he was in turn to persuade the pope to overlook two major objections to Animuccia and his appointment. First, that Animuccia was married; his ingenious solution to this problem—their married state had resulted in 1555 in a number of singers, among them Palestrina, being dismissed from the papal choir—is that he would never need to enter the chapel physically, as all his work could be done outside it. Second, that there was already a composer being paid to produce music for the papal chapel. This was, of course, Palestrina, the 'Gianetto' Animuccia mentions in a postscript as having composed 'I-don't-know-what' for the chapel (at least the first book of motets, the first book of masses and the *Missa Papae Marcelli*, no matter which of the proposed dates one chooses to accept), but who was being paid without (in Animuccia's opinion) having to work.[11] But for Animuccia this 'Gianetto' was clearly a minor figure, and he does not see—or does not choose to see—him as a major obstacle, pointing out that he (Animuccia) would be willing to work constantly at the job of seeing that the chapel did not 'go to ruin'.

It is perhaps not surprising, however, that the cardinal did not act on Animuccia's suggestion (at least, there is no further mention of the matter in the rest of the cardinal's correspondence, nor does any mention appear in other places, such as the *Diarii Sistini*). Boundless self-confidence will only carry a person so far, after all, and the cardinal must have known enough about music to be able to judge Palestrina's superiority to Animuccia. So in spite of his sensitivity to modern currents in music and his quickness in taking advantage of new opportunities, Paolo Animuccia remained in Urbino, leaving us, instead of the massive 'reform' he said he was contemplating, only a few works and this glimpse into his character and ambitions.

I wish to thank the Villa I Tatti and the Leopold Schepp Foundation for support in the research and writing of this article.

[1]This canon, which forms the basis of the final decree, is printed in L. Lockwood, ed., *Palestrina: Pope Marcellus Mass* (New York, 1975), p.19. See also K. Weinmann, *Das Konzil von Trient und die Kirchenmusik* (Leipzig, 1919).

[2]On Cardinal Borromeo and music, see L. Lockwood, *The Counter-Reformation and the Masses of Vincenzo Ruffo* (Venice, 1970), pp.74–135. In 1566, Animuccia was paid a number of times by the Cappella Giulia

for composing music 'secundum formam concilii'; see A. Ducrot, 'Histoire de la Cappella Giulia au XVIe siècle depuis sa fondation par Jules II (1513), jusqu'à sa restauration par Grégoire XIII (1578)', *Mélanges d'archéologie et d'histoire*, lxxv (1963), pp.179–240, 467–559, on pp.514–16.

[3] On Animuccia, see the articles by L. Lockwood in *The New Grove* and by L. Pannella in *Dizionario biografico degli Italiani*.

[4] Article in *The New Grove*

[5] Lockwood, ed., *Pope Marcellus Mass*, pp.21–2

[6] Lockwood, *The Counter-Reformation*

[7] I hope to publish elsewhere transcriptions of all the letters from composers. On Cardinal Giulio and Loreto, see E. Alfieri, *La cappella musicale di Loreto dalle origini a Costanzo Porta (1507–1574)* (Bologna, 1970); on the cardinal and Ravenna, see R. Casadio, 'La cappella musicale di Ravenna nel sec. XVI', *Note d'archivio*, xvi (1939), pp.140–54.

[8] Florence, Archivio di Stato [*I-Fas*], Archivio di Urbino [AU] filza 70, f.471r: letter dated 19 September 1565. The singers had been dismissed on 31 August 1565, though they continued to be paid pensions of varying amounts. See Lockwood, *The Counter-Reformation*, p.87, and F. X. Haberl, 'Die Kardinalskommission von 1564 und Palestrinas Missa Papae Marcelli', *Kirchenmusikalisches Jahrbuch*, vii (1892), pp.82–97.

[9] *I-Fas* AU filza 72, f.72r, letter of 9 October 1566; AU filza 73, ff.633r–633v.

[10] *I-Fas* AU filza 88, f.187r. See L. P. Pruett, *The Masses and Hymns of Costanzo Porta* (PhD diss., U. of North Carolina, Chapel Hill, 1960), pp.7–11.

[11] Beginning in August 1565, Palestrina was paid a monthly salary by the papal chapel 'ex causa diversarum compositionum musicalium quas hactenus edidit et est editurus ad comodum dicte capelle'. But Animuccia is correct when he says that Palestrina was not serving in the chapel, as Palestrina was at the time *maestro* of Santa Maria Maggiore.

VI

NOTES ON THE BIOGRAPHY AND MUSIC OF BERTRANDUS VAQUERAS (CA. 1450–1507)

BIOGRAPHY

As a contemporary of Josquin's in the papal chapel and as the composer of a *L'Homme armé* Mass, Bertrandus Vaqueras has earned some mention in standard texts and reference books. There has been some confusion about his origins, however, a confusion I can now clear up, as I can offer a fairly firm date for his death. While Spain, western France, and Flanders have all at various times been offered as Vaqueras' birthplace, it can now confidently be stated that he hailed originally from the south of France, and his autograph signature, *Bertrandus de Vaquerassio alias de Bessea*, can be explained.[1] The information provided by his beneficial documents (see Appendix) shows that although Vaqueras had strong ties both to the south of France and Flanders, he actually came from the area in southern France now known as the department of Vaucluse, and that Vaqueras was not his family name. It would seem, from the way he is designated in a number of documents, that his true name was Bertrandus Vassadelli or Bassadelli „de" Vacqueyras; (Bassadelli apparently then became „delli Bassa" or „della Bassa" or „de Bassea"). He was thus a member of the old noble Vassadel family of the Comtat-Venaissin (now part of the department of Vaucluse) who had since the 14th century been the Lords of Vacqueyras, a town situated not far west of Orange.[2] This, however, does not entirely clear up the problem of his birth. For one thing, Vaqueras consistently calls himself a cleric of the diocese of Cavaillon, while the town of Vacqueyras is in the diocese of Orange, and is quite a bit to the north of Cavaillon. Furthermore, Vaqueras never proclaims his noble birth through the common formula *de nobile genere ex utrusque parente procreatus*. Finally, Vaqueras sought and held benefices in Flanders, specifically in Liège, even though it was difficult for singers to possess benefices that were not in their home dioceses. A way of reconciling these contradictions would be to posit that he had been born in Vacqueyras and was perhaps illegitimate, then moved to receive his first tonsure somewhere in the diocese of Cavaillon, and then moved again to Flanders.

Vaqueras had a long distinguished career as a musician in Rome, most of it spent in the service of the papal chapel. He began in the choir of St. Peter's. Reynolds has shown that Vaqueras

---

[1] Early writers have suggested Spain because the name Vaqueras seems Spanish, Jose Llorens in *Die Musik in Geschichte und Gegenwart* read the *de Bessea* of the signature as Latin for Bresse, while Manfred Schuler read *Bassea* as Latin for the town of La Bassée in Flanders. See Manfred Schuler, „Die Kapelle Papst Pius III", *Acta Musicologica* 42 (1970), pp. 225–30. Vaqueras, as did most of the papal singers, became a member of the Confraternità di Santo Spirito in Sassia, signing his name upon his joining the confraternity on 7 June 1484. See, Rome, Biblioteca Lancisiana, Codex 328, fol. 93^v.

[2] See Jean-Antoine Pithon-Curt, *Histoire de la Noblesse du Comté-Venaissin d'Avignon et de la Principauté d'Orange Dressée sur les Preuves Dediée au Roy*, 4 vols., Paris 1743–50 (reprint 1970), vol. III, pp. 490–96. See also the map in Charles Perrin, *Etats Pontificaux de France su Seizième Siècle*, Paris, 1847. In 1490 a „Ludovicus Vassadelli" claimed to be the Lord of Vacqeyras. See Vatican City, Archivio Segreto Vaticano, Registra Supplicationum 916, fols. 111^v-112^r: supplication dated February 19, 1490.

was a member of that choir from December, 1481 to April, 1483.³ In November of that year, he joined the papal chapel and remained there for 24 years until his death shortly before April 21, 1507 (the date of the first supplication requesting a benefice made vacant by Vaqueras' death in Rome). At the time of his death, his accumulated salary and income from benefices was 274 ducats a year (about 2.8 times his regular salary of 96 ducats), and he may indeed have died in the vineyard he had purchased from the chapter of St. Peter's in 1498.⁴

Uniquely among the papal singers of his generation Vaqueras was apparently also an active humanist. The MS Vatican City, Biblioteca Apostolica Vaticana, Fondo Vaticani Latini [VatL] 2836, fols. 92ᵛ, 94Aʳ-94Bᵛ, 97ʳ, 100ʳ-102ᵛ, preserves two long classicizing Latin poems and a short dedicatory poem in what appears to be an autograph. One of the poems is entitled *Bertrandi de Vaquerassio in suam sortem brevis querela*, and seems to be a complaint addressed to a lady the author had left in France and had been expecting to join him in Italy; its mention of the „Gallic wars" may date it after 1494.⁵ A dedicatory poem shows that Vaqueras intended to send this to Barnabus Christino in the house of Camillus del Bene. The other poem, dedicated to Antonius Flaminio (*Bertrandus de Vaqueirassio Antonio Flaminio*) has been edited by Marco Vatasso who dates it in 1493–94. It shows Vaqueras connected with humanistic circles in Rome and its university.⁶ As we shall see, if Vaqueras was indeed a humanist, this did not inspire him to write „humanistic" music.⁷

WORKS

Vaqueras' most complicated work, the one that has earned him his place in the history of music, is his *Missa L'Homme armé*, preserved in VatS 49.⁸ Vaqueras may have been born in southern France and may have written humanistic poetry, but here, he shows himself to be a

---

³ Christopher Reynolds, *The Music Chapel at San Pietro in Vaticano in the Later Fifteenth Century*, Ph. D. Dissertation, Princeton University 1982, pp. 138–42.

⁴ See Reynolds for documents about the vineyard, which was in the area behind St. Peter's curiously known as „Egypt".

⁵ VatL 2836, 92ᵛ, lines 14–15: *Itala dispexi et devovi Gallica bella / Quippe* [?] *teneant cursus forsitan illa tuos*. The poem also states that Vaqueras had expected his love (named Laura) to set sail from Marseille, and was in constant anxiety about storms and shipwrecks. The poem is unedited.

⁶ See Marco Vatasso, „Antonio Flaminio e le Principali Poesie dell'Autografo Vaticano 2870", *Studi e Testi* 1 (Rome, 1900), pp. 60–4. I am grateful to Christopher Reynolds for bringing this to my attention; see Reynolds (n. 3 above), p. 139. There is, however, a problem. The poems in VatL 2836 seem to be autograph (there are many compositional corrections), yet the „humanistic" handwriting bears no resemblance to the handwriting of Vaqueras' 1484 signature (even allowing for the blurriness of my photograph of the Biblioteca Lancisiana MS.) which resembles the French bâtard script. But perhaps in the ten or more years which separate these manuscripts, Vaqueras changed his handwriting to go better with his humanistic pursuit. It also seems highly unlikely that there were two people named Bertrandus de Vaqueras in Rome at the same time.

⁷ On the type of music favored by humanists, see Edward E. Lowinsky, „Humanism in the Music of the Renaissance", *Medieval and Renaissance Studies*, Durham 1982, pp. 87–220.

⁸ Published in Richard Sherr, ed., *Bertrandi Vaqueras Opera Omnia*, Neuhausen-Stuttgart 1978 (= *Corpus Mensurabilis Musicae*. 78). I take this opportunity to indicate some corrections to my edition.

Credo
17/1   S   should be dotted quarter note.
19   B   The comma should be reversed C
23/2   A   should be f'f' instead of g'g'
70/3   S   b-flat quarter note should be b-flat eigth note.
142/1 A   b-flat for c'

true follower of the late medieval Franco-Flemish school of composition. His work has distinct points of reference with various *L'Homme armé* Masses of the 1460's and 70's, some of which Vaqueras could have known from the manuscript VatS 14;[9] in fact, his Mass could be viewed as a purposeful eclectic compilation of previously used techniques, with some added innovations. For instance, as in the Mass by Faugues (VatS 14, fols. 138^v-149^r) Vaqueras' work presents the cantus firmus in strict canon with the comes preceding the dux, although this is not true of every movement (in the Kyrie and Sanctus, and in the interior sections of the Gloria and Credo, the dux precedes the comes). And where Faugues used the canon to create four out of two voices, Vaqueras uses it to create five out of two voices (as in the last of the *L'Homme armé* Masses in NapBN 40). Vaqueras' use of canon is not consistent, however; in what may be a reference to the Kyrie of Josquin's *Missa L'Homme armé super voces musicales*, the second Tenor in Vaqueras' Kyrie, although written out, is actually created by a mensuration canon with the first Tenor (it is twice as slow),[10] while in all the other movements, the cantus firmus is written out once with instructions as to the point of the canonic entry. As in the Mass by Busnois (VatS 14, fols. 106^v-117^r), Vaqueras presents his cantus firmus without elaboration and in large note values indicated by augmentation time signatures (C-dot, O-dot), and changes the time signatures of the other voices in internal sections, consistently employing Busnois' „favorite" time signature of O2, but also presenting all voices in the „augmentation signature" of C-dot as in the Mass by Ockeghem.[11] As in other Masses in the tradition, Vaqueras divides the *L'Homme armé* melody into its usual A B A phrases, except for the Agnus where he divides the tune at the same strange spot Busnois did, ending the Agnus I with the beginning of the B section of the melody. In another reference to other Masses, Vaqueras uses sesquialtera proportions for extended passages in the Gloria and Credo movements, at one point even employing the proportion reversed-C to create an exceedingly awkward „octuplet" (Credo, mm. 19–20). Vaqueras may also be responsible for one innovation, however; each movement of the Mass uses a different pitch interval for the canon (as opposed to the upper fifth used consistently by Faugues), these different intervals identified by their Greek names (Busnois had also em-

---

[9] There is some controversy about the origins of this manuscript, but there is general agreement that it was in Rome by the 1480's at least.

[10] There is of course a problem of reference here since we don't know when Josquin composed his Mass. Maybe the „influence" went the other way; of course, Josquin's use of the mensuration canon in his Kyrie is more complicated than Vaqueras'. We can, though, be sure that Vaqueras and Josquin knew each other.

[11] The time signatures are:
Kyrie I: C-dot (canonic voices), O (other voices)
Christe: C-dot (canonic voices), O2 (other voices)
Kyrie II: cut-C3 (all voices)
Gloria: O-dot (canonic voices), O (other voices)
Qui tollis: C-dot (canonic voices), O2 (other voices)
Cum sancto: C-dot (all voices)
Patrem: O-dot (canonic voices), O (other voices)
Qui propter nos: C-dot (canonic voices), O2 (other voices)
Et in spiritum: C-dot (all voices)
Sanctus: O-dot (canonic voices), O (other voices)
Pleni: No canon, O (other voices)
Hosanna: C-dot (all voices)
Benedictus: No canon, C2 (all voices)
Agnus I: O-dot (canonic voices), O (other voices)
Agnus II: No canon, C2 (other voices)
Agnus III: C-dot (canonic voices), cut-O (other voices)
I do not intend here to enter into the controversy surrounding the implications these signatures have for tempo.

ployed Greek terms). As a result, three movements of Vaqueras' Mass (Credo, Sanctus, Agnus) present the cantus firmus in different modes simultaneously while the whole work stays clearly in G-Dorian.[12]

This is all very impressive, but perhaps we shouldn't be too impressed. Busnois might have been a model for the use of the cantus firmus material and time signatures, for instance, but one will look in vain in Vaqueras' work for the elaborate proportional system Richard Taruskin found in the structure of Busnois' Mass, or for more complicated cantus firmus manipulation such as the inversion employed by Busnois or the retrograde used by Du Fay and Josquin.[13] Actually, creating a strict canon out of the *L'Homme armé* melody was not such a big deal; in fact, the use of strict cantus firmus technique and canon could bring to a composer of modest abilities certain distinct compositional advantages. With two slow-moving voices easily „set" in advance, he only had to worry about composing three independent contrapuntal voices at the most. And, in fact, Vaqueras reduces even the situations of free three-voice counterpoint to the absolute minimum. His basic method of contrapuntal construction is quite clearly (and almost exclusively) the duet (either two free voices, or one voice against the cantus firmus), the genre of free counterpoint that is easiest to manage. The Mass abounds in duets: when there are more than two voices of the free voices in play, one is often presenting the cantus firmus (as in the three-voice beginnings of every movement – the melody in the Altus); and even when the full five-voice texture is reached with the entrance of the canonic Tenors, the Bassus reverts to a slow-moving harmonic support of the cantus firmus or actually enters into a triple canon with the Tenors, effectively leaving only two free elaborate contrapuntal voices to be composed (this treatment of the Bassus can be found in other Masses of the middle 15th century).

Another advantage to a composer of Vaqueras' abilities, I would argue, was brought by that part of the „*L'Homme armé* tradition" that called for the cantus firmus melody with its signature leaps of fourths and fifths (particularly the „doibt on douter" repetition in the A section of the tune) to invade all of the melodic material of the piece. Vaqueras pursues this with a vengeance, and thereby greatly reduces the compositional problem of what to write in the free contrapuntal voices: When in doubt, quote the tune, and even better, use those fourths and fifths to engender simple triadic elaborations of the basic harmonies (beginning every movement with nne measures of head motive also helps). In other words, Vaqueras was making things easy for himself by providing the opportunity for layered composition over a slow moving cantus firmus (represented by one melodic line and its harmonization) and reducing the amount of melodic material he actually had to think up. This was precisely the situation encountered by singers who sang „contrapunctus supra librum", improvisations above chant, a technique required of all members of the papal chapel.

Although we have evidence of the importance of contrapunctus in the period, its actual sound is (quite naturally) lost. There are, however, hints of it in the written record. One example of recorded contrapunctus, for instance, can be found in the written „improvisations" by Guillelmus

---

[12] Another reference to Josquin's Mass?
The disposition of the canon (the dux always presents the melody on G) is:

Kyrie	canon at the upper fifth.
Gloria	canon at the lower fourth.
Credo	canon at the lower fifth.
Sanctus	canon at the upper second.
Agnus	canon at the lower second.

[13] See Richard Taruskin, „Antoine Busnoys and the L'Homme armé Tradition," *Journal of the American Musicological Society* (*JAMS*) 39 (1986), pp. 255–93.

that accompany the Basse danse tenor La Spagna[14], others are given by Tinctoris in Book II of his *Liber de arte contrapuncti*.[15] Most of Tinctoris' examples of written counterpoint are apt for our purposes because they were designed first to show how singers could improvise above chant melodies organized in predictable patterns. Above the cantus firmus, Tinctoris constructs a single voice of counterpoint in an agitated, syncopated rhythmic style. This very style is to be seen in most of the free counterpoint in Vaqueras' Mass. Indeed, the constant use of syncopation and standard melodic gestures as well as occasional long chains of sequences – what Gombosi called the „imbecilities" of the post-Ockeghem generation[16] (sometimes blatant – see Gloria, mm. 82–5, Agnus I, mm. 16–19; sometimes more subtle – see mm. 151–61, Benedictus) – seem to arise out of the common language of an improvisatory tradition.

We can see this mode of composition operating very clearly in the Credo of Vaqueras' *Missa L'Homme armé*. Measures 73–89 of the Credo set the text: *Crucifixus etiam pro nobis. Sub Pontio Pilato passus et sepultus est. Et resurrexit tertia die secundum scripturas. Et ascendit in caelum sedet ad dexteram Patris*. This entire text segment is set to the first part of the B section of the tune. But because there was so much text – his Credo sets more text to this part of the tune than any other *L'Homme armé* Masses known to me – Vaqueras lengthened this section by introducing five measures of rest in the Tenor between the repetitions in the tune segment.

Vaqueras also introduces elided repetitions of the four notes of the segment (Tinctoris and Dufay did similar things in their *L'Homme armé* Masses), in a way that actually produces a repeating bass pattern tantalizingly close to the passamezzo antico. In fact, it may be that Vaqueras began to think of this segment as having a „life of its own" for instead of cadencing the segment on V of the mode (as might be expected), he brings the whole section to a cadence on G in measure 89 which actually feels more like a resolution of the newly created bass pattern than of the segment of the *L'Homme armé* melody, although it isn't so strong that the Mass cannot easily continue with the setting of the words *Et iterum venturus est*.

That Vaqueras may have recognized that he had created a bass pattern over which the improvisations of contrapunctus could be created is seen in the other voices which, in their quasi-repetitive aimless meandering, always keyed to the measure by measure changes in the basic harmonization of the cantus firmus, move in ways which give the impression of improvisatory variations on the basic pitches or „aria" accompanying the bass pattern, shared between the Superius and the Altus and Tenor and Bassus, as a comparison of the passage with the example showing its reduction will make clear.

EXAMPLE 1: REDUCTION OF MM. 73–89

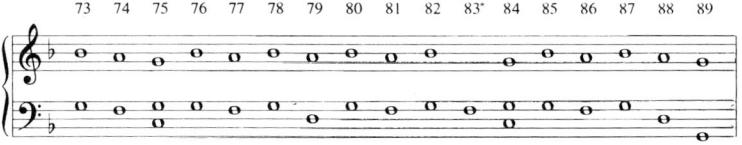

* See later discussion

---

[14] See Manfred Bukofzer, *Studies in Medieval and Renaissance Music*, New York 1950, pp. 199–200.
[15] Chapters 21 and 22. See Albert Seay, ed., *Johannis Tinctoris Opera Theoretica*, Vol. II, American Institute of Musicology 1975 (= *Corpus Scriptorum de Musica*. 22).
[16] Otto Gombosi, *Jacob Obrecht: Eine stilkritische Studie*, Leipzig 1925, pp. 13 ff.

Knowledge of the compositional technique governing this section provides an opportunity to see (I am going to argue) the effect of performance upon a completed composition. The inexorable musical logic which dictated to Vaqueras that every g in the cantus firmus be accompanied by b-flat'[17] in the Superius and every f in the cantus firmus or d in the bass should be accompanied by an a', allows us to find a self-correction where none is evident in the actual source of the Mass. In m. 82, the Superius is given a line that by this logic would require an a' on the first beat of m. 83:

EXAMPLE 2: CREDO, MM. 82–83

Yet, instead of that, there appears a rest which disturbs the melodic flow and seems completely arbitrary. To explain this, I suggest the following scenario: Vaqueras had indeed written an a' in the Superius at this point, but noticed (probably at a performance) that when the Bass sang an e-flat by musica ficta because of the b-flat in the Altus and Superius in the last beat of m. 82, parallel fifth motion would result between the Bass and Superius as m. 82 moved to m. 83. In fact, Vaqueras himself could have been that Bass singer (he is listed as „Contratenor" in the records of St. Peter's).[18] As the piece was already composed, Vaqueras corrected the mistake through the simple expedient of correcting not his own part by removing the e(flat), but by re-

---

[17] c' = middle c.
[18] Reynolds (note 3), p. 138.

moving the offending Superius a' in his exemplar which served as the exemplar for the copy in VatS 49 where there are no traces of corrections at this point.

Other examples of what might be called the common language of contrapunctus can be found in many of Vaqueras' works. And Vaqueras can get quite obsessive about them. For example, Vaqueras seems to have been struck by a particular feature of the cantus firmus of his *Missa Du bon du cœur* (drawn from the Tenor of an anonymous chanson): that it contains in it a number of examples of a stereotyped melodic phrase involving a descending fourth (in boxes in the Example).

EXAMPLE 3: *DU BON DU CŒUR*, TENOR, BEGINNING

This phrase can be found at some time or other in every piece by Vaqueras (and many other composers), but it does sometimes appear that there is not a measure of the *Missa Du bon du cœur* that is free of it. But whereas in other works it is merely a cliche of composition, in this Mass it is a cliche and a direct reference to the cantus firmus. It is almost as if Vaqueras committed the cantus firmus to memory, was so imbued with its melodic gestures that they entered every voice of his Mass in a way that indeed seems almost unconscious.

Another popular contrapuntal figure abounds in Vaqueras' works. It consists of a (usually) cadential phrase illustrated in the Example that must have been a kneejerk reaction to a particular configuration of breves in the Tenor or Bass line (although this was sometimes omitted).

EXAMPLE 4: CONTRAPUNTAL FIGURE

This figure can be found to some degree in the works of many important renaissance composers – it is less frequently used by Josquin (particularly in his Masses) than by Obrecht – but surely few use it as repetitively in a single work as Vaqueras does in his Missa *Du bon du cœur* (see the Credo, mm. 137–160). Interestingly, the figure is not to be found in any of the contrapuntal examples Tinctoris provides in his *Liber de arte contrapuncti*, nor (as far as I can tell) in any of his works, or in the works of Ockeghem and Du Fay. This would seem to indicate that it was part of the contrapuntal language of a younger generation of composers. In fact, its overuse in the *Missa Du bon du cœur* almost suggests that Vaqueras had just learned it and somehow could not get it out of his head.

Perhaps the most accessible of Vaqueras' works to modern ears (and perhaps his most successful work) is his motet *Ave regina caelorum*.[19] This four-voice setting of the Marian antiphon is notable particularly for its „C major" qualities (the 6th-mode melody is transposed to C) and for its concentration on the third of the C-major triad at cadences, even to the point of leaving out the fifth of the chord entirely.

The work begins with a technique which, although not its main means of articulation, is used at important structural points in the work: syntactic imitation of the opening notes of the chant melody, proceeding in the beginning through the four voices from lowest to highest. The only curiosity is that Vaqueras chose to begin the motet on f rather than on c or c', with the result that the first sonority in this clear „C" piece is the fifth f-c' (m. 5). Perhaps he meant this as a reference to the f-mode version of the chant, but there might be other reasons. To have begun the imitation on c or c' may have caused a certain awkwardness in vocal lines and in counterpoint; beginning on c' would have meant that the first sonority would have been a unison (or that the imitation could not be consistently at the octave), while choosing c to allow for that sonority to be an octave would have brought the Bass immediately down to G, not an impossible note, but one that is in fact totally avoided in the work. The implications of the f are actually reserved for the very end, the setting of „exora" (mm. 158–73). Here, the chant seems abandoned, and instead, four-voice imitation on f seems to repeat the opening notes of the piece, giving the work a kind of closed structure.

In spite of the use of the 16th-century device of imitation at the beginning and the end, the majority of the motet is organized along more 15th-century lines: a paraphrased chant setting moves among the voices in a series of duets, each culminating in a four-voice section. The music seems to divide the text into a number of separate sections.

---

[19] The motet has recently been recorded in *Ave Regina Coelorum: Marienantiphonen in Vertonungen des 15. Jahrhunderts*, Isaak Ensemble Heidelberg und Frankfurter Renaissance Ensemble (Bayer-Records, 1991).

mm. 1–24: sets the text *Ave regina caelorum* as four-voice imitation culminating in a four-voice drive to a cadence. The chant is paraphrased and appears in all the voices. All cadences are on C without the fifth but with the third.

mm. 25–49: sets the text *Ave Domina angelorum* as duets, culminating in a four-voice passage where the „drive" to the c cadence is sharpened by an explicit change from b-flat to b-natural in the Superius (mm. 45–46). The paraphrased chant appears in the Bass and Altus. The final cadence again leaves out the fifth.

mm. 50–63: sets the text *salve radix sancta, ex qua mundo* as duets leading to a four-voice passage with a cadence on c. But the differences here are the appearance of the first cadence on g (m. 54), that the final cadence contains the fifth as well as the third, and that this section does not set a syntactic textual entity. Also, the chant seems abandoned.

mm. 64–76: sets the text *lux est orta* as a long duet that does not culminate in a four-voice passage. At the cadence on c in m. 76, the word *Gaude* of the next passage is turned into an acclamation on the note g (on an open fifth). There seems to be no use of the chant here, except in the generalized move from c to g.

mm. 77–97: sets the text *gaude virgo gloriosa, super omnes*, again not a complete textual entity, first as a short duet which turns into a three-voice passage with a cadence on g (with an e in the bass), and then as another duet characterized by sequential repetition in both voices. The paraphrased chant returns at the beginning of each duet. The final cadence in m. 97, on c but with the fifth, really leads directly into the next section.

mm. 97–132: sets the word *speciosa*. This is the first section of the piece devoted to a single word of the text. Beginning first in four-voice imitation, Vaqueras places great emphasis on this word employing repetition and ostinato drawn from the chant melody, repeating *speciosa* over and over as he drives towards the cadence on c, once again without the fifth.

mm. 134–143: sets the text *vale valde decora* as a sesquialtera section in imitation, ending on a c cadence (with A in the Bass). The chant appears in all the voices.

mm. 145–157: sets the text *et pro nobis semper Christum* as block chords, ending on an f triad, leading into the last section.

mm. 158–173: sets the text *exora* in triple time (the signature is cut-O) as imitation at the octave of f, leading to the final cadence on c, without the fifth. The chant of *exora* is not used, but there is a hint of the notes of the opening of the melody.

These sections might be combined into larger ones, each of them distinguished by the introduction of a new compositional element: A (mm. 1–49) characterized by cadences on c without the fifth, four-voice imitation, duets, the use of the paraphrased chant, and „drives to the cadence"; B (mm. 50–97) characterized by cadences on g or cadences on c with the fifth, longer duets, absence of „drive to the cadence," sequence, and occasional abandonment of the chant; C (mm. 97–132) characterized by four-voice imitation, ostinatos and repetition used eventually to build up a „drive to the cadence", and use of the chant; D (mm. 134–143) characterized by sesquialtera and four-voice imitation; E (mm. 145–157) characterized by block chords; F (mm. 158–173) characterized by four-voice imitation on f. The work is thus a good example of the „varietas" championed by Tinctoris. While its emphasis on the third of the triad and its use of imitation at important structural points is striking, the work itself belongs to the tradition of the late 15th-century „Choralbearbeitung",[20] even though Vaqueras' dramatic introduction of *Gaude* (rejoice), his insistence on *speciosa* (beautiful) and the block chords when intercession is spe-

---

[20] See Stephan, *Die Burgundisch-Niederländische Motette zur Zeit Ockeghems*, Kassel 1937.

cifically requested imply further that he „read" the text as a particular kind of (flattering?) message to the Virgin (emphasizing her joy and her beauty, and then asking her to intercede for us), even as he ignored some of the text's syntax.

It can be gathered from the above that I am not at this point prepared to argue for the greatness of Vaqueras' music, although the *Ave Regina* has a certain definite interest and the œuvre as a whole is not at all incompetent.[21] The advantage to studying the works of composers of the second rank, it seems to me, is that it allows us more easily to see into their method of composition, as they do not have the talent of geniuses to embellish almost beyond recognition the relatively simple structures that lie behind their music (consider how difficult it is even today to come up with any convincing analysis of Josquin's works).[22] But with somebody like Vaqueras, it is possible to see (particularly in his Masses) the „background" of written compositions informed constantly by the work-a-day practice of contrapunctus in which Vaqueras probably excelled. As such, his compositions provide us with a window to this now lost improvisatory polyphonic art.

APPENDIX

Calendar of Documents Concerning Bertrandus Vassadel alias Vaqueras [or Vaqueras alias Vassadelli, Bassadelli, de Bessea], cleric of the diocese of Cavaillon, papal singer from November, 1483, died before April 21, 1507.

1. Vatican City, Archivio Segreto Vaticano, Registra Supplicationum [RS] 996, fol. 83^r-83^v: supplication dated April 28, 1495.

Canonries and prebends in the cathedral of Liege and the collegiate church of Notre Dame de Tongres had become vacant by the death of Petrus de Holy, and the Master of the Chapel, Bartholomeus, Bishop of Segovia, had been given the benefice, but now has resigned it. Vaqueras now asks for a new provision to the benefices. The total income was not expected to exceed 4 marks.

2. RS 1202, fol. 190^v: supplication dated May 9, 1505.

Vaqueras had engaged in a lawsuit concerning a canonry and prebend in the cathedral of Lausanne, and has agreed to resign the benefice. He and Johannes Grandis, canon of Sion ask that the resignation be allowed. The income was not expected to exceed 30 ducats, but Vaqueras is to be paid a pension of 46 ducats drawn from the fruits of the canonries and prebends of Lausanne and Sion and a parish church in Lausanne.

---

[21] For another, somewhat curious, discussion of Vaqueras as a composer see the recent exchange between Rob Wegman and Richard Taruskin. Rob C. Wegman, „Another Mass by Busnoys?", *Music and Letters* 71 (1990), pp. 1–19; Richard Taruskin and Rob C. Wegman, „Correspondence", *Music and Letters* 71 (1990), pp. 631–635.

[22] See most recently, Cristle Collins Judd, „Modal Types and *Ut, Re, Mi* Tonalities: Tonal Coherence in Sacred Vocal Polyphony from about 1500", *JAMS* 45 (1992), pp. 428–67.
A comparison of Vaqueras' use of sequences (another tool of *contrapunctus*) in the *Missa Du bon du cœur*, Agnus II, mm. 77–82 with a similar passage (using almost the identical melodic material) in Josquin's *Missa Gaudeamus* (Pleni, mm. 42–50) allows us almost at once to see what separates the great composer from the minor one; in a word: unpredictability. In Vaqueras, the sequences repeat regularly, but this could hardly be said for the Josquin example, where every effort is made to unbalance sequential patterns.

3. RS 1207, fols. 219r-219v: supplication dated May 26, 1505.

A Canonry and prebend in the cathedral of Avignon as well as the parish church St. Genesius in the diocese of Avignon had become vacant on the death of the papal singer Johannes Pintelli, and the Master of the Chapel, Antonius Ferreri, Bishop of Gubbio had presented Vaqueras for the benefices. He is reconfirmed („nova provisio") by motu proprio. The income was not expected to exceed 48 ducats (24 each).

4. RS 1254, fol. 277r: supplication dated April 21, 1507.

An Archdeaconry in the cathedral of Vaison as well as the priory of Sanbeler in that diocese had become vacant by the death of Vaqueras. Philippus de Primis, canon of Fano, papal singer and chamberlain has been presented for the benefices by Franciscus, Bishop of Sessa Aurunca, Master of the Chapel, and is granted them by motu proprio. The income was not expected to exceed 50 ducats, and Primis is also granted a dispensation from the requirement of being able to speak the language of the diocese.

5. RS 1253, fol. 72v: supplication dated May 4, 1507.

Egidius Caroiati, canon of Avignon, had been engaged in a lawsuit with Vaqueras [alias Vassadelli] concerning a canonry and prebend in the cathedral of Avignon which was at the collation of the chapter and had been held by Johannes Pintelli. Vaqueras is now dead, and the canons and chapter of Avignon ask that Caroiati be surrogated in Vaqueras' place. The benefice was worth 24 ducats.

6. RS 1254, fol. 8v: May 10, 1507.

A canonry and prebend in the church of Notre Dame de Tongres in the diocese of Liege had become vacant by the death of Vaqueras. By virtue of the indult allowing papal singers to receive the benefices of dead colleagues, Remigius de Mastaing, papal singer and cleric of Tournai, was presented for the benefice by Franciscus, Bishop of Sessa Aurunca, Master of the Chapel. Mastaing now asks for a new provision to the benefice. The income was not expected to exceed 24 ducats.

7. RS 1254, fols. 57v-58v: supplication dated May 10, 1507.

A canonry and prebend in the cathedral of Liege had become vacant by the death of Vaqueras. By virtue of the indult allowing papal singers to receive the benefices of dead colleagues, Johannes Gruter, cleric of Liege had been presented for the benefice by Franciscus, Bishop of Sessa Aurunca, Master of the Chapel. Gruter asks first for a dispensation to compensate for his illegitimate birth, and then he and Paulus de Trottis, papal singer and cleric of Alessandria, ask that the benefice, whose income was not expected to exceed 4 marks, be awarded to Gruter and that Trottis be awarded a pension of 20 ducats from the fruits of the benefice.

8. RS 1254: fols. 182r-182v: supplication dated May 10, 1507.

The parish church St. Eulalie in the diocese of Lausanne had become vacant by the death of Vaqueras. By virtue of the indult allowing papal singers to receive the benefices of dead colleagues, Jacobus Walpot, papal singer and cleric of Cambrai, had been presented for the benefice by Franciscus, Bishop of Sessa Aurunca and Master of the Chapel. Walpot asks for a new provision to the benefice. The income was not expected to exceed 20 ducats, and Walpot is also granted a dispensation from the requirement of being able to speak the language of the diocese.

9. RS 1255, fol. 33r: supplication dated May 10, 1507.

A perpetual vicary or simplex benefice *St. Andrea de numero viginti capellania in ecclesia metropolitana* had become vacant by the death of Vaqueras. By virtue of the indult allowing papal singers to receive the benefices of dead colleagues, Thomas de Jazanis [Fazanis], papal singer and cleric of Siena, had been presented for the benefice by Franciscus, Bishop of Sessa

VI

Aurunca and Master of the Chapel. Fazanis asks for the benefice, whose income was not expected to exceed 15 florins. He is also given a dispensation from the requirement of being able to speak the language of the diocese.

10. RS 1255, fols. 103^r-103^v: supplication dated May 31, 1507.

Remigius de Mastaing, who had been granted a canonry and prebend in the collegiate church of Notre Dame de Tongres in the diocese of Liege, vacant by the death of Vaqueras, has now ceded the benefice. Gerardus Dutry, member of the papal household at the insistence of the Cardinal of Santa Maria in Trastevere, asks for the benefice. The income was not expected to exceed 24 ducats, and Mastaing is awarded a pension of 14 ducats from the fruits of the benefice.

11. RS 1256, fols. 26^v-27^r: supplication dated June 4, 1507.

Michael Touppe, papal singer and cleric of Chartres, had been granted the parish church St. Genesius in the diocese of Avignon vacant by the death of Vaqueras [*alias Bassadelli*], but the letters conferring the benefice had not been written and Touppe had decided to resign it. He and the canons and chapter of Avignon ask that the parish church be united to the „mensa" of the chapter. The benefice was worth 20 ducats, and Touppe is awarded a pension of 25 ducats to be paid by Lodovicus Extoris, cantor and canon of Avignon, from the fruits of the church of St. Maria de Insula in the diocese of Cavaillon.

12. RS 1277, fol. 39^v-40^r: supplication dated February 14, 1508.

An archdeaconry in the cathedral of Vaison, vacant by the death of Vaqueras, had been awarded to Philippus de Primis, papal singer, by virtue of the indult allowing papal singers to receive the benefices of dead colleagues by Franciscus, Bishop of Sessa Aurunca and Master of the Chapel. But Primis had doubted his ability to take possession of the benefices and had himself died, so the Bishop had awarded the benefice to Remigius de Mastaing, papal singer and cleric of Tournai. But as the letters conferring the benefice had not been written, Mastaing had ceded it. He and Johannes Vassadelli de Vaqueratio, cleric of Orange and of noble birth, ask that the benefice be given to Vassadelli. The income was not expected to exceed 30 ducats, and Mastaing is awarded a pension of 10 ducats from the fruits of the benefice.

13. RS 1277, fol. 43^r: supplication dated February 14, 1508.

The parish church of Dinpuelon [?] in the diocese of Lausanne, vacant by the death of Vaqueras, had been given to Jacobus Walpot, papal singers and cleric of Cambrai, by virtue of the indult allowing papal singers to receive the benefices of dead colleagues by Franciscus, Bishop of Sessa Aurunca and Master of the Chapel. But the letters conferring the benefice had not been written and Walpot had ceded it. He and Petrus Marmad, cleric of Lausanne, ask that the benefice be given to Marmad. The income was not expected to exceed 24 ducats, and Walpot is awarded a pension of 7 ducats from the fruits of the benefice.

VII

The Relationship between a Vatican Copy of the Gloria of Josquin's Missa de Beata Virgine and Petrucci's Print

One of the things scholars who study the transmission of the music of the 15th and 16th centuries would most like to know is the exact relationship among or between extant sources; we would like to known particularly if one source is a direct copy of another or if one or more sources can be traced directly to a known exemplar. Occasionally, as Margaret Bent has shown in her studies of MSS Vg and B of the Machaut complex and the Trent MSS 90 and 93, direct copying relationships can be established by a careful consideration of musical readings and a host of seemingly unimportant details (spaces between notes, ornamental flourishes in the text, etc.)[1]. But many late 15th- and early 16th-century sources are not direct copies of each other, and the most scholars have been able to do with them is establish families of sources or posit stemmas showing relationship to lost exemplars[2]. In this regard, I would like now to offer some observations on the relationship of a Petrucci print to a Vatican manuscript.

Petrucci's print of the *Missa de Beata Virgine* in his Book III of Josquin's Masses (Fossombrone, 1514), contains some curious *signa congruenciae* in the Gloria, which might make some musical sense as a hold at the end of the phrase «propter magnam gloriam tuam» were it not that the sign in the Altus is misplaced (See Example 1). As it happens, the notes over which these signs appear are exactly those (including the mistake in the Altus) which begin a new opening in the copy of the Gloria in Vatican City, Biblioteca Apostolica Vaticana, Fondo Cappella Sistina, MS 23 [VatS 23], a copy made by the scribe of the papal chapel, Johannes Orceau who died in November, 1512[3]. What could this mean? Is it mere coincidence[4]?

In some of the copies of Josquin Masses made by Orceau (the *Missa Gaudeamus,* the *Missa Malheur me bat,* both in VatS 23) it is possible to see similar signs marking the same place in all voices; they come mostly in Gloria and Credo sections[5]. At first, we might be tempted to think that these are some sort of rehearsal marks, but in fact they generally only appear once in an opening, usually rather far down the part, and it is hard to see what rehearsal function they really could have had. Some time ago, a colleague suggested that the markings really were aids in the process of copying into choirbook format[6]. Obviously, in choirbook format, all the voices have to turn the page at the same time. The most practical way of insuring this when making a copy in that format is to copy one voice part until the page turn, mark the spot in the part, count the same number of breves or semibreves in the other parts and put in similar signs. The copyist would then know when to stop in the other parts. Unfortunately, I have not been able to find any choirbook copies that correspond exactly to the signs I found in the *Missa Gaudeamus* and *Malheur.* But I can demonstrate that a similar procedure was used for another piece. VatS 42 preserves a copy of the popular motet *Sancti dei omnes,* ascribed to Mouton. This copy contains slashes at corresponding spots in all voices (some in red pencil, some merely impressed in the paper), and numbers written in the margins (the number of semibreves up to that spot). These signs correspond exactly to the page turns in the late 16th-century copy of this motet in VatS 76 (they mark the end of each page in each part)[7]. So here we can prove that markings of this sort were intended to aid the copying process into choirbook format.

Given this particular use of marks in manuscripts, it seems to me that the most plausible explanation of the relationship between the signs in

Petrucci, and the page turn in Orceau (especially because of the mistake in Orceau's copy) is that Petrucci used the same exemplar of the Gloria as had Orceau, an exemplar in which the Vatican scribe had already noted the places for his page turn with *signa congruenciae,* those signs simply reproduced by Petrucci's compositor, who would not have known what they meant[8]. This hypothesis becomes even stronger when we realize that Petrucci and VatS 23 agree in almost all details (down to the placement of the text) and further, as Thomas Hall has shown, share a reading found only in those two sources, Petrucci derived prints, and two late manuscripts, Munich, Bayerische Staatsbibliothek, Handschriften-Inkunabelabteilung, MS Musica C (*olim* Cim. 210) (ca. 1544) and Budapest, Orszàgos Széchényi Könyvtár (National Szecheny Library), MS Bartfa 20(a-b) (after 1600), which most likely were also derived from Petrucci. All other sources of the *Missa de Beata Virgine* considered by Hall, including the other Vatican source (VatS 45), contain a different reading; VatS 45 also does not reproduce VatS 23's mistake in the Altus. As Hall remarked, this evidence suggests that there were two different exemplars of the Gloria circulating in Italy[9].

This hypothesis is plausible because the aggregate sources of the *Missa de Beata Virgine* indicate that the Mass was not originally conceived as a complete entity[10]. The Gloria and Credo seem to have had separate transmissions and were both copied into VatS 23 long before any source presents the entire Mass. I would date the VatS 23 copy of the Gloria in the middle of the reign of Julius II (1503-13), whereas the copy of the entire Mass in VatS 45 dates some time in the reign of Leo X (1513-21 – Jeffrey Dean thinks it is early in the reign or even at the end of the reign of Julius II)[11]. Petrucci's edition (the first securely datable source of the entire Mass) was published in March, 1514, but presumably was prepared earlier, perhaps in late 1513. The exemplar of the Gloria used by Orceau was therefore older (perhaps by as much as 7 years), separate, and different from the exemplar of the Gloria that served for the complete Mass in VatS 45. Its close relationship to the Gloria of the complete Mass in Petrucci suggests that Petrucci did not have access to an exemplar to the complete Mass, and instead constructed his publication of it from exemplars of individual movements, one of them found in the Vatican. Since the papal singers already had the Orceau copy of the Gloria, perhaps they felt no need to keep the original exemplar and simply gave it to Petrucci or allowed a copy to be made. When the exemplar of the complete Mass (with the altered reading in the Gloria) reached Rome and was used as the basis for the Mass in VatS 45, there likewise would have been no need to turn to the single copy of the Gloria the chapel already possessed[12].

But how could Petrucci have come upon Orceau's exemplar? Presumably, it would have had to have been in Rome, and there is no evidence that Petrucci visited the city before 1520. There is, however, reason to conjecture that he did. In October, 1513 (after his move back to Fossombrone), Petrucci received from Pope Leo X a monopoly on the production of organ tablature in a bull that he reproduced in many of his prints. It can now be demonstrated that he received this letter by following the normal bureaucratic procedures of the curia, submitting a supplication (the formal legal document prepared by all suppliants, submitted for papal approval and to serve as the basis of an eventual papal bull) which was duly registered in Vatican City, Archivio Segreto Vaticano, Registra Supplicationum 1430, fol. 22r, dated October 22, 1513, the same date as the letter (and does not differ markedly from the final bull)[13]. Dealing with the papal bureaucracy was a complicated, time consuming, and costly affair, and, while it was not absolutely necessary, it was always better for suppliants to be in Rome to watch over the progress of their supplications and the expeditions of their bulls. It seems quite possible that for something as important as a printing monopoly Petrucci journeyed from Fossombrone to Rome to confront the bureaucracy in person. When in Rome, he certainly could have gotten in touch with the members of the papal chapel and looked at its repertory (Book III was, in fact, the first publication Petrucci issued after receiving the monopoly).

Although I think that a direct connection between Petrucci and an extant Roman source has now been established in the case of the Gloria, it must be admitted that comparison of the rest of Petrucci's Book III of Josquin Masses with Masses which existed in older copies in the Vatican (the *Missa Faysans regretz*) in VatS 23 – copy of the first decade of the 16th century; the *Missa ad Fugam* in VatS 49 – a copy of the 1490's) show differences suggesting that there was no direct relationship between Petrucci and Vatican sources in these cases. Stanley Boorman has further shown, at least as far as the *Motetti de la Corona* volumes were concerned, that Petrucci did not seem to have used Roman sources there[14]. Considering the general divergences between Petrucci prints and Vatican sources, it would appear that the Gloria of the *Missa de Beata Virgine* was perhaps the only piece that Petrucci received directly from the library of the papal singers, and that this was the result of a unique circumstance: the need to create an entire Mass out of separately transmitted movements.

Thus, the relationship does not allow any kind of generalizations about the way Petrucci got his music. It merely serves to underscore what a number of scholars have recently been making clear: we must consider every case of the transmission of renaissance music (even down to individual movements) as a separate case to be examined on its own merits. The sources of most of Petrucci's repertory may have been extremely various, and they have yet to be uncovered.

---

[1] See Margaret Bent, "The Machaut Manuscripts Vg, B and E", *Musica Disciplina* 37 (1983): pp. 53-82; and "Trent 93 and Trent 90: Johannes Wiser at Work", in Nino Pirrotta and Danilo Curti, eds. *I codici musicali trentini a cento anni dalla loro riscoperta* (Trento, 1986), pp. 84-111.

[2] There are many such studies. For a partial bibliography, see Stanley Boorman, "Limitations and Extensions of Filiation Technique, in *Music in Medieval and Early Modern Europe: Patronage, Sources and Texts,* edited by Iain Fenlon (Cambridge, England, 1981), pp. 319-46.

³ See Richard Sherr, "The Papal Chapel ca. 1492-1513 and its Polyphonic Sources", Ph. D. dissertation, Princeton University, 1975; and Sherr, *Papal Music Manuscripts in the Late Fifteenth and Early Sixteenth Centuries,* Renaissance Manuscript Studies 5, American Institute of Musicology, forthcoming.

⁴ While there are other choirbook sources which turn the page at this spot, none that I have seen reproduces the mistake in the Altus. See Appendix for the sources examined for this article.

⁵ In the *Missa Gaudeamus,* the signs appear in all parts in the following places: Gloria, m. 34, m. 99; Credo, m. 36, m. 189.

⁶ I am grateful to Thomas Hall for making this observation many years ago.

⁷ On the date of VatS 76, see Mitchell Brauner, "The Parvus Manuscripts", Ph. D. dissertation, Brandeis University, 1982, pp. 290, 371.

⁸ Or if not that, Petrucci could have had an exact copy of Orceau's exemplar.

⁹ Thomas Hall, "Some Computer Aids for the Preparation of Critical Editions of Renaissance Music", *Tijdschrift van de Vereniging voor Nederlandse Muziekgeschiedenis* 25 (1975): pp. 38-53. This evidence also indicates that Petrucci was not the basis for most of the sources of this Mass.

¹⁰ I made this suggestion in my article "Notes on Two Roman Manuscripts of the Early Sixteenth Century", *The Musical Quarterly* 63 (1977): pp. 48-73.

¹¹ Richard Sherr, "The Papal Chapel, ca. 1492-1513 and its Polyphonic Sources"; Jeffrey Dean, "The Scribes of the Sistine Chapel 1501-1527", Ph. D. dissertation, University of Chicago, 1984.

¹² I do not mean to suggest, by the way, that Petrucci was actually responsible for "creating" the complete Mass; he may merely have heard that the Mass was being circulated in a complete form, and decided to make his own compilation of movements from various sources. It is even possible that the exemplar used for the complete Mass in VatS 45 was already in Rome, and the singers did not want to part with it, or even did not want Petrucci to see it.

¹³ It does contain one interesting detail. Originally, the supplication was signed with the remark "concessum ut petitur in presentia D.N. Papae", a formula used when someone other than the pope signed the supplication (although the pope was presumably present and approved). But this is crossed out and replaced with "Fiat ut petitur J", indicating that Leo (Giovanni de' Medici) had intervened and decided to sign the supplication with his own hand (popes signed supplications with the first initial of their Christian names). The exact implications of this are not clear to me, but it probably would have strengthened the supplication if it were really signed by the pope, and may also indicate that Leo took a personal interest in Petrucci's request.

¹⁴ Stanley Boorman, "Petrucci at Fossombrone: A Study of Early Music Printing, with Special Reference to the Motetti de la Corona (1514-1519)", Ph. D. dissertation, University of London, 1976.

VII

Ex. 1. Measures 48-49 of the Gloria of the *Missa de Beata Virgine* showing the placement of the *signa congruentiae* in Petrucci and the notes which begin the new opening in VatS 23.

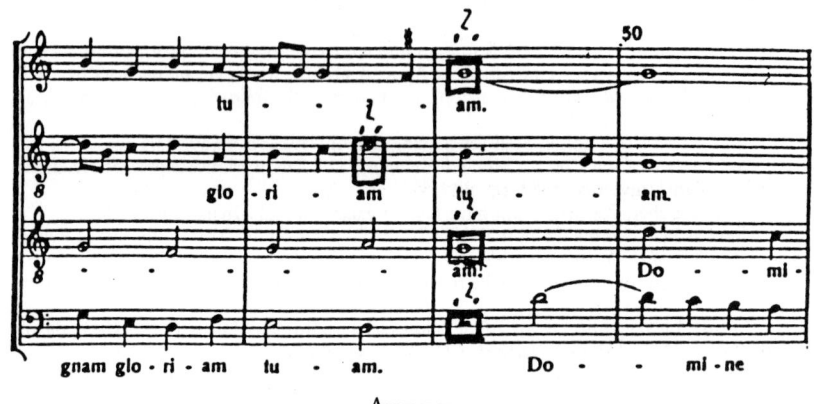

APPENDIX

Choirbook Sources of the "Missa de Beata Virgine" consulted for this Study

Cambrai. Bibliothèque Municipale. MS 18, fols. 200r-206v; 208v-241r; 215v-218r.
Jena. Universitätsbibliothek. MS 7, fols. 61v-77r.
Milan. Biblioteca Ambrosiana. MS E46, fols. 11v-22r.
Munich. Bayerische Staatsbibliothek. Handschriften-Inkunabelabteilung. MS Music C (*olim* Cim. 210), No. 2.
Munich. Bayerische Staatsbibliothek. Handschriften-Inkunabelabteilung. MS Musica 510, fols. 1v-23r.
Stuttgart. Württembergische Landesbibliothek. MS Musici folio I 44, fols. 57v-84r.
Uppsala. Universitetsbiblioteket. MS Vokalmusik i Handskrift 76b, fols. 97v-112r.
Uppsala. Universitetsbiblioteket. MS Vokalmusik i Handskrift 76c, fols. 1v-10r.
Vatican City. Biblioteca Apostolica Vaticana. Fondo Cappella Giulia. MS XII.2 (*olim* C.48), fols. 143v-159r.
Vatican City. Biblioteca Apostolica Vaticana. Fondo Cappella Sistina. MS 23, fols. 129v-132r; 135v-139r.
Vatican City. Biblioteca Apostolica Vaticana. Fondo Cappella Sistina. MS 45, fols. 3v-17r.
Vatican City. Biblioteca Apostolica Vaticana. Fondo Cappella Sistina. MS 160, fols. 33r-48r.
Vienna. Österreichische Nationalbibliothek. MS 4809 (*olim* Theol.35; VIII A 3), fols. 23v-46r.
Weimar. Bibliothek der evangelisch-lutheranischen Kirchengemeinde. MS B, fols. 76v-85r.
Liber Quindecim Missarum (Rome: Antico, 1516).
Glarean, Heinrich. *Dodekachordon* (Basel, 1547).

VIII

Illibata Dei Virgo Nutrix and Josquin's Roman Style*

Illibata Dei virgo nutrix is one of the few motets securely attributed to Josquin des Prez that has generated extended scholarly interest and debate in the twentieth century. The interest thus far has been motivated not primarily by the music of the motet, but by its text—specifically by the acrostics in the first and perhaps the second stanza (Smijers 1925, Titcomb 1963, Elders 1969 and 1970). This essay will consider the piece as a whole: what it shows about Josquin's approach to a text and where it might fit in the chronology of his works.

Most published discussions of Josquin's music assign *Illibata* a place among the composer's earliest works. Although there is some question as to what "early" means in the case of a composer presumably born ca. 1440 whose music seems not to have entered general circulation until the 1490s, most scholars have suggested the 1460s or 1470s for the composition of *Illibata*, dates which place the motet within Josquin's career at the court of Milan (ca. 1459-ca. 1479). The chronological designation "early" is based on an examination of the musical style of the piece, coupled with the widely-held assumption that the existence of certain style characteristics in a piece of Renaissance music allows one to assume that its was written close to the time when those characteristics were current.[1] Milan is the earliest place of production of Josquin's music we can target.

The motet does indeed exhibit musical traits associated with the middle fifteenth century. It is a five-voice motet in two parts, the first of which is in tempus perfectum, the second in tempus imperfectum diminutum. The fifth voice is a cantus firmus not derived by canon

---

* This article is an expanded version of a paper read at the Annual Meeting of the American Musicological Society held in New Orleans in October, 1987. I am grateful to Louise Litterick for many helpful comments and suggestions.

[1] Brown (1976, 122) writes: "It is clear from the few motets that can be safely be assigned to his Milanese years (1459-ca. 1479) that Josquin began his career by writing in the tradition of Dufay and Ockeghem. Dufay, for example, might almost have composed the duos formed of long melismatic lines that open *Illibata dei virgo nutrix* . . ."

© 1988 by the American Musicological Society. All rights reserved.

whose entry is delayed in the first part and which is clearly set off in the first part from the other voices by slower motion. *Illibata* is thus an example of a fifteenth-century genre, the five-voice Tenor motet. In what is perhaps still the most perceptive discussion of the music of the late fifteenth century, Wolfgang Stephan gives a convincing picture of the development of the five-voice Tenor motet (Stephan 1937, 24–50). At the center of the development is Johannes Regis (d. ca. 1485) whose five-voice motets constitute practically the whole of his output in the motet genre.[2] With Regis the five-voice motet, instead of an extreme rarity, becomes a regular (if small) part of a composer's total output. Regis also changes the general disposition of the five voices in his motets from "3+2" (as in Dufay's *Ecclesiae militantes*) to the "4+1" that became standard in the late fifteenth century (see also Blackburn 1976, 38). These works provided the general structural model adopted by Josquin's generation, particularly in the matter of large form, and in the notion that the fifth voice should be a *cantus prius factus*. The younger composers made their own contributions, of course; they added the idea that the fifth voice might be produced canonically or might be drawn from secular music or even solmization syllables, and they tended to reject Regis's habit of eventually integrating the Tenor into the contrapuntal complex, treating it more consistently as a slow moving cantus firmus (Stephan 1937, 34).[3]

Illibata clearly fits within a general conception of the Regis model as it was construed in the middle-late fifteenth century. It is the only one of Josquin's five-voice motets that begins, like the Regis model, in tempus perfectum. Furthermore, the melodic activity of its outer voices tends towards "wide-spanned melodic lines" (Wiora 1976) and complicated rhythms, without much use of syntactic imitation and with striking use of extended sequences and duets. This melodic style

---

[2] While everybody agrees with this assessment, few (to my knowledge) have remarked on how truly unusual such an oeuvre would have been in the later fifteenth century. What would we think, for instance, of a nineteenth-century composer who wrote nothing but wind octets?

[3] Regis's motets actually represent various ways of dealing with Tenor integration; but they almost always begin with the Tenor in long notes and end with the Tenor moving at the same speed as the other voices. A perfect example (almost an experiment) of different ways of treating the Tenor can be found in *Clangat plebs flores*, perhaps for that reason the most famous of Regis's motets. Composers of Josquin's generation also tend to reject Ockeghem's five-voice model, as seen in his *Intemerata dei mater*, in which the Tenor is fully integrated into the contrapuntal fabric (Stephan 1937, 37). The triumph of that idea had to wait until the adoption of the fully imitative style of the sixteenth century. See also Blackburn 1976, 38.

is often compared to the music of the pre-Josquin generation.[4] By contrast, the motet type popular in Italy in the late fifteenth century was for four voices, did not employ a slow-moving Tenor, and was made up of short phrases alternating duets and homophonic passages and quite often using syntactic imitation as a means of construction—a style that Finscher, Rifkin, and others have connected with the court of Milan in the 1470s, and with the works of Gaspar van Weerbecke and Loyset Compère, Josquin's colleagues in the Milanese chapel (Finscher 1964, 181–204; Rifkin 1978).

While the mid-fifteenth-century traits of the first part of the motet have been sufficient to convince scholars that the entire motet is early—for Osthoff (1965, 79), the motet was "one of [Josquin's] earliest works"—almost everybody has remarked that this style does not obtain even in the whole of the first part, and is scarcely to be found in the second part, for which Noble (1972) suggests "the influence of the Italian *lauda*." This, of course, does not really argue against an early date: we merely have to posit that the motet was written at the beginning of Josquin's career in Milan, when he still would have been imbued with the "Netherlandish" style, yet would have been picking up Italian musical techniques as well. In fact, for Gustave Reese/Jeremy Noble (1984, 30), the very abruptness of the stylistic discontinuity between parts "make[s] it probable that *Illibata* is a relatively early work." Against this chorus of opinion, only one voice has to date publicly been raised. Myroslaw Antonowycz suggested at the Josquin Conference in 1971 that the music of *Illibata* was "autobiographical," that the work contained not merely Josquin's name in its text, but represented a conscious borrowing of melodic fragments from works previously composed (Antonowycz 1976). And since Antonowycz identified such works as being (among others) the *Missa L'Homme armé super voces musicales*, the *Missa La sol fa re mi*, and the *Missa Hercules dux Ferrariae*, he could not believe that *Illibata* was early. This argument, however, has not been generally accepted, and the chronological indications of the "early" style of the motet have not been set aside.

But being archaic is not the same thing as being old, and, while admitting the correctness of earlier descriptions, various aspects of

---

[4] "The long duets in the first section with their cunningly cantilevered rhythms hark back to Dufay and the Burgundian school. . ." (Noble 1972); "the marks of the older style are especially noticeable in the first part of the work (which is in triple meter). Among other things, the rather bare sequences in imitation, the constant hemiola, and the other rhythmic groupings which tend to cover the basic meter may be pointed out. They indicate that this is a very early work." (Sparks 1963, 393)

TABLE 1

The Text of *Illibata Dei virgo nutrix*
from Albert Smijers, ed. *Werken van Josquin des Pres*, Vol. 1,
Bundel V, x.

Stanza 1	Stanza 2
1. Illibata Dei virgo nutrix, 2. Olympi tu regis o genetrix, 3. Sola parens Verbi puerpera, 4. Quae fuisti Evae reparatrix, 5. Viri nefas tuta mediatrix, 6. Illud clara luce dat scriptura.	13. Ave virginum decus hominum, 14. Coelique porta, 15. Ave lilium, flos humilium 16. Virgo decora.
7. Nata nati alma genitura, 8. Des, ut laeta musorum factura	17. Vale ergo, tota pulchra ut luna, 18. Electa ut sol, clarissima gaude.
9. Praevaleat hymnus, et sit ave, 10. Roborando sonos, ut guttura	19. Salve tu sola cum sola amica, 20. Consola "la mi la" canentes in tua laude.
11. Efflagitent, laude teque pura 12. Zelotica arte clamet ave.	21. Ave Maria, mater virtutum, 22. Veniae vena, ave Maria, 23. Gratia plena, Dominus tecum, 24. Ave Maria, mater virtutum.
	Amen.

Illibata suggest that it was not among Josquin's first works and was not composed in Milan. Consider first the music in relation to the structure of the poem, as far as it can be determined from what seems to be a corruptly transmitted text.[5] The poem consists of two stanzas. The first presents the acrostic in twelve 10-syllable lines with a recognizable rhyme scheme, the second seems to have a different structure (Table 1 presents the text as Smijers construed it).

Josquin responds to the poetic structure of the first part of the motet by articulating the 6+6-line, two-sentence text by a cadence at the end of the first sentence. The first six lines, governed by the "-*ix*" rhyme (Josquin is careful to make full cadences on *G* on that rhyme) are also each complete syntactic units. In setting these lines, Josquin

---

[5] The two sources of the motet (Vatican City, Biblioteca Apostolica Vaticana, Fondo Cappella Sistina, MS 15, ff. 243v-247v (C.S. 15), and Petrucci's *Motetti a cinque libro primo* [Venice, 1508]) disagree in a number of places, and a completely acceptable version of the text has yet to emerge. Noble 1972 accepts a number of words that Smijers rejects ("suave" for "sit ave" in line 9, for instance) and omits the redundant "cum sola" in line 19 (which has implications for those who would wish to treat the second stanza as an acrostic). Because of the difficulty of resolving this issue, my analysis of the text will not go beyond the broad outlines of its structure.

employs the long duets and sequences that have struck everybody as being "old" and "Netherlandish," and he elides the ends and beginnings of lines. But even with the elisions, the musical phrases clearly correspond to the poetic ones, so that the basic structure and meaning of the first part of the stanza is made clear.

In the next six lines of the first stanza everything changes. The "-*ix*" rhyme disappears, and the lines employ enjambment. Josquin responds to this structural feature of the text by abandoning the long duets and musical phrases corresponding to entire poetic lines. Instead (beginning in line 7), musical phrases divide each line of the text artificially into 4+6 syllables, and are organized in short imitative groupings in which the beginnings and ends of lines are increasingly confused (particularly in line 10); this is, in fact, a musical equivalent of the run-on lines, although it could not be claimed that it reflects the meaning or syntax of the text.

The second stanza is more problematic than the first, but it does seem to be made up of shorter phrases in the beginning and end (*Ave Maria . . . virgo decora* and *Ave Maria . . . Mater virtutum*) with longer lines in the middle (*Vale ergo . . . tua laude*). There also can be little doubt that the musical setting organizes the stanza into four clearly delineated sections corresponding to complete sentences (marked by boxes in Table 1). In setting the second stanza, Josquin also left behind the complications of the "Netherlandish style." The phrases of text are set using duets, imitative passages and homophony, and making all the sentences clear by coming to complete stops at the end of every sentence—the "Italian style" that everybody has noticed. In this second stanza Josquin served both the structure and the meaning of the text. In the motet as a whole, Josquin adopted different musical styles to illustrate the structure of the text. This stylistic mix surrounds a Tenor consisting of a three-note ostinato on the *soggetto cavato la mi la* (from "Maria") that recalls, in its construction, the old isorhythmic motet, but in a way that may go beyond even the complexities of fifteenth-century isorhythm described by Damman (1953) in his discussions of this and other isorhythmic motets.

The relationship between the Tenor ostinato and the structure of the text can be seen easily when the Tenor is presented in the original notation (See Example 1). For the first stanza (where the text is relatively regular), the presentation is straightforward: three statements consisting of three longs or nine breves, each separated by eighteen breves rest.

The ostinato in the second part, however, reflects that part's sectional structure in breves and semibreves that correspond to the

VIII

Example 1

Tenor of *Illibata dei virgo nutrix*

four musical sections (breves for sections 1 and 4, semibreves for sections 2 and 3). The Tenor also has three time signatures: ₵, ₵3 (sesquialtera to ₵), and ₵2 (proportio dupla to ₵); that is, one regular time signature and two proportional time signatures, the two proportional time signatures beginning the last two sections of the second part. But there are other levels of structure in the second part of *Illibata*, and these seem all to reflect the Pythagorean proportions of 1:1, 2:1, 3:2, 4:3, and 9:8 (see Table 2).

It is hard to believe that this insistence on Pythagorean proportions occurs by accident. Moreover, although proportions had always been an intrinsic part of the isorhythmic motet, it is possible to point to a specific piece using the very procedure Josquin employs. Antoine Busnois, who wrote motets with texts containing his own name (one of them—the motet *In hydraulis*—based on a three-note ostinato), was also concerned in at least one of his works with expressing the Pythagorean ratios through the durational proportions of sections of music; in his *Missa L'Homme armé*, as Taruskin (1986) has shown, the extraordinary method of expressing Pythagorean proportions through the temporal relations of the sections of the Mass is a basic feature of construction. This congruence is so compelling that Busnois's Mass could be claimed as one direct structural model for the second part of

TABLE 2
Proportions in the Tenor of *Illibata Dei virgo nutrix*

Section	Time Signature (a)	Number of Ostinato Statements (b)	Tempora (without Amen) (c)	Tempora (with Amen) (d)
1	¢	4	24	
	1:1	3:2	4:3	24+18 = 42
2	[¢]	6	18	
	3:2	4:3	9:8	1:1
3	¢3	8	16	
	4:3	1:1	3:2	16+48(24)+4(2) = 42
4	¢2	8	48(24)	
	2:1	2:1	1:1	

Column *a* shows the proportions (of semibreves) caused by the time signatures (comparing section 2 to section 1, section 3 to section 2, section 4 to section 3, and section 4 to section 1).

Column *b* shows the proportions caused by the number of statements of the ostinato in the 4 sections (again, comparing section 2 to section 1, section 3 to section 2, section 4 to section 3, and section 4 to section 1).

Column *c* shows the proportions of the *tempora* of the sections in the manner of Richard Taruskin in his provocative article of Busnois's *Missa L'Homme armé* (1986, 270), comparing section 1 to section 2, section 2 to section 3, section 4 to section 3, and section 4 to section 1, although we must agree that the final four breves of the piece are a coda, which they clearly are since they set the words Amen.

Column *d* compares the *tempora* including the final Amen in section 1 + 2 to those in sections 3 + 4.

Illibata, a claim strengthened by what appears to be a direct quote from the Mass in the first part of the motet.

Example 2 shows a small duet from the Christe of the Busnois Mass. Comparison of this with mm. 68–72 of the motet show a remarkable similarity. (Example 3 gives the two phrases in the original notation.)

This melodic concordance would probably not be worth mentioning if it were restricted to the first five notes of the example—a common phrase (in that exact rhythmic guise) found in many pieces including others by Josquin (most notably in his *Missa Hercules dux Ferrariae*, as Antonowicz noted).[6] But the concordance goes beyond those five notes, including a leap of a fifth, a return to the beginning note, and the reproduction of a contrapuntal imitative entry. Of course, this still might be coincidence, but, given the other affinities

---

[6] In fact, it was a happy coincidence for Josquin that the *soggetto cavato Hercules Dux Ferrariae* provided such a popular bit of melodic material. The motive can be found in much of the contrapuntal material in the Mass, and listeners could not but help relate it to the cantus firmus in spite of its being a melodic cliché.

Example 2

Busnois, *Missa L'Homme Armé*, Christe

Example 3
(a) Busnois, *Missa L'Homme Armé* (in the version C.S. 14)

(b) Josquin, *Illibata dei virgo genitrix*

between the Mass and the motet, it might also mean that Josquin wished to make a melodic reference to Busnois's Mass in the section of his motet that was not based on the proportional model of Busnois's *Missa L'Homme armé*.[7]

All of this looks like a case for the "early" date of the motet, but the situation is not so clear. We have in actuality no securely datable early motets by Josquin that exhibit the range of procedures and styles evident in *Illibata* (in fact, we have no securely datable early motets at all), and it may not immediately follow that a reference or modeling on Busnois must necessarily indicate an early work. In any case, we would have to know first of all when the Busnois Mass was written (or, more importantly, when it was first circulated), and we do not really know that, in spite of all the theories. We would also have to know when Josquin might first have been exposed to the work, and we don't really know that either. But there is one thing that we do know: when Josquin arrived in Rome in 1486, a copy of Busnois's *Missa L'Homme armé* was available in the library of the organization he joined, the papal choir, in what is now Vatican City, Biblioteca Apostolica Vaticana, Fondo Cappella Sistina MS 14 (C.S. 14), a manuscript that, according to recent theories, was copied in Naples

---

[7] I have seen the motive in similar guise only in another work by Busnois, the chanson *Quant se viendra*, mm. 10–13 and 23–27.

TABLE 3

The Sanctus of the *Missa L'Homme Armé* by Busnois in the Version of C.S. 14: Proportions of Tempora

Section	Tempora	Proportions
1. Sanctus [O]	36	
		4:3
2. Pleni [O]	27	
		3:2
3. Osanna [O2]	18	
		3:2
4. Benedictus [O2]	12	
		3:2
5. Osanna [O2]	18	

around 1480, and that was certainly in the hands of the papal singers before the end of the reign of Sixtus IV in 1484 (Roth 1982).

Taruskin has made an interesting point about the copy of the Mass in C.S. 14 by demonstrating that it belongs to a different tradition than the copy which exists in the Chigi codex—a tradition that might be labeled Neapolitan/Roman. One of the things that distinguishes the Neapolitan/Roman tradition is the time signatures of the Christe and the Benedictus (O2 rather than C). As Taruskin shows, this has important consequences for the proportions of the Mass (1986, 269–71). But consider what the proportions would be if the Neapolitan/Roman time signature were included in the only movement of the Mass to have more than three parts, the Sanctus (See Table 3 comparing sections 1 to section 2 and section 5 to section 4).

Admittedly, this may not be as satisfying as the proportions one gets if the Benedictus is read in C, but it does make the proportions of sections 1 to 2 and 5 to 4 of the Sanctus (4:3 and 3:2) exactly the same as the proportions of sections 1 to 2 and 4 to 3 of Part II of *Illibata* (See Table 2); in other words, if Josquin modeled the proportions of his motet on the proportions of Busnois's Mass, then the version current in Italy and preserved in Rome and not the one represented by Chigi might have provided the model. Now, I would be the first to admit that the theory that Josquin modeled his motet specifically on Busnois's *Missa L'Homme armé* and that he did so in Rome is highly speculative. But even if the Busnois connection turns out to be unconvincing, there are other good reasons for associating *Illibata* with Rome.

Consider the question of the genre of the motet in relation to its usual assignment to the 1470s and to Milan. If the Gaffurius Codices tell us anything at all, they should tell us something about repertories current in Milan in the late fifteenth and early sixteenth centuries (Jeppesen 1931, Ward 1986). The vast collection of motets in the Gaffurius Codices does not provide a single piece that fits the general five-voice tenor-motet model described at the beginning of this essay, although one finds an occasional four-voice tenor motet or motet with five voices. Instead, the vast majority of its motets are for four voices and are in the "new Italian" style represented only in the second part of *Illibata*. This would seem to indicate that in Milan there was no demand for the five-voice tenor motet. Would Josquin really have written in Milan a motet so at odds with the prevailing musical tastes (as illustrated by the Gaffurius Codices), especially considering how well he understood and adopted the Milanese style of the Gaffurius Codices as witnessed by *Qui velatus facie fuisti*, *Vultum tuum deprecabuntur*, and the *Missa D'Ung aultre amer*? On the other hand, as Gerhard Croll (1954, 243), and most recently Joshua Rifkin (1978) have remarked, Rome in the 1480s and 90s was a place where the five-voice tenor motet and the "Netherlandish style" can be said to have been not only accepted but cultivated.[8]

The few motets in surviving Roman sources of the 1480s and 90s (all but one written by composers who were members of the Papal Chapel during that period), indicate that the five-voice Tenor motet was an accepted genre in late fifteenth-century Rome. The motets are listed below.[9]

---

[8] The following continues arguments first made by Joshua Rifkin (1978). I am grateful to Prof. Rifkin for letting me consult an unpublished typescript of this paper.

[9] In this group, I am also tempted to place a motet which does not appear in a Roman source, Weerbecke's *Stabat mater*/T: *Vidi speciosam* (extant only in the Chigi codex). I do so first of all because it fits the pattern of the other motets, but also because of certain affinities it has with *Clangat plebs flores*, particularly that the tenor entry is delayed for exactly the same number of breves, and more strikingly that the second part of the motet begins by recalling the most unique audible feature of *Clangat*, the consistent alternation of short duets with homophonic five-voice sections. Now, one might argue that Weerbecke knew *Clangat* in the north or in Milan, but it cannot be denied that that particular motet was known in Naples (it is mentioned by Tinctoris in his *Liber de arte contrapuncti*) when Weerbecke joined the papal chapel in 1481, and that the repertorial links between Naples and Rome could have been very strong in the fifteenth century. Furthermore, the work was copied into C.S. 15, a manuscript that represents the chapel repertory in the 1490s (the motet was so popular in Rome that it was even recopied in the Leo X manuscript C.S. 16). The close affinity between these two motets is discussed by Stephan (1937, 36). There are also two five-voice motets in C.S. 15 which do not follow the Regis model in that they both begin in tempus imperfectum and derive their fifth voice by canon (*Inviolata integra et casta* by Basiron [ff. 250v-252r] and *Quis numerare queat* by Compère [ff. 196v-199r]). These motets, however, were written by composers who were not connected with the papal chapel.

Clangat plebs flores (T: *Sicut lilium*): Regis (Vatican City, Biblioteca Apostolica Vaticana, Fondo Cappella Sistina [hereafter, C.S.] 15, ff. 163v-166r)
Da pacem (T: *Da pacem*): De Orto (C.S. 35, ff. 192v-196r)
Dulcis amica Dei (T: *Da pacem*): Weerbecke (C.S. 15, ff. 204v-208r)
Rex fallax miraculum (T: *Apertis thesauris*): Vaqueras (C.S. 63, ff. 71v-75r)
Salve regis mater (T: *Hic est sacerdos*): [De Orto?] (C.S. 35, ff. 188v-191r; 196v-200r [another copy])

Although only one of these motets is by Regis—the only motet of his to appear in an Italian source before the publication of Petrucci's *Motetti a cinque* in 1508—all of these motets can be said to be in the manner of Regis; they adopt all the main characteristics of the Regis tenor motet:

-They are in two parts, the first in tempus perfectum, the second in tempus imperfectum diminutum.

-The fifth voice (the Tenor) is drawn from chant, and is not derived by canon.

-The entry of the Tenor is delayed by an introduction (see Examples 4–6 below), usually beginning as a shifting three-voice texture, but often containing extensive duets (e.g. Example 6 below).

-In the first part of the motet the Tenor remains separate from the other voices. To this can be added a tendency for the other voices to have "wide-spanned melodic lines" with complicated rhythms and some use of sequences, ie. the "Burgundian," "Netherlandish" style (see Example 7.a for an example from *Salve regis mater*, which bears a family resemblance to Example 7.b, from *Illibata*).

Two of these motets seem quite clearly to have been written during Josquin's tenure in the Papal Chapel; the others, with the exception of Regis, were probably written at about the same time. The text of Weerbecke's *Dulcis amica Dei*, in its second part, asks protection for a pope whose name is left blank in C.S. 15, but who must be, as Croll (1954) and Dunning (1970, 17–18) have pointed out, Innocent VIII, r. 1484–92, the pope during whose reign Weerbecke served the Papal Chapel.[10] The text of *Salve regis mater*, on the other

---

[10] Given the text of the motet, I would agree with Dunning (and disagree with Croll who thinks it was written for the pope's coronation in 1484) that the motet has something to do with the dire situation in which the pope found himself in 1487–88 when the armies of King Ferrante of Naples were practically at the gates of Rome, and there was real need for peace and protection.

Example 4

Opening of the motet *Salve Regis Mater* (VatS 35, fols. 188v–191r)

hand, makes clear reference to the coronation of Alexander VI (26 August 1492), and must have been composed for the occasion. Josquin first entered the chapel in September 1486. His name appears in the lists until January 1487, returns in September 1487, leaves the next month, and returns in June 1489 for a stay that lasted at least until 1495 (Sherr 1975, 28–37; Noble 1976, 78, 88). Both other motets, even though they cannot be connected with specific occasions,[11] were written by composers who were Josquin's direct contemporaries in

---

[11] De Orto's *Da pacem* might have had the same impetus as *Dulcis amica dei*.

Example 5

Opening of the Motet *Dulcis amica dei* by Weerbecke

Example 5 cont.

the chapel.[12]

All this indicates that the Netherlandish or Burgundian style in five-voice motets was alive and well in Rome in the 1480s and 90s (contrary to its position in Milan), and that composers who were members of the Papal Chapel during that period composed five-voice Tenor motets in that style in Rome (Weerbecke, de Orto, and Vaqueras were the most important chapel composers in the 1480s; the next important composer to join the chapel was, of course, Josquin). Furthermore, such motets were produced even when their style was

---

[12] De Orto and Vaqueras both joined the papal choir in 1483, and Vaqueras had been in Rome earlier as a member of the choir of St. Peter's—Sherr 1975, 62, 75; Reynolds 1982, 138–42.

VIII

Example 6

Opening of the motet *Rex Fallax miraculum* by Vaqueras (from CMM 78)

VIII

ILLIBATA DEI VIRGO NUTRIX

Example 6 cont.

Example 7

(a) From *Salve regis mater*

(b) From *Illibata*

manifestly different from a composer's "normal" motet style. One merely has to compare *Dulcis amica Dei* (and another motet, the *Ave regina coelorum* in C.S. 15) to all the other motets Weerbecke wrote, for instance, to agree with Croll that Weerbecke could compose in two radically different styles (in fact, Weerbecke was one of the most popular composers of the Milanese, "Italian" motet, as the Gaffurius Codices and Petrucci's *Motetti A* demonstrate).[13] But it does not seem in his case that the stylistic dichotomy is necessarily indicative of a chronological development, as one of the "old-style" pieces (*Dulcis amica Dei*) was certainly written after the "new-style" *motetti missales*. Rather it appears that Weerbecke changed styles because he moved to Rome, a musical milieu in which the "Netherlandish" style was admired and cultivated, and where the influence of Ockeghem and Regis was strong (particularly in the works of Vaqueras and De Orto).

If Weerbecke could adopt a style to fit new circumstances, could Josquin not do so as well? In at least one instance, in fact, he did. There was in Rome a particular tradition of polyphonic settings of the Tract *Domine, non secundum peccata* (see the Appendix to this article). What characterizes these Roman motets (and distinguishes them from Milanese motets) is a total reliance on paraphrased chant, on long duets, on setting off certain words that were important for the papal ceremonial, and a tendency to write in a style that (to quote Rifkin

---

[13] Interestingly, not one of these motets is preserved in an extant Vatican source, in spite of Weerbecke's long association with the papal chapel.

1978) "... displays a marked absence of cleanly articulated phrases, sharply profiled rhythms, and clear textual projection." Of the four earliest settings preserved in Vatican sources two are by Josquin's direct contemporaries in the chapel, Vaqueras and de Orto, one is anonymous, and one is by Josquin. Josquin's setting conforms in all its particulars to the general pattern set by the Roman tradition, and his work is so unlike the motets preserved in the Gaffurius Codices that it can be said to represent a true stylistic difference.

A comparison of Josquin's "Roman" setting of *Domine non secundum* with one by his colleague Bertrandus Vaqueras is instructive on another level. Both obviously proceed from the same compositional premises. Nonetheless, if one compares the manner in which Vaqueras paraphrased the chant melody with the inventive way Josquin combined two phrases of chant to form a single melodic arch (see Example 8), one sees that Josquin was in a sense "showing up" his colleague, demonstrating that, even in a bit of *Gebrauchsmusik* such as this, he could apply more imagination than anyone else. We may agree with Glarean (who also felt that the two motets were meant to be compared) that Josquin's setting of *Domine, non secundum peccata* is better than Vaqueras's (Miller 1965, II, 249).

It could be argued that exactly the same attitude of competition seen in Josquin's setting of *Domine non secundum* is present in *Illibata*. The motet could easily be viewed as Josquin's contribution to a Roman corpus of five-voice tenor motets, and another attempt to outdo papal composers at their own game. Yet, while demonstrating his compositional supremacy over his colleagues, he did not ignore them.

Consider Lines 19–20 of the poem (see Table 1), with the plea to the Virgin to console "those singing *la mi la*." Josquin here leaves no doubt who it is who is singing *la mi la*, for this is the only time that the ostinato leaves the Tenor and enters the other voices of the motet: the singers of the motet are singing "la mi la", and it is for them and by them that this direct appeal to the Virgin is made. The entire motet text is therefore not merely a personal embodiment of its composer, it is also a *Sängergebet*.[14] Of all the musical organizations of the fifteenth and sixteenth centuries, the papal singers had perhaps the strongest notion of corporate identity. They were called—and they were literally—the College of Singers; they had specific rights and privileges, a sense of history, and a feeling that they should "stick

---

[14] And a true prayer, rather than a simple list of singers as in Compère's *Omnium bonorum plena*, Josquin's *Nymphes des bois*, and Moulu's *Mater floreat florescat*.

Example 8

Paraphrases of the Tract *Domine, non secundum*
(a) Vaqueras, *Domine, non secundum*

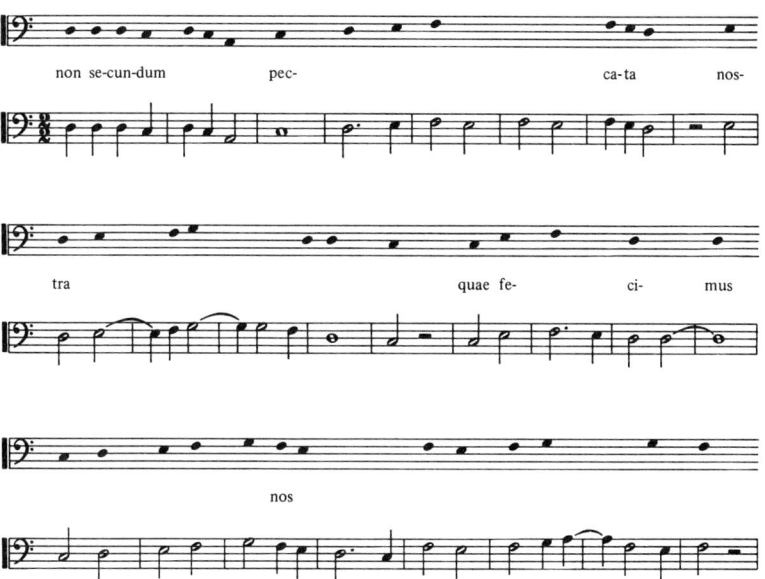

together." *Illibata* recognizes this communality; it prays for the papal singers at the same time as it declares the superiority of its composer over them.

All this suggests the following hypothesis concerning *Illibata Dei virgo nutrix*: When Josquin came to Rome, he found an acceptance of five-voice tenor motets in the style of Regis and a predilection for "Netherlandish" polyphony that had been absent in Milan.[15] He decided to provide his own contribution to this particular Roman style by composing a five-voice Tenor motet, just as he had contributed to the Roman tradition of *Domine, non secundum peccata* motets. However, although adopting the local genre, he deliberately chose to emulate a model different from the one employed by his colleagues (a Busnois Mass instead of Regis motets), and created a piece with many layers of style and construction, with a heightened awareness of the formal implications of its text—a piece the style of which is an actual fusion

---

[15] This can be observed in the majority of the motets that are preserved in the major fifteenth-century Roman manuscripts C.S. 35 and C.S. 15, as Rifkin (1978) demonstrates.

Example 8 cont.

(b) Josquin, *Domine, non secundum*

of the Netherlandish style and the style he had left in Milan. And at the same time that he was outdoing his colleagues, he included them as well as himself directly in the motet. It is small wonder that this work stands alone in his oeuvre, apparently had a limited circulation (it appears in only two sources),[16] and did not generate any theoretical comment; even Glarean, who delighted in telling tales of Josquin's ingenuity, does not mention the acrostic motet (in fact, the acrostic apparently was not noticed until Smijers 1925).

It remains to be seen whether the hypothesis put forward here about *Illibata* will in the long run seem more reasonable than our previous hypothesis about its place in the chronological development of Josquin's musical style. Two major objections can immediately be raised: 1) The Gaffurius Codices may not in fact represent all that was going on in Milan (considering the number of sources that are probably lost), and in any case may represent only tastes at the cathedral and not at the court.[17] 2) Josquin was not continuously in

---

[16] See note 5.

[17] As Bonnie Blackburn pointed out when this essay was originally presented, the cathedral choir consisted largely of Italians while the ducal chapel choir consisted largely of Northerners. Thus, the Gaffurius Codices, as representative of the

Milan even in the period ca. 1460–79, and apparently made a trip north (to Condé, where he could easily have come into direct contact with Busnois) in the 1480s before his move to Rome. Furthermore, the chronological hypothesis derived from musical style is based on venerable and extremely tenacious assumptions that sometimes turn out to be correct. But we can only deal with what we have. Rome in the 1480s, with its predilection for the Netherlandish style and for five-voice Tenor motets, provided both the motive and opportunity to compose *Illibata* which Milan did not. A later Roman provenance also supplies a better explanation for the eclectic musical characteristics of this piece than does the notion that it was an early work. What the study of *Illibata Dei virgo nutrix* may show is that place had as much an effect on Josquin's musical language as time.

---

cathedral, might be expected to contain more Italianate works, while court manuscripts might show that the Northerners continued to write in their own style. Unfortunately, no court manuscripts have been discovered to date, so what they might or might not contain remains in the realm of speculation. Furthermore, two of the most famous practitioners of the "Italian" style were Compère and Weerbecke, Northerners serving in the ducal chapel and not in the cathedral.

APPENDIX

Domine, non secundum peccata and a Roman Motet Tradition[18]

The Cappella Sistina collection of manuscripts contains many settings of the Tract *Domine, non secundum peccata*, a text used in the fifteenth and sixteenth centuries on Ash Wednesday and on various weekdays during Lent until Holy Week (see the text of *Domine, non secundum* in Table 4a). The polyphonic settings are preserved in sources ranging in date from the 1490s to the 1550s, and include works by Josquin, de Orto, Arcadelt, Festa, and other composers connected with the Papal Chapel. That there should be so many polyphonic settings of a single tract is in itself striking. More striking is that, of all the settings of the text I have uncovered to date (see Table 4b), those in the Vatican and connected with the Papal Chapel account for the majority, and provide what are perhaps the oldest pieces (the works by Josquin, de Orto, and Vaqueras, all members of the papal choir in the 1480s and 90s).[19]

TABLE 4a
The text of *Domine, non secundum peccata*

Domine, non secundum peccata nostra que
fecimus nos, neque secundum iniquitates
nostras retribuas nobis.

Domine, ne memineris iniquitatum nostrarum
antiquarum, cito anticipent nos misericordie
tue quia pauperas facti sumus nimis.

Adiuva nos deus salutaris noster, et propter
gloriam nominis tui domine libera nos
et propitius esto peccatis nostris, propter
nomen tuum.

Furthermore, the Vatican settings of *Domine, non secundum peccata* have remarkable musical similarities. Most of the motets begin with chant incipits (rare in the Italian motet repertory, but often used with liturgical pieces such as Magnificats, and in the liturgical motets written for the Imperial chapel). Many have duets or duet structures involving "wide spanned melodic lines," and almost all have some reduction of voices in the various *partes* (the model for this may have been Ockeghem's setting of the Tract in his *Requiem*). All

---

[18] This material was first presented in two unpublished papers: "Settings of the Tract *Domine, non secundum peccata*: Some Evidence of a Roman Motet Tradition," presented at the spring meeting of the New England Chapter of the American Musicological Society, Cambridge, MA, 1980; and "The Papal Singers and their Library," presented at the annual Conference on Medieval Studies, Kalamazoo, 1981.

[19] The setting by Anonymous 1 in Table 4b may be even older. Although the list in Table 4b is undoubtedly not complete, I think the general picture it paints is accurate.

VIII

TABLE 4b

A Preliminary Listing of Settings and Sources of *Domine, non secundum peccata*
(Manuscript sigla are those of the *Census-Catalogue of Manuscript Sources of Polyphonic Music 1400–1550*, 4 vols. [Neuhausen-Stuttgart, 1979–88])

	Settings Connected with the Papal Chapel		
Composer	Concordances	Sections	Voices
1. Anonymous 1.	C.S. 35, fols. 178v–181r, Anon.	Domine non secundum Domine ne memineris Adjuva nos	3 2 4
2. De Orto.	C.S. 35, fols. 181v–184r, Anon; 1503/1, Deorto.	Domine non secundum Domine ne memineris Adjuva nos	4 4 4
3. Josquin.[1]	BerlPs 40013, fols. 249v–252r, Anon; MunU322-5, No. 14, Iusquinus; SGallS 463, No. 97, Iosquinus Pratensis; C.S.P B80, fols. 32v–35r, Jusquin; C.S. 35, fols. 5v–7r, Judocus de Pratis; 1503/1, Josquin; 1547/1, pp. 246–50, Iodoco Pratensi; 1549/16, No. LXXX, Josquin.	Domine non secundum Domine ne memineris Quia pauperes Adjuva nos	2 2 4 4
4. Vaqueras.	LonBL 12532, fols. 35r-35v, Vacqueras; MunU 322-3, No. 13, Vaqueras; SGallS 463, No. 98, Vaqueras; C.S. 35, fols. 2v–5r, Vaqueras; 1503/1, Vaqueras; 1547/1, pp. 244–45, Vaqueras.	Domine non secundum Domine ne memineris Adjuva nos	2 2 4
5. Prioris.	C.S.63, fols. 55v–58r, Prioris.	Domine non secundum Domine ne memineris Adjuva nos	4 4 4
6. Michot.[1]	C.S. 55, fols. 111v–114r, A. michot.	Domine non secundum Domine ne memineris Adjuva nos	3 4 4
7. Anonymous 2.	C.S. 55, fols. 114v–118r, Anon.	Domine non secundum Domine ne memineris Adjuva nos	4 3 5
8. Anonymous 3.[1]	C.S.55, fols. 118v–122r, Anon.	Domine non secundum Domine ne memineris Quia pauperes Adjuva nos Et propitius esto Propter nomen tuum	2 2 4 4 4 4
9. Beausseron.[1]	C.S. 55, fols. 122v–125v, Jo. Beausseron.	Domine non secundum Domine ne memineris Adjuva nos	4 3 4

TABLE 4b, CONTINUED

Settings Connected with the Papal Chapel			
Composer	Concordances	Sections	Voices
10. Festa.[1]	C.S. 20, fols. 74v-78r.	Domine non secundum	2
		Domine ne memineris	3
		Adjuva nos	6
11. Arcadelt.[1]	C.S. 13, fols. 163v-167r.	Domine non secundum	3
		Domine ne memineris	4
		Adjuva nos	5
12. Escobedo.[1]	C.S. 24, fols. 146v-151r, Scobedo.	Domine non secundum	3
		Domine ne memineris	4
		Adjuva nos	5
Settings not Connected with the Papal Chapel			
Composer	Concordances	Sections	Voices
13. Martini.	ModE M.1.11, fols. 46v-49r, Io. Martini.	Domine non secundum	3
		Domine ne memineris	3
		Adjuva nos	3
14. Isaac.	I89 (Choralis Constantinus, vol. I)	Domine non secundum	4
		Domine ne memineris	4
		Adjuva nos	4
15. Maître Jan.[2]	VatG XII.4, fols. 63v-68r, Maistre Jan.	Domine non secundum	4
		Domine ne memineris	3
		Adjuva nos	5
16. Lebrun.[3]	CambraiBM 18, fols. 224v-229r, J. lebrung	Domine non secundum	3
		Domine ne memineris	3
		Cito anticipent nos	6
		Adjuva nos	6
		Et propitius esto	6
17. Jachet of Mantua.	1535/2, Jacquet.	Domine non secundum	6
		Domine ne memineris	3
		Adjuva nos	5
18. Clemens non Papa.	C2698 (1559).	Domine ne memineris	4
		Adjuva nos	4

[1] Begins with a chant incipit.
[2] An incipit has been added, even though it is not needed.
[3] There is no incipit in the manuscript, but the first words set are "non secundum;" presumably an incipit was sung.

the motets are chant based, and there are similarities in the method of handling the chant. In the earlier group of Roman motets in particular, the chant is often paraphrased, but in such a way as to be recognizable to anybody who knew the melody, and in later motets, written in a period where non-cantus firmus imitative motets were the rule, the chant is still used as a recognizable cantus firmus.[20]

More striking than these similarities of musical styles are certain similarities of text setting. All the motets are divided into three parts reflecting the three-sentence division of the text, and special care seems to have gone into the setting of the words *cito anticipent nos* (the end of the second part) and

[20] Many of the later settings have been published in Josephson 1982.

propter nomen tuum (the end of the third part). An attempt is made in many of these pieces, most clearly in certain Roman settings, to highlight these phrases—for example, by coming to a full stop before they begin, or by changing from duple to triple meter when they are sung, or by introducing a radical change in the polyphonic texture at that point. These similarities seem, in fact, to go beyond coincidence, and suggest that some Roman composers felt they had to approach the text in a certain defined way. Table 5 contains a list of these procedures.

Since so many of the motets come from sources and composers connected with the Papal Chapel, and since they have such musical similarities, one might wonder if they reflect something contained in the papal ceremonial. One might wonder if anything happened during the normal performance of the tract *Domine, non secundum peccata* that might have occasioned musical similarities in disparate polyphonic settings. Here, papal ceremonials and diaries provide an answer.

Table 6 presents a number of excerpts from papal ceremonials and diaries bearing on the ceremonies of the Mass of Ash Wednesday (the only occasion on which the tract was sung, in the presence of the pope, curia, and entire chapel assembled in the Cappella Sistina).

As can be seen, during the tract the pope had to move from his throne at the left chapel wall to the faldstool located in the center of the chapel. There he had to remove his miter and kneel during the singing of the third verse *Adiuva nos*, returning to his throne at the end in order to be ready for the Gospel reading. This in itself might not explain much about musical similarities, were it not for the pedantry of Paris de Grassis. In his Ceremonial and in his diaries, he is very specific about the actions during the performance of the tract, mainly because of his concern with timing: he wants the pope to get to the faldstool and kneel *exactly* when the singers sing *Adiuva nos*, not before, not after, and he wants the pope back on his throne *exactly* at the end of the tract. To make sure this occurs, he gives two directions: first, he suggests that the pope begin to leave the throne when the singers sing *cito anticipent nos*, and that he should rise and return when they sing *propter nomen tuum* (see Table 6, nos. 4–6). To make the timing even more accurate, he further instructs the singers to sing those last words slowly in order to give the pope enough time to get back to the throne. He does not mention polyphony, and, of course, polyphony was not essential to the service, but it is certainly more than a curious coincidence that precisely the words he mentions are those singled out for special treatment in almost all Roman settings of the tract. Obviously, if the pope or master of ceremonies had to hear certain words, extreme care had to be taken that they be understood, and this is what happens if they are set off in the manner utilized by many composers of the tract.

It would appear from this that the motet settings of *Domine, non secundum peccata*, unlike the majority of the motets in C.S. manuscripts, had a true liturgical function, since important parts of the musical form appear to have been dictated by liturgical action. This further explains the use of chant

TABLE 5

Musical Events At or Before the Words
Cito anticipent nos and *Propter nomen tuum*

Composer	cito anticipent nos	propter nomen tuum
1. Anonymous 1	Full stop (fermata). Change of time signature. Duet.	Full stop. Change of time signature (before "et propitius esto"). A *signum congruenciae* appears in the Superius above the note just before "propter nomen tuum."
2. De Orto	Cadence. Change of time signature. Duet texture. "Quia pauperes" begins a new section (a4).	Full stop (fermata). Change of time signature (before "tuum").
3. Josquin	Full stop (fermata). Change of time signature. Duet. "Quia pauperes" begins a new section (a4).	Full stop (fermata). Change of time signature.
4. Vaqueras	Full stop. Duet.	Full stop (fermata). Change of time signature.
5. Prioris	Full stop. Duet texture.	Full stop. Duet texture.
6. Michot	"Cito" embedded in polyphonic texture, but full stop (fermata) before "quia pauperes."	Cadence. Change of time signature (before "nomen tuum").
7. Anonymous 2	"Cito" embedded in polyphonic texture, but full stop before "quia pauperes."	Full stop (fermata). Change of time signature.
8. Anonymous 3	Full stop (fermata). Change of time signature. Duet. "Quia pauperes" begins a new section (a4).	Separate section
9. Beausseron	Embedded in polyphonic texture.	Embedded in polyphonic texture.
10. Festa	Full stop.	Cadence. Radical change in texture (from 6 voices to two groups of 3).
11. Arcadelt	Embedded in polyphonic texture.	Embedded in polyphonic texture.
12. Escobedo	Embedded in polyphonic texture, but the piece slows down dramatically through the use of long notes at "quia pauperes."	Full stop. Change of texture (from 5 voices to 3)
13. Martini	Embedded in polyphonic texture, but fairly distinct because of three-voice texture and homophonic writing.	Cadence
14. Isaac	Cadence.	Embedded in polyphonic texture.
15. Maître Jan	Cadence.	Cadence.
16. Lebrun	Separate section.	Cadence. Change of texture (from upper trio to lower trio of voices).
17. Jachet	Embedded in polyphonic texture.	Cadence.
18. Clemens	Cadence.	Cadence.

TABLE 6

Remarks in Papal Ceremonials and Diaries Concerning *Domine Non Secundum*

1. From a ceremonial of the time of the Avignonese Papacy. (See Schimmelpfennig 1973, 216–17)

In quadragesima et ferialibus diebus.

In quadragesima ad tractum cum dicitur: Adiuva nos deus salutaris etc., cum papa audit missam, descendit ad faldistorium, et diaconus deponit sibi mitram, et ipse faldistorio incumbit. Et statim, dicto usque ad partem illam: salutaris noster inclusive, resumit mitram, diacono ministrante, et ad sedem revertitur. Etiam cum celebrat in quadragesima et idem tractus fuerit dicendus, facit.

2. From a ceremonial of the time of Benedict XIII (1394–1409). (See Schimmelpfennig 1973, 301.)

Rubrica diei cinerum

Item in primis et ultimis orationibus papa genuflectit in cathedra cum cussinis per clericos capelle coram altari parata. Et similiter ibidem genuflectit, quando incipitur per chorum tertius versus tractus, videlicet: Adiuva nos deus, quod non faceret, si ipsemet celebraret, sed in faldistorio suo genuflecteret et non in cathedra coram altari.

3. From the diaries of Johannes Burkhard. (See Celani 1906-, 84)

Ash Wednesday, 1487 (February 22).

Incepto tracto, diaconus posuit librum evangeliorum super altare, osculatus est pedem pape, dixit Munda etc., et accepit benedictionem a pontefice antequam veniret ad genuflexionem pro versu Adjuva nos Deus etc.; quo versu finita, quamprimam papa esset in sede supra solium, incepit Dominus vobiscum pro evangelio.

4. From the Caeremoniale of Paris de Grassis [1505]. (See Vatican City, Biblioteca Apostolica Vaticana, fondo Vaticani Latini[VatL] 5634/II, ff. 213r and 214r.)

Die Cinerum

Cum autem dicendum est Dominus vobiscum ante primam orationem, papa cum mitra descendit ad faldistorium, ubi deponita mitra genuflectit et sic manet usque ad finem omnium quinque orationum. Idem facit antequam incohatur versus videlicet Adiuva nos, sic manens usque ad finem ipsius versus. Surgit autem descensurus quando cantores inchoant velle dicere videlicet Cito anticipent etc., super quo ipsi cantores advertantur ut sic lente aut expedite ipsum versum cantent, prout viderint quod papa similiter descendat ante versum ipsum videlicet Adiuva etc. quia inhonestus esset ut ipsi silerent si papa nondum venisset, sed inhonestius si pervenirent illud cantantes antequam papa illic esset. Papa quoque revertitur in verbis finalibus ipsius versus idest quando cantatur videlicet Propter nomen tuum. Quem versum cantores ita lente cantant quod papa sit firmatus in solio suo . . . et incepto tractu statim omnes descendunt ad locum evangelii ubi Diaconus petit et obtinet benedictionem a papa priusquam papa descendat ad faldistorium pro versu Adiuva nos, ad quod incipit venire quando cantores dicunt videlicet Citto [sic] anticipent. Et interim Diaconus cum omnibus aliis genuflexis expectat ibi post papam genuflexum. Itaque reverso papa ad solium in finalibus verbis versus predicti, ipse Diaconus commodissime incipit evangelium.

TABLE 6, CONTINUED

5. From the diaries of Paris de Grassis. (See VatL 5635, f. 80v.)

Ash Wednesday, 1505 (February 5).

Et cum cantores dicerent [gap] videlicet cito anticipent nos misericordiae tuae, papa surrexit et interim descendit sicque in tempore dicendi versus Adiuva fuit apud faldistorium et genuflexit. Et in finalibus verbis surrexit papa, itaque adhuc cum cantores finirent versum papa applicuit ad solium.

6. From the diaries of Paris de Grassis. (See VatL 12304, new ff. 140r, 140v.)

Item quam papa omnino debet venire ad faldistorium pro versu Adiuva nos etc., ideo provideatur quod veniat quando cantores cantant cito anticipent, et non tardius et etiam in hoc admoneantur cantores ut si papa lente veniret ipsi etiam lente cantent, alias si cessarent esset non bene factum.

Item similiter papa ex faldistorio revertatur quando ipsi cantores cantant ultimum Propter nomen tuum, quem versum trium verborum lente cantent ut papa sit in sede locatus, ne fiat silentium in capella, quod esse non debet.

---

incipits,[21] and the care given to the presentation of the chant melody, the better to remind listeners of the piece being replaced.

Actual use in the correct liturgy even suggests an explanation of the way some of the motets are transmitted. Of the eight motets transmitted in C.S.35 (four motets) and C.S. 55 (four motets), for instance, six appear to be in close relationship to a copy of a *Missa de Feria* (a Mass without Gloria or Credo). In C.S. 35, two *Domine, non secundum peccata* motets appear literally in the middle of one such Mass; in C.S. 55 the four motets appear as a group, following a *Missa de Feria*, while another motet (in C.S. 63) comes before a *Missa de Feria*. A *Missa de Feria* was the only type of Mass that could be performed on Ash Wednesday. Given the close physical proximity of *Domine, non secundum peccata* settings and *Missae de Feria* in three different manuscripts, the suggestion is strong that the motets and Masses were intended to go together, and that both were sung on Ash Wednesday. In this regard, it should be noted that, in his diary notation for Ash Wednesday 1495, Johannes Burkhard complained that the Tract *and* the Sanctus had been sung "in figuris," a possible direct reference to polyphonic performance.[22]

This reference can be amplified by one from 1578, which both attests to the tradition of singing the tract in polyphony and to the general disapproval of masters of ceremonies of that tradition. In his diary entry for Ash Wednesday 1578, Franciscus Mucantius wrote:

---

[21] Chant incipits usually indicate a liturgical function. Incipits were so clearly associated with *Domine, non secundum peccata* that, when the Vatican scribe Johannes Parvus copied Maître Jan's setting of the text into a Cappella Giulia manuscript (see Table 4b, no. 15) he added the incipit, even though one was not needed.

[22] Cantores non cantarunt antiphonam Exaudi, que etiam in libro pape male est scripta hoc est incompleto. Cantores cantarunt tractum et Sanctus in figuris etc.; et male fuit, quia ab omnibus blasphematus. Celani 1906-, 578.

The pope, after he read [to himself] the Epistle and Gospel and before he descended [from the throne] for the verse "Adiuva nos," incensed the Gospel, because this was more convenient than doing it after he descended (although it had been done in a different way by others), and immediately descended [to the place where he was] to genuflect. The singers sang this verse ["Adiuva nos"] in polyphony, which was seen to be inappropriate; rather they should have sung in ferial plainchant, since it was a ferial Mass and it was during the time of fasting, and further so that [the words] could be better understood.[23]

This late sixteenth-century concern for propriety and for intelligibility may explain why there are no settings of *Domine, non secundum peccata* by major contemporary composers in Rome such as Palestrina or Victoria, but it does seem that in the late fifteenth century and in much of the sixteenth there was a motet tradition in Rome of settings of *Domine, non secundum peccata*, and that the motets were actually performed in the correct liturgical place.

LIST OF WORKS CITED

Antonowycz, Myroslaw. "'Illibata Dei Virgo': A Melodic Self-Portrait of Josquin des Prez." In *Josquin des Prez: Proceedings of the International Josquin Festival-Conference*, ed. Edward E Lowinsky, 545–59. London, 1976.

Blackburn, Bonnie J. "Josquin's Chansons: Ignored and Lost Sources." This JOURNAL 29 (1976): 30–76.

Brown, Howard Mayer. *Music in the Renaissance*. Englewood Cliffs, 1976.

Celani, E., ed. *Joh. Burkardi Liber Notarum*. Rerum Italicarum Scriptores, T. 32, P. I (J. Burkardi Liber Notarum, vol. 1) Città di Castello, 1906-.

Croll, Gerhard. "Das Motettenwerk Gaspars van Weerbecke." Ph. D. diss. University of Göttingen, 1954.

Damman, Rolf. "Spätformen der isorhythmischen Motette im 16. Jahrhundert." *Archiv für Musikwissenschaft* 10 (1953): 16–40.

Dunning, Albert. *Die Staatsmotette 1480–1555*. Utrecht, 1970.

Elders, Willem. "Das Symbol in der Musik von Josquin des Prez." Acta Musicologica 41 (1969): 164–85.

———. "Josquin des Prez en zijn motet *Illibata Dei virgo*." *Mens en melodie* 25 (1970): 141–44.

Finscher, Ludwig. *Loyset Compère*. Musicological Studies and Documents, no. 12. n.p., 1964.

Jeppesen, Knud. "Die 3 Gaffurius-Kodizes der Fabbrica del Duomo, Milano." *Acta Musicologica* 3 (1931): 14–28.

Josephson, Nors S. ed. *Early Sixteenth-Century Sacred Music from the Papal Chapel*. 2 vols. CMM 95. Neuhausen-Stuttgart, 1982.

---

[23] Papa postquam legit epistolam et evangelium antequam descenderet ad versiculum *Adiuva nos* incensum inposuit pro Evangelio quia commodius quam post descensum; (licet alios diverso modo factum fuerit) et statim descendit ad genuflexionem. Cantores recitarunt dictum versiculum cantu figurato, quod minus convenire videtur, sed potius debuit cantare in cantu feriali, cum et missa sit ferialis, et tempore ieiunii, ac etiam ut melius intelligeretur (Rasmussen 1983, 120).

Kellman, Herbert, and Hamm, Charles, eds. *Census-Catalogue of Manuscript Sources of Polyphonic Music 1400–1550.* 5 vols. Neuhausen-Stuttgart, 1979–88.

Miller, Clement A., trans. *Heinrich Glarean: Dodecachordon.* Musicological Studies and Documents, no. 6, 2 vols. n.p., 1965.

Noble, Jeremy. Liner Notes for the recording *Josquin Des Prez, Mass L'Homme armé (sexti toni).* The Bach Guild HM.3 SD, 1972.

⸺⸺⸺. "New Light on Josquin's Benefices." In *Josquin des Prez: Proceedings of the International Josquin Festival-Conference*, ed. Edward E. Lowinsky, 76–102. London, 1976.

Osthoff, Helmut. *Josquin Desprez*, vol. II. Tutzing, 1965.

Rasmussen, Neils Krogh. "Maiestas Pontificia, A Liturgical Reading of Etienne Dupérac's Engraving of the Capella Sixtina from 1578." *Analecta Romana Instituti Danici* 12 (1983): 110–48.

Reese, Gustave and Noble, Jeremy. "Josquin Desprez." In *New Grove High Renaissance Masters*: 1–90. New York, 1984.

Reynolds, Christopher. "The Music Chapel at San Pietro in Vaticano in the Later Fifteenth Century." Ph.D. diss., Princeton University, 1982.

Rifkin, Joshua. "Josquin in Context: Toward a Chronology of the Motets." Unpublished typescript of a paper read at the annual meeting of the American Musicological Society, Minneapolis, 1978.

Roth, Adalbert. "Studien zum frühen Repertoire der päpstlichen Kapelle unter dem Pontifikat Sixtus IV (1471–1484). Die Chorbücher 14 und 51 des Fondo Cappella Sistina der Biblioteca Apostolica Vaticana." Ph.D. diss. Johann Wolfgang Goethe-Universität, 1982.

Schimmelpfennig, Bernhard. *Die Zeremonienbücher der Römischen Kurie im Mittelalter.* Bibliothek des Deutschen Historischen Instituts in Rom 40. Tübingen, 1973.

Sherr, Richard. "The Papal Chapel ca. 1492–1513 and its Polyphonic Sources." Ph.D. diss. Princeton University, 1975.

⸺⸺⸺. "Settings of the Tract *Domine, non secundum peccata*: Some Evidence of a Roman Motet Tradition." Unpublished paper presented at the spring meeting of the New England Chapter of the American Musicological Society. Cambridge, MA, 1980.

⸺⸺⸺. "The Papal Singers and their Library." Unpublished Paper presented at the annual conference on medieval studies, Kalamazoo, 1981.

Smijers, Albert. "Een kleine bijdrage over Josquin en Isaac." In *Gedenkboek an Dr. D. F. Scheurleer*: 313–19. The Hague, 1925.

Sparks, Edgar H. *Cantus Firmus in Mass and Motet 1420–1520.* Berkeley, 1963.

Stephan, Wolfgang. *Die Burgundisch-Niederländische Motette zur Zeit Ockeghems.* Kassel, 1937. Reprint. 1973.

Taruskin, Richard. "Antoine Busnoys and the *L'Homme armé* Tradition." This JOURNAL 39 (1986): 255–93.

Titcomb, Caldwell. "The Josquin Acrostic Re-examined." This JOURNAL 16 (1963): 47–60.

Ward, Lynn Halpern. "The Motetti Missales Repertory Reconsidered." This JOURNAL 39 (1986): 491–523.

Wiora, Walter. "The Structure of Wide-spanned Melodic Lines in Early and Later Works of Josquin." In *Josquin des Prez: Proceedings of the International Josquin Festival-Conference*, ed. Edward E. Lowinsky, 309–16. London, 1976.

IX

The Medici coat of arms in a motet for Leo X

1 Medici coat of arms: illustration from the Medici Codex (1518). (Laur. Ms. Acq e doni, f.2v; University of Chicago Press)

Following the election of Giovanni de' Medici as Pope Leo X on 11 March 1513, singers, instrumentalists and composers from all over Western Europe flocked to Rome in great numbers, apprised of new opportunities for employment.[1] Among the many specifically recruited to enhance the Pope's public and private establishment of musicians was the composer Andreas de Silva,[2] who remains a somewhat shadowy figure in spite of the esteem in which he was held at the time; very little is known about him except that in 1519 he was the first to hold the position of personal composer to the Pope. That his relationship to Leo must predate the document in which this is recorded[3] is demonstrated by his setting of the text *Gaude felix Florentia*, which clearly celebrates Leo's election, calling on his native city of Florence to rejoice, and wishing him a long and happy reign.[4] Works of this type, which set texts written for specific state occasions or to honour specific people, form a particular genre that may be named the 'state motet'.[5] I would like now to consider whether this motet might go further than its text in rendering homage to the most musical of popes.

Gaude felix Florentia is in three sections.[6] The first and last are scored for six voices and employ a cantus firmus; the second part is freely composed for four voices. In the opening section the cantus firmus (ex.1a) is repeated three times to the words 'Gaude felix Florentia', while in the third section it appears to consist of five different melodies (ex.1b–f), each with the words 'Salve pater sanctissime'; on examination, all these prove to be related in some way to ex.1a. (These relationships are indicated by arrows in ex.1a–f.)[7]

The cantus firmus is a curiosity: it cannot be identified with any pre-existing sacred or secular melody, and the way in which ex.1b–f are derived from ex.1a may be unique for the period. The most obvious explanation is that de Silva wrote the cantus firmus himself.[8] But why he should have done this, especially considering the established tradition of 'state motets' wherein the cantus firmus was not only drawn from a pre-existent melody, but from one with some relevance to the occasion at hand, is not clear.[9] I suggest that he

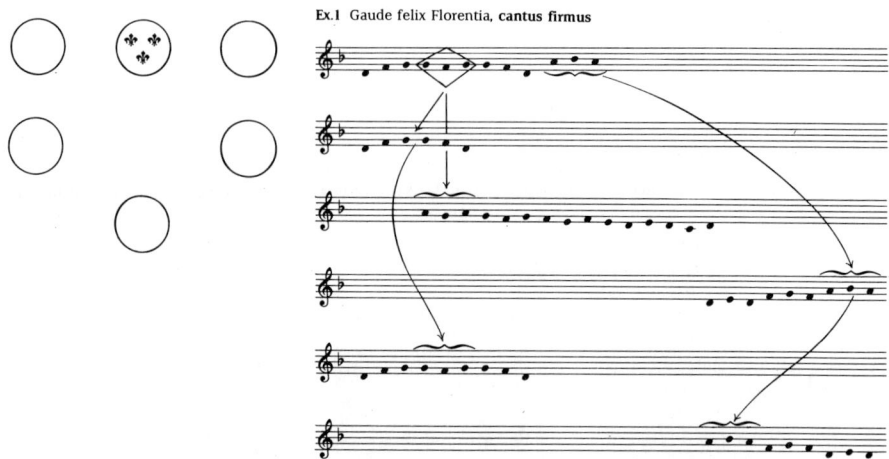

Ex.1 Gaude felix Florentia, cantus firmus

wrote a unique cantus firmus in order to give a special significance to his motet, to make it at its most fundamental level of construction a reference to Leo and to his house.

Ex.2 presents the cantus firmus of the first section in the original rhythmic notation. The symmetrical pattern of the first nine notes, emphasized by the three breves G F G, is striking in this form; indeed, those breves, in the midst of longs, are its most outstanding visual feature.[10] Given that the composer had chosen not only the pitch but also the rhythm of these notes, it follows that he created this visual image on purpose. He did so, I believe, because he knew that the configuration would suggest a symbol with undeniable relevance to the dedicatee. The Medici coat of arms or *stemma* (illus.1) is constructed of six balls or pills (*palle*) arranged in the configuration 3–2–1 (sometimes the middle ball of the top row is placed higher than the other two, giving the *stemma* an oval shape, but it was just as usual to present it with the top three *palle* in a single row, as in illus.2). The *palle* are red, with the exception of the middle one in the top row, which is blue and contains three gold *fleurs de lys* (a privilege granted to the Medici by King Louis XI of France in 1465).

Ex.2 Gaude felix Florentia, **cantus firmus**

If the first nine notes of de Silva's cantus firmus are considered in the light of the Medici *stemma*, they can be seen to form a perfect representation in musical notation of the *stemma* itself: the three breves standing for the three *fleurs de lys*, the F and G to each side for the other *palle*, while the repeated D represents the circular nature of the *stemma*, for returning to a note is the only way to suggest a circle in musical notation (see ex.3a). If this interpretation is correct, de Silva paid direct homage in his motet to Leo X and his family. In doing so, he may have had a historical model, for as Allan Atlas has shown, an instrumental work with cantus firmus by Heinrich Isaac, *Palle, palle*, also contains a striking reference to the *fleurs de lys* and the other Medici *palle*, although there the relationship to the *stemma* is rather less clear.[11]

Ex.3a **The Medici** stemma **in the cantus firmus**

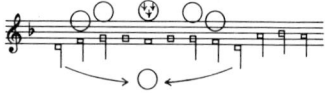

But what about the three extra notes at the end of the cantus firmus? If the cantus firmus is reduced simply to a succession of pitches (as in ex.3b), the three extra notes bring the number of pitches to ten; of course, Leo was Leo X. The application of simple

Ex.3b **Pitches of cantus firmus**

Ex.3c The cantus firmus, with rests

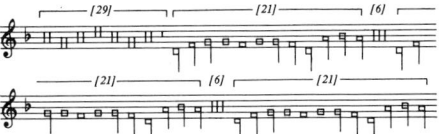

arithmetic can be taken even further. The three statements of the cantus firmus in the first part of the motet are separated by six breves' rest (ex.3c); there were six *palle* in the Medici *stemma*. Each statement of the cantus firmus contains 21 breves (ex.3c), and with two semibreves to each breve, the number of semibreves in each cantus firmus statement is 42; in the well-known system whereby each letter of the Latin alphabet is given a number, and the letters of a word then added together, 42 is the numerical representation of 'Medici'. Subtracting from the 21 breves of the cantus firmus the ten pitches leaves eleven. Eleven, as it happens, was the most important number in Leo's life. He had been born on the 11th (11 December 1475), he had been captured in the battle of Ravenna on the 11th (11 April 1512), he had been liberated from that captivity on the 11th (11 June 1512), and he had been elected Pope on the 11th (11 March 1513). He took the name of St Leo, whose feast day was the 11th April, and delayed his ceremonial possession of the Lateran to 11 April 1513. On his procession route, he was even greeted with a triumphal arch containing illustrations of his famous 'elevens' (along with a few false ones).[12] There can be no doubt that at the time the relationship of the Pope to the number eleven was widely understood. Can it then be a coincidence that this motet can also be seen to contain that number? Two of its fundamental elements—its length (determined in part by the number of breves in the cantus firmus), and its harmonic structure (determined by the notes of the cantus firmus)—are musical embodiments of its dedicatee.

Is all this crazy? Of course. Is it on that account also impossible? Not entirely. The Renaissance love for all kinds of arcane symbolism (especially numerical symbolism) is too well known for us to dismiss this out of hand, particularly when dealing with a special piece, written for a special person and a special occasion; especially when that person was an extremely knowledgeable musician.[13] A state motet was exactly the type of piece in which to employ such symbolism in the assurance that its dedicatee would enjoy the artifice.[14]

There remains the question of the occasion for which the motet was written. Kirsch, Lowinsky and Dunning agree that the text makes reference to Leo's election. Yet they all argue (because of the opening words 'Gaude felix Florentia') that there must also have been a connection with Florence, and try to identify occasions in Florence when the motet might have been performed. But it was not unknown in Rome that Leo was a Florentine; the city had a large Florentine population, and the Medici cry of 'palle, palle' was heard in the streets of Rome during Leo's procession to the Lateran. It is perfectly possible that this motet was written for the Roman celebrations at the beginning of Leo's pontificate. In that regard, some corroborative evidence from Leo's coronation ceremony may be considered.

Leo was crowned as soon as possible after his election on 11 March. Because he had to be consecrated a bishop (and a priest), the coronation was put off until 19 March, the feast of St Joseph; as the papal diarist Paris de Grassis reported, that day (Saturday) was chosen in preference to the Sunday, because Palm Sunday was too important a liturgical occasion to be obstructed by a ceremony of coronation. St Joseph was not an important feast, and had no special elaborate liturgy; the Introit for the Mass was that for the Common of Confessors not a Pope, 'Justus ut palma'. A comparison of its second phrase (ex.3d) with the cantus firmus of de Silva's motet shows that it is constructed largely of the same notes in the same order. This could, of course, be a coincidence, but the possibility of a significant connection cannot be ignored. If *Gaude felix Florentia* had been intended for Leo's coronation, de Silva might have turned to chants appropriate to the feast of St Joseph when searching for a cantus firmus, and the Introit might have then suggested to him a representation of the Medici *stemma*. The motet, then, could have been written for a Roman occasion, either to have been sung during the Mass itself, or (and I think this is more likely) to have been performed during or after the banquet that would have followed the ceremony (there was a long-established tradition of similar performances).[15] In that case, the 'familia' to which the third section of text

Ex.3d Introit, Justus ut palma, second phrase

IX

2 Adrian Willaert: Virgo gloriosa Christi, motet from the Medici Codex showing the Medici coat of arms (Laur. Ms. Acq e doni, f.3r; University of Chicago Press)

refers can be taken in its customary Renaissance sense, as 'household':[16] the Pope's household and musicians have gathered to perform in his honour a motet based on his personal coat of arms, in which he and his family are represented through the application of numerical symbolism to the musical fabric. It was a musical honour that Leo might even have suggested; he would certainly have understood and appreciated it.

Richard Sherr received his Ph.D. from Princeton University and is currently Professor and Chair of the Department of Music at Smith College. He is working on a major study of music and musicians in Rome in the early 16th century.

This article is a revised version of a paper read at the symposium 'Culture and Spectacle in Rome: 1400–1700: a symposium with Nino Pirrotta', held at Smith, Mt Holyoke and Amherst Colleges in April 1986. I would like to thank Nino Pirrotta for the helpful comments and suggestions he made on that occasion.

[1] See A. Pirro, 'Leo X and Music', *MQ*, xxi (1935), pp.1–16, and H. W. Frey, 'Regesten zur päpstlichen Kapelle unter Leo X und zu seiner Privatkapelle', *Die Musikforschung*, viii (1955), pp.58–73, 178–99, 412–37; ix (1956), pp.46–57, 139–56, 411–19.

[2] See W. Kirsch, *Die Motetten des Andreas de Silva* (Tutzing, 1977), for a general biography.

[3] This *motu proprio* (*I-Ras* Camerale I 859 bis, f.37r) addresses de Silva as 'cappelle nostre cantori et compositori nostro nuper in eadem capella nostra per nos admisso et recepto'.

[4] The original text is preserved in the Vallicelliana partbooks, while a Vatican source contains the motet as a religious contrafactum. See E. Lowinsky, 'A Newly Discovered Sixteenth-Century Motet Manuscript at the Biblioteca Vallicelliana in Rome', *JAMS*, iii (1950), pp.173–232. For transcriptions and discussion of the texts, see Lowinsky, *op cit*, and Kirsch, *op cit*, pp.168–74.

[5] A. Dunning, *Die Staatsmotette 1480–1555* (Utrecht, 1970); this motet is discussed on pp.32–35.

[6] Transcription in *Andreas de Silva: Opera omnia*, ii, ed. W. Kirsch, Corpus Mensurabilis Musicae, xlix (American Institute of Musicology, 1971)

[7] Also noted in Kirsch, *op cit*, p.352

[8] See Kirsch, *op cit*, pp.352–53

[9] For instance, Isaac's motet in honour of Leo, *Optime pastor*, is based on two plainchant cantus firmus melodies, 'Da pacem domine' and 'Sacerdos et pontifex', both singularly appropriate to its papal dedicatee and to the warlike times. See Dunning, *op cit*, pp.47–53.

[10] That de Silva thought of this sequence of notes as a separable entity is demonstrated by his use of them in the cantus firmus in the third section of the motet.

[11] A. Atlas, 'Heinrich Isaac's *Palle, Palle, Palle*: A New Interpretation', *Analecta Musicologica*, xiv (1974), pp.17–25. It was Atlas's discussion that first drew my attention to the possible symbolism of de Silva's cantus firmus.

[12] See J. Cox-Rearick, *Dynasty and Destiny in Medici Art: Pontormo, Leo X and the Two Cosimos* (Princeton, 1984), pp.51–52.

[13] On symbolism and 'double meaning', see the classic studies of E. Lowinsky, *Secret Chromatic Art in the Netherlands Motet* (New York, 1946), and W. Elders, *Studien zur Symbolik in der Musik der altern Niederländer* (Bilthoven, 1968). The study of symbolism can be, and has been, carried to extremes which stretch credibility, but I do not believe that to be the case here.

[14] It is a relatively simple matter to visualize the cantus firmus while hearing it, as can be done also with certain examples of late 16th-century 'Augenmusik'. Simple counting leads to the rest of the symbolic meaning.

[15] See A. Tomasello, 'Ritual, Tradition, and Polyphony at the Court of Rome', in preparation in *The Journal of Musicology*.

[16] In Kirsch's transcription the last line reads 'Exultent vocem praesens familia dicens: Vivat Leo decimus, vivat, regnet feliciter multis annis'. He translates 'familia' as 'Familie (Gemeinde)' (*op cit*, pp.168–69).

X

Ceremonies for Holy Week, Papal Commissions, and Madness (?) in Early Sixteenth-Century Rome

Early on 11 March 1513 (the day of his lucky number), Giovanni de' Medici, Cardinal Deacon of Santa Maria in Domnica and the person responsible for announcing the vote talleys at the conclave held on the death of Julius II, announced his own election as pope to the assembled cardinals. He took the name Leo, the saint whose feast day of April 11 also recalled his lucky number. And even if it turns out not to be true that he said "Let us enjoy the papacy, since God has given it to us,"[1] we certainly have in Leo X perhaps the most artistically sensitive of all the popes. That this sensitivity involved painting, sculpture, architecture, and literature was not so surprising in a pontiff, but truly unique was Leo's passion for music; as is well known, his patronage of that art far outstripped that of his predecessors and was rarely equalled by his successors.[2]

Also important to Leo, as his master of ceremonies Paris de Grassis tells us, was the demonstration of the papal majesty, its primary locus the Sistine Chapel with its newly-painted ceiling, its tapestries (soon to include new ones on designs by Raphael), and the glittering assembly of the entire papal court during the celebration of the mass.[3] It was here, of course, that music played its most conspicuous role, the papal choir singing the various musical items of the mass in chant and polyphony. And, indeed, it was for the celebration of the mass that the great monuments of late fifteenth-century sacred music had been written. We know further from the testimony of Paolo Cortesi that Cardinal Giovanni de' Medici had preferred the music of the mass above all others.[4]

As pope, Leo moved quickly to augment the musical element of the papal majesty. During his reign, the papal choir expanded to its greatest number ever, eventually reaching about thirty-one members; he

---

This article was originally read as a paper at the colloquium "Pageantry and Ceremony in the Middle Ages and the Renaissance," Princeton University, 1 May 1992.

[1] "Godiamoci il papato poichè Dio ce l'ha dato." Quoted in John Addington Symonds, *Renaissance in Italy*, 2 vols. (New York: Modern Library, n.d.), 1:219, who gives as his source a report by Marino Giorgi, the Venetian ambassador, dated 17 March 1517.

[2] See André Pirro, "Leo X and Music," *Musical Quarterly* 21 (1935): 1-16. Indeed, his musical reputation persisted long after his death. Whereas Raphael had depicted him admiring the miniatures in a Bible (open, not by coincidence, to the beginning of the Gospel according to John, with its double reference to his own given name and the patron saint of Florence, John the Baptist), a late sixteenth-century copy of the portrait by Leonardo Buti, now in the Uffizi Gallery, shows the pope with an open book of (unfortunately undecipherable) music before him.

[3] On the term "papal majesty," see John Shearman, *Raphael's Cartoons in the Collection of Her Majesty the Queen and the Tapestries for the Sistine Chapel* (London: Phaidon, 1972), 1-20.

[4] See Nino Pirrotta, "Music and Cultural Tendencies in 15th-Century Italy," *Journal of the American Musicological Society* 19 (1966): 127-61, esp. 154.

supplemented this with a corps of private singers and instrumentalists whose numbers were approaching twenty by the end of his reign.[5] And he took a further decisive and unprecedented step when he decided that the *maestro* of the papal chapel, the official with executive authority over all the chapel personnel (not merely the singers in the choir), who by long tradition had been a prelate, was to be a singer/composer.[6]

When he decided to appoint a musician to his post, however, Leo did not act as we might have expected, given his musical proclivities. Ercole d'Este of Ferrara (another melomane) had recruited and appointed (in order) Johannes Martini, Josquin des Prez, and Jacob Obrecht to head his singers.[7] But when the pope, the ruler of a much more prestigious and powerful court, wished to appoint a composer to lead his chapel, he turned instead to a relative unknown, Elzéar Genet, known as Carpentras. Genet was probably born around 1470 in the city of Carpentras in the south of France, near the papal see of Avignon. Perhaps at the urging of Pope Julius II (who had resided in Avignon as archbishop for a number of years), the composer went to Rome and joined the papal choir sometime between September 1507 and June 1508. He stayed in Rome until May 1512, when he announced his intention of leaving the city, and we know from his own account that he joined the chapel of Louis XII of France, from there to be recalled by Leo to Rome, specifically to be appointed papal protonotary and *maestro* of the papal chapel on 5 November 1513.[8]

On the surface, Carpentras seems an odd choice for a patron who presumably could have had his pick of the best composers of the day. However, it should be pointed out that the established composers with whom Leo would have been acquainted at the time that he was making his decision were either dead, too old, or ensconced in far-away places (Josquin was 73 and provost in Condé, Isaac was four years away from death, Obrecht was dead, Brumel may have been dead, Mouton was firmly established at the French court, Févin was dead, Gaspar van Weerbecke was probably still alive and in the papal chapel but also was old and basically forgotten), while the major composers of the younger generation (Willaert, Festa, Jacquet of Mantua) were just beginning their careers. Furthermore, the *maestro* of the papal chapel had to be more than a major composer; he had to be an administrator, a recruiter, and also a teacher.[9] This required a certain kind of personality, and if Leo had examined the careers in Ferrara of the famous composers Josquin and Obrecht, he might have become a bit leery of entrusting his chapel to such people.[10] With his choice thus restricted, perhaps it is not strange that Leo turned to someone he had known as a singer in the papal choir and perhaps as a member of his private circle.[11]

---

[5] See Hermann-Walther Frey, "Regesten zur päpstlichen Kapelle unter Leo X un zu seiner Privatkapelle," *Die Musikforschung* 8 (1955): 58-73, 178-99, 412-37; 9 (1956): 46-57, 139-56, 411-19.

[6] This idea did not occur to him immmediately. In fact, he first made a more conventional appointment, giving the position of *maestro* to Gabriele Anconitano, Archbishop of Durazzo, who had been the sacristan of the chapel. The bull of appointment is dated 6 April 1513—Vatican City, Archivio Segreto Vaticano, Registra Supplicationum 1406, f. 105v.

[7] See Lewis Lockwood, *Music in Renaissance Ferrara, 1400-1405* (Cambridge: Harvard University Press, 1984).

[8] Richard Sherr, "The Membership of the Chapels of Louis XII and Anne de Bretagne in the Years Preceding Their Deaths," *Journal of Musicology* 6 (1988): 67. The most complete biography of Carpentras is still Lee Rigsby, "The Sacred Music of Elzéar Genet" (Ph.D. diss., University of Michigan, 1955).

[9] Carpentras in fact arrived in Rome with three choirboys who lived in his house. And he was almost immediately engaged in recruiting singers from the chapel of Francesco Gonzaga; see William Prizer, "La cappella di Francesco II Gonzaga e la musica sacra a Mantova nel primo ventennio del Cinquecento," in *Mantova e i Gonzaga nella civiltà del Rinascimento* (Mantua: Città di Mantova and Arnoldo Mondadori Editore, 1977), 267-76.

[10] As is well known, Josquin stayed in Ferrara only one year, while Obrecht was summarily dismissed in 1505 for reasons that are not entirely clear but may have been political; see Lockwood, 196-212.

[11] Indeed, Carpentras's settings of Petrarch texts represent what James Haar and Iain Fenlon have described as "a fairly localised and short-lived taste associated with Leo X's circle." See Fenlon and Haar, *The Italian Madrigal in the Early Sixteenth Century* (Cambridge:

Early Sixteenth-Century Rome 393

Still, it is not clear why Carpentras would have come readily to mind. The papal chapel sang sacred music, so it would seem logical that an experienced composer of sacred music would have been chosen to lead it. But there are only two extant sacred works by Carpentras that can be dated before 1513, and they, settings of the Marian antiphons *Salve Regina* and *Regina cœli*, would not have made one optimistic about the future. However, at least the *Salve Regina* does perhaps tell us something about Carpentras's character: that he was a self-critical reviser of his own works.

As I have pointed out elsewhere, the copy of the *Salve Regina* that appears in the manuscript VatS 42, ff. 154v-157r, contains many changes in hands different from that of the main scribe.[12] These changes are compositional corrections; that is, they alter in significant ways the contrapuntal structure of the piece, and they extend even to the addition of accidentals and changes in the placement of text to help text setting.[13] I suggested that the only person who would have taken the trouble to produce such emendations (even if he was not the one who wrote them into the manuscript) would have been their composer. Interestingly, VatS 42, f. 154v, actually has the date 1507 added after the composer designation. It is tempting to view this as the date of the copy of the date of the revisions, but a study of the manuscript shows that the *Salve Regina* was most likely copied in its original form sometime toward the end of the reign of Julius II, certainly before the end of 1512, possibly between 1510 and 1512.[14] However, if 1507 cannot be the date of this copy, it is a possible date for the first entry of Carpentras into the papal chapel and may therefore be the actual date of the composition of the piece. The revision may have taken place when Carpentras returned to the chapel after his sojourn in France (perhaps the date was recorded there by the composer so that the singers would know that it was an early work when they looked at all of the emendations).[15]

Indeed, the alterations suggest that the Carpentras who composed this *Salve Regina* was not totally at home in the world of four-part sacred polyphony. Two passages in their original and altered form are shown in exx. 24.1 and 24.2. Two observations suggest themselves immediately: that the heaviest changes are to the melodic shape of the altus (presumably the last voice composed in "layered" composition) and that the tenor (defined as the foundation of a composition by Tinctoris) basically is not touched, suggesting indeed that Carpentras agreed that it was the most important voice regardless of whether it was the first to be composed.

It can be further suggested that the compositional process used in producing the first passage was a three-part texture to which the altus was added (see ex. 24.1). The chant is quoted in the superius, suggesting that this was the first voice to be written, while the relationship of this voice to the tenor and bass suggests that those two voices were conceived together as accompaniments to the superius.[16] These three voices are in fact almost self-sufficient, although the idea that there would be a fourth voice probably was present

---

Cambridge University Press, 1988), 22. But considering that Carpentras's music was first published in the very year that Leo became pope and the very year the composer returned to Rome (in Antico's *Canzoni sonetti et strambotti, libro tertio*, RISM 1513[1]), it is very likely that he wrote the pieces as a member of Cardinal Giovanni de' Medici's circle before 1512.

[12] Transcribed in Albert Seay, ed., Elziarii Geneti (Carpentras): *Opera omnia*, 7 vols., Corpus mensurabilis musicæ, 58 (American Institute of Musicology, 1972), 5:100-10.

[13] Sherr, "Notes on Two Roman Manuscripts of the Early Sixteenth Century," *Musical Quarterly* 63 (1977): 48-73.

[14] See Sherr, *Papal Music Manuscripts in the Late Fifteenth and Early Sixteenth Centuries*, Renaissance Manuscript Studies, 5 (Neuhausen: American Institute of Musicology/Hänssler-Verlag, forthcoming); and Sherr, "Notes."

[15] This conclusion is shared by Jeffrey Dean, who considers the revisions to be in hand of Claudius Gellandi (scribe of the papal chapel in the reign of Leo X), possibly assisted by Carpentras. See Dean, "The Scribes of the Sistine Chapel, 1501-1527" (Ph.D. diss., University of Chicago, 1984), 187-94.

[16] For instance, the cadence on A on "nostra" is made between the superius and bass, while the following cadence on D in meas. 2 is made between the superius and tenor, while the tenor is written so as to negate the implied parallel fifths A-e, Bb-f with the bass and the fifths f-c', g-d' with the superius that would have occurred when "fixing" the fifths with the bass by substituting parallel sixths.

Ex. 24.1. Carpentras, *Salve Regina*, original and altered versions, meas. 22-27.

Ex. 24.2. Carpentras, *Salve Regina*, original and altered versions, meas. 34-39.

in the composer's mind, since the superius, tenor, and bass often do not form full triads, the missing note being added by the altus. Yet problems occur when the altus is added to the texture: it adds a 3-2 suspension with the superius to the already awkward 5-4 suspension of the superius with the tenor and bass in meas. 3 and later has an awkward line leaping from c' to b' (flat) in meas. 26.[17] None of this is particularly troubling, but Carpentras was clearly dissatisfied with the altus line.

The revision adds much of interest. The altus repeats a newly-composed figure in meas. 22-23 and 24-25, which implies in both cases a cadence on D that is never supported by the other voices. Meanwhile, the repeat in the altus phrase is "uncoordinated" *à la* Josquin, with a pseudo-repeat of material in the tenor, which, by the addition of a sharp to the c' in meas. 24, which necessitated a change in the bass note, creates another false cadence on D. Meanwhile the superius was rewritten to reinforce the cadence on A in meas. 5 with a 7-6 suspension over the bass, which then finally moves to the true cadence with the tenor on D in meas. 6 (typically made a deceptive cadence by the $B\flat$ in the bass). And, finally, the text setting in the superius is changed to one that almost any modern editor would have chosen as "right" for this passage.

In ex. 24.2, the changes come exclusively in the altus. The first version has the "busy" feel that this voice often has, but as a result, it contains instances of writing that come close to being contrapuntal errors, even in pre-Palestrinian polyphony: the barely-disguised parallel fifths between altus and bass in meas. 35 and the 7-8 suspension with the superius in meas. 39. Carpentras's solution here was to simplify the altus drastically, strengthening the cadence on D in meas. 37 and introducing a bit of four-voice imitation on the word "exules," thereby truly integrating that voice into the four-part texture. Indeed, integration of the altus into the texture is one of the achievements of the revision in ex. 24.1. In fact, these changes are so clearly improvements that they seem to justify Leo's opinion, stated in a letter of 1518 concerning one of the many benefices with which the pope rewarded his *maestro*, that the composer had made "great progress" in the art of composition before becoming the *maestro* of the papal chapel.[18]

The difficulties with four-part polyphony also bring to mind Carpentras's own admission that early in his career he was not principally a composer of sacred music. According to the dedication to Cardinal Ippolito de' Medici in his volume of hymns and Magnificats, Carpentras had spent his time composing secular music (much of which could have been in three parts and almost all of which is lost), and it was Leo himself who turned him to the composition of sacred music:

> There was a time, most Illustrious Lord, when, in youthful years and being a slave to the customs of the court, and—as one says—the world, I thought no occupation more beautiful than that of placing popular rhythms and amorous poems in music. . . . But after Louis XII . . . had sent me to Leo X . . ., who called me to him by letter during the first days of his pontificate and . . . made me the master of his chapel, which this good pope maintained so flourishingly, I perceived that he was so pleased and charmed with no type of song . . . as much as with the types . . . used for sacred things. . . . Then I began to give a different direction to my thoughts.[19]

This is actually a startling bit of evidence (if true—one always has to be careful about autobiographical statements), for it shows the direct influence of a patron, not merely by commissioning a single work but actually changing the direction of a composer's entire output. And in this admission we may find the real

---

[17] The revision of this measure suggests that Carpentras wanted the note to be $b\natural$.

[18] Quoted in M.-L. Pereyra, "Elzéar Genet di il Carpentrasso per le chanoine Requin," *Revue de Musicologie* 3 (1918): 139-44.

[19] Translated by Albert Seay in *Opera omnia*, vol. 5, part 1, p. xiii (with emendations to Seay's translation made here and elsewhere).

reason why Leo X chose Carpentras: the composer might have been selected precisely because Leo perceived in him a malleable and hardworking individual who, because he had little reputation as a composer of sacred music, would act diligently on papal advice, which someone like Josquin would almost certainly not have done.

Carpentras's *œuvre* as a whole shows further that Leo did not merely wish to turn Carpentras to the composition of sacred music; he also had a particular type of sacred music in mind. What the pope inspired (or ordered) his *maestro di cappella* to write were not the great mass settings that Leo himself preferred, or elaborate motets, but music of a much "humbler" yet more useful, and for that reason perhaps even more valued, kind: polyphonic settings of liturgical texts appropriate, not for the great celebration of the papal majesty (the mass), but for the Office, the liturgical services that constituted the day-to-day devotions of members of cathedral chapters, monastic communities, and the clerical residents of the Vatican Palace — liturgies that (while provided with an old corpus of polyphony) had been generally neglected by the composers of the late-fifteenth century.[20] It further appears that the pope wanted a coherent body of music for these services, that he told Carpentras to compose not merely one or two settings but large cycles of related compositions, for the bulk of Carpentras's work consists (besides a few motet-like settings of entire psalms — also connected to the Offices, of course) of cycles of hymns and Magnificats to be sung at the daily office of Vespers, as well as complete polyphonic settings of the Lamentations of Jeremiah. Carpentras was, in fact, the first composer in a long time to have produced cycles like these.[21] This made him something of an expert in setting reciting tones, the basis of Magnificats and the Lamentations; that is, he spent most of his compositional career constructing works based on the most formulaic and uninteresting of musical materials.

The first commission was apparently for the Lamentations of Jeremiah, which formed part of the ceremonies of Holy Week in the three days before Easter Sunday known as the *triduum sacrum* (Maundy Thursday, Good Friday, and Holy Saturday). This is actually an odd commission. If any period of the church year was endowed with a distinct affect, it was the *triduum sacrum*. That affect was sorrow, because of the commemoration of the Crucifixion. Ceremonies were long and taxing, and they were also austere. This was not a period of the year that was an auspicious occasion for elaborate ornament, particularly of the musical kind; indeed, one would have thought that polyphony was completely out of place. In fact, Paris de Grassis states unequivocally that polyphony was to be banned from Palm Sunday to Easter Sunday. Nonetheless, it was allowed, according to him, on Maundy Thursday, the first day of the *triduum sacrum*.[22]

The liturgical ceremonies of Maundy Thursday began with what was known as the Tenebræ service (actually celebrated towards morning on the previous Wednesday and combining the Offices of Matins and Lauds). The service was extremely long and also very dramatic. The basic structure of Matins and Lauds for the *triduum sacrum* was as follows: for Matins, three Nocturns, each containing three psalms with their antiphons, three lessons each followed by a Great Responsory, and various other readings; for Lauds, five psalms with antiphons and the Canticle of Zachary, *Benedictus Dominus Deus*, and Psalm 50, *Miserere mei Deus*, at the end. In Rome, the Sistine Chapel was lit by six large candles placed on the rood screen along with six candles on the altar and a special triangular candelabrum containing fifteen candles placed to the side of the altar. After each of the fourteen psalms that constituted part of the services (nine

---

[20] There was another composer "on staff": Andreas de Silva, who produced masses and motets. De Silva may have been in Leo's employ much earlier than the first documentary reference to him as papal composer in 1519. See Sherr, "The Medici Stemma in a Motet for Leo X," *Early Music* 15 (1987): 31-35.

[21] This is very unlike the output of someone like Josquin, who wrote mainly masses and motets with only a few hymn settings and possibly no Magnificat settings to his credit.

[22] See Richard Sherr, "The Singers of the Papal Chapel and Liturgical Ceremonies in the Early Sixteenth Century: Some Documentary Evidence," in *Rome in the Renaissance, the City and the Myth*, ed. P. A. Ramsey (Binghamton, N.Y.: Center for Medieval and Early Renaissance Studies, 1982), 249-64.

psalms in Matins and five in Lauds), one of the candles in the candelabrum was extinguished, so that at the point of reciting the Canticle of Zachary, the *Benedictus*, only one candle in the candelabrum was burning. After each verse of the *Benedictus*, one of the candles on the altar and one of the torches on the rood screen was extinguished, so that by the end of the canticle the chapel was lit only by the one candle in the candelabrum. Still lit, this was then placed under the altar so the chapel was in semi- or complete darkness. At this dramatic point, out of the darkness, the singers were supposed to recite ("alte legendo sine nota" or "reading aloud without music," according to all of the papal ceremonials of the period) Psalm 50, *Miserere mei Deus*. Then the one candle was brought out, and everyone scraped his feet on the floor, making a noise symbolic of the commotion that occurred when Christ was arrested, and made a silent exit.[23]

This service drew Leo's attention early on. By 1514 at the latest, we have evidence of a new method of singing the *Miserere* at the end of the Tenebræ by alternating chant and polyphony.[24] This clearly contradicted ceremonial practice, and Paris de Grassis was none too pleased when he remarked in 1518 that the polyphony consisted of *falsobordone*, but that the pope wanted it.[25] Of course *falsobordone*, which consisted basically of harmonizing a reciting tone in triads, could be easily memorized, as would have been necessary for the rendition of the *Miserere* that was taking place in darkness. It was thus Leo X who established the tradition of the *falsobordone* renditions of the *Miserere* that in the eighteenth and nineteenth centuries were one of the great tourist attractions of papal Rome.[26]

Falsobordone was at heart an improvisatory practice. The subject of Leo's compositional commission to Carpentras was performed earlier in the Tenebræ. The first three readings of Matins of all three days of the *triduum sacrum* were drawn from the Lamentations of Jeremiah (or Threni), for just as the Prophet lamented the destruction of Jerusalem, so did Christians lament the coming Crucifixion. There was, however, no uniformity in the choice of verses to be read; it varied widely from place to place until the Council of Trent imposed order upon it. Similarly, there was no universal melody or recitation tone attached to the readings: the Council of Trent fixed that as well by mandating the use of the "Roman" reciting tone. At the end of the fifteenth century, composers begin to produce polyphonic settings of verses from the Lamentations (with very little agreement among them); in 1506, Petrucci published two books of polyphonic Lamentations. There might also have been a Vatican tradition of singing at least the Lamentations of Maundy Thursday in some sort of polyphony, a tradition that may have begun during the reign of the Spanish Pope Alexander VI (1492-1503).[27]

It is possible that Leo wished to build on this tradition, and also to impose some order of his own, by having his *maestro di cappella* create polyphonic settings of all the Lamentations of the *triduum sacrum* (thereby breaking the ban on polyphony for days other than Maundy Thursday), because in fact Carpentras composed polyphonic settings not only for Maundy Thursday but also for Good Friday and Holy Saturday. If these settings were then the only ones to be used by the papal singers, the choice of verses would also always be the same, thereby bringing order to what was a somewhat chaotic situation.[28]

---

[23] See Marc Dykmans, *L'Œuvre de Patrizi Piccolomini ou le cérémonial papal de la première Renaissance*, 2 vols., Studi e Testi, 294 (Vatican City: Biblioteca Apostolica Vaticana, 1982), 2:365-67.

[24] Sherr, "Singers of the Papal Chapel," 25.

[25] "In fine officii mihi non placavit quod cantores cantassent psalmum Miserere per falsum bordonum licet devote et papa sic voluit." Diary entry of 31 March 1518 – Vatican City, Biblioteca Apostolica Vaticana, Ms. Vaticani Latini 5636 (henceforth, VatL 5636), f. 232v.

[26] See Richard Boursy, "The Mystique of the Sistine Chapel Choir in the Romantic Era," *Journal of Musicology* 11 (1993): 277-329.

[27] See Sherr, "The 'Spanish Nation' in the Papal Chapel, 1492-1521," *Early Music* (1992): 601-09.

[28] According to Baini (Palestrina's nineteenth-century biographer and *maestro* of the papal chapel), the papal singers sang Carpentras's Lamentations continually until 1587, when they were replaced by the Lamentations of Palestrina, but I have been unable to find any corroboration of this claim; indeed, the many settings of Lamentations that exist in the Cappella Sistina collection argue against it. See Giuseppe Baini, *Memorie storico-critiche della vita e delle opere di Giovanni Pierluigi da Palestrina*, 2 vols. (Rome, 1828), 2:190ff.

We may also have a description of the sound of Carpentras's music. In his diary entry describing the Tenebræ for Maundy Thursday in 1518, Paris de Grassis says that the choir broke up into national groups for the Lamentations, the Spaniards singing the first reading of the Lamentations "lamentabiliter," while the French sang the second reading "docte," and the Italians sang the third reading "dulciter."[29] It would seem logical to suppose that the Lamentations sung in 1518 were those composed by Carpentras, and, in fact, his setting of the three Lessons of Maundy Thursday are qualitatively different. The first (this is what the Spanish would have sung in a lamenting manner) is distinguished by its low tessitura; the "Roman" Lamentation reciting tone is transposed down a fifth. The second (sung by the French) brings the Lamentation tone to its original pitch of A, usually places it very clearly in the top voice, and harmonizes it in the 6th mode (on F) — it is just possible that this use of the "correct" reciting tone is what de Grassis means when he uses the word "docte," which could mean "strict." The third reading (sung by the Italians) is the most striking. Built on a different reciting tone (A with an ending on E), it emphasizes major triads with the pointed use of explicit sharps. Was this what was de Grassis meant when he spoke of Italian "sweetness"?[30]

Unfortunately, we cannot be certain that the Lamentations by Carpentras we now have were indeed the ones composed for Leo X. Carpentras's Lamentations turned out to be a major irritant to the composer. When Leo X died in 1521, Carpentras was in Avignon, where he had substantial benefices. He did not return to Rome upon the election of Leo's successor Adrian VI, and gave up his position as *maestro* of the papal chapel. It is usually asserted that Carpentras did go back to Rome in 1524, when another Medici was elected pope as Clement VII, although I know of no actual evidence of this (he does not appear in any of the extant lists of the chapel for the years 1525-26, for instance). In any case, it does appear that it was around this time that the composer was made aware in some way (possibly by hearing a performance, possibly by seeing copies) of "corruptions" in his Lamentations. This elicited exactly the critical stance he had applied to his earlier *Salve Regina*. As he says in the dedication to Clement VII of the elaborate manuscript copy of his pieces that he himself commissioned (VatS 163, probably dating from 1524-27):

> The Lamentations that hitherto were pleasing to Leo X and favorable to your ears were so corrupted that your ward Carpentras, who was the composer of the work, scarcely recognized them. For that reason, he has not merely restored them as they were but has presented them in a much better form.[31]

This is expanded somewhat in the dedication to the print of the Lamentations of 1532 (also dedicated to Clement VII):

> By order of our most Holy Lord Leo X, I at one time had set the Lamentations of Jeremiah the Prophet to music, but having seen that after a number of years they had been corrupted in many places and were being circulated in such a form that I myself scarcely recognized my own product, I thought I would achieve something notable, most Blessed Father, if, to please Your Holiness, I should restore anew those songs that had pleased you no less

---

[29] Entry for 31 March 1518: "Tres primæ lamentationes recitata fuerunt primo per Hispanos lamentabiliter, secunda per Gallos docte, tertia per Italos dulciter et bene." VatL 5636, f. 232v. Johannes Burkhard also refers to national groups and has a similar opinion of the Spaniards. He relates, for instance, that everybody was pleased with the performance of the Lamentations and Passion by Spaniards because there was something in the quality of their voices that was deemed appropriate to the solemn and sad occasion being commemorated (the Crucifixion). See Sherr, "'Spanish Nation,'" 603-04, for an interpretation of that remark.

[30] Of course, it is perfectly possible that he, like Burkhard, was merely remarking on the sound of the voices of the different nationalities.

[31] *Opera omnia*, 2:xiv.

than Leo X himself and also (if it could be done by me) render them better. And so, some
time ago, I set my hand to the task and presented them, restored and (if I am not mistaken)
better, to Your Holiness, for whose favor especially my labor had been expended. And,
indeed, that effort has turned out not unsuccessfully, since I am informed that our little
work pleased Your Holiness himself tremendously and that you honored it abundantly with
flattering words.[32]

This is not the place to consider what could possibly have happened in only a few years so thoroughly to "corrupt" this music on which the papal choir traditionally lavished the greatest care.[33] Indeed, "corruption" may not have taken place at all, Carpentras merely having decided (as he had with his *Salve Regina*) that the works could be and should be improved (or "rendered better," as he says), but this is where the "madness" to which my title alludes comes into play. Enter that remarkable individual Girolamo Cardano, a man who, it seems, had something to say about absolutely everything.[34] In 1972, Clement A. Miller discovered a reference in Cardano's *Liber de sapientia* to Carpentras. The theme is the danger of overwork, and Cardano says (in Miller's translation):

You must take care not to work with such excessive mental strain that you become insane,
so that the remedy becomes a poison; for it is said that when the musician Carpentras labored
too strongly in that art (to which the Pope was very devoted), he lost his reason. Yet he
composed (in imitation of a swan) nothing more pleasing than his last song.[35]

Now, this description of madness is a little different from a general allusion to the "melancholy" temperament of creative artists. It adduces a specific cause (overwork) that might affect anybody and in this case just happened to affect a composer. The statement suggests, therefore, a more "clinical," cause-and-effect connection between the act of composition and madness—the last sentence could even be read to assert that madness does not even interfere with good composition. Of course, there is no *a priori* reason to believe Cardano. Although he did live in Rome in the last years of his life, he almost certainly never met Carpentras and could merely be reporting gossip. On the other hand, he was a shrewd observer and successful physician who probably knew doctors in Rome who had talked to the composer; or, perhaps, he learned of the case through one of the many printed medical *consilia* published in the sixteenth century.[36] What is more interesting is that there is seeming confirmation of this diagnosis from Carpentras himself. In the dedication to Pope Clement VII of the first volume of the complete edition of his works (*Liber primus missarum*, 1532), Carpentras acknowledges that he had suffered some affliction affecting his head above five years previously (ca. 1526 or 1527), and gives a remarkably clear description of what had troubled him:

---

[32] Ibid.

[33] The music for Holy Week is the only music for which we have evidence of rehearsals. The source situation for the Lamentations is, in fact, extremely complicated, but it is possible that the "original" versions can be recovered. I am grateful to Gayle Sherwood for pointing this out in a paper written for a seminar at Yale University.

[34] See Girolamo Cardano, *The Book of My Life*, transl. Jean Stoner (New York: Dutton, 1930), and Ore Øystein, *Cardano, the Gambling Scholar* (Princeton: Princeton University Press, 1953).

[35] "Cave, ne nimia etiam animi intentione laborans, insanias, fiatque remedium venenum: fertur enim Carpentratem Musicum, dum nimis ad artem, cuius studiosissimus erat Pontifex elaboret: e proprio sensu decidisse: nec tamen quicquam iucundus aedidit (imitatus olores) extrema illa cantione." *Liber de sapientia*, in *Hieronymi Cardani Mediolensis: Opera omnia* (Lyons, 1663), vol. 1, p. 575. See Clement A. Miller, ed., *Hieronimus Cardanus (1501-1576): Writings on Music*, Musicological Studies and Documents, 32 (American Institute of Musicology, 1973), 211 and 220, and Miller, "Jerome Cardan on Gombert, Phinot, and Carpentras," *Musical Quarterly* 58 (1972): 412-19.

[36] See Richard J. Durling, *A Catalogue of Sixteenth-Century Printed Books in the National Library of Medicine* (Bethesda: National Library of Medicine, 1967).

> Already the fifth year is passing, most Blessed Father, since a disease (hitherto unheard of, unless I am mistaken), which I should truly call serious, so suddenly attacked my head, the most noble part of the body, that it does not cease to torment it with continuous hissing and to agitate the brain like winds fighting among themselves. I have had recourse to medical aid and have not neglected to call upon eminent doctors for the purpose of alleviating the disease. But such is my misfortune that up to now no one has been found who has recognized the cause of the disease, much less dispel it. For that reason, I concluded that I had to put any hope of recovering my health in God alone.[37]

The onset of this disease seems to have corresponded in time to Carpentras's problems with his Lamentations. Did the strain and annoyance of having to revise and even recompose the whole set drive him to the brink of nervous collapse? Was the frustration of having spent a career setting reciting tones under the most musical of popes too much to bear? Eight years as head of the papal chapel and never once having been asked to compose a mass! (It is something like serving as chair of a department for five years and having nothing to show for it but some cleverly-crafted memoranda.) Most scholars who discuss this, of course, are circumspect, referring merely to a "mysterious illness."

But, in fact, the condition for which Carpentras consulted the doctors was most likely not a hallucination caused by "loss of reason." *Post facto* diagnosis is dangerous, but Carpentras's description of the constant noises in his head corresponds very well to a condition known as tinnitus (or constant noises in the head), which comes on suddenly, often for no particular reason. Tinnitus afflicts millions of people today and has generated a vast literature. In 1960, G. F. Reed reported that many of his patients described the sound they heard as "steam," which is remarkably like Carpentras's complaint of constant "hissing."[38] In a very recent article in a popular music magazine, the author, Michael Church, another tinnitus sufferer, described his symptoms as "a cacophony of whines, bleeps, and hisses," and pointed out that modern musicians (particularly members of orchestras) are often affected by tinnitus.[39] Tinnitus is also incurable, and even today doctors do not exactly know what causes it, although it is often related to hearing loss, exposure to loud noises, or Meniere's disease.

It is also possible to get an idea of what Carpentras would have enountered when he consulted doctors about his ailment (as he said he did) and why Cardano might have heard stories about insanity. Both Hippocrates and Galen, the ancient authorities whose writings formed the basis of all medical thought in the Renaissance, were aware of a condition they described as "sounds (or echoes) in the ears" (in the Latin translations that would have been consulted by Renaissance doctors, "sonitus aurium [or "in auribus"]" or "tinnitus").[40] Galen says that these sounds are generated by "windy spirits" (vapors that somehow get trapped in the head) and may be acute or chronic. He suggests that it is not easy to make a diagnosis of direct cause, which might involve sickness, fever, drunkenness, vomiting, or even medicine for the ears, and he gives examples of medicines in whose ingredients one can identify substances like vinegar, honey,

---

[37] *Opera omnia*, 1:xiii.

[38] G. F. Reed, "An Audiometric Study of Two Hundred Cases of Subjective Tinnitus," *Archives of Otolaryngology* 71 (1960): 94-104; quoted in Dennis McFadden et al., *Tinnitus: Facts, Theories, and Treatments* (Washington, D.C.: National Academy Press, 1982), 33.

[39] "Aural Torture," *BBC Music Magazine* 2 (1994): 30-32.

[40] See Karl Gottlob Kühn, ed., *Claudii Galeni: Opera omnia*, 20 vols. (Leipzig, 1883; reprint, Hildesheim: G. Olms, 1965), which presents the Greek and Latin texts, and Emile Littré, ed., *Oeuvres complètes d'Hippocrate*, 10 vols. (Paris: J. B. Bailliere, 1846), vol. 5, which presents the Greek with a French translation. I am grateful to Nancy G. Siraisi for directing me to the first of these sources; I rely heavily on her interpretation of the passages from Galen.

and the juice of wild cucumbers.[41] Galen was also of the opinion that if the symptoms of "sonitus" persist, the reason is an acute sense of hearing, and he prescribed stupefacients as medicine. But more to the point, Hippocrates (and Galen agrees) points to sounds in the ears as a symptom of delirium or impending delirium (at one point the Latin translation even uses the word "melancholia"), mostly in the context of a severe fever (that is, as a temporary symptom).[42] Nonetheless, we can imagine, then, what Carpentras encountered when he, presumably not feverish, complained of sounds in the ears (or head). It certainly could have been bruited about that this was one of the signs of "delirium" (which could then have become "madness" or "loss of reason"); indeed, he may even have said something to the effect that "This is driving me crazy." And a little imagination suffices to permit one to sympathize with Carpentras's sense of hopelessness as he had wild concoctions poured into his ears in vain attempts at a cure.

Carpentras's next statement in this dedication is of greater interest:

> Meanwhile, in order that continuous sadness might not consume my heart, I turned my mind, thus afflicted, to the composition of music, and I have compelled it even against its will to serve the task, not, to be sure, without the greatest effort.[43]

I would suggest that this statement shows that this Renaissance composer was not only self-critical with regard to his own music; he was self-aware. For what he describes as having noticed in himself are two of the most prevalent signs of depression. First is what one authority has called "the only invariant symptom of depression": dysphoria or "an unpleasant mood-state, experienced as a feeling of sadness, hopelessness, and helplessness which is subjectively different from anxiety"[44] or the "continuous sadness" (Carpentras, incidentally, uses the word "tristitia," not "melancholia") that was consuming his heart. Second is another prevalent symptom, "passive inertia," i.e., the inability to do anything, or "slowing down of psychomotor activity," for Carpentras admits that he had to force himself to work "against his will" and "with the greatest effort."[45] What all of this means, it seems to me, is that Carpentras felt himself sinking into a serious depression because of his unexplained physical affliction, that he felt he had to do something about it, and that he took a "common sense" route that the best way to fight an overwhelming tendency to do nothing is to "get busy." In so doing, he happened upon one of the techniques of what modern clinical

---

[41] See Kühn, 12:642-46, from *De compositione medicamentorum secundum locos*, Lib. III, a section entitled "De sonitu in auribus": "Sonitus quidam ex flatuoso spiritu generantur. Quidam ob exquisitam sensus audiendi subtilitatem fiunt, quemadmodum in oculis imaginariæ suffusiones propter vapores ex ore ventris exhalantes." One of the prescriptions reads as follows: "In sonitibus repentinis acetum cum rosaceo instilla. Aut cuminum et oleum crassitudine mellis. Aut radicis cucumeris silvestris succum. Aut ipsam radicem oleo incoctam."

[42] Kühn, 16:553, *Galeni in Hippocratis prædictionum, librum I: Commentarius II*, 18: "In ardente febre si aurium tinnitus cum visus hebetudine fuerit proveneritque in naribus gravitas, mente ex melancholia aberrant." Ibid., 589 (37): "Si quid in urina innatarit dissipato femoris dolore delirium portendit; et que circa aurium sonitus talia existunt." Vol. 15, p. 599, *Galeni in Hippocratis de auctorum morborum victu liber et Galeni Commentarius I*: "[As a symptom of delirium] Consimiliter autem et aures sonitu implentur, tum propter elatos a ventre sursum vapores, tum propter flatulentum spiritum in capite ipso orborientem."

[43] *Opera omnia*, 1:xiii.

[44] Peter Lewinsohn and Paul Rhode, "Psychological Measurement of Depression," in Anthony J. Marsella et al., eds., *The Measurement of Depression* (New York: Guilford Press, 1987), 243.

[45] Aaron T. Beck, "The Development of Depression: A Cognitive Approach," in Raymond J. Friedman and Martin M. Katz, eds., *The Psychology of Depression: Contemporary Theory and Research* (Washington, D.C.: W. H. Winston & Sons, 1974), 3-28. The relationship of tinnitus with depression is also fairly well known. See, for example, Jonathan B. Anderson and Stewart D. Anderson, "Anxiety and Depression in Tinnitus Sufferers," *Journal of Psychosomatic Research* 35 (1991): 383-90; Jane Harrop-Griffiths et al., "Chronic Tinnitus: Association with Psychiatric Diagnoses," *Journal of Psychosomatic Research* 31 (1987): 613-21; and Mark D. Sullivan et al., "Disabling Tinnitus: Association with Affective Disorder," *General Hospital Psychiatry* 10 (1988): 285-91.

psychologists call "cognitive therapy," a therapy related directly to "common sense" by one of its main proponents, and one that has met with some success in treating emotional disorders, particularly depression.[46] According to Aaron Beck, a cognitive therapist confronted with a patient depressed to the point of inertia will devise "graded task assignments" that will encourage the patient to "get busy" while providing a "series of successes." Now, if this were easy, we would not need therapists, yet this is precisely what Carpentras accomplished by sheer force of will; he decided on a task that he knew he could complete in stages and that would be assured of success.[47]

The task Carpentras set himself consisted of forcing himself to engage in a massive and previously-unheard-of musical project: composing new works, revising others, and overseeing and paying for the publication of four deluxe volumes in choirbook format, which in fact comprise the first complete works edition of a single composer ever printed.[48] With this, Carpentras presumably composed himself out of his depression, so to speak, and, indeed, may also have found while doing so that thinking about music "masked" the noises in his head.[49] And he is not the only composer to have used composition in this way. When Beethoven sank into a suicidal depression upon the realization that he was going irreversibly deaf, he stopped himself. As he says in the Heiligenstadt Testament of 1802, "it was only my art that held me back. Ah, it seemed impossible to leave the world until I had brought forth all that I felt was within me."[50] The result of Beethoven's compositional effort was the Second Symphony. The first types of pieces Carpentras composed in his attempt at self-therapy were the very ones that he had not been permitted to compose at the court of Leo X: the first volume of his complete works contains five masses, which he offered to Clement VII in the hope that they might be used in the papal chapel. He then followed these with a volume of his Lamentations (in their new version), a volume of hymns, and a volume of Magnificats and settings of Office antiphons as motets. This comprised, as he tells us, "all ecclesiastical music" and completes the systematic program he had started under the auspices of Leo X. The publication was complete by about 1535, and Carpentras, presumably still suffering from tinnitus, retired to the life of a rich cleric, dying in Avignon in 1548.

Carpentras is forgotten as a composer today, but he clearly had a strong personality and was an influential person in his own time. His Lamentations were eventually superseded in Rome by those of Palestrina and others, but, in fact, it was Carpentras who produced the first coherent sets of polyphonic renditions of all these readings of the *triduum sacrum* (creating the tradition these composers followed). His cycles of hymns and Magnificats were followed by similar cycles produced by the younger generation, including his colleague in the papal chapel Costanzo Festa, as well as Jacquet and Willaert. It could in fact be argued that Carpentras, with Leo X in the background, led the way in reviving a neglected genre of sacred music.

---

[46] Aaron T. Beck, M.D., *Cognitive Therapy and the Emotional Disorders* (New York, 1976), 266, 272. His first chaper is entitled "Common Sense and Beyond," and he defines the therapist's task as inducing "the patient to apply the same problem solving techniques he has used throughout his life to correct his fallacious thinking" (p. 20). According to a recent article, "cognitive therapy has emerged as one of the most promising psychosocial interventions for the treatment of depression." Steven D. Hollon et al., "Cognitive Therapy for Depression: Conceptual Issues and Clinicial Efficacy," *Journal of Consulting and Clinical Psychology* 61 (1993): 270-75.

[47] And he was undoubtedly neither the first nor the last person to have taken the "self-help" route out of depression. Robert Burton's *Anatomy of Melancholy* (1621) comes immediately to mind.

[48] For a discussion of the contractual arrangements for this edition, see Daniel Heartz, *Pierre Attaingnant, Royal Printer of Music* (Berkeley: University of California Press, 1969), 110-17.

[49] A cognitive approach known as "distraction." See Per Lindberg et al., "The Psychologial Treatment of Tinnitus: An Experimental Approach," *Behaviour Research and Therapy* 27 (1989): 593-603.

[50] Alexander Wheelock Thayer, *Life of Beethoven*, ed. Elliot Forbes (Princeton: Princeton University Press, 1967), 305. Beethoven was also afflicted by tinnitus.

His *magnum opus* was also inspiring. In 1536, Costanzo Festa was planning to publish hymns and Magnificats, and in 1538 he apparently wished to publish all his works, including masses, motets, madrigals, Lamentations, hymns, Magnificats, even contrapuntal exercises, a project that far outstripped Carpentras's in scope, but which Festa, unlike Carpentras, did not have the money to continue beyond the publication of two books of madrigals.[51] Quite astounding is the (surely purely fanciful) plan of the theorist and soon-to-be papal singer Ghiselin Danckerts (from whom almost no music is preserved) to publish in 1537 (two years after the completion of the Carpentras edition) and at his own expense, "Masses, motets, hymns, psalms, orations, *laude,* readings, Lamentations, chansons, dialogues," as well as intabulations of these pieces for lute, viols, harpsichords and organs.[52] It would be a while before other composers of the Renaissance began to equal Carpentras's achievement.[53]

Behind all of this is the patron and the ceremonies he wanted to embellish. Leo X appointed Carpentras to his position, gave him the charge to compose music for the Offices, and further rewarded him with the benefices that turned him into a wealthy man who could afford to publish four volumes of his own works. But, I would suggest, without Carpentras's particular introspective nature, we would have no evidence of this patron/composer collaboration and the mental investment the composer made in it. Ceremony and two forceful personalities combined here to give us a small glimpse into the world of music-making during the Renaissance.

---

[51] See Richard J. Agee, "Filippo Strozzi and the Early Madrigal," *Journal of the American Musicological Society* 38 (1985): 227-37; Mary S. Lewis, *Antonio Gardano, Venetian Music Printer 1538-1569: A Descriptive Bibliography and Historical Study*, vol. 1 (1538-1549) (New York: Garland, 1988), 673; and Iain Fenlon and James Haar, *Italian Madrigal*, 73-74. Although the present Cappella Sistina collection does not contain the Carpentras edition, it almost certainly once did. In any case, the edition was known in Rome by 1537 at the latest, when the trio sections from the hymns were published in *Libro de canti a tre di Carpentras* (Rome: Valerio and Luigi Dorico, 1537). See Donna G. Cardamone, "*Madrigali a Tre et Arie Napoletane*: A Typographical and Repertorial Study," *Journal of the American Musicological Society* 35 (1982): 436-81.

[52] On 22 March 1537 (predating his entry into the papal chapel on 21 March 1538), Danckerts received a privilege from Paul III to publish at his own expense: "missas, moteta, hymnus, psalmos, orationes, laudes, lectiones, lamentationes, cantiones, dialogos et alias huius generis plura . . . ac ea seu eorum partem ad intabulaturam liuti seu vyole ac cimbali et organi consimiliumque instrumentorum musicalium." See Jose Maria Llorens, "Cantores pontificos colegas de Cristóbal de Morales," *Inter-American Music Review* 10 (1989): 3-18.

[53] In the mid- to late-sixteenth century, various "complete works" editions were published. For instance, in 1560 and 1561, Giovanni Contino brought out 10 separate publications (two are lost) of motets, masses, madrigals, Lamentations, introits, and hymns. See Richard Sherr, ed., *Ioannis Contini ecclesiæ cathedralis Brixiæ magistri modulationum quinque vocum, liber primus* (Venice: Scotto, 1560), The Sixteenth Century Motet, 25 (New York: Garland, 1994), introduction.

XI

The Singers of the Papal Chapel and Liturgical Ceremonies in the Early Sixteenth Century: Some Documentary Evidence

THE PAPAL CHOIR, still in existence and with a history stretching at least as far back as Gregory the Great, can certainly claim to be among the Western World's most durable musical institutions.[1] In the late fifteenth and early sixteenth centuries, it was also among the world's most important, with many famous singers and composers (among them, Dufay and Josquin) flocking to Rome for a chance to serve the Vicar of Christ. Renaissance popes rewarded the choir through the issuance of bulls and constitutions which eventually allowed the singers to form a self-governing college with wide privileges, and a large library of manuscripts (now the Cappella Sistina Collection of the Vatican Library)[2] testifies to the great quantity of music they had at their disposal. But there is still very little direct evidence of what the singers sang or how they actually participated in liturgical ceremonies in Rome. Most of what we have must be drawn from documents closely connected with the papal choir: through them it is possible to come to some understanding of the role the singers played in papal ceremonies and of the extent to which they performed polyphony.

A primary document helpful in determining certain aspects of the daily life of the singers and of their participation in papal ceremonies is the Constitution of the Chapel. The most famous constitution, one that has been published several times and further exists in a sumptuous manuscript, is dated 1545,[3] but there are two older manuscript constitutions (one a fragment) in VatS 687, new fol. 146–53 and 156–66v. Both of these contain inscriptions in other hands indicating that they represent constitutions previous to the one of 1545 and implying that they were consulted in the preparation of the new document.[4] That they do represent pre-1545 stages of the constitution is, in fact, supported by internal evidence.

This is clearest in the second of the documents (eleven folios written in humanistic script) because certain papal singers are mentioned by name. In a chapter concerning the distribution of the gift of money that each new singer had to make to the entire college, there is a discussion of the rights of singers who might be ill:

> ... these gifts are divided among the singers present and participating in the admission of the said [new] singer, that is [those] who

---

'The Singers of the Papal chapel and Liturgical Ceremonies in the Early Sixteenth Century: Some Documentary Evidence', in *Rome in the Renaissance, the City and the Myth*, edited by P.A. RAmsey, MRTS vol. 18 (Binghamton, NY, 1982), pp. 249–264. Copyright Arizona Board of Regents for Arizona State University.

are present and living in Rome, even if they are sick, as long as the sickness is not so grave or perilous to life that the singers cannot participate in or attend the daily Office, as was [the case] of Gaspar Weerbecke and Matheo de Alzate. And whoever is so sick shall not receive such gifts nor any other gifts during the said infirmity. . . .[5]

This seems to refer to a fairly recent case in which Gaspar van Weerbecke and Matheo de Alzate had not shared in the gift because they were so ill at the time that they could not participate in chapel activities. Weerbecke had joined the chapel in the reign of Sixtus IV,[6] and Alzate had become a member in the reign of Julius II;[7] both singers have been shown to have been in the chapel during the reign of Leo X, and both are absent from a list of the chapel dated December, 1526.[8] It would appear, then, that the incident described above would have occurred in the first two decades of the 16th century.

The next mention of a singer occurs in a chapter concerned with the reading of the constitution to new singers. It begins by stating that "Dominus Johannes Scribanus, canon of Salamanca . . . Secretary of the College of Singers . . ."[9] is to read the constitution to new singers. Scribano joined the papal chapel in the reign of Pius III,[10] can be shown to have been a member during the reign of Leo X, and is second in the list of singers of December, 1526.[11] But he had left the chapel by 1529, and did not return until 1531, immediately moving to the head of the list of singers as their dean (a position awarded him in 1527).[12] As it seems unlikely that he would ever have been secretary after becoming dean, the date of the second of the two constitutions can be placed before 1527; indeed, the document could even date as early as the reign of Leo X.

The first of the constitutions in VatS 687 is probably later than the second. Mention is made, for instance, of the *ducatus auri in auro*, a coin created by the currency reform of Clement VII in 1530.[13] But the document was most likely written before 1540: chapter 7 specifies that the singers' monthly salary should be eight ducats; in December, 1540, this salary was raised to nine ducats, the level it retained for the rest of the century.

A comparison of these two documents shows that neither is a direct copy of the other—indeed, they are almost complementary, each containing things absent in the other—and that both of them taken together agree more than they disagree with the Constitution of 1545. From this it may be surmised that the Constitution of 1545 continues many of the earlier customs and regulations of the singers.

Both the Constitution of 1545 and the second of the two earlier constitutions specify in almost the same words the duties of the singers regarding the daily canonical hours. The singers were to assemble in the smaller of the two first-floor chapels of the Vatican Palace, the Capella Sancti Nicolai (in 1545, changed to Capella Sancti Pauli[14]), when they heard the ringing of the palace bells. They were to be present at all the daily offices, including Mass, presumably said in this same chapel, and they were fined very modest amounts for coming in late or missing any of the offices. Nothing is said about the singing of psalms, but they probably performed all the antiphons, responsories, hymns etc., in the offices as well as all of the chants of the Mass. The sopranos among the singers seemed to have had a special role in these ceremonies. It was a soprano who intoned the "Domine labia mea" at the beginning of the offices and the "Jube Domine benedicere" at the beginning of Compline, and two sopranos were to sing the Versicles during the various offices. No mention is made of polyphony at any of these services.

At papal ceremonies, the singers were to be present and waiting in the singers' box of the Cappella Sistina before the pope and cardinals entered, and were fined much greater amounts—up to one ducat (an eighth of a month's salary)—for being late or absent. Special attention was also given to the Office of Christmas Matins. Two sopranos were to sing the beginning of the Invitatorium "Christus natus est," which was then repeated and continued by the rest of the singers in "cantu plano maiori." But the first three antiphons of the first Nocturn as well as the first and eighth responsory were to be sung in contrapunctus (an improvisitory practice of singing polyphony). This is the only mention of any kind of polyphony in relation to papal ceremonies to be found in the constitutions.

In papal matins there was also a particular method of chanting the Lessons and Prophecies. The singers sang these one at a time in order of seniority, beginning with the last (hired) singer, and the manner of chanting these Lessons and Prophecies had to be taught to new singers as soon as they joined the chapel. And mention should also be made of the one reference to cantus figuratus as part of a service which occurs only in the Constitution of 1545 in a chapter entitled, "De cantore mortuo," where it is stated that the singers should follow the body after the funeral, two by two in order of seniority, singing "in cantu figurato" the responsory "Libera me Domine."

Thus, the constitution is of little help in answering the major question of how much polyphony was performed at papal services, although it does state that all singers before they could be accepted had to be tested to see if they had good voices, could sing cantus figuratus, could sing contrapunctus, could sing chant, and could read. To discover if they took much advantage of the ability to perform polyphony, we must turn to another type of document of papal ceremonies, the diaries of the papal masters of ceremonies.

In fact, most of our knowledge of the daily activities of the papal singers in the late fifteenth and early sixteenth centuries is drawn from the writings of the masters of ceremonies. During the reign of Alexander VI and at the beginning of the reign of Julius II, the senior magister ceremoniarum was Johannes Burkhard, who left a diary, available in modern editions, which is an important and much cited source of the history of the period, and contains many descriptions of papal services.[15] In general, music is not discussed, although a motet is mentioned once, and there are descriptions of the singing of the Passion.[16] Somewhat more interesting are the writings of Paride de Grassis, Burkhard's colleague and successor.

De Grassis, one of the most important Roman commentators on events during the papacy of Julius II, came from an old noble Bolognese family, and was probably born before 1450. He apparently made a visit to Rome as early as 1474, but did not leave Bologna for good until 1494, when he became the papal governor of Orvieto. In 1499, he was given a canonry in the church of San Lorenzo in Damaso, and officially joined the chapel on 26 May 1504 on the resignation of Bernardus Gutteri, becoming the second of two masters of ceremonies (Burkhard was the first). On Burkhard's death, de Grassis became the senior master of ceremonies, and remained in that position during the reigns of Julius II and Leo X. On 4 April 1513, apparently at his own request, he was made Bishop of Pesaro. Exactly when he left the chapel is not clear—he was not there in December 1526, and, although he did not die until 10 June 1528, his diaries only cover the years from 1504 to the end of Leo's reign (1521).[17]

Like Burkhard, de Grassis kept a detailed diary of the ceremonies of the papal court, although these diaries have never seen a complete modern edition. He was also the author of other works—the Vatican Library contains several manuscripts of a *Caeremoniale* by him, one with a dedication to Cardinal Petrus Isvalies dated 17 May 1505, and his *Ordo Romanus* is published in Martène's *De antiquiis Ecclesiae ritibus*. The dedication of the latter work to Cardinal Guillaume Briçonet places its probable origin before 1511, when that cardinal was excommunicated for having taken part in a council directed against Julius II. A further treatise from de Grassis's pen is the *De Caeremoniis Cardinalium et Episcoporum*, published posthumously in Venice in 1564. Other miscellaneous writings are preserved in the Vatican Library.[18]

All these works are given over to detailed descriptions of liturgical ceremonies, particularly those concerning the papal chapel. The *Ordo Romanus* and manuscript *Caeremoniale* specify the occasions when the entire chapel (pope, curia, etc.) assembled. These were fifty in all—five matins, ten vespers, and thirty-five masses—and de Grassis further indicates if the ceremonies were to take place in the Sistine Chapel (the "palace chapel") or in Saint Peter's, and indicates whether the celebrant was to be pope or cardinal.[19]

De Grassis's writings make it clear that he takes music very much for granted, or at least did not consider it to be a very important part of the ceremony, and he is much more concerned about when people had to stand or sit, what they were to wear, and where they were to be at certain times. For instance, a long chapter in the manuscript *Caeremoniale* is devoted to the celebration of the Mass.[20] Taking the Mass for the Feast of Circumcision as a model, de Grassis runs through all the liturgical actions that must be performed by the celebrant. The singers are, in fact, mentioned a number of times, but mainly so that the celebrant can be advised to wait until they finish singing before going on with the service. Apparently, the singers sang

Table I
Occasions Requiring Participation of the Full Chapel
(* = Mass celebrated by the Pope; ** = Mass celebrated by a cardinal)

Matins (5)
All Souls Day
Christmas Eve
Wednesday, Thursday, and Friday of Holy Week

Vespers (10)
(The vespers were celebrated on the day previous to the feast listed [Vigilia])
Christmas (in Saint Peter's)
The Apostles Peter and Paul (in Saint Peter's)
All Saints
All Souls
Circumcision
Epiphany
Ascension
Pentecost
Trinity
Corpus Christi

Masses (35)
All Saints (in Saint Peter's)**
All Souls**
1 Advent
2 Advent
3 Advent**
4 Advent
Christmas Eve**
Christmas (in Saint Peter's)*
Saint Stephen**
Saint John the Evangelist**
Circumcision**
Epiphany (in Saint Peter's)**
Purification**
Ash Wednesday**
1 Quadragesima
2 Quadragesima
3 Quadragesima
4 Quadragesima (de Rosa)**
Passion Sunday
Palm Sunday**
Maundy Thursday**
Good Friday**
Holy Saturday**
Easter*
Monday after Easter**
Tuesday after Easter**
Saturday after Easter
Ascension (in Saint Peter's)**
Pentecost**
Trinity Sunday**
Corpus Christi (in Saint Peter's)**
Apostles Peter and Paul (in Saint Peter's)*
Anniversary of the death of the preceding pope
Creation and coronation of the present pope** (two separate Masses)

over the reading of the celebrant. In his description of the Introit and Kyrie, for instance, de Grassis says that the celebrant reads the Introit and Kyrie while the singers sing the Introit and Kyrie and the pope reads the Introit. The celebrant then has to wait until the singers can finish before he can intone the Gloria. The Gloria is also said while the singers perform, and the celebrant again has to wait until they are finished. The actions of the Credo are somewhat more complicated. The celebrant reads the Credo. At the words "Et incarnatus est . . . Et homo factus est," he and his assistants kneel. When he has finished, he sits down. When the pope and cardinals get to "Et incarnatus est" they kneel, but the celebrant does not. But when "Et incarnatus est" is sung, the celebrant inclines his head towards the altar. There is nothing in the chapter to indicate if the singing was entirely in chant or polyphony or in any combination. What is clear, however, is that from a ceremonial and liturgical point of view it did not much matter whether the singers were there or not, the important thing being that the sacred words were said by the celebrant. There was no reason, then, for de Grassis to include detailed discussions of the singers' role in his manual for papal masters of ceremonies.

More information about the singers can, fortunately, be gleaned from the diaries. According to Table I, the chapel only assembled on the most important feast days of the church for mass, and rarely met for the daily offices, and this is generally confirmed by the diaries. But even though the papal court did not attend, the daily offices were celebrated anyway, as the constitutions of the chapel demonstrate, and the pope even attended daily mass in a private chapel of his own. De Grassis refers several times to the pope's "parva capella superiore," the chapel of Nicholas V on the second floor of the Vatican Palace, used by Julius II for daily mass:

> Today, the pope wanted to have the papal Mass in his small daily chapel with himself, some Palatine cardinals, and the Duke of Ferrara present, and it was done (8 September 1508).[21]

> On the vigil and feast of St. Thomas the Apostle, the pope ordered me to prepare for the vigil and thereafter for the solemn Mass in his small daily chapel on the upper floor; accordingly it was done (21 December 1508).[22]

But if the singers were involved in singing the daily offices in the Chapel of Saint Nicholas, it does not seem likely that the pope's private masses were particularly elaborate, and the schedule of fines in the constitutions even implies that missing anything but papal ceremonies was a relatively minor offense.[23] It is possible, though, that a number of pieces preserved in papal manuscripts which seem appropriate only to the daily offices (the series of vespers hymns in VatS 15, for instance) were actually performed at these smaller services. De Grassis, however, does not describe the ceremonies.

Although the main business of the singers was the performance of chant,[24] there are certain times when de Grassis feels constrained to mention polyphony — usually when something new, strange, or incorrect has occurred. For instance, in 1505, he had cause to remark on the mangled performance of the Credo:

> . . . in the Credo none of the chapel knelt when the words "Et homo factus est" were sung; and this was the fault of the singers whose Dean usually lets us know when they sing those words because we do not always understand [them] very well (27 December 1505).[25]

De Grassis does not specifically mention polyphony here, but I do not see how the problem could have arisen if the singers were not singing in polyphony. The words "Et homo factus est," the cue for people in the chapel to kneel, obviously had to be understood. Another reference to the Credo is clearer:

> As is the custom, the singers sang in Gregorian chant, all except the Credo, which was sung in such a confused manner that many did not understand the words, especially "Et incarnatus est" (17 March 1510).[26]

These quotations suggest that a polyphonic Credo with its attendant problem of intelligibility must have been a fairly regular occurrence — so much so that the master of ceremonies actually seems to have worked out a signal system with the dean of the singers to avoid mistakes. In yet another reference to the Credo, de Grassis states that, on 10 April 1507 (Saturday of Easter Week), the singers performed a "Credo with 16 voices," wishing to honor, "in this new way," the maestro di cappella who was celebrating mass that day.[27] Unfortunately, it is not clear whether the novelty was that sixteen people were singing or that the Credo was actually written for sixteen parts.

With regard to motets, de Grassis is not much more help than Burkhard, and I have been able to find only one mention of a motet:

> After the Gospel is sung, the Pope kisses and incenses the book, and it is well [done]. Although the *officium* is omitted, yet the singers with our consent might have sung one of their motets so there would not be silence in the chapel until it was time for the Preface (22 April 1508).[28]

The motet, in this case, is being used as a filler to avoid silence in the chapel, and in this sense de Grassis's description is close to Burkhard's which had mentioned a motet to be placed in the service at the initiative of the singers themselves.[29] The implication here that motets could be sung *ad libitum* during the Mass may reflect actual Roman practice, as it agrees with the pronouncement of Paolo Cortese in his *De Cardinalatu Libri Tres*. Cortese, writing in the first decade of the sixteenth century, objected to motets because they did not have a regular place in the service:

> Then, those songs are called precentorial, which although mixed with propitiatory singing, can be seen to be supernumerary (*ascriptitia*) and ingrafted (*astitia*), since for them there is free option of choice. . . .[30]

This attitude may indeed explain why there are so many motets from this period with non-liturgical (but religious) texts vaguely associated with certain feasts (as in VatS 42, for instance), and why it is practically impossible to demonstrate that motets with liturgical texts were performed at the correct spots in the liturgy. The answer may be that the singers simply did not know themselves when to sing the pieces.

Another discussion of polyphony (during a Tenebrae service in the reign of Leo X) concerns a psalm:

> At the end, the singers sang the psalm *Miserere* in a new way—after the first verse they sang in symphony, and then *alternatim*, which was good and devout (12 April 1514).[31]

Two other statements from diaries of the reign of Leo X mention polyphonic performances of the same psalm:

> The singers today began to sing the psalm *Miserere mei Deus* in figural music and symphony (20 March 1516).[32]

> At the end of the Office, I was not pleased because the singers sang the psalm *Miserere mei* in falsobordone, and the pope wanted it thus (1 April 1518).[33]

What is evident is that in 1514, presumably a number of years after the composition of Josquin's famous *Miserere*, relatively simple alternatim polyphonic renditions of the same text were a novelty at the papal court.

De Grassis and Burkhard are at their most specific when describing the performance of the Passion. In his discussion of the Passion on Palm Sunday, 16 March 1505, de Grassis states that it was sung by three people, each taking a different part (Evangelist, Christ, crowd), and then continues:

> Each one sang his own part, but sometimes they all sang in figural music, that is: at the words "Tristis est anima mea," etc., until the end of the verse; and "Mi pater si possibile est," until the end of the verse; and "Pater mi si non potest," etc., the whole verse; and "Flevit amare;" and "Eeli Eeli Lama Zabathani;" and "Deus meus, Deus meus, ut quid," etc.; and at the words "Emisit spiritum."[34]

He relates later on in the diary that the Passion was performed in the same way on Good Friday, 21 March 1505, and Burkhard's shorter descriptions of the same ceremonies of earlier years suggest a long standing custom. Although an alternatim performance of the Passion was no novelty at this time, it is striking that the words of the Evangelist and Christ are performed polyphonically while those of the turba are not. Manfred Schuler has tried to make the point that this custom relates to the Spanish influence of the court of Alexander VI — in one description Burkhard mentions that the Passion was sung by Spaniards — and, in fact, de Grassis says as much in his manuscript *Caeremoniale*.[35]

In at least three places, de Grassis mentions that no polyphony was to be performed during certain periods of the year. In the diaries, the *De Caeremoniis Cardinalium* and the *Ordo*, he states that no polyphony was to be sung from Passion Sunday to Easter with the exception of Maundy Thursday:

> And note that the singers from today until Easter, with the exception of Maundy Thursday, sing in Gregorian chant, with no figural music, and the pifari, tubae, and tibiae of the Castello cease to play (9 March 1505).[36]

The *De Caeremoniis Cardinalium* adds Ash Wednesday to those days without polyphony (even the musicians of the Castel Sant'Angelo were to be silent). While it may be hard to find a reason for this ban (it may relate to Lent), and while there is evidence in de Grassis's Diaries that the ban was not followed strictly, it does confirm the supposition that polyphony was being performed at all other periods of the church year.[37]

In fact, de Grassis at one point refers to the papal singers specifically as singers of polyphonic music — the statement is found in a chapter of the manuscript *Caeremoniale* entitled "Concerning Choruses in the Papal Chapel [and] Finally the Instruction of the Choristers."[38] De Grassis is using the word "chorus" here in an architectural sense, and is describing various sections of the papal chapel, including one where "soli simphoniaci cantores" are placed. Later on, he talks about the "ultimo simphonizantium choro."

> Concerning the last chorus of symphonizers, nothing pertains to our ceremonies, as these [singers] stand or sit or do anything else according to what pleases or is suitable for them.[39]

He goes on to say that the master of ceremonies should watch to see if the singers are going to take a breath, this signifying that they are going to sing in symphony which ". . . consists of harmony (concentu) and of many voices."[40] He thus seems to be indicating that the singers in papal ceremonies sang polyphony when it pleased them. If this is really what he means, then this statement becomes the only clear contemporary account of the regular participation of singers of polyphony in papal services.

Certain assumptions about the state of polyphony in the chapel can be drawn from the above:

1. Singers of polyphony were present at all papal ceremonies.

2. Occasionally, single polyphonic Mass movements (particularly Credos) were sung.

3. Motets did not form a regular part of the service, but could be inserted.

4. The Passion was performed with certain sections in polyphony.

5. There were periods of the year when polyphony was banned altogether.

6. The practice of singing a polyphonic or half-polyphonic psalm during Holy Week was new in 1514.[41]

But while de Grassis may write sparingly of polyphony, he is not so silent on other matters concerning the singers. Some of his information is financial. From the diaries, we learn that the singers were paid ten ducats for participating in the funerals of cardinals, and that newly created cardinals were expected to tip the same amount. The singers were not always given money, though, as it was the custom for the prelate celebrating a mass in which they took part to provide a meal for them before the ceremony. Such meals are mentioned frequently in the diaries, although on at least one occasion (1 November 1508) the celebrating cardinal offered cash instead—de Grassis grumpily remarks that ". . . the singers always want to have money (cantores semper volunt habere pecunias)."[42]

On more than one occasion, de Grassis also expresses his displeasure, stating that the singers sang badly, and he is particularly concerned with the amount of time taken up by singing. According to the manuscript *Caeremoniale*, for instance, a good deal of action took place during the Kyrie of a pontifical mass. De Grassis says that it may be necessary to repeat the Kyrie as many as twenty times or as few as three, as the occasion demanded (and such occasions are reported in the diaries).[43] Other times, he instructs the choir to sing slowly, or quickly, or even to repeat chants, when accompanying ceremonial actions—the music could neither end before nor continue beyond the termination of the actions. At one point he says that the singers sang the Alleluia in long notes (or very slowly—"tenendo longum cantum") in order to take up time.[44]

Once in a while, accidents would occur, as when the singers, thinking the pope had finished the incipit of a hymn, began to sing before he actually stopped ". . . cum risu papae et alorium."[45] Once the singers did not return to the palace for Lauds and the second Mass of the Christmas Vigil because they did not want to leave the house of the cardinal who was to feed them on Christmas Day.[46] On another occasion, they were so angry when the executors of a cardinal's estate refused to give them a meal, that they nearly refused to sing at the funeral.[47] Some mishaps did not concern them directly as when the pope sang an incorrect intonation or when the subdeacon, Bernardus Gambara, began an antiphon badly to the amusement of the pope and the assembled chapel (". . . quam quam male et cum risu Papae et omnium de capella").[48] These incidents, however, demonstrate a spirit of independence among the papal singers that was to grow more pronounced as the century progressed.[49]

The papal singers existed, then, to serve not only the pope, but the entire Vatican establishment, and were required to participate in the daily canonical hours held for members of that establishment. When they attended the pope at papal ceremonies, they performed chant, but were also considered by the master of ceremonies to be singers of polyphony, although they seem to have had the choice of when to sing it and of how much to sing. And finally, from the music preserved for them in their library, from the calibre of the people employed as singers, and from their great reputation, it can be seen that, in spite of the general neglect and even contempt with which they are treated by Burkhard and de Grassis, the papal singers were a necessary fixture, and indeed one of the glories, of liturgical ceremonies in Rome during the Renaissance.

Notes

1. For a history of the papal choir, see Franz Xaver Haberl, *Die Römische "schola cantorum" und die Päpstlichen Kapellsänger bis zur Mitte des 16. Jahrhunderts*, Bausteine für Musikgeschichte, vol. 3 (Leipzig, 1888).

2. Vatican City, Biblioteca Apostolica Vaticana, fondo Cappella Sistina (hereafter VatS).

3. VatS 611. The document is published in Haberl. Beginning in 1535, many things regarding the daily life of the singers were recorded in documents now known as the Diarii Sistini. See Raffaele Casimiri, *I Diarii Sistini, i primi 25 anni (1535-1559)* (Rome, 1939), and Josef Llorens, "Reglamentación del Colegio de Cantores Pontificios, Las *Constitutiones Apostolicae* y el *Liber Punctorum Capellae*," *Anuario Musical* 30 (1975): 97-108.

4. "Constitutionum Fragmentum, quae antiquiores in nostro archivio reperiuntur, unde Novae constitutiones Pauli III tempore, exhavitae fuerunt, quare in hisce nonnullae apparent liturae constat capit. 41" (VatS 687, fol. 146v). "Fragmentum nonnullarum constitutionum quae ante Pauli tempora in usu habitae fuerunt, et ex quibus plura novarum constitutionum capitula tempore

ipsius Pauli III cura Lodovi Episcopi Assisiensis Capella Magistri labere, et diligentia cantorum exhavit fuerunt" (VatS 687, fol. 157). Both constitutions contain corrections and marginalia in other hands.

5. ". . . Ipsa regalia dividantur inter cantores participantes et interessentes admissioni cantoris predicti et inter presentes hoc est Rome commorantes etiam si infirmitate constituti essent dummodo ipsa infirmitas non esset tam grandis seu periculosa ad vitam quod non possent cantores infirmi servire nec accedere ad quottidianum offitium ut fuit in Domino Gaspare vebret et in domino Matheo de Alzate. Et quiunque constitutus in tali infirmitate non percipiet de talibus regalibus nec de aliquibus aliis regalibus durante ipsa infirmitate. . ." (VatS 687, fol. 160v).

6. He first appears in a list of the chapel in February, 1481. See Rome, Archivio di Stato, Camerale I, *Mandati Camerali* (hereafter, *Mandati*), 847.

7. He first appears in a list of April, 1507. See *Mandati*, 857.

8. See Hermann-Walther Frey, "Regesten zur päpstlichen Kapelle unter Leo X und zu seiner Privatkapelle," *Die Musikforschung* 8 (1955): 70–71, 189; and Richard Sherr, "New Archival Data Concerning the Chapel of Clement VII," *Journal of the American Musicological Society* 29 (1976): 472–78.

9. "Dominus Johannes Scribanus canonicus Salamantinus . . . Secretarius collegii cantorum . . ." (VatS 687, fol. 162).

10. He first appears in a list of October, 1503. See Vatican City, Biblioteca Apostolica Vaticana, MSS Vaticani Latini (hereafter, Vat. Lat.) 9027, fol. 163v.

11. See Frey, "Regesten", p. 184, and Sherr, "New Archival Data."

12. *Mandati*, 864. See also Josef Llorens, "Juan Escribano Cantor pontifico y compositor," *Anuario Musical* 41 (1957): 99.

13. I am grateful to Mr. Jeffrey Dean for pointing this out to me.

14. See Franz Ehrle S.J. and Hermann Egger, *Der Vaticanische Palast in seiner Entwicklung bis zur Mitte des XV Jahrhunderts* (Vatican City, 1935).

15. Burkhard was the most important of two or three masters of ceremonies—the chapel generally employed more than one at a time. He died on 17 May 1506. For more on the masters of ceremonies and the papal *ceremoniale*, see the introduction by Msgr. Jaoquin Nabuco to *Le Cérémoniale Apostolique avant Innocent VIII, Texte du manuscrit Urbinate Latin 469 de la Bibliothèque Vaticane établi par Dom Filippo Tamburini*, Biblioteca "Ephemerides Liturgicae" Sectio Historica, vol. 30 (Rome, 1966).

16. See Alexandre Thuasne, ed., *Diarium sive urbanarum commentarii* (Paris, 1883-85), and E. Celani, ed., *Joh. Burkardi Liber Notarum*, Rerum Italicarum Scriptores, vol. 32, Tl. I (Città di Castello, 1906ff.). Concerning Burkhard and music, see Arnold Schering, "Musikalisches aus Joh. Burkhards Liber Notarum," *Festschrift Johannes Wolf* (Berlin, 1929), pp. 171–75; and Helmut Osthoff, *Josquin des Pres* (Tutzing, 1962).

17. Most of the biographical details are taken from L. Frati, ed., *Le due spedizioni militari di Giulio II trati dal Diario di Paris de Grassis Bolognese con documenti* (Bologna, 1886), Introduction.

18. The manuscripts in the Vatican Library containing de Grassis's works are catalogued and described in Pierre Salmon, *Les Manuscrits Liturgiques Latins de la Bibliothèque Vaticane, III, Ordines Romani Pontificaux Rituels Cérémoniaux*, Studi e Testi, vol. 260 (Vatican City, 1970).

The manuscripts consulted for this study are:

The Diaries of the Reign of Julius II

Years	Call Number
1504-06	Vat. Lat. 4739
	Vat. Lat. 5635
	Vat. Lat. 12303
	Vatican City, Biblioteca Apostolica Vaticana MS Chigi (hereafter, Chigi), L.I. 17
Itinerarium 1506-09	Vat. Lat. 12304
	Vat. Lat. 12411
	Vat. Lat. 12413
1506-08	Chigi L.I. 18
1509-12	Vat. Lat. 12305
1510-13	Vat. Lat. 12414
	Vat. Lt. 12415
1509-13	Chigi L.I. 19

Diaries of the Reign of Leo X

1513-21	Vat. Lat. 5636
	Vat. Lat. 12274

(All these manuscripts transmit the same text, some more legibly and accurately than others.)

Caeremoniale

Vat. Lat. 5634

This manuscript is in three parts. The first, with 250 folios, is described by Salmon as a "Traité du cérémonial" (p. 126). The second part, with 382 folios, contains de Grassis's reworking of the Caeremoniale of Patrizi, and has the dedication to Cardinal Isvalies dated 1505. The third part, with 19 folios, is titled *Tractatus de equitatione papae per urbem in solemnitate non pontificali.* . . . According to Salmon, the second and third parts were owned by de Grassis himself, and have autograph corrections.

Some modern publications of de Grassis include:
Frati.
Paris de Grassis, *Il Diario di Papa Leone X*, ed. M. Armellini (Rome, 1884).
Vincenzo de Brognoli, ed., *Il Diario di Paride Grassi* (Rome, 1884).
Also, excerpts in Döllinger, *Beiträge zur Politischen Kirchlichen und Kultur-Geschichte*, 3 (Vienna, 1882): 363-433.

19. See Martène, and Vat. Lat. 5634, part I.

20. Vat. Lat. 5634, part II, fols. 51-66, a chapter entitled "De Ceremoniis quibus solus celebrans utit in sua missa."

21. "Hodie Papa voluit habere missam pontificalem in sua quotidiana parva capella coram se, et aliquibus palatinis cardinalibus ac etiam Duce Ferrariae et sic fuit" (Vat Lat. 12304, fol. 304).

22. "Die vigiliae, et festi Sancti Thome Apostoli Papa mihi mandavit, ut pararem pro vesperas in vigilia, deinde in die festi missam solemnem in sua quotidiana parva cappella superiori prout factum fuit" (Vat. Lat. 12304, fol. 338v).

23. See Haberl, and VatS 687.

24. Time and time again the singers are described as singing antiphons, Te Deums, and other sections of the services not normally in polyphony.

25. ". . . ad credo nulli de capella geneflexerunt cum diceretur versus Et homo factus est, fuit per culpam cantorum quorum Decanus solet nobis significare quando ipsi cantant dictum Versum quod nos non bene semper intelligimus" (Vat. Lat. 5635, fol. 178v).

26. ". . . more solito cantores cantarunt cantum Gregorianum excepto credo quem sic confuse cantarunt ut multi non intellexerunt verba maxime illa videlicet et incarnatus est" (Vat. Lat. 12414, fol. 17).

27. "Credo cantatum fuit hodie nescio qualiter per cantores ut dixerunt per XVI voces . . ." (Vat. Lat. 12413, fol. 156v).

28. "Post cantatum evangelium Papa osculatur librum, et incensatur et bene, licet officium non dicatur, tamen cantores de consensu nostro unum suum mottetum cantarent, ne esset tantum in capella silentium usque ad praefationem" (Vat. Lat. 12304, fol. 277v).

29. See Osthoff and Schering. Apparently, the singers were encouraged by Ascanio Sforza to sing a motet with a text by Tinctoris in honor of Alexander VI after the Offertory, but the pope decided to hear it later "in camera sua."

30. Nino Pirrotta, "Musical and Cultural Tendencies in 15th-Century Italy," *Journal of the American Musicological Society* 19 (1966): 154. In the article Pirrotta also explains Cortese's somewhat convoluted terminology.

31. "In fine cantores dixerunt Psalmum Miserere cum novo modo, nam primam versum cantarunt symphoniando et deinde alternatim, quod fuit bene et devote" (Vat. Lat. 12274, fol. 120v). This really must have been something new. In his *Caeremoniale*, de Grassis had specified this psalm to be "read aloud without music" ("Cantores dicunt pater noster sub silentio: et demum psalmum Miserere, alte legendo sine nota usque ad finem," Vat. Lat. 5634, part II, fol. 245).

32. "Cantores hodie inceperunt cantare psalmum Miserere mei Deus partim cum cantu figuratu et simphonia . . ." (Vat. Lat. 12274, fol. 192).

33. "In fine officii mihi non placavit quod cantores cantassent psalmum miserere mei falsum bordonum, et Papa sic voluit" (Vat. Lat. 5636, fol. 232v). This quotation is of special interest in that it contains one of the first uses of the term *falsobordone* (referring to a particular manner of singing psalms in polyphony). In fact, Leo X may have been responsible for introducing this practice to Rome. There is no mention of it in de Grassis before his reign, yet almost as soon as Leo ascended the throne, the diarist begins complaining about *falsobordone*. For instance, he mentions something that occurred during the Mass of the Feast of Saint John the Baptist (24 June, 1513):

> . . . cantores nescientes regulas ceremoniarum prepararunt cantum per falsum Bordonum sic dictum, et multi murmurarunt, aliqui riserunt de natura quasi ignorantia . . . (Vat. Lat. 12274, fol. 60v).

Unfortunately, this reference is unclear. *Falsobordone*, as a technique for performing psalms, had no place in the Mass, and I do not quite understand what is meant by "prepararunt cantum." Nevertheless, this does become the first recorded instance of the term. See Murray C. Bradshaw, *The Falsobordone: A Study in Renaissance and Baroque Music*, Musicological Studies and Documents, vol. 34 (Neuhausen-Stuttgart, 1979).

34. "Unusquisque cantabat partem suam sed in aliquibus omnes simul can-

tabant in cantu figurato videlicet, versum tristis est anima mea etc. usque ad finem versus. Item: mi pater, si possibile est, usque ad finem versus. Item: pater mi si non potest etc. totum versum. Item flevit amare. Item Heli, Heli lamazabatani. Item: Deus meus, Deus meus, ut quid etc. Item: ad haec verba videlicet emisit spiritum" (Vat. Lat. 5635, fol. 93).

35. See Manfred Schuler, "Spanische Musikeinflüsse in Rom um 1500," *Anuario Musical* 25 (1970): 27–36. Further evidence for the Spanish origin of this technique is presented in Theodor Göllner, "Unknown Passion Tones in Sixteenth-Century Hispanic Sources," *JAMS* 28 (1975): 46–71. In Vat. Lat. 5634, part II, fol. 238, de Grassis says:

> Verumtamen Alexander papa VIa qui fuit hyspanus statuit quod cantores sui indigene hyspani: qui naturaliter cantando magis flere videntur quam vociferari: in aliquibus clausulis sive partibus passionis simul tres omnes per cantum figuratum pientissime quidem: ac devotissime cantarent quasi lamentarentur hec partes videlicet Tristis est Anima mea usque ad mortem. Item mi Pater si possibile est etc. usque ad finem clausule. Item pater mi, si non potest etc. Item flevit amare. Item Deus meus, Deus meus ut quid etc. Item emisit spiritum, et similes passionis partes, quae notabiles ad pietatem in hoc actu excitant audientes. Idem etiam servabunt ipsi cantores in parasceve sequenti inter passionem decantandam.

36. "Et nota quod cantores ab hodie usque ad pascha praeterquam in die Jovis Sancti cantant gregorianum, & nullo modo figuratum, & pifari, ac tubae, & tibiae Castelli cessant" (Vat. Lat. 5635, fol. 89v).

37. For instance, on Passion Sunday in 1513 (reign of Leo X) he complained:

> . . . cantores in introitus et offertorio cantarunt per cantum Gregorianum et bene sed alia symphonisando et male, cum in die usque ad Pascha semper Gregorianum soleant, praeterquam in cena Domini (Vat. Lat. 12274, fol. 119).

38. "De choris in capella papali denique choristarum disciplina" (Vat. Lat. 5635, part I, fols. 27r–28v).

39. "De ultimo simphonizantium choro nihil ad nostras ceremonias pertinet, qualiter ipsi stare, aut sedere, vel aliquod facere, quod eis aut liceat" (Vat. Lat. 5635, part I, fol. 28).

40. ". . . nam multorum concentu vocibusque constat" (Vat. Lat. 5635, part I, fol. 28). I am grateful to Professor Marie-Louise Martinez Göllner for supplying me with translations of these and other passages.

41. It is interesting to note that the Constitutions of 1545 and VatS 687 both specifically forbid any polyphony during the Tenebrae Services (see chapter LV of the 1545 Constitution). Could this have been in response to what was going on in the reign of Leo X?

42. Vat. Lat. 12413, fol. 313v.

43. "Kyrie eleison novies, sive decies, aut duodecies vel vigeties repetierit, sive minus novem numero nam quandoque ter, aut quater, seu quinquies . . ." (Vat. Lat. 5634, part I, fols. 120r–120v).

44. Vat. Lat. 5635, fol. 117v.

45. Vat. Lat. 5635, fol. 5v.

46. Vat. Lat. 5635, fol. 177.

47. Vat. Lat. 12414, fol. 204.
48. Chigi L.I. 17, fol. 667.
49. This spirit is demonstrated most clearly in documents of the later sixteenth century. See, for instance, Richard Sherr, "From the Diary of a 16th-Century Papal Singer," *Current Musicology* 25 (1978): 83–98.

XII

Speculations on Repertory, Performance Practice, and Ceremony in the Papal Chapel in the Early Sixteenth Century

Ceremony and Specific Works of Polyphony

One of the frustrating things about dealing with the actual repertory of the papal singers in the early 16th century is our inability to connect any specific pieces (particularly the settings of the Ordinary of the Mass) with specific occasions. I would like to suggest now two times when I think this can be done. On Christmas Day, 25 December, 1514, the papal Mass in St. Peter's was attended by a distinguished visitor, Isabella d'Este. According to Paris de Grassis, on this occasion:

The singers sang the third psalm of Terce in polyphony.[1]

Since de Grassis specifically uses the term *cantus figuratus*, when, as we will see, he knew the term *falsum bordonum*, I would suggest that he is not talking about a falso bordone recitation of the psalm, but rather about what we now call a psalm-motet; a new and increasingly popular genre in the early 16th century. The *"third psalm"* of Terce consisted of verses 65–80 of Psalm 118 (which is broken up to provide all the psalms of the Little Hours) beginning with the words *"Bonitatem fecisti"*. As it happens, there is a psalm-motet setting of these words including a *Gloria patri* that without question was known in Rome in 1514; the setting by Elzéar Genet, called Carpentras, who had moved back to Rome to become the maestro of the papal chapel by November, 1513[2], and whose motet had just

---

[1] "Cantores cantarunt tertium psalmum tertiae in cantu figurato." Vatican City, Biblioteca Apostolica Vaticana, Fondo Vaticani Latini (hereafter, BAV, Vat. lat.), MS 5636, fol. 102ᵛ.

[2] Genet was made maestro of the papal chapel on November 5, 1513. See SHERR 1988A, p. 67.

been published by Petrucci in the first book of the *Motetti dela corona* (dated 17 August, 1514). *Bonitatem fecisti* was not a Vespers psalm, there are probably very few other settings of the text; I think the conclusion is almost inescapable that this was the piece that was performed at this special occasion, perhaps to add even greater musical glory to a service attendend by Isabella d'Este.

Carpentras' *Bonitatem fecisti* also brings up the question of the *second* psalm of Terce, lines 49–64 of Psalm 118 beginning with the words "*Memor esto verbi tui*" whose setting by Josquin was published in the same volume of the *Motetti dela corona*. In fact, these two motets are transmitted in series (*Bonitatem* following *Memor esto*) in every extant source in which they both appear; indeed two sources ascribe *Bonitatem* to Josquin.[3] This has long been known, but I don't think the liturgical connection of the texts has been noticed before. Instead, they have been related because of an anecdote told by Glarean, one of the several that have been interpreted to show that Josquin had some official connection with the court of Louis XII.

Glarean's story (related on p. 440 of the *Dodekachordon*) as we have always understood it is as follows. Josquin was promised a benefice by King Louis XII of France, but the king was slow to deliver on his promise, so Josquin composed a setting of the psalm verses of Psalm 118 beginning with the words "*Memor esto verbi tui servo tuo*," (be mindful of your word to your servant) which goaded the king into awarding the benefice. In gratitude, Josquin then composed a setting of the verses of Psalm 118 beginning "*Bonitatem fecisti cum servo tuo Domine*" (Lord, you have done a good thing with your servant). This implies that at some unspecified date, Josquin was in the employ of Louis XII. The problem is that a version of this story has also been told about an entirely different composer and king, and that while Josquin's authorship of *Memor esto* is secure, the source situation comes down on the side of Carpentras as the composer of *Bonitatem fecisti*.[4] As it happens, Glarean's tale of the com-

---

3 See OSTHOFF 1962A, vol. 1, p. 41–42. The two sources ascribing *Bonitatem* to Josquin are: Kassel, Murhard'sche Bibliothek der Stadt Kassel und Landesbibliothek, MSS 4.o Mus.24/1–4 and Saint Gall, Stiftsbibliothek, MS 463 ("Tschudi Liederbuch"). *Memor esto* appears by itself in a number of sources. For concordances, see CUMMINGS 1980, p. 447–8, to which can be added for *Memor esto* Buffalo, State University of New York, Music Library, MS M/O2/A3/p, No. 51.

4 The story concerning *Memor esto* is also told about the composer Dionisio Memmo and King Henry VIII (See OSTHOFF 1962A, p. 42). The two sources that ascribe the *Bonitatem*

position of *Memor esto* is curiously ambiguous in naming the person who was promised the benefice by Louis XII. We have assumed it to be Josquin, but in fact, Glarean does not say that specifically. He writes:

> In primis vero de Jodoci Pratensis, ut Cantorum coryphaei ingenio de quo non semel in prioribus. Is multa iucunda relatu fecisse dicitur, antequam in hominum noticiam venerit. Inter alia multa et hoc fuerunt: Francorum Regem Lutuichum XII. haud scio quod sacerdotium homini promisisse. Verum cum promissa leviter, ut in Regum aulis fieri solet, caderent, ibi commotum Jodocum psalmum composuisse, Memor esto verbi tui servo tuo, tanta maiestate ac elegantia, ut ad Cantorum collegium relatus ac deinde iusto iudicio excussus, admirationi omnibus fuerit. Regem suffuso pudore promissionem diutis differre non ausum, beneficium quod promiserat, prestitisse, Ibi vero virum, Principis liberalitatem expertum, continuo alterum per gratiarum actione orsum esse psalmum, Bonitatem fecisti cum servo tuo Domine. Verum inter duas Harmonias videre licet, quanto dubia premiorum spes plus urgeat, quam certo depositum beneficium. Neque enim paulo venustior est, meo quidem iudicatu, si affectus spectes prior quam posterior editio.[5]

Glarean does not actually say that it was Josquin who was promised the benefice. He says that "*a man*" or "*someone*" was promised the benefice ("*sacerdotium homini promisisse*"). And it was this man ("*virum*") who composed *Bonitatem fecisti* (by contrast, Glarean does say specifically that Josquin wrote *Memor esto*). When we consider that Carpentras is most likely the composer of the setting of *Bonitatem* that is always coupled with Josquin's *Memor esto*, a different interpretation of the story might be made. Carpentras was promised the benefice, and Josquin composed his motet in Carpentras' behalf

---

fecisti to Josquin (see note 3) are both late and German, and could have arrived at their ascriptions by interpreting Glarean exactly in the way we have done.

5   GLAREAN 1547, p. 440. Clement Miller translates this as follows:
"But first of all we speak about the genius of Josquin des Prez as chief of singers, whose skill we have mentioned frequently in the preceding. Before becoming generally known, he is said to have done many things. Among many others, the following story is told: Louis XII, the French king, had promised him some benefice, but when the promises remained unfulfilled, as is wont to happen in the courts of kings, Josquin was thereupon aroused and composed the Psalm *Memor esto verbi tui servo tuo* with such majesty and elegance that, when it was brought to the college of singers and then examined with strict justice, it was admired by everyone. The king, filled with shame, did not dare to defer the promise any longer and discharged the favor which he had promised; but then Josquin, having experienced the liberality of a ruler, immediately began, as an act of gratitude, another Psalm, *Bonitatem fecisti cum servo tuo Domine*. Yet between these two harmonies one can see how much more of a stimulus is the uncertain hope of a reward than is a securely established benefice. For in my opinion, if one considers the affections, the first composition is much more beautiful than the second." GLAREAN 1965, p. 271–272.

to shame the king into granting the favor to the other composer (the unexpected repetition of the opening words instead of the expected end of the *Gloria patri* certainly gives credence to this point of view). And it was Carpentras who in gratitude composed the other motet, which Glarean did not feel to be as effective as Josquin's. Furthermore, if it is true, we can be fairly specific as to when these compositions were written; Carpentras was a member of the French royal chapel from ca. June, 1512 – ca. November 1513.[6] Josquin was in Condé at this time, but until we can document every minute and day of his life there, a visit to the French court (or a visit of Carpentras to Condé) at some point cannot be ruled out entirely. Quite possibly, the two motets travelled to Italy with Carpentras when he returned to Rome.

Yet it does not seem as if the liturgical connection of the two texts had anything to do with the paired transmission of the works. For one thing, de Grassis states that the third (but not the second) psalm of Terce was sung in polyphony, so we cannot argue that *Memor esto* was performed on the same occasion as *Bonitatem fecisti*; furthermore, the Vatican source of Josquin's motet (Vatican City, Biblioteca Apostolica Vaticana, Fondo Cappella Sistina (Hereafter, CS), MS 16, copied during the reign of Leo X) does not include *Bonitatem* (in fact, there is no copy of Carpentras's motet in extant Sistine manuscripts). And the repetition of the opening words in place of the end of the *Gloria patri* in all sources of *Memor esto*, argues against a "liturgical" performance. That the two motets are connected in some sources may indeed be entireley a result of the circumstances of their composition as suggested above, remembered by Carpentras, and transmitted by him to Petrucci, the earliest source to couple the works.[7]

Another reference to polyphony during a papal ceremony is problematic. In his diary entry for the feast of St. John the Baptist,

---

[6] Carpentras had been a member of the papal chapel from ca. 1507. On 21 May, 1512, he announced his intention of leaving Rome, and he was appointed maestro of the papal chapel on 5 November 1513. During the interim, by his own admission, he was at the court of Louis XII. After a second stint in Rome, he returned to Avignon. See SHERR 1988A, p. 67

[7] That the first book of the *Motetti dela corona*, with its emphasis on French court composers (including the otherwise obscure Hilaire Bernoneau, master of the French chapel) should have followed so soon on the return of Carpentras to Rome is an interesting coincidence.

June 24, 1513, de Grassis makes a curious remark about the *Credo*. First of all, he does not like it that the *Credo* was used at all (it was supposed to be omitted, but Pope Leo X specifically ordered that it be included)[8], and to add to his displeasure, the singers did something strange:

> The Credo, which should not have been sung, was sung entirely because the pope wanted it, and it was badly done because the singers, not knowing the rules of the ceremonies, prepared the music with falso bordone [falsum bordonum], as it is called, and many murmured and others laughed as if at our ignorance, but the Pope wanted that which he should not have.[9]

This remark is of especial interest as the apparent first use of the term *falso bordone*.[10] But there are problems. For one thing, falso bordone is almost exclusively connected with the singing of psalms, yet here it is specifically connected with a *Credo*, so it is possible that de Grassis uses it here really to mean fauxbourdon (an extremely archaic technique in 1514). Yet in 1518, he used *falsum bordonum* to indicate what must have been a falso bordone performance of the *Miserere*; this is the first unequivocal appearance of the term.[11] And then there is the use of the verb *"praepararunt."* What can de Grassis have meant by that? If he had meant to say that the entire *Credo* was sung in falso bordone, why didn't he use the word *"cantarunt"* as he did in his description of the *Miserere*? Of course, he might have meant that, but it is just possible that he is referring to something else, something like the *Credo* in Example 1.

This is the beginning of Josquin's *Credo De tous biens plaine* as it appears in Petrucci's *Fragmenta Missarum* (Venice 1505). It begins by

---

8   This feast had been dropped from the calendar under Julius II and Leo, for obvious reasons (his own name and the Florentine connection) had reinstated it. Apparently, in the papal ceremonial, the *Credo* was not to be sung that day. However, when the feast was celebrated outside of the papal chapel, in St. John Lateran, the *Credo* was sung, much to de Grassis's displeasure (see BAV, Vat. lat. 5634, Part 2, fol. 344^v–345^r. In 1512, de Grassis got into a big fight with the canons of St. John Lateran over this issue; see BAV, Vat. lat. 12305, fol. 302^v–303^v).

9   "Credo quod non debuit dici fuit sic omnino volente papa dictum et male quia cantores nescientes regulas ceremoniarum praepararunt cantum per falsum bordonum sic appellatum et multi murmurarunt aliqui riserunt de nostra quasi ignorantia, sed papa sic voluit quod non debuit velle." (BAV, Vat. lat. 5636, fol. 43^v.) I am grateful to Karalee Strieby for help with with this and other translations of Latin.

10 See SHERR 1982A, p. 262, n. 33.

11 "In fine officii mihi non placavit quod cantores cantassent psalmum 'Miserere mei' per falsum bordonum licet devote, et Papa sic voluit." BAV, Vat. lat. 5636, fol. 232^v. See BRADSHAW 1978, p. 43–45.

setting the words *Patrem omnipotentem* in the melody of *Credo I* in the Superius (which continues to quote Credo I throughout the piece) in four voices with each note of the chant harmonized by a root position triad; in other words in something very like falso bordone.[12] It was so unusual to begin a polyphonic *Credo* in this way that this might have been what de Grassis had in mind when he uses "*praepararunt*" (in the sense of beginning, or getting ready to sing the mensural polyphony or *cantus figuratus*).

It would be nice to state further on the basis of this evidence that Josquin's *Credo* was the one sung at this occasion; no other *Credo* in the *Fragmenta* begins this way, and the piece also existed in the singers' library in what is one of the earliest sources for any sacred work by Josquin, CS 41, fols. 185^v–187^r (with the chant incipit only in the Superius). Certainty eludes us, but I would like to suggest that this *Credo* might have been a good one to choose for the celebration of the feast of St. John the Baptist. The reason lies in the *cantus firmus*, the well-known chanson *De tous biens plaine*. On looking at the liturgy for the Feast of St. John, one is immediately struck by the emphasis that is given to the womb in its texts (for instance, the Introit: *De ventre matris meae vocavit me Dominus*; the first reading from Isaiah 49: *Audite insulae et attendite populi de longe: Dominus ab utero vocavit me*; the Gradual: *Priusquam te formarem in utero*). This of course relates to the Biblical account of John's mother Elizabeth, a barren women who miraculously became (we would say in an English euphemism) "*big with child;*" and who indeed might have felt herself to be "*filled with all good things*" (de tous biens plaine). Now it is true that in modern French to use "*pleine*" to refer to a woman's pregnancy is extremely vulgar (it is used in connection with animals); yet a look at Godefroy shows that many of the word's derivatives had the meaning of "*fécondité*," so the implication of the text might well have been recognized. If I am right, then this is a bit more evidence that there was perhaps more to the choice of particular secular *cantus firmi* than we have thought, and that polyphonic settings employing them might have been chosen because of some relevance to a particular liturgical occasion.

Having presented this fantasy, I am obligated to present an opposing view suggested to me by Stanley Boorman.[13]

---

12 See BRADSHAW 1978.

XII

Speculations on repertory 109

If we look at the passage translating *"dictum"* literally, *"preparaunt"* as the pluperfect, and *"cantum"* as *"a song,"* we get:

> The Credo which should not have been said, was said, entirely because the Pope wished it, and badly, because the singers, not understanding the (changed) rules of the ceremonies had prepared a song in falso bordone (or faux-bourdon).

This might mean that the singers, not knowing or forgetting that the *Credo* had become part of the Mass of St. John the Baptist, had decided to perform something using the new technique of *falso bordone* (or the old technique of fauxbourdon) before the Offertory, which should have immediately followed the Gospel in this Mass (and was a spot in the ceremony where there was a lot of action that could be accompanied by music)[14], and actually began singing it, interfering with the recitation of the *Credo* by the celebrant, Pope, and congregation. This explanation has a more logical ring to it, but I think my previous interpretation is more fun.

Ceremony and Preserved Repertory

I wish to make an observation now about the works preserved in the manuscripts in the singer's library. Although we do not know exactly who chose these works, it is true that in 1564, Antonio Calasanz stated that it was the feeling of the singers that "the scribes should only copy music that has been approved by the College," so it seems likely that the singers themselves had control over the preservation of their repertory.[15] But did anything influence the order of pieces in manuscripts? True, some motet manuscripts and fascicles are ordered according to the liturgical year, but one would think that would not affect the order of settings of the Ordinary. Yet it has been noticed by Joshua Rifkin, and possibly others that a surprising number of Mass manuscripts beginning with the earliest

---

13 In private conversation at this Conference.
14 During the reign of Leo X there was no sermon at the Mass of St. John the Baptist. See O'MALLEY 1979, p. 15. It seems unlikely that the Offertory itself would have been performed in "falsum bordonum." The Offertory later became the traditional spot to interpolate motets into the Mass service (sung after the Offertory); see ADAMI 1711.
15 Calasanz was a papal singer. This statement appears at the end of a series of notes apparently taken at a meeting the singers had on July 24, 1564; see CS 680, fol. 98^r. For a discussion of others of his remarks, see SHERR 1987B.

(CS 14, CS 35), and consistently in those from the reign of Leo X on begin with one or more *Missa[e] de Beata Virgine*.[16] Is this just coincidence? Rifkin suggests that this may have something to do with the fact that the Sistine Chapel was dedicated to the Assumption, thus relating it to a liturgical occasion; a reasonable suggestion, except when confronted with the unimportance of the Feast of the Assumption to the papal ceremonial of the early 16th century.

It seems clear from a reading of Paris de Grassis that the Feast of the Assumption (which had been important to Sixtus IV, and was in fact the occasion on which the first Mass was celebrated in the newly built and decorated Sistine Chapel) figured only barely in the liturgical calendars of Julius II and Leo X, and in fact in Julius's reign had been superseded as a papal event by a Roman festival. As de Grassis says in his MS *Ceremoniale* of about 1505:

> In the Vigil of the feast of the Assumption of the Blessed Virgin Mary there used to be a papal vespers and solemn Mass on the day of the feast usually celebrated by a cardinal-priest, but this is not done in Rome today because of the solemn feast of the Roman citizens which they celebrate in the basilica of Santa Maria Maggiore.[17]

And indeed de Grassis's diaries for Julius's reign, when they mention the Feast of the Assumption at all, state that the pope travelled to Santa Maria Maggiore for the celebration of the Vigil and the Mass[18]; one major exeption (probably not coincidental) was on August 15, 1511, when the first half of Michelangelo's ceiling was revealed for the first time.[19] Leo X apparently only at the beginning of his pontificate celebrated the Vigil and Mass of the Assumption in the papal chapel (on August 15, 1513, see BAV, Vat. lat. 12274, fols. $73^r - 74^r$); or at least there are no more references to it as a pa-

---

16 Joshua Rifkin, in private communications to me.
17 "In vigilia assumptionis Beatae Mariae Virginis solebant esse vesperae papales et in die missa solemnis quam solebat presbiter cardinalis ... sed Romae hodie non fit propter festum solemne romanorum quod ipsi celebrant in dicta basilicha Sancte Mariae Maioris." (BAV, Vat. lat. 5634, vol. 2, fol. $345^v - 356$) See also PATRIZI, vol. 2, p. 432, where the exact same wording is used. A reading of Burkhard confirms this: there is no mention of the Assumption in the diaries from 1487–1504.
18 He did so in 1505 and in 1509. See Vat. lat. 5635, fol. $132^v - 133^v$; BAV, Vat. lat. 12305, fol. 2^v.
19 See BAV, Vat. lat. 12305, fol. $171^r - 171^v$. Julius may have wanted to start a tradition, however. He apparently was planning to celebrate the feast of the Assumption in the chapel in 1512, but the ceremony was cancelled because of bad weather (thunderstorms and hail). See BAV, Vat. lat. 12305, fol. 334^v: "Missa in dies assumptionis parata fuit sed non celebrata propter tempestate et grandinem inaudita." Julius died in February, 1513.

pal ceremony (there are, of course, many gaps in de Grassis's diaries for the reign of Leo X). But that does not mean that nothing happened in the chapel on that feast day. In fact, although the Assumption had lost its importance for the papal ceremonial, it remained important to two groups of people. The first of these were the singers themselves.

In 1517, de Grassis had occasion to mention the Feast of the Assumption, not because it was a papal ceremony, but for purely personal reasons. He had announced to Leo X his decision to resign his position as Master of Ceremonies to his nephew Ippolito de Grassis, and had further resigned to him the archpriestship he held in the church of St. Celsius. Ippolito apparently had just become a priest, and de Grassis was looking for a suitable church in which Ippolito could celebrate his first Mass; St. Celsius would not do (it was "nullorum capax"). At this point, the papal singers had a suggestion:

> *The singers, however, whose colleague Ippolito was, invited him to sing his first Mass on the day of the Assumption of the Virgin Mary in the papal chapel which is dedicated to the Assumption; because if another prelate is not named by the pope, this Mass may be sung by one of the singers on condition that the Sacristan is not present.*[20]

De Grassis checked with Leo, who gave his approval, and even attended the Mass (this clearly as a favor to de Grassis, who remarks proudly that "quasi omnes sicut in diebus quibus fit missa et capella ordinaria"). This incident points to a personal relationship the singers had to the Feast of the Assumption, specifically that one of their number had the right to celebrate the Mass itself on that day (it also implies that Ippolito de Grassis had been a singer, although there is no documentary confirmation of this). In fact, in his *Ceremoniale* of the time of Julius II, de Grassis already hints that the Assumption was important to the singers, and also to another class of people who were normally excluded from the Sistine chapel entirely:

> *It should be known, however, that under Sixtus IV who built the palace chapel, it was instituted that women, who otherwise in general were not permitted to enter the palace chapel and attend divine services, could be given free entry to attend the first vespers*

---

20 "Cantores autem quorum ipsi Hippolitus est collega, eum invitaverunt ut in die Assumptionis Virginis Marie missam novam suam cantaret in capella papali quae est dicata assumptioni, quia si alius prelatus non sit a Sua Sanctitate deputatus, missa ipsa per aliquem ex ipsis cantoribus cantaretur, ex quo sacrista non est presens." (BAV, Vat. lat. 5636, fol. 194^r).

through the second vespers inclusively that is solemnly sung there [ie. including Mass], and it is said that he gave a plenary indulgence to all who were visiting the chapel at this time. Indeed, it was usual for Pope Sixtus along with cardinals to attend the divine service, but his successors stopped attending. The singers, however, did not stop singing both vespers and the Mass, and women did not stop following the old custom.[21]

Thus, for one day a year, women had a chance to attend a Mass in the Sistine chapel, and that day was the very day that the singers (at least in the reign of Leo X) had the right to have one of their number celebrate. The day was further the day of the Feast to which the chapel (apparently) had always been dedicated. Given the control the singers could have had over their manuscripts, is it now so strange that so many of them begin with a Mass that would have been perfect for this very special and personal occasion?[22] It would appear that the papal singers considered themselves as we consider them, related in some way to the edifice that was the Cappella Sistina.

---

21 "Sciendum tamen est quod a Sixto Quarto qui maiorem capellam in palatio extruxit institutum fuit ut mulieres quibus antea communiter sacram palatii capellam religionis et rei divinae audiendae gratia ingredi non licebat, a primis ad secundas inclusive vesperas quae ibi solemniter cantantur libere ingredi possint quibus etiam ac omnibus eam capellam tunc visitantibus indulgentiam plenariam concessis se dicitur. Quin etiam ipse, Sixtus papa cum cardinalibus ire ad rem divinam solitus erat, sed successores eius deinde cessarunt. Cantores tamen ab utrarunque vesperarum et missae cantu, mulieres quoque ad additu et cultu pristino non cessarunt." This is confirmed by Jacopo Gherardi da Volterra's description of the first Mass in the chapel on August 15, 1483: "Die solemni assumptionis Mariae Virginis in coelum, qui evenit in sabbato processit pontifex in novum maius sacellum ibique divine rei interfuit [...] pontifex indulgentiam sacellum visitantibus pronuntiavit etiam feminis [...] Cum tota urbe percrebuisset rumor indulgentiam ad sacellum instauratum etiam feminis concessarum mirum dictu quam celeriter tota civitas commota fuerit prae multitudine vix iri aut exiri poterat nec cessavit frequens concursus priusquam noctis medium transactum fuisset." See GHERARDI, p. 121–122.
22 Manuscripts that begin (or originally began) with a *Missa da Beata Virgine* are: CS 14, 35, 16, 26, 45, 55.

Ceremony and Practical Matters of Performance

A Mass in the papal chapel in the presence of the pontiff in the 16th century was extremely elaborate, and was governed by strict procedures embodied in the papal ceremonial and entrusted to the care of the papal master of ceremonies. The singers were required to sing the texts of the Proper and Ordinary either in chant, polyphony (*cantus figuratus*) or improvised polyphony over chant (*contrapunctus*) — the ceremonials never specify which — at the same time that the celebrant read those texts, although they may have had some choice when it came to the performances of motets. But although a study of the liturgy as it was celebrated in Masses in the presence of the pope will not answer most questions about repertory, it does provide some insights into the practical matters of how the music actually sounded. The key here is provided by the one aspect of papal liturgy that was unique; the presence of the Vicar of Christ.

The pope's participation in a papal Mass, even when he did not celebrate, was an active one, and this constitutes the element of the papal ceremonial with real effect on musical performance. For the pope was required to read (at his own pace, of course) most of the major texts of the Proper and Ordinary at the same time as the celebrant read the text and the singers sang the text, and further, on certain occasions had to move from the throne to the faldstool in the middle of the chapel and back again. This in itself would mean little, were it not abundantly clear from the writings of people concerned with ceremony and the singers' part in it from the 16th to the 18th century, that timing of the music to coincide with papal actions was crucial. The singers had to be constantly aware of the speed at which the pope read certain key texts of the Mass, they had to know when he was standing or sitting, they even had to be concerned with the amount of time it took him to get to the faldstool and back again. In the 18th century, the maestro di capella had the job of coordinating the singing with papal actions, indicating to the choir when they should start, when to stop, and when to slow down or speed up. Andrea Adami in his *Osservazioni per ben regolare il Coro della Cappella Pontificia* (Rome 1711), provides many examples of the way this coordination was supposed to operate in his day (and there is reason to believe that things had not changed very much in this regard from the 16th century).

In fact, one of de Grassis's major concerns is that the music intended to accompany liturgical actions last for *precisely* the length of the action. This concern is expressed time and time again in the diaries and ceremonials. When the pope read sections of the Mass or had to move from the throne to the faldstool, it was de Grassis's job to see that the singers did not finish singing before the pope finished reading or before he had reached the faldstool, and it is clear from his writings that he controlled the situation by communicating with the singers, sometimes telling them to repeat sections, and sometimes by warning them that they would have to sing slowly in order to take up enough time.[23]

The *Credo*, in particular, created a problem of timing with regard to the words "*Et incarnatus est ex Maria Virgine, et homo factus est*", because various people in the chapel had to kneel at different times. In his manuscript *Ceremoniale*, de Grassis devotes a very long chapter to a description of the Mass of the Circumcision, as a general guide for what the celebrant must do during a Mass in the presence of the pope.[24] Every action, every text, every motion of the celebrant is described as the Mass is carried forth from its beginning to

---

[23] De Grassis's concern with timing has led me recently to posit that there was a Roman motet tradition of polyphonic settings of the Lenten tract *Domine non secundum peccata*, performed at the proper place in the liturgy precisely because certain words in settings by chapel composers are set off in a very particular way; and these words are the very ones singled out by de Grassis as cues for papal actions so that there would not be silence in the chapel after the action was completed. The problem was caused because the pope had to move to the faldstool and kneel during the singing of the last sentence of the tract, the verse "Adiuva nos", and then had to return to the throne before the next liturgical action began. What de Grassis says is that the pope should begin to move towards the faldstool when the singers sing "cito anticipent nos" (the last three words of the second sentence of the text — the second part of all polyphonc settings), and that he should move back to the throne when the singers sing "propter nomen tuum" (the last three words of the text). As it happens, these words are generally set off in the settings of the Tract produced by Vatican composers from the fifteenth and early sixteenth centuries. De Grassis also says that the singers should be sure to sing "propter nomen tuum" slowly in order to give the pope enough time to get back to the throne in time for the Gospel and so there would not be silence in the chapel before he reached the throne. We must assume then that the words "propter nomen tuum" would always have been sung slowly, even when they are written in sesquialtera proportion, which always suggests to us a faster tempo with regard to the preceding sections. See SHERR 1988B.

[24] "De ceremoniis quibus solus celebrans utitur in sua missa," BAV, Vat. lat. 5634, vol. 2, fol. $51^r - 67^v$.

its end. During the *Credo*, the celebrant has to be cognizant both of what the pope is doing and of what the singers do. The key words, "*Et incarnatus est ... et homo factus est*", required various responses by the celebrant: kneeling when he says them, listening for when the pope says them and remaining motionless, and bowing (while seated) towards the altar when the words are sung, which is assumed to occur after the Pope had finished reading the *Credo* and had sat down. The pope, reading the *Credo* with his assistant cardinals, also knelt when he came to those words (which de Grassis expected to be said after the celebrant had said them). But the celebrant also has to listen for the words to be sung.[25] And so did the rest of the congregation, for it was here that they were to kneel. The implication in de Grassis that the singers sing the "*Et incarnatus*" after the pope has sat down, is made explicit in the description given by Adami which, although from the 18th century, deals here with a problem that had remained unchanged since the 16th.[26] The implications of these descriptions are clear: the "*Et incarnatus est*" has to be understood, and it must be reached by the singers after the pope has finished reading the entire *Credo*. And this obviously applied to performance of polyphony as well as chant, although polyphonic performance sometimes caused difficulties.[27]

In fact, the necessity of making clear the beginning of the "*Et incarnatus est*" was not ignored by most composers of polyphony. It is probably not a coincidence, for example, that there are many Renaissance Masses in which the "*Et incarnatus*" is a separate section,

---

25 "Et cum incipit dicere 'Et incarnatus est de spiritu sancto ex Maria virgine, et homo factus est', manens in eisdem modo et loco genuflectat usque ad terram cum suis ministris donec omnia supra dicta verba dixerit, deinde surgat et similiter prosequatur usque ad finem videlicet 'Et vitam venturi seculi, Amen', quae verba dicendo, signet se a fronte, ad pectus, et sic stet quo usque papa dixerit totum simbolum et sederet, et similiter ipse celebrans tunc sedeat cum mitra. Et nota quod cum papa et cardinales cum eo dicentes praedictum versum genuflectunt, ipse celebrans cum suis ministris non genuflectit sed omnino immotus manet. Dum autem cantant supradictum versum, videlicet 'Et incarnatus est de spiritu sancto ex Maria, etc', celebrans sedens iungit manus et vertit caput cum mitra versus ad altare et caput profunde inclinet donec sit finitus versiculus 'Et homo factus est', et iterum ut prius manet."
26 "Avverta il signor maestro di non far dire "Et incarnatus est" fin che il papa, terminata il Credo, non si sia posto a sedere insieme con gli altri cardinali che assistono al soglio perché di poi può farlo proseguire con qualche solicitudine." ADAMI 1711, p. 9.
27 On at least two occasions, de Grassis complains that there was difficulty in understanding the words "Et incarnatus est", a difficulty that only can be ascribed to a polyphonic rendition of the *Credo*. See SHERR 1982A, esp. p. 255.

and that even when it is not (and there are many Masses in which this is true), it is generally preceded and/or followed by such a strong cadence that it *could* be treated as a separate section. This was true in and out of Rome of course (as was the custom of kneeling at those words), but I would suggest that the singers there, confronted with the commanding and pedantic presence of the master of ceremonies and the necessity of not making liturgical mistakes in the presence of the Vicar of Christ were under special pressure and would have made an extra effort in performance to highlight the text (even though they clearly did not always succeed), either by slowing down before and after it, or perhaps actually by coming to a halt.

Even more important in Rome was the necessity of not reaching the "*Et incarnatus*" before the pope had finished reading the *Credo* and had sat down. This has clear implications for tempo. It would mean, for instance, that if the *Credo* was in chant, that the first part of it would have been sung slowly, and that the tempo of a polyphonic rendition would also have to be adjusted constantly depending on what the pope was doing. As it turns out—and this might be the reason polyphonic *Credos*, even as single movements, were popular in the papal chapel—most polyphonic settings up to "*Et incarnatus est*" were long enough (in fact, it is amazing how many of them are long enough) so that the singers could be assured that the timing would always work out, but even so the tempo could not be too fast.[28] And, since it is virtually impossible to listen to music while you are reciting a text at the same time, this aspect of the papal ceremonial means that the pope, at whom presumably all of the music was directed, did not get to hear much of it during Mass. That would not have bothered someone like Julius II, but Leo X was a different matter. Leo, of course, was the first pope to have a corps of private singers who could sing anything for him at anytime he wanted it.

Strangely though, the Sistine chapel itself was perhaps not the most ideal place for the performance of music. In 1615, Paul V began construction in the Quirinale Palace of a chapel built on the pro-

---

28 A little experiment will show that the tempos picked by some modern groups would have caused serious problems in the papal chapel. An obvious candidate for a slow tempo under these conditions would be the *Credo* of Josquin's *Missa D'Ung aultre amer*, which does exist in a Vatican manuscript (CS 41).

portions of the Sistine (the Cappella Paolina), and we have an interesting document recording some advice that the papal singers wished to give to the architects.[29]

> May 3, 1615. *Before Mass there was a meeting. Signor Paolo Facchonio, maestro di cappella, told us that there will be built in the new chapel in Monte Cavallo [The Quirinale Palace] a cantoria just like the one in the Vatican [and because] that cantoria is far away both from the pope and the celebrant, also, because of the noise of the congregation, it is extremely difficult to make responses [to the pope and celebrant] since they can barely be heard, it was decided by unanimous consent that the maestro will negotiate with the Congregation [of prelates who were overseeing the construction] to see that [the cantoria] is placed 12 or 16 palmi closer to the altar, that it is made larger, that the balustrade is pushed further out and is larger, and that the ceiling is smooth without any carvings, so that the music can make good effect.* [30]

The singers in 1615, therefore, had long been aware of the problems of coordination of music and liturgical action and that they had become dissatisfied with the solutions they had to adopt in the Sistine Chapel. So they suggested that the cantoria of the Quirinale Cappella Paolina be placed closer to the altar and papal throne, and in fact, that is exactly what happened.

Even more fascinating, however, is the second part of the singer's complaint about the ceiling of the cantoria and the extension of the balustrade. Here they seem really to be concerned with acoustics. The cantoria of the Sistine is a rectangular box with a carved ceiling. Now, I know very little about acoustics, but I do know that a rectangular box is more likely to hold sound in than to project it forward (that is why curved shell structures are so often used to project the sounds of orchestras). I am not sure about the real effect of the ceiling, but the singers clearly thought that the carvings somehow trapped the sound, and they therefore asked for a smooth ceiling in the new cantoria.

Unfortunately, unlike the forms and colors of renaissance paintings, the actual sound of this music is lost for ever; we can never

---

29 I want to thank Jean Lionnet for giving me this reference.
30 "Prima della Messa si fece congregatione. Il signor Paolo Facchonio, Maestro di Cappella, proporse come in Monte Cavallo ne la cappella nova si farà un coro come in quella di San Pietro, per essere il coro lontano e da N.S. e dal celebrante, per il rumore ancora del popolo, da grandissimo impedimento per rispondere che appena si sentono, con consenso di tutti viva voce il signor maestro tratarà nella Congregatione di veder che si facia 12 o 16 palmi più in su acanto l'altare et più largo e la ballagrostrata più in fora et più largo et il ciello in nicchia lissa senza lavoro alcuno perché la musica faccia bono effecto." DS 34, fol. 18^r.

recapture renaissance polyphony the way Michelangelo's colors have been recaptured by restorers, and musical notation provides only the bare skeleton of musical practice. We will never hear the music as it was performed then, but we can try to appoximate it and the glory can still be imagined; even dry documents permit in the mind's eye and ear a reconstruction of the full visual and aural effect of the Papal Majesty in the Cappella Sistina.

Speculations on repertory

Example 1

Literature

ADAMI 1711	Adami, Andrea, detto "Il Bolsena", *Osservazioni per ben regolare il Coro dei Cantori della Cappella Pontificia* [...]. Roma 1711 (repr. ed. Giancarlo Rostirolla, Lucca 1988 = *Musurgiana*, vol. 1).
BRADSHAW 1978	Bradshaw, Murray C., *The Falsobordone. A Study in Renaissance and Baroque Music.* Neuhausen-Stuttgart 1978 (*Musicological Studies and Documents* 34).
CUMMINGS 1980	Cummings, Anthony M., *A Florentine Sacred Repertory from the Medici Restoration (Manuscript II.I.232 of the Biblioteca nazionale centrale, Firenze).* Diss. Princeton University 1980.
GHERARDI	*Il Diario Romano di Jacopo Gherardi da Volterra.* Ed. Enrico Carusi. Cittá di Castello 1904 (*Rerum Italicarum Scriptores, nuova edizione*, 23, 3).
GLAREAN 1547	Glarean, Heinrich, *Dodekachordon.* Basel 1547.
GLAREAN 1965	Glarean, Heinrich, *Dodekachordon.* Trans. Clement A. Miller. American Institute of Musicology 1965 (*Musicological Studies and Documents* 6).
O'MALLEY 1979	O'Malley, John W., *Praise and Blame in Renaissance Rome.* Durham, N.C. 1979.
OSTHOFF 1962A	Osthoff, Helmuth, *Josquin Desprez.* 2 vol., Tutzing 1962.
PATRIZI	*L'Oeuvre de Patrizi Piccolomini ou le Cérémonial Papal de la Première Renaissance.* Ed. Marc Dykmans S.I., 2 vol., Città del Vaticano 1980/82 (*Studi e Testi* 293–294).
SHERR 1982A	Sherr, Richard, *The Singers of the Papal Chapel and Liturgical Ceremonies in the Early Sixteenth Century: Some Documentary Evidence.* In: *Rome in the Renaissance. The City and the Myth. Papers of the Thirteenth Annual Conference of the Center for Medieval & Early Renaissance Studies.* Ed. Paul A. Ramsey. Binghamton, NY 1982, p. 249–264.
SHERR 1987B	Sherr, Richard, *Performance Practice in the Papal Chapel during the 16th Century.* In: *Early Music* 15, 1987, p. 453–462.
SHERR 1988A	Sherr, Richard, *The Membership of the Chapels of Louis XII and Anne de Bretagne in the Years Preceding their Deaths.* In: *The Journal of Musicology* 6, 1988, p. 60–82.
SHERR 1988B	Sherr, Richard, *Illibata Dei Virgo Nutrix and Josquin's Roman Style.* In: JAMS 41. 1988, p. 434–464.

XIII

Performance practice in the Papal Chapel during the 16th century

The suggestion was recently made in this journal by Jean Lionnet that polyphony in the Papal Chapel was normally performed by soloists during the 17th century.[1] My purpose in this article is to consider similar questions of performance practice for the 16th century, by examining documents from that period (often unspecific and ambiguous) in conjunction with some from the 18th century (generally specific and unambiguous).

A 16th-century memorandum preserved in the archives of the Cappella Sistina in the Vatican Library appears to contain notes taken by Antonio Calasanz, one of those who attended a meeting of the papal singers on 24 July 1564. The purpose of the meeting, which was called by the *maestro di cappella*, was to reinstitute certain practices that had been usual in the papal choir but had fallen into disuse (hence, practices that could have been followed in the early 16th century). One of these concerned the way the singers grouped themselves around the music lectern:

Antiquitatus ad decantandam musicam cantores prout D. Decanus petulit costruebant [ante legium seu facistorium hoc videlicet modo: – in the margin] suprani ad sinistram et contralti ad dexteram prope legium seu facistorium, et tenores ad sinistram retro suprani et bassi ad dexteram retro contralti.[2]

Formerly, when music was sung, the singers, as the dean requested, stood in front of the lectern in this way: sopranos on the left and contraltos on the right of the lectern, and tenors on the left at the back of the sopranos and basses on the right at the back of the contraltos.

This is, of course, precisely the grouping that would be expected, for it exactly mirrors the layout of the parts in the manuscripts. As well as providing documentary confirmation, even of the obvious, it also explains various references in the *Diarii Sistini*[3] to the fining of contraltos for not turning the page in time.[4] But the contraltos seem to have had several specific functions, for Calasanz went on to discuss another practice whose neglect was causing difficulties:

Officium contraltorum erat in servire pro ebdomad[ari]us et querere divina officia diei [illegible word] *tam in cantu plano quam figurato.*

The office of the contraltos was to act as the hebdomadarius, and to find out the [pieces to be sung during] Divine Office of the day, whether in chant or in polyphony.

He added that because the contraltos had not been carrying out this duty there were daily errors and incidents in the chapel.[5] Chapter XV of the 1545 Constitution of the Chapel also refers to the contraltus hebdomadarius, stating specifically that he was responsible for indicating which books were to be put on the lectern.[6] The *Diarii Sistini* testify further to the special function of the contraltos by recording times when they failed in their duties.[7] The hebdomadarius was normally the person chosen on a weekly basis to celebrate the liturgy; in the case of singers, the term appears to refer to the person who chose the polyphony and made sure that the correct order of pieces was followed. Why this person had to be a contralto, however, is not clear.

The instruction 'Let this custom be observed by the most senior and expert [singers]' was added in the margin beside another of Calasanz's comments:

Antiquitatus in decantanda musica, vox que primo incipiebat [cuiuslibet vocis—in margin] *videlicet supranus, tenor, altus, vel bassus intonabat ad libitum suum.*[8]

Formerly when singing music, the voice which began first whatever it is—that is, soprano, tenor, alto or bass—intoned as he wished.

Though it is not at first clear what is meant by 'intoning', it is most likely that Calasanz is talking about setting the pitch level (the main function of an intonation) both in chant and in polyphony (hence, his use of the general term 'musica', instead of 'cantus planus' or 'cantus figuratus'). When they performed in the Sistine Chapel, the papal choir sang without the accompaniment of instruments. There was thus no

XIII

1 The canonization of Carlo Borromeo, 1610: interior of St Peter's, Rome. Engraving by G. Maggi (Biblioteca Angelica, Rome)

way of giving the pitch to the choir (through an instrumental toccata, for instance), and the solution seems to have been to allow whoever began to choose the pitch level. This is implied also by a decision recorded after an apostolic visitation of the choir in 1630:

Quando si ha da cominciare a cantare, ciascuno lasci cominciare il più vecchio, quale se non intonarà bene, doverà essere punctato con rigore.[9]

When the singing begins, everyone will allow the oldest singer [of his voice part] to begin, and if he does not intone well, he should be severely fined.

18th-century documents clarify the meaning of 'intoning', and demonstrate that the pitch level was determined by the first singer, who began without any reference to an absolute pitch. The problems that could arise concerning pitch level were addressed by Matteo Fornari, who in the midst of a general discussion about castrati in the Papal Chapel attempted to explain why there were no contralto castrati in the choir.[10] The reason he gave was that their level tessitura was not low enough, so that:

Nelle cantilene dove i contralti danno il primo regolamento della voce al rimanente del coro, si prendesse il tuono dai contralti non naturale, questo riuscirebbe alto in forma si disadatta alle altre parti che renderebbe, anziché armonia, una notabile confusione, et così derogherebbesi affatto a quella gravità ecclesiastica con cui si è sempre conservato il canto della pontificia cappella.[11]

In the music where the contraltos give the first indication of the pitch to the rest of the choir, if one were to take the pitch from the unnatural contraltos [castrati], this would turn out to be so high in such bad relation to the other parts that it would cause notable confusion instead of harmony, and would thus detract from the ecclesiastical gravity which the music of the pontifical chapel has always maintained.

Another treatise, the *Istruzione per gl'officiali della cappella pontificia*, contains a passage that must refer to the same problem; that of the singers starting at an inappropriate pitch level:

Alli 28 di Gennaro 1718 fu stabilito che in qualsivoglia cantilena o di canto figurato o di canto fermo, quando si prendesse la voce troppo alta o troppa bassa, e conoscendo non poterla seguitare, sia obligato l'anziano che prende la voce a calare o crescere, ma prima deve avvisare il coro. Quando poi entrassero tutte le parti assieme, o fosse nel canto fermo, sia obligato l'anziano de' bassi sempre dando prima l'avviso al coro, e non facendolo sia sotto posto al punto.[12]

On 28 January 1718, it was decided that in whatever music whether in chant or polyphony, when the pitch chosen is too high or too low, and realizing that he cannot continue, the senior singer who chose the pitch is obliged to lower or raise [it], but first he must advise the choir. When all the parts enter together [that is, at the same time], or in chant, the senior bass is obliged, always first advising the choir, and if he does not do this let him be fined.

References in the *Diarii Sistini* of the early 18th century (including Diary 147 of 1728 compiled by Fornari himself) also show that the word 'intonare' is to be read in its usual sense. All pieces, whether chant or polyphony, apparently began with an intonation; that is, the senior bass intoned the beginning of the chant[13] and the senior singer of whichever part began the polyphony sang the first few notes as a means of giving the pitch (rather than humming or singing a single note as might be done today); this was followed by a new start from the beginning either by the whole choir for chant or by all the singers of the appropriate part for polyphony.[14] This seems to be the only explanation for problems such as that recorded in the *Diarii* for 2 November 1700:

L'Antiano, nel principiare la Gloria, non tenne la prima nota, la quale valeva due battute, benché da suoi compagni fosse stata tenuta giusta, onde rese qualche sconcerto, & perciò – si punta solo il Signor Gagliardi.[15]

The senior singer, when beginning the Gloria, did not hold the first note which was worth two beats [long enough], although it was held correctly by his companions; this caused some confusion and therefore only Signore Gagliardi [the senior contralto] was fined.

The reference to 'battute' suggests that this was 'measured music' or polyphony, and the senior contralto must have begun by singing the actual music; furthermore, there would have been no way of knowing if he had held the first note for a different length of time than the others if he had not sung it first and they followed. Another reference is even clearer:

Nel principiar la Messa, cioè il primo Chirie, toccava a principiare alli signori tenori. Il signor Mezzoni, toccando a lui a pigliare come primo anziano, invece di principiar Chirie disse A quasi volesse dire Amen o Alleluia, per tale inavertenza si punta il signor Mazzoni 05.[16]

At the beginning of the Mass, that is, the first Kyrie, the tenors were to begin. It fell to Signor Mazzoni to choose [the pitch], as he was the senior singer, [but] instead of beginning with 'Kyrie', he sang 'A', almost as if he wanted to sing 'Amen' or 'Alleluia'. For such negligence, Signor Mazzoni is fined 5 [baiocchi].

Similarly, on 8 September 1728, four sopranos were fined:

Per aver alterato il tuono della voce presa dall'anziano al mottetto, che cagionò molto stonamento.[17]

For having altered the pitch taken from the senior singer in the motet, which caused much disharmony.

Altering a pitch given as a single note would hardly cause 'disharmony', but repeating at a different pitch the opening of the piece would surely be noticed. And it would be easier to alter the pitch if a piece was actually begun anew, rather than for the alteration to occur as other singers joined a piece that had already begun.

There was sometimes confusion when singers forgot who was to perform the intonation.

Avendo presa al motetto O magnum il Sig. Baldini anziano la voce, la presse nell'istesso tempo ancora il Sig. Resi sottoanziano un tuono più basso, di modo che obligò l'anziano a cedere, con qualche sconcerto; ondo è puntato il Sig. Resi b. 20.[18]

The senior singer Signor Baldini, having begun to give the pitch [that is, begun singing] for the motet O magnum, the vice-senior Signor Resi began singing at the same time a whole step lower and forced the senior singer to stop singing, which caused certain confusion; for which Signor Resi is fined 20 baiocchi.

Nell'agnus dei della messa a 4 voce del Pelestrina, dovendo il Sig. Bastianelli anziano de'contralti pigliar la prima voce al cenno del sig. maestro, e avendo negligente tardato, pigliò il Sig. Mattia la voce col quale si seguitò la cantilena, ma per avere il Sig. Bastianelli sopragiunta la voce dissonante, si punta il medemo S. Bastianelli bai. 20.[19]

In the Agnus Dei of the 4-voice Mass by Palestrina, Signor Bastianelli, senior contralto, was supposed to give the pitch at the cue of the maestro, but as he waited negligently, Signor Mattia gave this pitch with which the singing continued. But because Signor Bastianelli added a dissonant pitch, he is fined 20 baiocchi.

A reference for 6 April [Good Friday] 1703 concerns the occasion mentioned by Fornari when all the parts entered together and the responsibility for intoning fell on the senior bass. The piece being performed was the *falsobordone* setting of the *Improprerii* by Palestrina.

Incominciato l'Improprii, cioè Popule meus a due chori a 8. finito che hebbe il primo choro il primo verso, attacò il secundo choro l'altro verso Quia eduscit te, pigliando la medesima voce che lasciò il primo choro, dove dovevano pigliare nel lasciar che fece il primo choro una quarta sopra. Ma l'errore lo fece il basso che si pigliò male l'intonatione, dunque per tale errore vien puntato solo il signor Spinacciati 20.[20]

We began the Improprerii, that is 'Popule meus' *a* 8 for two choirs. The first choir had sung the first verse, the second choir began the next verse 'Quia eduscit te', taking the same pitch on which the first choir ended, instead of beginning a 4th higher than the ending pitch of the first choir. The error

2 Detail from illus.1, showing the five singers

was made by the bass who sang the intonation incorrectly, therefore for that error only Signor Spinacciati will be fined 20 [baiocchi].

An incident that occured on 1 March 1700 points again to the duties of the senior singer of each voice, and also to those of the contraltus hebdomadarius, with regard to repertory.

Questa mattina per esser giornata feriale, è solito cantarsi, solamente il Sanctus e l'Agnus Dei. Il contralto edomadario inavertentemente prende la messa a quatro intitolata Missa paris vocibus di Vincenzo Pellegrini, con un mezzo soprano, due tenori, et un basso. Terminato il Prefatio, toccava a principiare il Sanctus alla parte del tenore, la quale era situata nel luogo del contralto, e per esser la chiave in terza riga, il suddetto, susponendo che fosse la sua parte, la principiò come anziano in voce di contralto, dal che ne nacque grandissimo sconcento, onde per tale inavertanza non essendo mai solito cantarsi niuna Messa senza contralto, e per essere l'errore molto sensibile, il puntatore in vigore del capitolo 3. a delli novi regolamenti, punta il Signor Gagliardi 20.[21]

This morning, since it was ferial feast day, it is the custom to sing only the Sanctus and Agnus Dei. The contraltus hebdomadarius, without thinking, chose the Mass for four voices entitled 'Missa paris vocibus' by Vincenzo Pellegrini, with a mezzo-soprano, two tenors and one bass. After the Preface, the tenor part was supposed to begin the Sanctus, which was placed [in the choirbook] in the position of the altus,[22] but because the clef was on the third line, the above mentioned [contralto], thinking that it was his part began it, as [he was] the senior contralto. Great disharmony came from this mistake, it never having occurred that a Mass was sung without the contralto part, and because the error was very obvious, the punctator, according to Chapter 3 of the new regulations, fined Signor Gagliardi 20 [baiocchi].

What this seems to mean is that Signor Gagliardi had momentarily forgotten that he had chosen a Mass *a voci pari*, in which the contralto part appeared on the upper left of the choirbook in the space usually reserved for the soprano. Instead, following the tradition whereby the senior singer of the part that began the piece 'intoned' the beginning, he started to read from the normal place for the contralto part (upper right), which in this case was occupied by one of the tenor lines. But the real problem here (that the Sanctus was sung without the contralto part) is best explained by assuming it was being performed with one singer on a part, so that when the one contralto began singing the tenor part, there was no other contralto to sing the correct part.

The question of solo performance is, of course, the crux of the matter. The use of the word 'intonare' implies continuation by a choir, and the fact that countless fines are recorded in the 18th-century *Diarii* to groups of singers on the same part for making mistakes in the performance of polyphony suggests strongly that choral performance was by then the rule.[23] Occasionally, however, the pattern of fines suggests performance by soloists: this tends to relate to *terzi e quarti* (trio and quartet sections).[24] As Lionnet has pointed out, the *Diarii Sistini* and other documents from the 17th century are full of references to *terzi e quarti*, phrased in such a way as to indicate that they were sung by soloists. Mention is made of fines for singers who refused to sing them, and exhortations that the Master of the Chapel be very careful in choosing the right singers.[25] Corroboration that this continued in the 18th century comes from Matteo Fornari who described the process of auditioning for a bass for the Sistine Chapel in 1737:

Invocato dal signor maestro lo spirito santo, si chiamono uno per volta dal custode li concorrenti videlicet per la voce di basso, e fatto salire sul coro dove si ritrovano alcuno signori cantori, stando gli altri a sedere al bancone dell'emminentissimi cardinali. Si trova un terzo col basso, e gli si fa cantare in concerto.[26]

The Custode calls the applicants for the position of bass one by one, and has them ascend to the singers' box where a few other singers are, the rest of the singers sit on the benches reserved for the cardinals. A trio is found to sing with the bass, and they sing in concert.

Since the point of the audition was to judge the applicant's voice, the *terzo* must have consisted of soloists: presumably it allowed the singers to hear how well the applicant blended with others.[27]

But can this have any relevance for the 16th century? Although we must proceed cautiously in attempting to extrapolate backwards from a period of the papal choir's decadence (the 18th century) to the period of its greatest glory, Calasanz's 1564 statements concerning the contraltus hebdomadarius and the intonations are a direct link between those two centuries, and imply that those practical matters of performance had not changed. On the question of solo performance in the 16th century, however, there is evidence both to support and to contradict the hypothesis defended by Lionnet. First of all, Calasanz's use of 'intonare' implies that some sort of choral performance was contemplated.[28] On the other hand, there is evidence that the use of solo singers was also an option.

For instance, one document shows that in music for double and triple choir in Rome in the late 16th century, at least one of the choirs was made up of soloists (as in Venice).[29] This is demonstrated through a dispute the Master of the Chapel had with one of the singers, Giovanni Santos, about a botched performance of the motet during the Mass of the Feast of St James on 24 July 1594, when the singers went, as they did every year, to sing at San Giacomo degli Spagnoli. Santos took charge of distributing the parts for the motet without consulting the Master, and since the Master (who had to conduct the performance) thought the motet was for two choirs when in fact it was for three, 'notable confusion' arose. The Master accused Santos of usurping his authority to control the music and demanded that he be fined. Santos claimed that the Master knew about the motet since he had already sent

quattro cantori all'organo per cantar il motetto.[30]

four singers to the organ to sing the motet.

As the Master thought the motet was for double choir, it follows that one of those choirs had to be made up of soloists. And as only 23 singers were present, there cannot have been more than two on a part in the other two of the three choirs, once the problem had been

XIII

3 Coronation of Charlemagne (Vatican Palace, Stanza dell'Incendio, fresco by Raphael, Penni and others (Monumenti, Musei e Gallerie Pontificie)

resolved.[31] Similarly, in his autograph of a setting of the *Improprerii* to be used in the Cappella Giulia in the 1570s, Palestrina carefully indicated the names of the eight singers who were to make up the two 'choruses'.[32]

It also appears that soloists were used in the performance of the *terzi* and *quarti* included within the music for five and more parts that was usual in the late 16th century. On 31 May 1583, the punctator of the College of Singers noted the following incident:

Ad Benedictus D. Cesar Bellucius incepit canere, quia D. Marinus Luppus ei precipit. D. Johannes Baptista Martinus eciam ipse cantavit, quia D. Paulus de Magistris cani ei dixit, adeo quod ambo derelinguere nec cedere alter alteri voluerunt. D. Cesar Bellucius ordinem capelle nesiebat, sed D. [Marinus Luppus – crossed out] Johannes Baptista Martinus dolose egit, ut D. Marinus retullit, quia multocies precipit ut canaret et nunquam canere voluit, hodie quia D. Marinus dixit D. Cesari cani, ipse cantare voluit; unde post Benedictus multa verba inter eos habuerunt propter hoc.[33]

At the Benedictus, Cesare Bellucius [a bass] began to sing because Marinus Lupi [another bass] told him to. Johannes Baptista Martini [a bass] also sang because Paulus de Magistris [a bass] told him to sing, such that neither one of them wanted to stop or make way for the other. Cesare Bellucius did not know the rules of the chapel, but Johannes Baptista acted badly, as Martinus reported, because he was often told to sing and never wanted to, but today because Marinus told Cesare to sing, he [Martini] wanted to sing; thus, after the Benedictus they had much discussion about this.

A Benedictus in 1583 was likely to be a *terzo* or *quarto*, and the problem was clearly caused when two and not one of the basses began to sing.[34]

But what about music that was not *terzi* or *quarti* (or music that was entirely *terzi* and *quarti*, as was most of the music of the early 16th century)? Again, an entry from the *Diarii Sistini* suggests soloistic performance. On 1 November 1583, the same Cesare Bellucius was fined

Quia D. Cesar Bellucius in Gloria in excelsis que cantare oportebat non cantabat, et propter disonantiam causa magne subversionis fuit.[35]

Because Cesare Bellucius in the Gloria in excelsis which he was supposed to sing, did not sing, and because of the dissonance was the cause of great subversion.

Now, the absence of one voice from a choir might be noticed, the absence of a soloist singing an intonation or chant would of course be noticed, but only the absence of the bass voice from a polyphonic work sung by soloists could cause 'dissonance'. The Gloria was not normally a *terzo* or *quarto*, so this entry seems to suggest that all polyphony was sung soloistically. Similarly, on 25 May 1577, Francesco Druda was fined because he refused to sing the motet and the Agnus Dei, surely a greater offence if these were to be performed by single voices and another singer was forced to take his place.[36]

There is also contradictory evidence. Following a very old tradition, on special feast days a motet was sung for the pope as he was dining; the descriptions of this event in the *Diarii Sistini* are always phrased 'we sang the motet', implying that all the singers took part. On the other hand, on 18 August 1585, the *Diarii* specify that eight singers were sent to sing a motet for the pope (two on a part for a four-part piece, but it was almost certainly a piece in more than four parts).[37] And on 4 February 1596, mention is made of four singers who went to sing a motet at the pope's private Mass: here, certainly one on a part.[38]

Even more conflicting evidence exists. It can be demonstrated, for instance, that in the 1530s and 1540s the chapel employed a more or less equal number of sopranos, altos, tenors and basses, all of them men, the soprano part being taken by falsettists.[39] In February 1544, the breakdown was 7 sopranos, 14 contralto/tenors and 8 basses.[40]

The *Diarii Sistini* also indicate that between one and three to a part was considered an acceptable ensemble. On 5 August 1546, four singers (S, 2C/T, B) were given permission to perform at Santa Maria Maggiore, and on 10 February 1544, eight (2S, 4C/T, 2B) were given permission to sing Mass at a convent to celebrate the admission of the daughter of the singer Blasio Nunez. On a similar occasion on 11 June 1546, the eight singers were disposed 2S, 4C/T, 2B, and earlier that year, 21 January, six singers (2S, 2C/T, 2B) were sent to the Council of Trent, then meeting in Bologna. When Paul III made a pilgrimage to Loreto, he took twelve singers (3S, 6C/T, 3B).[41]

Another entry in the Diary for 1545 shows what was unacceptable. On 30 August 1545 (13th Sunday after Pentecost), Mass was not sung, but was read, 'because of the scarcity of singers, mostly sopranos, caused by the rain'. It was decided that all those absent would be fined, and nine singers are listed. This is approximately a third of the choir, and includes only two sopranos, but considering that three other sopranos were sick, one was away, and another had been banned from the chapel, this left only one soprano, and he clearly was not judged to be enough.[42]

But what does all this mean? If these numbers indicate a desire for an equal number of singers on each part, this would run counter to the idea that more soprano falsettists were needed in order to balance the lower parts in choral music.[43] On the other hand, if solo performance was the norm, the concern would only be that enough singers be available to share the load by taking turns, and that it was considered unacceptable for one singer to shoulder the entire burden (hence the problem on 30 August 1545). The documents do not give a clear answer. In 1630, it was agreed by the singers that the absolute minimum needed was three to a part. Does this say something specific about performance practice, or were they merely trying to provide enough singers if two- and three-part choral music was to be performed, and otherwise sang with one to a part?[44] Does the great concern for choosing the right singers to perform *terzi* and *quarti*, a concern not expressed for other parts of Masses and motets, indicate that only those sections were sung by soloists?[45] Or does it simply mean that trios and quartets naturally appear more exposed in music for five to eight voices sung one on a part?

But even if performances were generally given with more than one singer on a part, there is evidence to indicate that the massed singing of the entire choir in the 16th century was extremely unusual. Take, for instance, a remark made by Paris de Grassis, papal master of ceremonies during the reigns of Julius II and Leo X, concerning the Credo of the Mass on the Saturday after Easter (Sabbato in Albis), 10 April 1507: a Mass celebrated by Francesco Guastaferro, Bishop of Sessa Aurunca and Master of the Papal Chapel:

Credo cantatum fuit hodie nescio qualiter per cantores ut dixerunt per xvi voces quia celebrans est magister capellae ideo voluerunt eum hoc novo modo honorare.[46]

The Credo, I don't know which one, was sung today by the singers, which they sang in sixteen voices because the

XIII

4 The canonization of Diego d'Alcala, 1588 (Vatican Library, fresco by Nebbia and Guerra) (Monumenti, Musei e Gallerie Pontificie)

celebrant was the Master of the Chapel; therefore, they wanted to honour him in this new manner.

Either de Grassis is referring here to a genuine 16-part Credo (practically, if not totally, unheard of in 1507) or he is referring to the 'new manner' of having 16 people singing at once (four to a part in a four-part piece). I would opt for the latter interpretation; what was new, what honoured the Bishop of Sessa Aurunca, was the massed sound of all or almost all the singers present (the choir at the time numbered about twenty) in a period when it was usual for only a few of them to sing at any given time (and de Grassis never mentions this 'new manner' again).

Also suggestive is some evidence from the reign of Leo X. When Leo made his first and only state visit to Florence in November 1515, on his way to Bologna to meet François I, the whole papal court went with him, including, naturally, the choir (which then numbered about 30). In Florence, he chose not to stay at Santa Maria Novella, the usual residence of visiting pontiffs, but instead resided in the family palace, now the Palazzo Medici-Riccardi. After he had ordered that the family parish church of San Lorenzo should serve as the papal chapel, his sister-in-law Alfonsina Orsini ordered building work in the church: the enlargement of the choir, the construction of a platform for the papal throne, benches for the cardinals, and so on. The payments for this work are quite detailed and show the setting up of two bronze pulpits (which must be those made by Donatello). One of these was without question used as a singers' box. The payments for erecting it refer to the work of putting it on its stand, attaching it to the pilasters, and also to five planks of beechwood purchased

per fare le spalliere et agiunta a dicto pergamo in modo fusse capace de' cantori.[47]

to make the railing and addition to the said pulpit so that it could hold the singers.

459

XIII

5 The canonization of Francesca Romana, 1608, showing five singers (Vatican Library, fresco by G. B. Ricci) (Monumenti, Musei e Pontificie)

It seems to me that an addition to either of the Donatello pulpits to make it large enough to hold over 30 grown men at one time would require more than five planks of wood, even long ones;[48] furthermore, it would be expected that some mention of it would be found in the accounts, as with the other works carried out in the church.[49] This suggests that the 'bellissima messa di figurato' sung every morning by the papal singers in San Lorenzo was performed by a small group, possibly only one to a part.[50] It may be, then, that Raphael's depiction of singers at a papal ceremony in his *Coronation of Charlemagne* in the Vatican Stanze is truer to life than might appear at first glance, considering the awkwardness of their positions and placement (see illus.3).[51] Performance of polyphony in the chapel of Leo X (musically the most brilliant in Italy, if not Europe) may then have consisted of only a few singers on a part, with soloists certainly performing duet and trio sections and perhaps all the polyphony as well, in spite of the large number of singers (at one point over 35) that belonged to the choir.

Some tentative conclusions may be drawn from this evidence:

It does not seem to me that knowing either the size of the papal choir or the number of singers on each part can be used as evidence of the numbers who sang at any given time.

Nor can the word 'coro' be taken to mean more than one singer on a part; in the 16th century it merely designated more than one person singing at the same time (for example, four soloists singing four-part polyphony formed a 'coro').

It is almost certain that duet, trio and quartet sections of Masses were sung by soloists.

The evidence for the use of soloists in other parts of Masses and motets is ambiguous; nevertheless, it suggests that only rarely if ever did all the singers perform together, and that the use of soloists was

460

always an acceptable possibility.

But if performances did involve more than one on a part, polyphony in the Sistine Chapel from the 16th to the 18th centuries (and probably also in the 15th) would still have begun with a solo intonation. Solo singing in that sense would have then formed a constant part of what the 'period ear' (to borrow a term from Michael Baxandall) heard during papal ceremonies in the Renaissance.

---

[1] J. Lionnet, 'Performance practice in the Papal Chapel during the 17th century', *EM*, xv/1 (Feb. 1987), pp.4–15

[2] The MS is part of the *fondo Cappella Sistina, I-Rvat* S [hereafter VatS] 680, f.98r.

[3] On the *Diarii*, see Lionnet, 'Performance practice', *op cit.*

[4] For instance:
  D. Johannes Lucas Confortus [a contralto] propter folium quos tempore non vertit mulctatus est' (*Diarii* 12, f.12v: 6 April 1585
  'D. Thomas Benignus [a contralto] ex quo dum sacrum celebraretur coram S.mo ni volvendo folium cantus firmi decepit aperiendo unum pro alio non sine magna omnium pertubatione, ideo fuit acetu omnium absque alia dissentione mulctatus in julios quinque' (*Diarii* 14, f.7r: 10 March 1585)
  That the singers still used this configuration in the 18th century is implied by Matteo Fornari, a papal singer and author of several manuscript treatises concerning practices there, when he writes in VatS 606 that 'Un contralto nelle cappelle papali se non volta in tempo la carta si punta ex costitutione ducati 20'.

[5] VatS 680, f.98r.

[6] 'Ad ultimum cantorem pertinet amovere libros et ad penultimam cantorem ipsos situare in legio seu facistorio, juxta ordinationem cantorum, videlicet contralti hebdomadarii seu decani dictae capellae.' The Constitution is published in F. X. Haberl, *Die römischer 'schola cantorum' und die päpstliche Kapellsänger bis zur Mitte des 16. Jahrhunderts*, Bausteine für Musikgeschichte, iii (Leipzig, 1888).

[7] For example:
  'Dedit corectionem D. Agostino [Martini, a contralto] quia in matitutinis Natalis Domini non providit himnum, et in contrapunctum fuit cantatum.' (*Diarii* 11, f.12v: 12 February 1577
  D. Augustinus [Martini] hodie ad missam cum esset ebdomadarius fecit cantare un introitum pro alio.' (*Diarii* 11, f.41v: 1 October 1577)
  'Austino [Martini] fece levare il libro dal ligio quale ci era cantato li Kirie et la Gloria et era a preposito, et ne fece mettere un altro di nota piccola che per rispetto del tempo non era a preposito: il decano gli disse che ne mitesse un altro, non la volse mai mettere in questo contrasto; venne l'ora da cantare il Sanctus non era trovato niente, et ci fu fatto gran dissordine.' (*Diarii* 11, f.92v: 9 March 1579
  That all these references concern the same person may not be coincidental.

[8] VatS 680, f.98r

[9] Another reference reads: 'Nel cominciare a cantare ciascuno lasci nella sua parte cominciare al più vecchio.' See S. M. Pagano. 'Una visita apostolica alla Cappella dei cantori pontifici al tempo di Urbano VIII (1630)', *Nuova rivista musicale italiana [NRMI]*, xvi (1982), pp.40–72, esp. pp.69 and 52.

[10] VATS 606. See discussion in Helmut Hucke, 'Die Besetzung von Sopran und Alt in der Sixtinischen Kapelle', *Miscelanea en Homanaje a Monsenor Higinio Angles* (Barcelona, 1958–61), i, pp.379–406.

[11] VatS 606, pp.33,-4. Whether Fornari gives the real reason that alto castrati were not admitted to the chapel is not at issue here.

[12] VatS 639, p.22

[13] It was sometimes specified that the chant be intoned by sopranos or contraltos, however.

[14] The senior singers would be experienced enough to know what a comfortable pitch level was, although, as Fornari's statement, and many entries in the *Diarii Sistini* show, sometimes they erred and chose a pitch level that was not practicable. At that point, I assume that they were supposed to stop, tell the choir they were beginning the intonation again, and start again on a different pitch.

[15] *Diarii* 119, f.112r–112v

[16] *Diarii* 122, pp.108–9: 13 May 1703

[17] *Diarii* 147, f. 35r

[18] *Diarii* 147, f.9v: 1 January 1728

[19] *Diarii* 145, f.11r: 2 February 1726

[20] *Diarii* 122, pp.45–46. In the *Improprerii* preserved in VatS 205-206, the first verse ends on *C* and the second verse begins on *f*.

[21] *Diarii* 119, f.34r–34v

[22] That is, at the top of the right hand side of the opening, in the printed choirbook of Pellegrini's Masses that the chapel owned and must have used in this occasion. See VatS 79, V. Pellegrini, *Missarum Liber Primus* (Coenobio, 1604).

[23] One example of many: 'All mottetto del'Offertorio li secondi signori soprani entrorno mezza battuta dopo che non dovevano, per non esser stati attenti vengono puntati, e sono li signori Adami, Monaci, Marchitelli, e Pippe'. *Diarii* 122, p.63: 18 March 1703 (Fourth Sunday of Quadragesima, celebrated in the Sistine Chapel).

[24] For example: 'Al Domine Jesu Christe, cioè l'offertorio, vi fu un quarto. Per esser uscito di tuono due volte che fu rimesso dall signor Adami come antiano, si punta in baiocchi cinque per volta il signor Francesco Besci'. *Diarii* 122, p.7 (7 January 1703, special funeral services in the Chiesa Nuova).
'Al terzo dell Benedictus, per non haver contato le battute giuste che cantava una battuta indietro, si punta il signor Petrucci 05.' *Diarii* 122, p.148 (2 July 1703: Visitation of the Blessed Virgin).

[25] See Lionnet, 'Performance practice', *op. cit.*

[26] VatS 639, p.201

[27] It is also highly likely that the *Improprerii* and *Lamentations* were sung by soloists in the 18th century as they were in the 17th. See Lionnet, *op cit.*

[28] Unless, of course, he used the term only in the sense of beginning a piece.

[29] See J. H. Moore, 'The *Vespero delli Cinque Laudate* and the Role of *Salmi Spezzati* at St Mark's', *JAMS* xxxiv (1981), pp.249–78, and D. Bryant. 'The *cori spezzati* of St Mark's: Myth and Reality', *Early Music History*, i (1981), pp.165–86.

[30] VatS 678, f.112r–112v

[31] See H. W. Frey, 'Das Diarium der Sixtinischen Sängerkapelle in Rom. für das Jahr 1598', *Analecta Musicologica*, xiv (1974), p.479.

[32] See R. Casimiri, *Il 'codice 59' dell'Archivio musicale lateranense autografo di Giovanni Pierluigi da Palestrina* (Rome, 1919), pp.17–19.

[33] *Diarii* 12, f.19r

[34] For another incident suggesting that *terzi* and *quarti* were sung by soloists, see Lionnet, *op cit*, p.7.

[35] *Diarii* 12, f.35v

[36] 'D. Druda non cantavit motetum neque agnus absque ulla cause vel necessitate sed qui aspiciebat D. N. et colegium ill.orum punctatur in uno julio.' *Diarii* 11, f.26r

[37] 'Eodem die DD. cantoribus congregatis ordinarunt otto cantores eorum coram pontifice inter sciiphos mottecta canere, quorum nomina sunt videlicet:
D. Honofrius
D. Jacobus Gallus
D. Horatius
D. Tomas Benignus

XIII

D. Ippolitus
D. Vincentius Musactus
D. Vincentius Zambonus
D. Decanus [Petrus Bartholomuccius]
D. Johannes Maria Nanino si placet sibi ipsi tamen ad libitum'
[Nanino was probably the composer.] *Diarii* 14, f.19v

[38]'M. Leonardo [Crescenzio], Messer Antonio [Manni]. [Pietro] Montoya, et M. Hercole [Ferrucci] sono andati a cantare il motetto alla Messa di N. Sig. mentre faceva communione alla famiglia et sono tornati in Cappella mentre si diceva prima.' H.-W. Frey, 'Das Diarium der Sixtinischen Sängerkapelle in Rom für das Jahr 1596 (Nr.21)'. *Analecta Musicologica*, xxiii (1985), p.145

[39]The first castrato apparently entered the chapel in 1558.

[40]These figures result from a comparison of the chapel list of February 1544 in RAS, Camerale I 878 with the voice designations of the individual singers as determined by Josef Llorens. (See 'Cristobal de Morales, cantor en la Capilla Pontificia de Paulo III (1535–1545)', *Anuario Musical*, viii (1953), pp.39–69, esp. p.46.) The ingenious way Llorens arrived at his voice designations should not go unremarked. While it is true that only a few of the singers are specifically designated as 'soprano', 'tenore', etc. in the documents, Llorens noticed through a careful reading of the *Diarii Sistini* that singers often deputized for colleagues (each singer was allowed one day a week off excluding Sundays and certain feasts, and sometimes a singer would work on his day off in place of a colleague). The *Diarii Sistini* are full of references to this, and by comparing the substitutions with what we know about voice designations, it can be seen that singers only substituted for colleagues of the same voice. By extension, then, it was possible to learn the voice parts of almost all the singers in the chapel. Llorens considered contraltos and tenors as one part, and I have followed this in my estimations.

[41]The sources for this are the *Diarii Sistini* as published by Casimiri in *Note d'Archivio*, where the names of the singers are given, and Llorens, who gives the voice designations. See *Note d'Archivio*, xi (1934), p.77; x (1933), p.149, 342, 335; iii (1926), p.259.

[42]'Propter inopiam cantorum maxime supranorum ob pluviam non fuit cantata missa sed plane celebrata, ideo ordinatum fuit ut quia non compuerunt punctarentur.

(Antonius) Calasans (B)
Genesius (Bultheti T)
(Antonius) Loyalis (B)
Jo. Abbat (T)
Matheus Floranus (B)
Paulus Bursanus (S)
Virgilius Amanditis (T)
(Petrus) Ordognez (B)
Octavianus (Gemelli S)
Federicus Algisius (T)

Of the other sopranos, Simon Perusinus had received permission to absent himself from Rome; Johannes Le Conte, Blasius Nunez and Virgilius Fortin were sick; and Bernardo Pisano had been banned from the chapel by the Master. This left only Stephanus de Thoro to sing on that day. Details are in the Diary for August 1545; see *Note d'Archivio*, x (1933), pp.263, 275–76.

[43]As argued by D. Fallows, 'Specific information on the ensembles for composed polyphony 1400–1474', in *Studies in the Performances of Late Mediaeval Music*, ed. S. Boorman (Cambridge, 1983), pp.109–60.

[44]See Pagano, 'Una visita apostolica alla Cappella dei cantori pontifici al tempo di Urbano VIII (1630)', *op. cit.*

[45]Many singers consulted as part of the Apostolic Visitation of the chapel in 1630 declared that the Master of the Chapel should exercise great care in choosing singers to sing *terzi e quarti*; see Pagano, 'Una visita apostolica', *op cit.* On 20 November 1584, the Master of the Chapel reported complaints that he had received 'de aliquibus nostris senibus qui in tertiis et quartis malum agunt effectum. Itaque ut magis S.mo D.no N. et Ill.mi Cardinalibus placere ut ipsi senes in tertiis et quartis taceant'. *Diarii* 13, f.33r

[46]See VatL 12413. f.156v. Mentioned in R. Sherr, 'The singers of the Papal Chapel and liturgical ceremonies in the early sixteenth century: some documentary evidence', in *Rome in the Renaissance: the City and the Myth*, ed. P. A. Ramsey (Binghamton, 1982), pp.249–64.

[47]*I-FR* Archivio di San Lorenzo [AL] 2471, f.306r

[48]The entry refers to the planks being '11 b', which may mean 11 *braccia* or about 20 feet. But these were certainly cut up in order to make the railing and the addition.

[49]See *I-FR* AL 2471, f.305r. The pulpits are 280cm (9.33 feet) and 292cm (9.73 feet) wide; in order to accommodate 30 singers standing around a lectern, they would have had to be made wider, thus separating the sculpted panels. This does not seem likely.

[50]See F. A. D'Accone, 'Heinrich Isaac in Florence: New and Unpublished Documents', *MQ*, xlix (1963), p.482.

[51]The fresco shows three singers singing in a pulpit at the far left overlooking the scene (which presumably is taking place in St Peter's rather than in the Papal Chapel), but the arch of the top of the fresco itself makes it impossible for the artist to have included many more singers. A recent article by Neils Rasmussen provides further pictorial evidence. Rasmussen presents a number of late 16th- and early 17th-century frescos and engravings showing in accurate details various ceremonies of canonization. Three of his illustrations also show singers (always standing in pulpits), and in each case they are few in number. Considering the general attention to the detail of the rest of the ceremony being depicted, we could perhaps conclude that the representation of the number of singers also reflects reality. See Neils Krogh Rasmussen, O.P., 'Iconography and Liturgy at the Canonization of Carlo Borromeo', *Analecta Romana Instituti Danici* 15 (1986), pp.119–50: fig.2 (canonization of Diego d'Alcala, 1588, showing 3–5 singers), fig.4 (canonization of Francesca Romana, 1608, showing 5 singers; see illus.1 and 2 of my article). All of these ceremonies took place in St. Peter's, but the singers must have been members of the papal choir. Furthermore, Rasmussen's fig.2 takes place in a portion of the church that has the aspect of the Sistine Chapel (see illus.4).

XIV

Competence and incompetence in the papal choir in the age of Palestrina

In 1581 the English Catholic expatriate Gregory Martin wrote a book, *Roma Sancta*, in praise of religious life in Rome, where he had lived for about a year and a half between 1576 and 1578. Its first volume is devoted to churches, relics and ceremonies, and contains two descriptions of ecclesiastical music, one pertaining to the churches of Rome and one specifically mentioning the papal choir in the Sistine Chapel. Neither refers to a specific occasion, yet they appear to be true reflections of Martin's musical experiences.[1]

It is the most blessed varietie in the world, where a man may goe to so many Churches in one day, chose where he wil, so heavenly served, with such musike, such voices, such instrumentes, al ful of gravitie and majestie, al moving to devotion and ravishing a mans hart to the meditiation of melodie of Angels and Saintes in heaven. with the Organs a childes voice shriller and louder then the instrument, tuneable with every pipe: Among the quyre, Cornet or Sagbut, or such like above al the other voices. Wherein this is singular and much to be noted, that they deliver every word and everie syllable so distinctly, so cleane, so commodiously, so fully, that the hearers may perceave al that is sung. And that Verse which the Organs doth playe, one of the quyre in the meane time with a base voyce very leasurely, rather sayth then singeth which there is common in other places I have not seene it. (bk.1, chap.33: 'Solemnitie of Divine Service')

The quyer standeth a loft at one side with voices like so many belles tuneable one to another. No organes bycause the quyer is so ful for al partes. No descant, but such pricke song as every syllable may be heard in thy eares like a Preachers voice. (bk.1, chap.34: 'The Popes Chappel and Solemnities in the Palace')

As Christopher Reynolds has pointed out, Martin's observations are useful for the mention of instruments other than the organ in the churches of Rome and for confirmation that the papal choir sang without instrumental accompaniment of any kind. More striking, as Reynolds also notices, is Martin's emphasis on the clarity of diction of church choirs and of the papal choir; indeed, that is really all he has to say about the sound of those singing ensembles.[2] In fact, this particular observation, coming as it does in a book that was, after all, partly propaganda, is so clearly an affirmation that the ideals of the Council of Trent regarding sacred music were indeed being put into practice in the Holy City that we should perhaps take it with a grain of salt.

1 *(opposite)* The Sistine Chapel in the early 16th century: the choir is in the box on the right: engraving by Etienne Dupérac (1578) (Biblioteca Apostolica Vaticana, Ris. Strag. 7, f.16) **see now p.619**

2 St Peter's basilica, from Antonio Tempesta's map of Rome (1593)

Actually, it is evident from other sources that loudness or full sonority, not good diction, was the sound ideal of a church or chapel choir in the late 16th century, while clarity of pronunciation and refined expression were ideals of *musica da camera*.[3] Confirmation that this view of cappella singing was indeed held in the Vatican is found in papal bulls and *motu proprii* spanning 200 years in which the preferred term for describing the desired sound of the papal choir is 'sonorous' (*sonora, canora*). Now, papal letters also have to be taken with a grain of salt; they were, after all, legal documents and their repetition of certain terms might be a matter of custom rather than a reference to reality. Yet it would not be surprising that the papal chapel would share the same sound ideal as other cappella groups. What is surprising, perhaps, is the number of papal singers throughout the 16th century who were thought by their contemporaries not to have been competent to produce this sound; singers who indeed may never have sung in the choir in spite of being 'on the books'. These people definitely did not have 'sonorous' voices; adjectives used to describe them include 'harsh' (*aspra*), 'hoarse' (*rauca*), 'dissonant' (*disona*: 'untuned'—i.e. unable to keep the pitch?), and they are occasionally associated with the noun *imbecillitas* ('weakness'). Furthermore, the papal choir could have had at any given time as many as five singers who had been active for 25 years or more, with the concomitant decline in their singing ability (although this obviously varied from person to person). At one time the proportion of such people (bad and/or old singers) in the premier choir in Christendom might have approached 40 per cent. I suggest that this would have produced a surprising level of incompetence for a major professional singing organization in the late 16th century.[4]

But how could this have happened? In particular, how could this have happened in an organization whose constitution specified that singers were to be admitted after an audition that tested the quality of the voice and ability to sing chant, polyphony and contrapunctus, and then by a 2/3+1 vote of the singers themselves?[5] The presence of older singers is explained by a phrase in the constitution that declares that membership in the papal choir carried lifetime tenure,[6] but the presence of acknowledged incompetents is a hint that something had gone wrong in the quality-control department. And, indeed, there is ample evidence that subversion of the constitutional practices regarding the admission of singers had become standard in the 16th century. In short, the papal choir, like every other bureaucratic institution in the Roman Curia, became in the 16th century a haven for deadbeats who, through the influence of patrons, were given jobs for which they were not qualified and awarded salaries for which they were not expected to work.[7] Periodically this state of affairs caused consternation at the highest levels, which in turn produced a reaction, which in turn would prove to be inefficacious, which would in turn produce more consternation, and so on and so on.

The first documented indication of subversion can be found in the bitter dispute between the singers and their hated *maestro di cappella* Ludovico Magnasco, Bishop of Assisi (*maestro* 1540–50), a dispute too complicated to go into here except to mention that the singers in the end managed to get their administrator dismissed. One of the complaints against Magnasco was that he was populating the choir with people entirely of his own choosing (most likely as favours for powerful individuals) completely ignoring the audition process prescribed in the constitution. Things became so bad that in 1553 Pope Julius III decided or was persuaded to take serious action to purge the choir of incompetents. His opinion of the state of the choir is found in an undated *motu proprio*, the original of which is preserved in the *fondo Cappella Sistina* of the Biblioteca Apostolica Vaticana (see illus.4; the text is transcribed in appendix 1).[8]

The gist of the document is as follows. In the past singers had been brought from all over the world to the papal chapel who were not only expert in the art of music but had sweet and sonorous voices. But now, by subverting the constitutions of the chapel, a number of singers had been placed in it, bypassing the audition process merely to please powerful patrons so that the total complement of singers was approaching 35, the majority of whom because of

3 The Cappella Sistina presenting Paul III with the constitution of 1545 (Rome, Cappella Sistina, Ms 611, f.1v)

their weak voices were 'totally useless' as singers ('imbecilitate vocum ad cantandum penitus inutilis'). The pope observes that unless something is done about this, in the future the papal choir, which had been first in the world, would become inferior to all the other chapels. Wishing to reform the choir by removing those who had not entered it legally, Julius orders that the number of singers be reduced to 24 in perpetuity. Presumably the result of this drastic reduction of 30 per cent, most of whom were incompetent anyway, would have been a choir that was 'mean and lean'. It might also not be a coincidence that 24 is precisely the number claimed for the choir in the reign of the Medici pope Clement VII (1524–34), which is put forth in one document as a sort of 'golden age' in which the choir had just the right number and balance of singers (specifically, seven sopranos, seven contraltos, four tenors and six basses, all personally auditioned and approved by the pope himself).[9]

But there were two glaring weaknesses in this *motu proprio*. First, although Julius declared that his intention was to remove those singers who were not competent, he did not in fact require their removal. Instead, he simply ordered that no new singers be admitted for whatever reason until the desired number of 24 had been reached by attrition.

4 Original *motu proprio* (?1553) in which Julius III orders the reduction of the papal choir to 24 members (Vatican City, Biblioteca Apostolica Vaticana, fondo Cappella Sistina 646, f.84r). (Transcribed as appendix 1.)

This goal could take a very long time to achieve and would not even guarantee that the incompetents would leave the choir. In refusing to dismiss singers outright, the pope was undoubtedly responding to manoeuvring behind the scenes by the other singers who would have been very concerned about the precedent that would be set if the right of lifetime appointment was abrogated—even for good reason—by papal authority. At the very least, as we later find out, they insisted that those who would be removed be given some permanent monetary recompense in the form of a pension or benefice.[10]

That may have been a point gained by the singers. But, as they soon found out, a more drastic loophole had been inserted into the *motu proprio*. Read literally, the papal order would have made it impossible to accept any new singers into the choir for years. This clearly was not a good situation, so the pope allowed for exceptions: if a singer could be shown to have passed the required audition and received express papal permission in the form of a *motu proprio* (that would abrogate the 'rule of 24'), then he could be admitted to the choir. Presumably this would account for the rare situation where a really terrific singer came upon the scene and it would have been idiotic not to allow him to join a choir consisting mainly of incompetents.

This loophole proved to be the undoing of the entire attempt at reform. What Julius III actually had done was strengthen the patronage system. Anybody who knows anything about the actual process of getting *motu proprii* will have no trouble imagining the ease with which powerful cardinals or other members of the Curia could sneak the requisite supplications past the pontiff. And, in fact, Julius himself was the first person to abuse his own reform, when on 13 January 1555 he ordered the choir to accept a favourite musician, none other than Giovanni Pierluigi da Palestrina, as a member without examination ('absque ullo examine secundum motum proprium quod habebamus et absque consensu cantorum', grumpily remarks the diarist of the papal choir recording the entrance of the man who more than any other composer was to personify music in the Sistine Chapel).[11]

Things got worse and worse. Rather than being reduced to 24, the choir still had 31 members at the end of Julius's reign (although it had never had the 35 members that his *motu proprio* claimed). And while Julius's successor, the reforming Paul IV (1555–9), had by the end of his reign managed to order the expulsion of nine singers, the reasons adduced were never primarily musical and in any case the singers were replaced, so that by the end of his reign the membership of the choir stood at 29.[12] Time and time again in the following years, as the ever more specific *Diarii Sistini* report and as the existence of actual *motu proprii* attests, singers were able to bypass the order that the choir could not exceed 24 members, and frequently were able to avoid the audition as well, merely by obtaining a *motu proprio* with the appropriate language, usually by enlisting the aid of a cardinal.

This all came to a head in 1565, when Pius IV decided the papal choir should be evaluated as part of the general reform of the Curia taken in response to the Council of Trent, and appointed cardinals Borromeo and Vitelli to a commission to examine the state of the College of Singers with the object of correcting abuses.[13] This task force generated (as such committees always do) a flood of documents from the examined party, many outlining in detail the sorry state of the papal choir.[14] One constant complaint concerns the evil wrought by the misguided loophole in the 1553 *motu proprio* of Julius III. For instance, we learn that by 1565, nine singers in the choir had been admitted without audition merely by *motu proprio*; furthermore, it is claimed that these men were in fact singers 'in name only'.

Cantores admissi sine examine vigore motu proprii volunt percipere et cum effectu percipiunt partem suam de omnibus regalibus et emolumentis provenientibus ex missis papalibus et consistoriis publicis prout alii cantores canonice admissi percipiunt quod videtur absurdum quod illi qui nomine tenus sunt cantores gaudeant de emolumentis huiusmodi prout alii qui serviunt.[15]

Singers admitted without audition on the strength of *motu*

XIV

Document 1 A report on the abilities of certain singers (1565)
(Vatican City, Archivio Segreto Vaticano (ASV), Misc. Arm. XI, xciii, f.151r)

M Ant.o villadiego voce mediocre. [suprani—in margin]	M. Antonio Villadiego: moderate voice.
M. Pietro Aretino questo per bisogno fu pigliato per servitio del concilio.	M. Pietro Aretino [Scortecci]: This one was hired because he was needed at the Council [of Trent].
M. Symon Perugino questo è infirmo et fuor di Roma et ha servito molti anni con bone voce.	M. Simone [Bartolini] Perugino: This one is ill and away from Rome and has served for many years with a good voice.
M. Stefano Fornarino M. Fermino Label questi non hano voce bona ma hano bona intelligenza nella musica.	M. Stefano [Betti] Fornarino, M. Fermin Lebel: These do not have good voices but are good musicians.
M. Ghisilino [Danckerts]: ha servito molto ma non ha voce però è buon musico et è infirmo.	M. Ghiselin Danckerts: Has served for many years but has no voice; however, he is a good musician and is ill.
M. Joan de Monte ha servito sempre la capella con bona voce et è stato exemplatto di vita et costumi ma hora gli è mancato la voce.	M. Jean de Monte has always served the chapel with a good voice and has been exemplary in his life and manners, but now his voice is gone.
M. Bart.o del Conto è fuor di Roma ne so rendere conte di lui, ma si dice che non ha molto bona voce.	M. Bartholomé Le Conte is away from Rome and cannot be accounted for, but it is said that he does not have a very good voice.
M. Mateo Albo ha grandissima voce ma poca scientia et fa male effetto.	M. Mattia Albo [Bianco] has a very loud voice but little knowledge and makes a bad impression.
M. Christiano [Ameyden]: ha voce mediocre et quasi tollerabile.	M. Christian Ameyden has a moderate voice which is almost bearable.
M. Jo Aloysio [de Épiscopis]: ha voce assai trista [bona—crossed out] ma vale molto più perché è sicuro cantore et fa grandissimo effetto nella parte del baritonans.	M. Giovanni Luigi de Espiscopis has a voice which is rather disappointing, but he is more greatly valued because he is a secure singer and makes a very great impression in baritone parts.
M. Jo Ant.o Latino ha voce assai grande ma si potrebbe migliorare.	M. Giovanni Antonio Latino has a fairly loud voice but it could improve.
M. Bartolomeo Bartolo il medesimo.	M. Bartlomeo Bartolo: The same.
M. Jo Batt.a Precacese il medesmo.	M. Giovanni Battista Precacese [Aspra]: The same.

proprii wish to partake and indeed do partake of their share of all gifts and tips given out at papal Masses and consistories as do the other singers who were legally admitted, which may be seen to be absurd that those who are singers in name only should enjoy the same emoluments as those who really serve.

The singers also submitted to the cardinals two copies of a list of the choir members, indicating both the year of entry and the diocese of each singer.[16] The preamble to the list indicates that the state of the choir membership was as follows: there were 37 singers officially in the choir, but of these, five were away on various leaves of absence and one had been extremely ill for two years, so in effect there were 31 singers present in Rome. We know that of the total of 37 as many as nine (24 per cent) had been admitted without having passed an audition, and it appears those singers did not in fact

XIV

5 The facade of St Peter's. The 'Domus Capellae Juliae' stands to the left of the Constantine portico.

sing at all; we might add also that four singers in the list had served the choir for 25 years or more and presumably their voices had lost some of their original qualities. The singing component of the choir, then, actually consisted of fewer than 30 men.

There is more. The cardinals' commission did not merely collect documents, it proceeded to an actual examination of the abilities of the singers in the choir, paying special attention to those singers who had been admitted simply by *motu proprio*. The notes of these examinations are preserved,[17] and what they reveal about 14 of the singers in the papal chapel is shown here as document 1.

It is stated outright that four of these singers have bad voices. Two others were not in Rome (one of these was said not to have a good voice), and seven others had voices that were more or less acceptable (one was 'almost tolerable'), although some 'might improve' (one is valued specifically for being a baritone, that is, was capable of singing throughout the bass and tenor range, perhaps even higher—a voice designation that was rare at the time and much prized—even though he did not have a good voice),[18] while one other had been admitted merely to be sent to the Council of Trent.[19] More information is presented in annotations added after the names of practically every singer in one of the copies of the submitted chapel list, annotations that seem to represent an examination of morals and religious orthodoxy as well as vocal abilities (see table 1).[20]

Fourteen singers in this list have crosses in front of their names and/or 'recompensa' added after, and on 31 August 1565 an order was signed and transmitted to the College of Singers on 17 September and recorded in the *Diarii Sistini* for that year,

613

XIV

Table 1 The list of papal singers submitted to the cardinals' commission of 1565
The date of entry of each singer is given together with his diocese; annotations are in a different hand.*
(Archivio Segreto Vaticano, Misc. Arm. XI, xciii, ff.174r–175r)

1529	Antonius Calasans Decanus Illerden [Lerida] diocesis *bonus*	Acceptable.
1535	Joannes Abbatte nullius diocesis *lusor sed† eviliens‡ musicus vocis mediocris pauper*	Gambler and a weakening musician of moderate voice at that; poor.
+1538	Ghisilinus Dankerts Leodien [Liège] diocesis *non habet vocem sed eccellens dives et mulieribus deditus inutilis propter infirmitatem*	Has no voice but surpassingly rich and devoted to women; useless because of illness.§
1538	Virgilius de Amanditis Romanus [Rome] *lusor bonus pauper*	Gambler, acceptable, poor.
+1542	Joannes Mont Leodien [Liège] diocesis *pauper sed surdus et bonus*	Poor, but deaf and acceptable.
+1543	Simon Bartholinus Perusinus [Perugia] *infirmus, infamus et pauper*	Ill, infamous and poor.
1546	Federicus Lazizius Romanus [Rome] *dives bonus concubinarius*	Rich, acceptable; keeps a mistress.
1547	Joannes Aloisius de Episcopus Napolitanus [Naples] *pauper utilis et bonus non habet vocem*	Poor, useful and acceptable; has no voice.
+1547	Franciscus de Montaluo Abulen [Avila] diocesis *bonus sed absens dives*	Acceptable but absent; rich.
1547	Vincentius Bimercato Brixien [Brescia] *bonus examinatus non habet vocem*	Acceptable, examined; has no voice.
1547	Petrus de Sancto Germano nullius diocesis *bonus*	Acceptable.
1547	Annellus de Antignano Nolan [Nola] diocesis *bonus*	Acceptable.
1549	Petrus Paulus Caraceus Maceraten [Macerata] *bonus*	Acceptable.
1551	Joannes Antonius Merula Roman [Rome] *bonus pauper*	Acceptable; poor.
+1555	Bartholomeus Leconte Novionen [Noyon] *hereticus pessimus*	The worst kind of heretic.
+1555	Franciscus de Talavera Seguntin [Siguenza] *fugitivus propter es alienum*	Has fled because of debts.
+1556	Mathias Albus Fulginaten [Foligno] *lusor sed vastus et incompositus recompensa*	Gambler and a wastrel [?] and disorderly [?] at that; pension.
1556	Marinus Luppi Asculanus [Ascoli] *pauper bonus*	Poor, acceptable.
1558	Franciscus de Bustamente Palentin [Palencia] diocesis *pauper et nunc bonus*	Poor and now acceptable.
1559	Joannes Antonius Latinus Beneventan [Benevento] *recompensa*	Pension.
1560	Franciscus Druda Forosempronien [Fossembrone] *bonus examinatus*	Acceptable, examined.
1560	Jacobus Celius Romanus [Rome] *bonus sed mulierum appetitor admoneatur*	Acceptable but desires women; he is to be warned.
1561	Franciscus Nardus Bononien [Bologna] *bonus*	Acceptable.
+1561	Bartholomeus de Bartholis Urbinaten [Urbino] *recompensa*	Pension.
1561	Lucas de Longinquis Ambianen [Amiens] *bonus*	Acceptable.
+1561	Firminius Lebell Novonionen [Noyon] diocesis *recompensa non habet vocem*	Pension; has no voice.
+1561	Antonius de Villadiego Segobien [Segovia] *apostata non habet vocem*	Apostate; has no voice.
1561	Petrus de Arrozco Aretinus [Arezzo] *bonus novus tridentinus*	Acceptable; the new singer for Trent.
1561	Christophorus Hoseda Corduben [Cordoba] *bonus*	Acceptable.
1561	Alexander Merolus Roman [Rome] *bonus*	Acceptable.
1562	Benedictus Archadio Spoletanus [Spoleto] *bonus*	Acceptable.
1562	Franciscus de Torres Toletan [Toledo] diocesis *bonus*	Acceptable.
+1562	Stephanus Fornarinus Bononien [Bologna] *bonus non habet vocem recompensa*	Acceptable; has no voice; pension.
1562	Franciscus de Sotto Oxomen [Osma] diocesis *bonus*	Acceptable.
1563	Joannes de Figueroa Toletan [Toledo] diocesis *bonus*	Acceptable.
+1563	Christianus Amayden Leodien [Liège] *recompensa*	Pension.
+1563	Joannes Baptista Aspra *recompensa*	Pension.

expelling 14 singers (not entirely the same group that is marked in table 1, however).²¹ On 1 October 1565 the Camera Apostolica was instructed to remove 13 singers from the regular lists of the choir, to place those who were in Rome in a category labelled 'second class', and to pay those singers monthly pensions of varying amounts depending on whether or not they had been admitted originally by audition.²² These documents, added to the information presented in document 1, provide the following concerning the abilities of approximately a third of the papal choir. Nine singers (Christian Ameyden, Mattia Bianco, Bartolomeo Bartholi, Stefano [Betti] Fornarino, Giovanni Antonio Latino, Firmin Lebel, Giovanni Battista

Precacesa [Aspra] and Antonio Villadiego) had been admitted without audition and had bad or barely tolerable voices. Of four singers admitted by audition, Jean Mont had lost his voice (was, in fact, deaf), Ghiselin Dankerts had lost his voice and was too ill to be of any use, Simone Bartolini was ill and Pietro Scorteccia (Aretino) had been hired merely in order to be sent to the Council of Trent. Bartholomé Le Conte and Francisco Talavera were not assigned pensions since they had both left Rome under a cloud (Le Conte was a heretic and Talavera had fled Rome because of debts); nor was Antonio de Villadiego given a pension (as a member of the regular clergy, he had been ordered back to his monastery). All these singers were expelled from the choir with the exception of Christian Ameyden, who was formally readmitted in spite of his weak voice because of a special petition by the other singers who probably valued him more for his character and administrative skills than for his vocal ability.²³ The final result, by subtracting 13 singers from the choir of 37, reduced it exactly to the 'ideal' number of 24. By the end of 1565, three singers listed in table 1 (Pietro Paulo Caraceno, Francisco Bustamante and Francesco Nardo) had either left the chapel or died, so that the membership of the chapel in 1566 was that shown in table 2.

If we consider that this list of 23 names contains four singers who were said to have weak voices yet were retained on the books (Giovanni Abbate, Giovanni Luigi de Episcopis, Vincenzo Vimercato, Christian Ameyden) and two who had served for 25 years or more (Antonio Calasans, Virgilio Amanditis), we get a total 17 singers who could be presumed to be competent. And if we assume that two or three of these would be on leaves of absence at any given time, we get a total of about 15 singers who could constitute the actual singing component of the papal choir in 1566, and also in the years before the reform.

This, then, was the effect of the patronage system first introduced by Magnasco, unknowingly abetted by Julius III and shamelessly manipulated by following popes and cardinals. A choir that had

---

Notes to table 1

* It appears that Casimiri published either this entire list or part of it, since J. de Bruyn gives some of the annotations in his article, 'Ghisilinus Danckerts, kapelaan-zanger van de Pauselijke kapel van 1538 tot 1565). Zijn leven, werken en onuitgegeven tractaat', *Tijdschrift der Vereinigung voor Nederlandse Muziekgeschiedenis*, xvi (1946), p.251, with references to Casimiri, but I have not yet located the publication. The annotations are written in an extremely sloppy cursive which, however, is usually (but not always) decipherable and understandable.

† It is not at all clear what *lusor* (a word applied to Mattia Bianco and Virgilio de Amanditis) is supposed to mean here. If considered as Classical Latin, it should mean 'player', 'trifler', even 'gambler'. Of these, 'gambler' might be the best meaning in context (since morals was one of the things being examined by the commission). The *sed* which follows would seem to make little sense when translated as 'but'; however, I am informed by Leofranc Holford-Strevens, to whom I am indebted for advice concerning Latin words and usage, that it could also have the meaning of 'and ... at that'. I suggest that this is the meaning that the writer of the marginalia had in mind when he coupled *sed* with *lusor*; the other uses of *sed* mkae best sense when translated as 'but'.

‡ I probably have not read this word correctly, since it appears not to exist in Latin, but it is fairly close to other Latin words meaning 'cheapening' or 'weakening', concepts that do make some sense in context.

§ De Bruyn omits the last two Latin words, giving a slightly different picture of the judgement of Danckerts's abilities: see G. Reese, *Music in the Renaissance*, rev. edn (New York, 1959), p.364.

Table 2 Membership of the choir in 1566 (after the expulsions) listed by seniority within voice part (derived from Rome, Archivio di Stato, Camerale I (mandati camerali) 917 and other sources)

Name	Admitted	Years of service
Sopranos		
Pietro Bartholomuccio	1547	19
Agnello Antignano	1547	19
Francisco Torres	1562	4
Francisco Sotto	1562	4
Juan Figueroa	1563	3
Altos		
Federigo Lagisio	1546	20
Giovanni Antonio Merlo	1551	15
Luc de Longuignis	1561	5
Giacomo Celio (?)	1560	6
Cristobal Hoyeda (?)	1561*	5
Tenors		
Giovanni Abbate	1535	31
Virgilio Amanditis	1538	28
Francisco Montaluo	1547	19
Vincenzo Vimercato	1547	19
Mattia Bianco	1556†	10
Alessandro Merlo	1561	5
Benedetto Archadio	1562	4
Christian Ameden	1563	3
Basses		
Antonio Calasans	1529	37
Giovanni Luigi de Episcopis	1547	19
Nicolo Barono	1566‡	
Marino Lupi	1556	10
Francesco Druda	1560	6

* Died 23 September 1566.
† Expelled 1565, readmitted February 1566.
‡ Admitted November 1566.

become bloated to its greatest number ever in fact only had as many working members as the choir of Julius II at the beginning of the century.[24] Such was the state of the most important musical organization in Italy, if not in Europe, at the time that is assumed by many to be the period of its greatest glory.

Of course, the reform of the Cardinal's Commission did not work out exactly as planned. As mentioned above, the singers successfully petitioned to have Ameyden readmitted to the choir in spite of his bad voice. Pius IV died in 1565, and in the next year Mattia Bianco managed to get himself readmitted also. Nonetheless, the reform (plus the fact that some singers left the choir of their own accord) had by the end of 1566 reduced the number of 'active' singers on the books to 22. During the reign of Pius V (1566–72) the number stayed within the boundaries of the ideal 24. There is a gap in the chapel lists for the years 1571–80; when they resume, the number of singers wavers between 24 and 27 until the decisive action of Sixtus V reduced the choir to 21.[25]

The problem of bloated membership had apparently been solved, but the problem of incompetence had not been. In 1573, eight years after the reform of Pius IV, yet another reform of the choir was contemplated, generating another pointed evaluation of the singing abilities of certain members, although this attempt at reform apparently was not carried out, since the singers mentioned remained in the chapel (see document 2).

Let us return now to Gregory Martin. As it happens, the exact membership of the choir, their voice designations and their length of service can be reconstructed for July 1577, one of the months that Martin spent in Rome. The choir was in fact representative of the ideal, consisting of six sopranos, six altos, five tenors and seven basses for a total of 24 (see table 3).

However, this list contains five people who had served for 25 years or more (four who had served for 30 years or more). If we add to this the specific comments about certain of these singers (see documents 1, 2 and table 1) we find that, of the five senior singers, two (Bartolomuccio and Antignano) had in fact been judged to have bad voices in 1573, but were useful because of their status as priests and their experience, while Episcopis had been said to be 'disappointing' in 1565 (12 years earlier), but was valued then because of his voice range (and was now the most senior singer and therefore the Dean of the College of Singers). Furthermore, among the less senior singers, Ameyden's voice had been said

Document 2 Remarks on the abilities of certain singers (1573)
(Archivio Segreto Vaticano, Miscl. Arm. XI, xciii, f.152r–v)

Li cantori infrascitti sono a chi si potrebbe dare ricompensa per havere qualche diffetto nella voce, et in cambio loro rimettere alla giornata degli altri, che non habbiano voce aspra o rauca ne disona, ma canora, suave, et chiara

Matthias Blancus. Questo fa tenore, et perché entrò in capella per un Motu proprio di Paulo iiii, ne fu levato nel tempo di Pio iiii, et è ritornato poi con un'altro motu proprio di Pio Quinto. Il salario suo è salario morto, perché essendo beneficiato in S. Pietro poco et quasi niente serve la capella; sta bene et ha altri beneficii ancora nella voce sua è molto buona.

Vincen.s Vimercatus. Questo ancora fa tenore, et entrò in collegio de cantori col Motu proprio nel tempo del pontificato di Paulo iii. Ha una voce senz'anima che non fa effetto nissuno; si dice ch'è fatto spenditore del collegio Germanico et è Mastro di casa del Cardinal Chiesa et che va cercando di esser esente i giorni feriale dell'ufficio della capella.

Augustinus Martini. Questo fa contralto, et è familiare del Cardinal Sermoneta, più volte si è provato per entrare in capella ma non ha potuto non perché non fusse valent'huomo in musica et persona molto da bene, ma perché non havea buona voce per contralto; l'anno passato fu data comissione, che si pigliasse, et così fu pigliato.

Ant.s Vimcercatus. Questo fa tenore, et ha una cattiva voce, entrò ancora lui l'anno passato con molti favori, et fu ricevuto da cantori si, et in quantum, senza che fusse passato secondo la forma delle constitutioni.

Petrus Bartholmucius et Agnellus de Antignano. Questi fanno soprano et hanno la voce più presto rauca et disona che altrimenti, ma sono molto utili per esser sacerdoti, et sempre uno di loro ordina il choro, et sono de vecchi che stiano in capella.

Joannes Paredes. Questo è castrato et fu preso per necessità de soprani, non ha molto buona voce, si può però tenere fin che compariscano buoni soprani di Spagna, et darli di poi buona ricompensa, ch'è giovane molto da bene et non ha cosa alcuna.

Hippolitus Gambotius. Questo fa contralto et è entrato secondo la forma delle constitutioni del collegio, ma in vero non ha molto buona voce et più presto disona che altrimenti

Joannes Aloisius de surento [nothing further]

The singers listed below could be given pensions because of various defects in their voices, and in exchange get others whose voices are not harsh or hoarse or dissonant, but sonorous, sweet and clear.

Mattia Bianco: This one is a tenor, and because he entered the chapel with a *motu proprio* from Paul IV, he was dismissed in the time of Pius IV, and he returned with another *motu proprio* from Pius V. His salary is wasted because, having a benefice in St Peter's, he almost never serves the chapel. He is well off and has other benefices and also has a very good voice.

Vincenzo Vimercato: This one also is a tenor, and entered the College of Singers with a *motu proprio* in the pontificate of Paul III. His voice is without substance and makes no impression whatsoever. It is said that he has become the bursar of the German College and the major domo of Cardinal Chiesa, and that he is trying to be absent on ferial days in the chapel.

Agostino Martini: This one is an alto, and is in the household of Cardinal Sermoneta. He tried many times to enter the chapel, but was not able to, not because he was not a good musician and a very worthy person, but because he did not have a good alto voice. Last year it was ordered that he be admitted, and he was.

Antonio Vimercato: This one is a tenor and has a terrible voice. He also entered last year with many favours and was accepted by the singers without having been judged according to the rules of the constitutions.

Pietro Bartolomuccio and Agnello Antignano: These are sopranos and have voices that are more hoarse and dissonant than not, but they are very useful because they are priests, and one of them always orders the choir and they are among the senior singers in the chapel.

Juan Paredes: This one is a castrato and was taken because there was a need for sopranos. He does not have a very good voice, but he can be kept on until good sopranos arrive from Spain; and he should then be given a good pension because he is a worthy young man and doesn't have anything.

Ippolito Gambuccio: This one is an alto and entered according to the rules of the constitutions of the college, but he does not have a very good voice and is more dissonant than not.

Giovanni Luigi from Sorrento [de Episcopis]

617

Table 3 Membership of the choir in July 1577, listed by seniority within voice part (derived from *Diarii Sistini*, xi, f.31r and other sources)

Name	Admitted	Years of service
Sopranos		
Pietro Bartolomuccio	1547	30
Agnelo Antignano	1547	30
Francisco de Soto	1562	15
Juan Figueroa	1563	14
Gabriele Carloval	1574	3
Jacobus Albano	1574	3
Altos		
Giovanni Antonio Merlo	1551	26
Miguel Peramato	1569	8
Annibale Zoilo	1570	7
Ippolito Gambuccio	1571	6
Agostino Martini	1572	5
Alessandro Barre	1574	3
Tenors		
Francisco Montaluo	1547	30
Mattia Bianco	1556	21
Benedetto Archadio	1562	15
Christian Ameyden	1563	14
Vincenzo Musatto	1571	6
Basses		
Giovanni Luigi de Episcopis	1546	31
Marino Lupi	1556	21
Francesco Druda	1559	18
Paolo Fumone	1569	8
Santo Gherlino	1571	6
Cesare Misserio	1575	2
Pietro Paulo Sanna	1575	2

to be almost bearable 12 years previously and he had actually been dismissed from the chapel at that time; Bianco admittedly had a good loud voice but was useless to the choir in 1577 since he was never there; while Gambuccio and Martini had been simply defined as 'bad' in 1573. There is also some doubt about the alto Annibale Zoilo, since on 1 August 1577 he requested to be allowed to retire from the choir because of a *rottura* (hernia) that was making it impossible for him to sing.[26] So it could be said that in 1577 nine or ten singers (38 or 40 per cent of the choir) probably could not really sing. That leaves four (two-thirds) of the sopranos, four or three (two-thirds or less) of the altos, two (one-third) of the tenors, and six (100 per cent) of the basses as competent singers. One wonders what a choir so constituted sounded like when all the singers were singing at the same time; such an unbalanced group (only two competent tenors) does not seem ideal for the performance of late 16th-century polyphony, and lends credence to the idea that if Gregory Martin was impressed by ringing clarity ('like so many belles tuneable one to another') then it probably was because he was listening to the choir singing with only a few of the competent singers on each part (possibly with only one on a part).[27]

Unfortunately singing one to a part was not in itself a guarantee of good performance. Let us take those situations where it can be proven that soloists did perform: the trio and quartet sections of the five- and more- voiced works that the choir sang in the late 16th century.[28] It turns out that these soloistic sections were rotated among singers in order of seniority, which meant that the older singers would always get a chance at it. This provoked a negative reaction in 1584, one that demonstrates also the existence of a sentient audience for the performance of the choir, as the following extract from the *Diarii Sistini* (xiii, f.33r. 20 November 1584) relates.

Post sacrum R.mus D.ns magister cappelle congregationem petiit, et postquam omnes cantores cum omni charitate hortatus est ut propter Adventu et festum Nativitatis D.ni N.ri Redemptoris se ad confessionem preparent, dixit sibi relatum fuisse quod aliqui ill.mi de concertis quibus in missis et vesperis papalibus fiunt lamentatus, et presertim de aliquibus nostris senibus qui in tertiis et quartis malum agunt effectum. Itaque ut magis S.mo D.no N. et ill.mis cardinalibus placere et satisfacere possimus, fuit decretum, ut ipsi senes in tertiis et quartis taceant, et quia D. Benedictus Archadius nominatus fuit cum omni humilitate respondit et paratum esse dixit omnibus mandatis R.mi D. magistri et collegii obedire, in hac congregatione omnes presentes fuerunt preter D. Alexandrum Merlum D. Jacobum Brunettum et D. Jo. Lucam Confortum.

After the service the *maestro di cappella* called a meeting, and, after having exhorted all the singers with all charity because of Advent and Christmas, to prepare themselves

XIV

6 Original *motu proprio* (undated, but promulgated 30 July 1555) in which Paul IV orders the expulsion of married singers (Vatican City, Biblioteca Apostolica Vaticana, fondo Cappella Sistina 646, f.92r). The crossed-out lines concern a pension of 6 ducats a month to which the pope had apparently agreed and then changed his mind. (Transcribed as appendix 2.)

for confession, he said that he had been told that certain cardinals had complained about the polyphony in papal Masses and Vespers and particularly about certain of our senior singers who sounded bad in trios and quartets. Thus, so that we might better please His Holiness and the illustrious cardinals, it was decreed that these senior singers should be silent during trios and quartets. And because D. Benedetto Archadio had been named, he responded in all humility that he was ready to obey all the orders of the *maestro* and the College; and at this meeting all were present except Alessandro Merlo, Jacques Brunet and Giovanni Luca Conforti.

This discussion leads to a few concluding comments. First, it appears that by the middle of the 16th century an ideal configuration of the Sistine choir, inspired by the situation in the third decade of the century, had been established as 24 men divided more or less equally among voice parts with all singers having the sonorous voices required for projection in churches and chapels (although the relationship of this to the actual number of singers who sang at any one time is still not clear).

But it also appears that the Sistine choir never achieved this ideal in the 16th century, and it seems increasingly evident that at least by the middle of the century it was bloated in size through the admission of people with limited or no vocal abilities who had not auditioned and were imposed on the choir by papal authority; furthermore these singers did not and were not expected to perform, causing tensions within the choir and official embarrassment. And even when these people had been purged and the size of the choir brought under control, there still remained an uncomfortably high number of voices that were inadequate for the type of cappella singing that was the ideal. In short, we may really not want to hear the music the Sistine choir sang in the Age of Palestrina in the way that they sang it. (So much for 'authenticity'.)

Second, if we consider the singers who over the years were considered to have weak voices, it is striking how many of them were composers. The most famous, of course, is Palestrina, who along with his colleagues Leonardo Bonot/Barre and Domenico Ferrabosco (also composers), was dismissed from the papal choir by a *motu proprio* of Paul IV promulgated on 30 July 1555 (illus.6; the text is transcribed in appendix 2).[29]

The main reason for the dismissal, as is well known, was the maintenance of ecclesiastical propriety. Considering the types of services that the choir attended, it was imperative from a strict point of view that its members be in holy orders; in spite of this, the papal choir had for years occasionally welcomed into its ranks singers who were not only laymen but were even married.[30] In 1555 there were three married singers (Palestrina, Barre and Ferrabosco—the progenitor of the Ferrabosco clan of Elizabethan fame) and the austere, reforming, intolerant Paul IV was not going to stand for such 'scandal'. Out they went, soon to be followed by another 'scandalous' singer, Charles d'Argentil, a member of the regular clergy.[31] This might be construed as a 'reform' of the organization, but it is clear that it had nothing to do with music.

Nonetheless, within the *motu proprio* of July 1555 is a musical reason for the dismissal of the three married singers; that they 'never were and are not now competent to be members of the choir because of their weak voices' ('attento quod nunquam fuerunt prout nec sunt ad presens ad officium cantorum in eadem capella exercendum habiles et idonei propter imbecillitatem vocis'). It might at first be tempting to dismiss this as merely some legal language, but in light of the evidence presented in this study, it should come as no surprise that 'weak' singers were members of the papal choir in 1555.[32] Palestrina, it seems, did not have the 'sonorous' voice required for the papal chapel.[33] Neither did the following composers: Leonardo Bonot/Barre, Domenico Ferrabosco, Ghiselin Dankerts, Agostino Martini, Firmin Le Bel, Stefano Betti (Fornarino), Christian Ameyden.

Talent in composition (and, in the case of Palestrina, Barre and Le Bel, talent as *maestri di cappella*) and talent (or even plain competence) as a choral singer clearly did not always go together in late 16th-century Rome. In fact, one gets the impression that these men had been hired, most in direct contravention of the constitution, precisely because they were composers, or perhaps more importantly, because they could be counted on to understand the techniques of composition and the intricacies of theory and notation, could 'help out' when needed.[34] The papal choir, after all, prided itself on always having one or two composers among its members, a pride that might have been shared at the highest levels. Indeed, Agostino Martini (who had consistently been rejected by the audition process—see document 2) was so grateful to Gregory XIII for placing him in the chapel that he dedicated a manuscript copy of what appears to be his complete works to that pope.[35] This may be indicative of a trend; certainly does seem to be the case that more and more composers in Italy (especially the important ones) do not rely on jobs as choral singers in order to make their primary living, and apparently those who did were often given such jobs as special favours. That composition should have become more of a 'profession' at this time is

XIV

7 A fresco by Bernardino Pinturicchio dating from the late 1480s: a lunette of the Loggetta at the Villa Belvedere, the Vatican

not surprising, of course; we have ample evidence from at least the end of the 15th century that composers (one thinks of Josquin, Isaac, Obrecht) were valued almost exclusively for their compositional talents, with not a word said about their singing abilities. But it is only the 16th century that provides evidence of how little singing ability actually counted.

Lest we think that incompetence and dissatisfaction with the papal choir was merely a problem of the 16th century, let us consider some evidence from an earlier time. The volume in the Archivio Segreto which contains the miscellaneous 16th-century documents related to various reforms of the papal chapel also has two extended excerpts regarding the chapel and its personnel copied in a late 16th-century hand from the writings of Johannes Burkhard (d 1506), the master of ceremonies in the reigns from Innocent VIII to Julius II. One of these excerpts can be traced to a Burkhard autograph miscellany produced between 1484 and 1488;[36] more interesting are the excerpts said to have been copied from various folios of Burkhard's writings, which I have not yet been able to track down (although they may also be in the miscellany).[37] For in these sections, Burkhard talks about the entire personnel of the chapel, and specifically about the singers, even referring to numbers of people on voice parts (the entire text is given in appendix 3, the sections about the singers are transcribed below).

Item sunt xii cantores videlicet duo tenoristae, 4.or contratenores, et sex voices altae, quae debent esse clarae et melodiosae non raucae, nec asperae: Nimia enim multitudo vocum melodiam tollit, et confundit auditum. Isti non sunt officiales sed simplices servitores; et istos semper consuevit magister cappellae ponere, et deponere, et mutare; quotiens visum est esse expediens honori, aut necessitati cappellae aut paci vel quieti.

Item. There are twelve singers, that is, two tenors, four countertenors and six high voices, who should have clear and melodious voices, and not hoarse or harsh ones; indeed, too many people singing distort melody and confuse hearing. These are not officials but simple servants, and the *maestro di cappella* has been accustomed to hire, fire and change them as often as it is deemed expedient for the honour or necessity of the chapel or its peace and quiet.

Cantores debent esse honesti, et moderati, in musica experti, habentes voces idoneas ad serviendum cappellae et practicam bonam, et qui tales non sunt debent expelli, et alii bene qualificati subrogari. Quo ad numerum verum est quod nunquam aliquis papa habuit ultra xii et aliquando viii et ix praeter D. Nicolam papam Vtum qui habuit magnum numerum sine causa, ex quo generatur confusio et tollitur melodia, experientia quotidiana hoc probat: Et nunquam fuerunt ita ineptae et viles voces in cappella sicut hodie; provideat magister cappellae quia de honore papae et ipsius magistri cappelle agitur.

The singers should be honest and modest, expert musicians, having voices appropriate for singing in the chapel and good experience, and those who are not, should be expelled and replaced with others who are well qualified. As to the number, it is true that popes never had more than twelve and at other times had eight and nine, except for Nicholas V who had a larger number for no reason, out of

622

which confusion is generated and melody is distorted, as daily experience shows. And there have never been such inept and ugly voices in the chapel as there are today: the *maestro di cappella* should take care, because this concerns the honour of the pope and of the *maestro di cappella*.

It seems clear that Burkhard, writing in the late 15th century, is here drawing on much older documents and customs. The proportions of the voice ranges, with its emphasis on the high voices, match almost exactly those in the Burgundian Ordinances of 1469 reported by David Fallows as at least: 'six high voices, three tenors, three contrabasses and two moiens [presumably countertenors]' for a total of 14 singers.[38] And the 'ideal' number of 12 or fewer seems to reflect the actual state of the chapel in the very first decades of the 15th century, in particular the choir of Eugene IV, which ranged between eight and 12 members.[39] Burkhard is, however, correct in asserting that it was Nicholas V who increased the number of singers thereby starting a trend that continued to Burkhard's own day; in the first year of Nicholas's reign the choir grew from 10 to 15 singers and the average size of the choir from then until the reign of Pius II appears to have been 16.[40] Under Sixtus IV (1472–84) the number of singers rose into the middle 20s and between 1484 and 1513 the number of singers ranged from 17 to 20.

What is interesting, of course, is Burkhard's dislike of choirs containing more than 12 members (that is, the papal choir of his own day) because of what so many singers do to the 'melody.' It is not at all clear what he means, but even if we assume that he was taking a theoretical position based on some idealization of choral sound, it would appear that he expected all the singers to be singing at the same time. This would run counter to arguments put forth by Jean Lionnet and myself that all the members of the choir rarely sang together.[41] At the moment, I am not prepared to try to reconcile the two positions. It is possible that things changed radically from the late 15th to the 16th century; for instance, Burkhard's view of the powers of the *maestro di cappella* to accept and remove singers runs contrary to the singers' constant reiteration in the 16th century that their own corporate privileges in that regard had existed since time immemorial. The point is that, even in the late 15th century, the papal choir inspired negative comment, to the extent of Burkhard's complaining about the quality of the individual voices. Burkhard's day was, of course, the 'Age of Josquin'; indeed, for all we know, Josquin's was one of the inept and ugly voices to which he refers. On the other hand, Burkhard was a notorious curmudgeon who did not care much about music anyway, so until more evidence emerges perhaps we can keep our illusions (if we have any left) about the papal choir during that particular 'Golden Age.'

Appendix 1

Julius III reduces the number of singers to 24 and declares that henceforth singers may be admitted to the choir in excess of that number only if they pass an audition and obtain a *motu proprio* from the pope (Vatican City, Biblioteca Apostolica Vaticana, fondo Cappella Sistina 646, f.84r: *motu proprio* without date (1553?)).

Inhibitio pape ne decetero sub pena excomunicationis aliquem cantorem admittant donec numerus cantorum ad xxiii.or reducatur[42]

Julius Papa iii.s

Motu proprio etc. Licet tam Nos quam predecessores nostri Romani Pontifices pro divini cultus in capella nostra conservatione et augmento ipsiusque capellae et in ea pro tempore celebrati divini officii venustate et decoro, sepe ad diversas orbis partes cum in urbe deessent ad inquirendum et inventos ad ducendum cantores non solum artis musices peritos sed qui essent canoris vocibus dulcissimoque concentu prediti ad dictae cappellae deservituram destinare consueverimus. Ac propterea in eadem capella dictorum cantorum certus numerus hactenus determinatus non fuerit, nihilominus tamen a certis annis citra tot cantores magnatum et aliarum personarum favoribus et precibus eiusdem capellae constitutionum et statutorum forma non servata in dicta capella recepti immo intrusi fuerunt, quod ad presens numerum triginta quinque efficiant eorumque maior pars (quod non sine animi nostri displicentia referimus) est imbecillitate vocum ad cantandum penitus inutilis. Brevique futurum est quod nisi de opportuno remedio de super provideatur eadem capella sicut concentu et musice melodia in toto terrarum orbe primatum obtinuit ita vilior et inferior omnibus aliis efficietur. Nos capellam ipsam in melius reformare et inutiles palmites ex ea amputare volentes, eosque qui non per ostium neque iuxta constitutionum et statutorum predictorum formam sed aliunde ingressi sunt et idoneorum loca indebite occupant a dicta capella amovere et ipsos cantores ad numerum vigintiquatuor reducere volentes, motu simili et ex certa scientia maturaque deliberatione nostra venerabili fratri nostro Hieronimo Episcopo Castrensis moderno et pro tempore existenti magistro necnon decano et cantoribus capellanis etiam pro tempore existentibus dicte capelle in virtute sanctae obedientiae et sub indignationis nostrae nec non excomunicationis late sententie a qua preterquam in mortis articulo constituti absolvi non possint nisi per nos aut romanum pontificem ipso facto totiens quotiens incurrendis penis districte precipiendo inhibemus ne aliquem etiam quantuncunque idoneum et sufficientem in dicte capelle cantorem capellanum quocunque etiam Sanctae Romanae Ecclesiae cardinalium intuitu etiam si id eis per nos viva voce aut alium seu alios etiam eosdem cardinales relatione vive vocis nostre oraculi etiam sub quavis pena quantuncunque gravi mandaretur, decetero recipere vel admittere audeant sive presumant donec et quousque dictorum cantorum numerus sive per obitum sive locorum dimissionem vel amissionem aut quamvis aliam vacationem ad vigintiquatuor reducatur, nisi servata forma statutorum et constitutionum huiusmodi et nisi hoc eis per motum proprium manu nostra signatum eis specialiter directum expresse commisserimus. Decernentes aliter pro tempore admissos dicte capelle cantores nec esse et de salariis et emolumentis aliis cantoribus dari solitis eis responderi non debere. Sicque per quoscunque judices etc. sublata etc. iudicandum etc. fore irritumque etc. Non obstantibus constitutionibus et ordinationibus apostolicis ac dicte capelle etiam juramento etc. roboratis statutis et consuetudinibus privilegiis quoque indultis et litteris apolstolicis eidem ac illius magistro decano et cantoribus predictis et quibusvis aliis quomodolibet et cum quibuscunque etiam derogatoriarum derogatoriis clausulis irritantibusque et aliis decretis etiam motu proprio etc. concessis confirmatis et innovatis. Quibus illorum tenores etc. hac vice derogamus. Ceterisque contrariis quibuscunque presentis motus proprii solam signaturam sufficere et ubique fidem facere regula contraria non obstante decernentes.

[signature] Placet et ita decernimus J

Appendix 2

Motu proprio without date (but promulgated on 30 July 1555). Paul IV removes married singers from the choir (Vatican City, Biblioteca Apostolica Vaticana, fondo Cappella Sistina 646, f.92r).[43]

Paulus Papa iiii
Motu proprio etc. Licet capelle nostre cantores sint etiam nostri et pro tempore existentis Romani pontificis cappellani consueverintque in eiusdem pro tempore Romani pontificis ac venerabilium fratrum nostrorum sancte Romane ecclesie cardinalium et prelatorum aliarumque diversarum urbis ad ipsam capellam confluentium personarum presentia lectiones prophetias ac evangelia et capitula aliaque divina officia decantare et recitare. Et propterea cum etiam per sacros canones spiritualia per laicos tractari prohibitum existat indecens sit ut aliqui ex eisdem cantoribus coniugati existant, nichilominus tamen accepimus quod inter eosdem cantores capellanos dilecti filii Leonardus Barre et Dominicus Ferrabosco ac Petrus Aloysius de Palestrina viri coniugati Pauli III et Julii etiam III Romanorum pontificum predecessorum nostrorum temporibus in cantores capellanos recepti cum aliis eiusdem capelle cantoribus capellanis preter et contra eosdem sacros canones et ipsius capelle statuta et consuetudines divina officia decantantes reperiuntur in divini cultus villipendium et scandalum plurimorum. Nos qui cultum et servitium divinum nostris presertim temporibus ea qua decet sinceritate semotis etiam quibuscunque scandalis celebrari toto desideramus affectu volentes in premissis opportune providere Motu simili et ex certa scientia maturaque deliberatione nostra prefatos Leonardum Dominicum et Petrum Aloisium ut prefertur coniugatos attento quod nunquam fuerunt prout nec sunt ad presens ad officium cantorum in eadem capella exercendum habiles et idonei propter imbecillitatem vocis[44] neque etiam in cantores dicte capelle servatis servandis accepti et ei admissi fuerunt ab exercitio officii in eadem nostra capella cantorum capellanorum necnon ab aliorum eorumdem cantorum capellanorum numero et consortio[45] cassamus eiicimus et amovemus ac cassatos eiectos et amotos esse cassarique eiici et amoveri debere decernimus. Mandantes eiusdem capelle magistro et cantoribus capellanis quatenus visis presentibus eosdem Leonardum Dominicum et Petrum Aloisium ab eadem capella ac a divinorum officiorum et in ea decantatione et aliorum cantorum capellanorum numero et consortio cassent eiiciant et amoveant nec eos de cetero in eadem cappella divina officia aut aliud decantare permittant[46] districtius etiam illis sub excomunicationis late sententie ipso facto incurrenda pena inhibentes ne de cetero aliquos coniugatos in cantores capellanos dicte capelle recipere audeant. Non

XIV

yhs

MANDATA **M**ENSIS DECEMBRIS
DNI THESAVRARIJ

R. S^{ti} Georgij ad velum aureum Ste Rom̄n ec̄lie Dioconus Car^{lis}
D̄ñs p̄p Cōmunibus R^{do} p̄ dño Aleandro Farnesio protoñ et
Thesaurario a^pt^{lico} Salu^{tē}. p . v . Tenore p̄ntium Committimus
et mandamus ut ex p̄dmissis (cum applic^{ne} p manibus Spect^{lium}
virore heredum e quondam Ambrosij de Spannochiis cliuum
Gmalium Depositariorū Solui facias infrascriptis cantoribz
et officialibus Capelle . S . D . N . Summam pecuniae infrascriptā
pro eorum provisione al Salario p̄ti mensis Novembris et p̄mo
R^{do} p̄ri ep̄o Bartholomeo Magro Capelle ————————— fl. x
R^{do} p̄ri d. Abbati S. Sebastiani Sens̄ Capelle ————————— fl. x

Jo. Monstroel	Jo. Barbe	
Jo. Rodulphi	Jo. Balmsir	
R. Masnini	Geor de Divris	
An. Bruston	Ju . de Spreo	pro quolibz flore otto aurj in auro de Cam
Ju. Coffe	Jo. Juvenis	Sunt in Totum flore c . L x
Jo. Menem	Ray deodona	
Ber Vacqueras	Phi . di Primo	
Mar de Orto	Jo. de Lanis	
De. Lofranch	Do felyx	
Gi. Ronspon	Jo. de Verona	

ho Rassi) Capellanis m̄ssarū pro quolibz flore qumqz sunt intotu fl x
f Carrera)
Jo. Brochardi) dⁿis Cerimoniare pro quolibz flore qumqz sunt intotu fl . x
Jo. Mario)
fras Nicolai) pro quolibz flore duobs sunt intotum ———————— fl iiij^{or}
Ni. Jacomini)

Custodum m̄ Totum Summam flore duarentosequatuor aurj in auro de Camera
quos in vris Computis admitti facies). Dat^m R^{ome} in Camer
pie pmo Decembris 14 . 92 . pont. S . D . N . D Alexandri
p̄p — vi   Anno   p̄mo

List of papal chapel, November 1492 (Vatican City, Archivo Segreto Varticano, Misc. Arm. XV, vol. 161, f.9 r)

XIV

obstantibus constitutionibus et ordinationibus apostolicis dicte capelle etiam juramento etc. roboratis statutis et consuetudinibus privilegiis quoque indultis et litteris apostolicis eisdem Leonardo Dominico et Petro Aloisio quomodolibet et cum quibuscunque etiam derogatoriarum derogatoriis clausulis irritantibusque et aliis decretis etiam per eosdem predecessores etiam motu proprio etc. concessis confirmatis et innovatis etiam iteratis vicibus quibus latissime extendentur tenores illorum etc. hac vice latissime derogamus. Ceterisque contrariis quibuscunque presentis motus proprii etiam non registrati neque datati solam signaturam sufficere et ubique fidem facere regula contraria non obstante decernentes.

[signature] Placet et ita mandamus J

Appendix 3

Excerpts from the writings of Johannes Burkhard concerning the number, voice designations and ideal vocal sound of the papal singers (1487?) (ASV Misc. Arm. XI, xciii, ff.132v–134r).

[f.133r] Insuper inter annotationes et scripturas praefati Jo. Brurchardi collegi sparsim infrascripta, quae ad materiam de qua agitur pertinere videntur, licet sint admodum antiqua.

Magister cappellae consuevit deputari a pontifice suo arbitrio sive cappellanus, seu cubicularius secretus, qui debet esse prudens, et magnae reputationis, cuius officium est gubernare cantores.

Cantores debent esse honesti, et moderati, in musica experti, habentes voces idoneas ad seviendum cappellae et practicam bonam, et qui tales non sunt debent expelli, et alii bene qualificati subrogari. Quo ad numerum verum est quod nunquam aliquis papa habuit ultra xii et aliquando viii et ix praeter D. Nicolam papam Vtum qui habuit magnum numerum sine causa ex quo generatur confusio et tollitur melodia, experientia quotidiana hoc probat: Et nunquam fuerunt ita ineptae et viles voces in cappella sicut hodie; provideat magister cappellae quia de honore papae et ipsius magistri cappelle agitur.

Omnes de cappella debent omni mense habere summam quae sequitur. Primo Dominus sacrista duc. x, Magister Cappellae x, subsacrista iiii, clerici cerimoniarum semper habuerunt x duc. pro quolibet, usque ad tribulationem Eugenii iiii; postea fuerunt reducti ad v, super hoc videatur ceremoniale quod est in libreria papae. Cantores nunquam habuerunt nisi quinque duc. usque ad Nicolam papam Vtum qui cantoribus doctis et aptas voces habentibus dabat viii duc., aliis dabat iii, iiii, v similes, quod plus aut minus merebantur, et nunquam habuerunt omnes simul octo nisi tempore Calisti pp iii. Videatur libri camere de tempore dictorum pontificum.

[ff.133v–134r] Ex alio folio sumpta sunt infrascripta, videlicet.

Modus quo cappella D. N. Papae regulari et ordinari consuevit ad laudem dei et honorem praefati D. N. Papae.

In primis est unus sacrista, qui consuevit esse episcopus, estque officialis perpetuus, et papae immediate subiectus. Cui quidem cura est de omnibus paramentis cappellae tam secretae quam communis et de omnibus libris utriusque cappellae calicibus, et aliis ornamentis, et quidquid ministrant campanarii, ministrant pro sacrista.

Item est unus magister cappellae immediate subiectus papae, qui debet diligenter attendere, ut per cantores horis debitis, debitaque cum reverentia, et silentio, horae canonicae nocturnae pariter et diurnae cantentur. Iste magister cappellae est officialis ad vitam papae, alias ad beneplacitum papae, et per solum papam ponitur et mutatur.

Item sunt duo clerici cerimoniarum, qui missas habent ordinarium et alternis ebdomadis servire, cerimoniasque facere ab omnibus observari. Isti sunt officiales perpetui, ut sacrista, et per solum papam creantur.

Item sunt duo cappellani alternis septimanis missas quotidianas celebrantes, qui debent esse viri honesti, habentes voces mediocres, bene legentes, et pronuntiantes, et bene scientes cantum Gregorianum. Isti non sunt officiales, sed simplices servitores ad nutum mutabiles, et per magistrum cappelle possunt institui et mutari.

Item sunt xii cantores videlicet duo tenoristae, 4.or contratenores, et sex voces altae, quae debent esse clarae et melodiosae non raucae, nec asperae: Nimia enim multitudo vocum melodiam tollit, et confundit auditum. Isti non sunt officiales sed simplices servitores; et istos semper consuevit magister cappellae ponere, et deponere, et mutare; quotiens visum est esse expediens honori, aut necessitati cappellae aut paci vel quieti.

Item sunt duo campanarii, qui debent esse iuvenes humiles, et apti ad serviendum cappellae, et debent obedire officialibus cappellae in his solum, quae concernunt divinum officium. Isti sunt simplices servitores, et ad nutum revocabiles.

Item omnes de cappella tenentur omni die venire ad officium divinum, videlicet unus clericus cerimoniarum et unus cappellanus ad missas tamen; cantores, et campanarii ad missas, et omnes horas: et qui defuerint debent mulctari, seu puniri secundum ordinationes olim factas. Multae autem, seu poenae deficientium debent ad thesaurarium venire; si enim applicarentur personis cappellae, facile possent inter se colludere.

XIV

1 Gregory Martin, *Roma Sancta* (1581), ed. G. B. Parks (Rome, 1969), pp.96, 101. Quoted in C. Reynolds, 'Rome: a city of rich contrast', *Man and music: the Renaissance*, ed. I. Fenlon (Englewood Cliffs, NJ, 1989), pp.75–6. Martin's description of the Sistine Chapel when occupied by the entire Curia corresponds very well (but not exactly) with the engraving by Etienne Dupérac of about the same time (shown here as illus.1), *Maestatis Pontificiae dum in Capella Xisti Sacra Peraguntur Accurata Delineatio* (Biblioteca Apostolica Vaticana, Ris. Strag. 7, f.16).

2 Reynolds, 'Rome: a city of rich contrast', p.76.

3 See M. Uberti, 'Vocal techniques in Italy in the second half of the 16th century', *Early music*, ix (1981), p.494. See also R. Wistreich, ' "La voce è grata assai, ma . . .": Monteverdi on singing', *Early music*, xxii (1994), pp.7–20; and A. Cavicchi, 'Appunti sulla prassi esecutiva della musica sacra nella seconda metà del XVI secolo con riferimento alla musica del Palestrina', *Atti del Convegno di Studi Palestriniani 28 settembre–2 ottobre 1975*, ed. F. Luisi (Palestrina, 1977), pp.295–312.

4 There is not much evidence, of course, but we do know, for instance, that in the 1590s, of the 13 members of the choir of S. Marco, only one was judged by the *maestro di cappella* to have had 'not much of a voice'; all the others were judged to be competent or better. See J. H. Moore, *Vespers at St Mark's: music of Alessandro Grandi, Giovanni Rovetta, and Francesco Cavalli* (Ann Arbor, MI, 1981), i, pp.75–6, 246.

5 *Constitutiones capellae pontificiae*, promulgated in 1545, chap.3: 'Modus examinis'; chap.4: 'Scrutinum super admissionem novi cantoris'. The original constitution is preserved in Vatican City, Biblioteca Apostolica Vaticana, fondo Cappella Sistina [VatS] 611 and is transcribed in F. X. Haberl, 'Die römische "schola cantorum" und die päpstliche Kapellsänger bis zur Mitte des 16. Jahrhunderts', *Bausteine für Musikgeschichte*, iii (Leipzig, 1888), pp.96–108.

6 In chap.5: 'Modus dandi cottam et jurmanetum novo cantori': 'Novi cantori approbato sufficienter, Magister dictae Capellae eidem novo cantori approbato cottam tradere tenetur in signum verae receptionis et admissionis ad vitam.'

7 Although it should be acknowledged that there is as yet no evidence that membership in the papal choir had become a venal office—it was practically the only office in the Curia that was not. See P. Partner, *The pope's men: the papal civil service in the Renaissance* (Oxford, 1990).

8 A copy of this *motu proprio* in VatS 684, f.114r–v has the date '5 Agosto 1553' added at the top in pencil. The text is transcribed in Haberl, 'Die römische "schola cantorum"', pp.92–3, n.3, and partially transcribed in G. Baini, *Memorie storico-critiche della vita e della opere di Giovanni Pierluigi da Palestrina*, 2 vols. (Rome, 1828), i, pp.42–3, n.59. Both transcriptions differ in minor details from the text of the original *motu proprio*. In particular, regarding the size of the choir as stated in the document, they both render the very clear 'triginta quinque' as '33.' It is likely that the transcriptions were made from a copy of the *motu proprio*, not the original reproduced in illus.4.

9 VatS 657, f.7r–v. 'Prefatus vero Clemens prefixit numerum xxiiii cantorum videlicet septem supranos, septem contraltos, sex vassos et quatuor tenores sed cum esset expertus in arte musicis ipsemet pontifex examinabat cantores admittendos sed non exclusit aliquem cantorem ad effectum reducendi cantores ad huiusmodi numerum et sic tempore suo fuit cappella illustrata et dechorata tam de vocibus quam de sufficientia cantorum.' Quoted in H.-W. Frey, 'Regesten zur päpstlichen Kapelle unter Leo X und zu seiner Privatkapelle', *Die Musikforschung*, viii (1955), p.199, and Frey, 'Klemens VII und der Prior der päpstlichen Kapelle Nicholo de Pitti', *Die Musikforschung*, ii/iii (1951), p.180. See also F. A. d'Accone, 'The performance of sacred music in Italy during Josquin's time', *Josquin des Prez: Proceedings of the International Josquin Festival-Conference*, ed. E. E. Lowinsky and B. Blackburn (London, 1976), pp.601–18. This paragraph is part of a memorandum prepared with regard to the reform of the chapel in 1565. Not all the chapel lists of Clement's reign are extant. Those that are show that the choir had an average of 20 members during the period. On the other hand, the most senior singers would have known colleagues who were members of Clement's choir.

10 Consider the administration of a college deciding to revoke the tenure of certain individuals on grounds of 'incompetence'. It would immediately find that its faculty, which up until then had been unable to agree on anything, suddenly had found solidarity. If, however, the crafty administrators promised the fabled 'golden handshake' to those it wanted to let go, things might be easier.

11 *Diarii Sistini*, iv, f.74v. See R. Casimiri, 'I Diarii Sistini', *Note d'archivio*, xiii (1936), p.209.

12 Paul IV had ordered the dismissal of: three married singers (Palestrina, Leonardus Bonot/Barre and Domenico Maria Ferrabosco); Charles Argentil because of his status in the regular clergy; Nicolò Clinca and Giovanni Antonio Merlo because of disobedience; further, he had banished Nicolò Barono and Giovanni Luigi de Episcopis from Rome (probably because of their relationship to Cardinal Carlo Caraffa); and he had expelled Giovanni Antonio Latino (another Caraffa protégé) because the singer had falsified the *motu proprio* ordering his admission to the choir and had been admitted without examination through the cardinal's influence.

13 On this commission and the unlikelihood that it was concerned with 'reforming' music, see F. X. Haberl, 'Die Cardinalskommission von 1564 und Palestrinas Missa Papae Marcelli', *Kirchenmusikalisches Jahrbuch*, vii (1892), pp.82–97. The singers were aware of the contemplated reform as early as January 1565, and appointed representatives to deal with the commission. See *Diarii Sistini*, vii, ff.119v–120r.

14 Some of these documents are preserved in a special volume in the Archivio Segreto (Vatican City, Archivio Segreto Vaticano [ASV], Misc. Arm. XI, xciii) containing miscellaneous documents related to the papal chapel and its membership, others are preserved in the *fondo Cappella Sistina* collection of the Vati-

can Library. Most of the documents are undated, but can be related to the 1565 reform through context.

15 ASV, Misc. Arm. XI, xciii, f.172r–v.

16 The first copy is in ASV, Misc. Arm. XI, xciii, ff.156r–157r.

17 ASV, Misc. Arm. XI, xciii, f.151r.

18 See Wistreich, ' "La voce è grata assai, ma . . .'".

19 Eight singers had been sent to the Council in 1560. By 1565, they had, of course, returned to Rome.

20 The word *bonus* is sometimes paired with 'non habet vocem': it would seem that something beside musical ability was deemed to be 'good'; I have therefore translated it as 'acceptable'. Further references to the singers' financial state or the remarks *apostata, concubinarius, hereticus pessimus* prove that something more than vocal abilities was being tested.

21 *Diarii Sistini*, vii, f.153r. See Haberl, 'Die Cardinalskommission', p.86.

22 Rome, Archivio di Stato, Camerale I 917, ff.28r–v.

23 Ameyden's career in the choir included repeated stints in the choir's main administrative offices, including that of *maestro di cappella*. See Haberl, 'Die Cardinalskommission', p.87.

24 During the reign of Julius II (1503–13), the choir ranged from 17 to 21 members.

25 In the bull *In supremis militantis ecclesiae* of 1 September 1586.

26 See *Diarii Sistini*, xi, ff.33v–34v, and R. Casimiri, 'Annibale Zoilo (1540?–1592) e la sua Famiglia', *Note d'archivio*, xvii (1940), pp.1–25.

27 J. Lionnet, 'Performance practice in the papal chapel during the 17th century', *Early music*, xv (1987), pp.4–15.

28 See Lionnet, 'Performance practice', and R. Sherr, 'Performance practice in the papal chapel in the 16th century', *Early music*, xv (1987), pp.453–62.

29 Transcribed in Baini, *Memorie . . . di Giovanni Pierluigi da Palestrina*, i, pp.53–5, n. 82. Translated (with omissions) on pp.53–5.

30 The earliest married singer known to me was Paolo Trotti (*d* 1523).

31 But the other singers made sure that those who were expelled were granted permanent monthly pensions to compensate for their loss of employment. Accordingly, for the rest of his life, Palestrina was paid 5 ducats 87 baiocchi a month (approximately two-thirds of the normal monthly salary of 9 ducats), and continues to be carried in chapel lists in a category labelled 'coniugatos'. Argentil got a better deal; the pope actually agreed to continue paying him 9 ducats a month. But he did not enjoy it for long, since he died in 1557.

32 The words 'propter imbecillitatem vocis' are actually an addition to the *motu proprio*, found in the middle of the last line and connected via a signum congruenciae to the middle of line 13. This might indicate that they are an afterthought; but they are in the hand of the scribe of the *motu proprio* and most likely were left out as the result of a copying error.

33 This, by the way, was too much for Palestrina's hagiographer Giuseppe Baini: consciously or unconsciously, he omits the offending judgement of Palestrina's singing abilities in the translation he gives of the entire *motu proprio* (although he kept it in the Latin text he supplies in a footnote), although the phrase in the *motu proprio* may have been the motivation behind Baini's statement earlier on in his book that Palestrina had a 'wretched voice' (*meschino di voce*) from whence, like so many other of Baini's opinions and fantasies, it entered general Palestrina lore (i.e. people have a vague notion that Palestrina had a bad voice, but they don't quite know how they came by it). Baini, *Memorie . . . di Giovanni Pierluigi da Palestrina*, i, pp.53–5, 44.

34 It may be significant that the negative evaluations of the voices of some of these men stress that their 'good knowledge of music', not that they are composers. See the discussion of the *rimettitore* in B. Blackburn, 'Luigi Zenobi and his letter on the perfect musician', *Studi musicali*, xxii (1993), pp.61–114. As is well known, beginning in June 1565, Palestrina was paid an extra monthly amount 'ex causis diversorum compositionum quas hactenus edidit et est editurus ad commodum dicte capell', thus becoming the official composer of the papal chapel practically ten years to the day from the date of his expulsion from that body.

35 VatS 58.

36 Vatican City, Biblioteca Apostolica Vaticana, fondo Vaticani Latini [VatL] 5633. See M. Dykmans S.I., *L'œuvre de Patrizi Piccolomini ou le cérémonial papal de la première renaissance*, Studi e Testi 293, 2 vols. (Vatican City, 1980), i, pp.78*–90*. The excerpts on ff.131–2 are copied from VatL 5633, ff.90– and followed by f.132v: 'Fuerunt suprascripta omnia excerpta de verbo ad verbum ex quibusdam annotationibus Jo. Brurchardi olim apostolicarum cerimoniarum magistri et episcopi ortani, et iuxtam praedictam ordinationem fuerunt transmissae cedulae omnibus R.mis tunc Cardinalibus ut illam observuarent prout in eisdem annotationibus scriptum reperitur. Quam quidem reformationem atque ordinationem fuisse usu receptam testatur Paris Crassus variis in locis.'

37 VatL 5633, f.133r: 'Insuper inter annotationes et scripturas praefati Jo. Brurchardi collegi sparsim infrascripta, quae ad materiam de qua agitur pertinere videntur, licet sint admodum antiqua.'

38 D. Fallows, 'Specific information on the ensembles for composed polyphony, 1400–1474', *Studies in the performance of late mediaeval music*, ed. S. Boorman (Cambridge, 1983), p.110. See also d'Accone, 'The performance of sacred music in Italy during Josquin's time', pp. 601–18.

39 See Haberl, 'Die römische "schola cantorum"'.

40 See P. Starr, *Music and music patronage at the papal court, 1447–1464* (PhD diss., Yale U., 1987), pp. 82–3.

41 Lionnet, 'Performance practice'; Sherr, 'Performance practice'.

42 Written in another hand in the upper left margin.

43 Transcribed in Baini, *Memorie . . . di Giovanni Pierluigi da Palestrina*, i, pp.53–5, n.82. Translated (with omissions) on pp.53–5.

44 Inserted at the bottom in another ink but in the same hand.

45 Three lines are heavily crossed out here.

46 Et nichilominus mensium salarium predictum persolvere pro illi incipiendo in eadem mandato describi mandent et faciant—crossed out.

XV

MECENATISMO MUSICALE A MANTOVA: LE NOZZE DI VINCENZO GONZAGA E MARGHERITA FARNESE

Di tutti gli scandali del tardo Cinquecento, quello provocato dal matrimonio *manqué* di Vincenzo Gonzaga e Margherita Farnese è certo uno dei più singolari. Non è necessario, qui, riportare nei particolari la vicenda, ben nota ai cronisti dell'epoca e forse narrata meglio da Maria Bellonci nei *Segreti dei Gonzaga*.[1] Basti ricordare che Margherita, nipote del duca di Parma Ottavio Farnese, sposò il 2 marzo 1581 il futuro sovrano di una delle più brillanti corti italiane, ma non riuscì ad avere figli. I Gonzaga, invece, avevano un disperato bisogno di eredi, per scongiurare la caduta di Mantova nelle mani dell'odiato ramo francese della famiglia (che oltre tutto, come Guglielmo Gonzaga faceva presente al papa, avrebbe portato con sé in Italia il « contagio » del protestantesimo), per cui fu necessario far annullare il matrimonio e dare a Vincenzo un'altra moglie. Margherita, sottoposta ad umilianti visite mediche e a crescenti pressioni da parte dei suoi e dei Gonzaga, dopo due anni di resistenza, finalmente acconsentì ad entrare in convento il 30 ottobre 1583. Scandalo a parte, le nozze Gonzaga-Farnese ebbero tuttavia delle ripercussioni sulla vita musicale della corte di Guglielmo Gonzaga, padre di Vincenzo e terzo duca di Mantova (dal 1550 al 1587).

I Gonzaga erano stati – già dal XV secolo – importanti patrocinatori di musica, e Guglielmo, compositore di non trascurabile talento, continuava la tradizione familiare.[2] All'epoca del matrimonio

---

[1] M. BELLONCI, *Segreti dei Gonzaga*, Milano-Verona, Mondadori 1947.
[2] Su Guglielmo e la musica cfr. C. GALLICO, *Guglielmo Gonzaga signore della musica*, « Nuova rivista musicale italiana », XI, 1977, pp. 321-334 (anche in *Mantova e i Gonzaga nella civiltà del Rinascimento*, Mantova, Accademia Virgiliana - Mondadori 1977, pp. 277-283); R. SHERR, *The Publications of Guglielmo Gonzaga*,

Farnese, il duca mostrò un notevole interesse sia nei confronti della vita musicale di Parma, sia nei confronti delle inclinazioni musicali della nuora. Una serie di lettere, scritte fra marzo e giugno 1581, ci documenta questo interesse: in quel periodo, non solo Guglielmo si mantiene costantemente informato sulle capacità musicali di Margherita e si dà da fare per assumere una musicista che l'intrattenga piacevolmente, ma cerca di attirare a Mantova due dei migliori cantanti di Parma. Notizie sui famosi musicisti impiegati a Parma vengono fornite a Guglielmo dagli ambasciatori inviati al matrimonio. Aurelio Zibramonti scrive da Piacenza, il 25 febbraio 1581, di aver ascoltato una « bellissima musica di instromenti et voci » (doc. 1), e Cesare Cavriani riferisce, il 5 marzo, di aver ascoltato a messa un'eccellente esecuzione di tromboni e cornetto mentre, tra i musicisti di Parma, definisce « molto rari » due cantanti: un basso e Orazio della Viola (Orazio Bassani; doc. 9).

Guglielmo, poco interessato agli strumentisti, desidera però assumere il basso e un castrato (all'epoca ogni corte ne aveva almeno uno),[3] e ordina pertanto a Zibramonti di prendere all'uopo contatto con il duca di Parma. Zibramonti risponde il primo marzo: basso e castrato sono troppo importanti per la musica di Parma, il duca non può farne a meno (doc. 2). La risposta viene ampliata in una lettera del 4 marzo: il duca di Parma non può rinunciare ai suoi cantori, ma è disposto a concedergfieli in prestito almeno « finché V. A. non sia provista de altri » (doc. 6). Guglielmo scrive il 6 marzo accettando l'offerta (doc. 10). Se il 20 aprile Cavriani lamenta il ritardo nella partenza dei musicisti (doc. 29), il 22 aprile scrive che stanno ormai per mettersi in viaggio (doc. 31). Eppure, il 2 luglio, Galvano Cantello, il funzionario incaricato del viaggio a Mantova, riferisce che i musicisti sono disposti a lasciare Parma solo per poco tempo, visto che il soggiorno presso i Gonzaga comporterebbe per-

---

« Journal of the American Musicological Society », XXXI, 1978, pp. 118-125. Più in generale sulla musica a Mantova cfr. A. BERTOLOTTI, *Musici alla corte dei Gonzaga in Mantova dal sec. XV al XVIII*, Milano, Ricordi 1890; P. CANAL, *Della musica in Mantova*, « Memorie del Reale Istituto Veneto di scienze lettere ed arti », XXI, 1879, pp. 655-774 (rist.: Genève, Minkoff 1978); e il più recente I. FENLON, *Music and Patronage in Sixteenth-Century Mantua*, 2 voll., Cambridge, Cambridge University Press 1980-1982.

[3] Cfr. R. SHERR, *Guglielmo Gonzaga and the castrati*, « Renaissance Quarterly », XXXIII, 1980, pp. 33-56.

dite di denaro particolarmente pesanti per il basso, che ha una famiglia di otto persone da mantenere, e per Gottifredo Palmartz, che guadagna a Parma 28 ducati al mese e altri 5 per il servizio d'organo in cattedrale (doc. 35). Infine, il 4 luglio, Cantello scrive che « i musici » partiranno entro tre giorni, ma non esistono tracce del loro arrivo a Mantova; evidentemente Guglielmo non riuscì ad averli se nel 1586, alla morte di Ottavio Farnese, tentò di assumere quegli stessi musicisti, ancora una volta senza risultati.[4]

Se questi tentativi non ebbero esito positivo, Guglielmo fu un po' più fortunato in un'altra trattativa: volendo compiacere Margherita, cercò di procurarle una fanciulla di buona famiglia che entrasse a far parte del suo seguito come musicista. Questa ricerca occupò larga parte del marzo e dell'aprile 1581, e coinvolse Guglielmo, i suoi ministri, il suo funzionario a Bologna Federico Pendaso, il duca di Parma e i cardinali Cesi e Paleotti.[5] Guglielmo, che aveva saputo da Annibale Capello di una eccellente cantante e strumentista bolognese, nipote del primicerio Bovio (quasi certamente Laura Bovio),[6] desidera che entri al suo servizio come damigella della principessa « che si diletta molto di musica ». Ordina quindi a Pendaso di informarsi sulla reputazione della fanciulla e di avviare eventualmente le trattative con la famiglia, ricorrendo, se necessario, all'appoggio del legato papale cardinal Cesi e del cardinal Paleotti (doc. 4). Nello stesso tempo Guglielmo scrive a Zibramonti per chiedere l'aiuto del vescovo di Osimo (doc. 3), e il 3 marzo Zibramonti risponde ponendo un problema: secondo il vescovo, la ragazza è in realtà la figlia illegittima di monsignor Bovio, non la nipote (doc. 5). La stessa informazione Guglielmo la riceve il 4 marzo da Cavriani (doc. 7); come se non bastasse, Zibramonti scrive, il 9 marzo, che a Parma si osteggiava la « nipote » di Bovio perché era figlia di un ecclesiastico e probabilmente era stata mandata in convento per nascondere qualche scandalo (doc. 12). Evidentemente solo una dama di assoluta integrità avrebbe potuto servire la giovane principes-

---

[4] Cfr. *Ibid.*, p. 55 sg.
[5] Quanto segue vuole ampliare e correggere i brevi accenni di P. CANAL, *op. cit.*, p. 700 sg., e di I. FENLON, *op. cit.*, I, p. 134.
[6] È vero che il suo nome di battesimo non compare mai nei documenti, ma la persona in questione che non può che essere la famosa cantante Laura Bovio; tuttavia sia P. CANAL, *loc. cit.*, che I. FENLON, *loc. cit.*, la confondono con qualcuno della famiglia Mezzovillani.

sa, per cui, l'11 marzo, Pendaso viene incaricato di sospendere le trattative, almeno fino a che non si sia accertato che « in lei non solamente sia effetualmente alcuna machia ma ne anco sospetto » (docc. 17, 20 e 24). Nel frattempo, tuttavia, sia Guglielmo che il duca di Parma ricevono dai due cardinali lettere che non mettono minimamente in dubbio la rispettabilità di Laura (docc. 13, 14 e 15), anche se Zibramonti ha, al riguardo, le sue riserve (doc. 19). Sembra che il cardinal Cesi, in particolare, si sia interessato personalmente alla faccenda; convocato Bovio, cercò di convincerlo a far entrare la nipote al servizio di Guglielmo, presentandogli l'offerta come un dono mandato dal cielo (doc. 15). Ma Bovio, dal canto suo, è poco entusiasta della proposta. Sembra poi di capire dalle lettere di Pendaso che Guglielmo gli abbia posto due condizioni. La prima riguarda la questione della nascita illegittima (doc. 21). A quanto pare, Guglielmo aveva chiesto a Bovio di dichiarare Laura sua figlia, e forse di legittimarla; Bovio aveva rifiutato, evidentemente offeso dai dubbi avanzati nei confronti della nipote (doc. 22). La seconda condizione è di carattere economico: Guglielmo aveva chiesto a Bovio di caricarsi in parte delle spese per il soggiorno della nipote a Mantova; ma Bovio, « molto parco nel spendere », aveva rifiutato. Nonostante lo scoraggiante atteggiamento di Bovio, Pendaso non dispera. Il 24 marzo arriva da Parma la buona notizia: sembra che i dubbi sulla reputazione di Laura siano risolti (doc. 23). Nel frattempo, Laura si trova nel convento di San Lorenzo, dove in molti si recano per ascoltarla cantare e suonare (in tutta la vicenda sembra non ci sia mai stato il minimo dubbio sull'abilità musicale della ragazza; doc. 25). Ma la questione della rispettabilità è il pensiero dominante di Guglielmo (doc. 26), anche se Pendaso assicura l'onestà della ragazza, invocando a sostegno della sua opinione anche l'autorità del cardinal Paleotti (doc. 27). A questo punto Guglielmo deve aver lasciato cadere la questione – o forse Bovio deve aver rifiutato ogni patto – se il 2 giugno 1581 vengono avviate le trattative per assumere un'altra musicista, probabilmente Ippolita Mezzovillani.[7] Anche questa volta, la possibile obie-

---

[7] Sia Laura Bovio che Ippolita Mezzovillani sono citate in un poema di Giulio Cesare della Croce, in lode delle cantanti, datato 15 luglio 1590. Cfr. A. NEWCOMB, *The Madrigal at Ferrara: 1579-1597*, I, Princeton, Princeton University Press 1980, p. 93.

zione riguarda la reputazione della ragazza più che la sua abilità musicale, e Guglielmo ordina che sia controllata in questo senso anche tutta la famiglia (doc. 32). Il controllo ha esito positivo, e Ippolita Mezzovillani risulta già assunta il 25 giugno 1581 (docc. 33 e 34). Ma il servizio di questa musicista, l'unica donna musicista impiegata alla corte di Guglielmo,[8] dura poco: Ippolita viene licenziata dopo un anno appena, perché « la Serenissima Signora Principessa per servitio della quale fu presa non s'è dilettata della musica come si credeva » (doc. 39). La spiegazione è sorprendente, visto che l'unica ragione per cui la musicista era stata assunta era il supposto amore di Margherità per la musica: impressione che lei aveva deliberatamente dato agli ambasciatori mantovani intervenuti al suo matrimonio. Infatti Margherita, sprovvista di reale talento, deve aver compreso chiaramente l'importanza che veniva attribuita alla musica presso la corte di Mantova, e deve aver tentato, attraverso la musica, di mostrarsi all'altezza della sua nuova famiglia. Tutto questo risulta da due lettere che Guglielmo aveva ricevuto da parte dei suoi ambasciatori il 4 marzo 1581. Cavriani scrive di averla sentita cantare: la voce non è perfetta, ma deve essere un « defetto naturale » dei Farnese (doc. 7); e Zibramonti, che pure non s'intende molto di musica, nota la debolezza della sua voce (doc. 6). Ma la vera abilità della principessa – suggeriscono i due ambasciatori per rassicurare Guglielmo – deve essere nella composizione. Interpellata esplicitamente da Zibramonti, Margherita esprime infatti il suo desiderio di studiare musica e composizione, magari sotto la guida del duca, famoso per le sue « cose » musicali.[9] Questa sua richiesta, unita a una certa adulazione nei confronti di Guglielmo, mostra chiaramente che Margherita cercava così di guadagnarsi la considerazione del suocero; Zibramonti, favorevolmente colpito dalla sua abilità in questo senso, osserva: « io stupisco ch'in così tenera età ella sappia tanto et sia così manerosa » (doc. 6).

---

[8] Concordo con I. FENLON, loc. cit., secondo cui Guglielmo non aveva intenzione di costituire un « concerto delle dame » sul modello di quello ferrarese.

[9] A Guglielmo sono attribuiti un libro di madrigali e uno di mottetti pubblicati anonimi a Venezia nel 1583 presso i Gardano (cfr. R. SHERR, *The Publications of Guglielmo Gonzaga* cit., p. 119 sgg.); Guglielmo è altresì indicato tra i probabili autori della raccolta *Villotte mantovane* pubblicata a Venezia nello stesso anno (cfr. C. GALLICO, *Damon pastor gentil. Idilli cortesi e voci popolari nelle « Villotte mantovane » (1583)*, Mantova, Arcari 1980, p. 6).

Un ulteriore indizio dell'interesse musicale di Margherita è la scelta di Cavriani come suo gentiluomo d'onore proprio perché questi era un buon esecutore e compositore (docc. 37 e 38).[10] Nondimeno il licenziamento di Ippolita Mezzovillani ci rivela il sostanziale disinteresse di Margherita per la musica che emerge nel momento in cui, nel 1582, ella si rende conto che non resterà ancora a lungo nella famiglia Gonzaga. Invece, il suo interesse più vero può essere stato di carattere letterario tant'è che spesso esprimeva i propri sentimenti con la poesia, e particolarmente con la poesia di Ariosto (doc. 37). Nei suoi giorni più cupi, quando ormai tutto era perduto, il suo stato d'animo si rispecchiava nei versi dell'*Orlando furioso* che ella recitava o intonava (doc. 40).[11]

(*Traduzione dall'inglese di Nicoletta Guidobaldi*)

---

[10] Si tratta senza dubbio del «Cavaliere Cavriani» citato nell'ultima delle *Villotte mantovane* (cfr. C. GALLICO, *Damon pastor gentil* cit., p. 7).

[11] Nonostante Margherita conoscesse – quasi sicuramente – le numerose composizioni polifoniche realizzate su questi versi, è probabile che ella li cantasse su una delle arie impiegate per la recitazione dei testi ariosteschi (cfr. J. HAAR, *Arie per cantar stanze ariostesche*, e M. A. BALSANO - J. HAAR, *L'Ariosto in musica*, in *L'Ariosto la musica i musicisti*, a cura di M. A. Balsano, Firenze, Olschki 1981 («Quaderni della Rivista italiana di musicologia», 5), pp. 31-46 e 47-88.

APPENDICE DOCUMENTARIA

I documenti qui riportati in ordine cronologico sono conservati nelle seguenti buste dell'Archivio di Stato di Mantova, Archivio Gonzaga:

   201   Affari di famiglia - matrimonio di Vincenzo
   202   Affari di famiglia - matrimonio di Vincenzo
1161   Lettere da Bologna, 1581
1379   Lettere da Parma, 1581
1380   Lettere da Parma, 1582
2211   Minute cancelleresche, 1581
2213   Minute cancelleresche, 1582
2952   Registri di lettere, 1571-1584
2953   Registri di lettere, 1577-1581.

1: Aurelio Zibramonti a Guglielmo, 25 febbraio 1581.

Finita la festa et ritiratisi in camera, è stata fatta una bellissima musica di instromenti et voci, mancandone Fabritio Denteci Farneto, il quale morì hieri a Parma. (1379)

2: Zibramonti a Guglielmo, 1 marzo 1581.

Il castrato et il basso che servono a S. Ecc.a le sono cari, siché quando ella ne restasse priva la Ecc.a S. lo sentirebbe male. (1379)

3: Guglielmo a Zibramonti, 2 marzo 1581.

Ho inteso esser in Bologna una giovane nipote di Mons.r Bovio, molto virtuosa nella musica, et perché stimo ch'ella debba apportar qualche passatempo alla sposa, mando Antonio con lettere a quelli S.ri Card.li Ill.mi in credenza del lettor Pendaso per haverla; et perché mi viene detto ch'ella è ricercata altrove, sarà bene che dandone parte a S. Ecc.a procurate ch'ella aiuti questo mio giusto desiderio. [Se] Lo Mons.r de Osmo vi potesse aiutare, credo che gioverà assai. Il luogo sarà di Damigella. (2952, libr. 379, c. 43).

4: Minuta di Theodoro di San Giorgio a Federico Pendaso, Bologna 2 marzo 1581.

È stato riferito al S.r mio Ser.mo da D. Annibale Capello, altre volte capellano dell'Al. S. et hora dell'Ill.mo S.r Card. d'Este, ch'essendo egli stato a questi giorni passati in cotesta città, ha udito cantare et sonare molti stromenti una giovine da màrito, nata nobilmente et d'ottimi costumi, nipote di Mon.re Bovio, celebrandola per cosa quasi che miracolosa. Il che ha acceso l'animo dell'Al. S. di desiderio d'haverla per damigella della Ser.ma Prencipessa sua nuora che si diletta molto di musica. Perciò m'ha commandato ch'io scriva a V.S. in nome dell'Al. S. che vogli informarsi se veramente la detta giovine ha queste virtù et qualità, et trovandola tale, che V.S. procuri colli suoi che s'accontentino di darla alla sodetta servitù; ma che V.S. non vi perda e questo perché s'intende ch'altri prencipi la ricercano, et a fine che nascendovi qualche difficoltà V.S. possa tanto meglio levarla, l'Al. S. scrive le lettere che serano qui alligate all'Ill.mi SS.ri legato e Paleotto in credenza di V.S. acciò aitino la prattica co'l loro favore, le quale se bisognerà V.S. puotrà presentarle, et non bisognando le rimanderà. (2952, lib. 381, c. 9r-v; riportato parzialmente in I. FENLON, *Music and Patronage* cit., qui a nota 2, I, doc. 69)

5: Zibramonti a Guglielmo, 3 marzo 1581.

Mons. Vescovo di Osmo dice che quella giovane è figlia non nipote di Mon. Bovio, et per antequente naturale ch'ella nodrita in un monastiero, et che S. S.ria R.ma non s'intende bene col Bovio, onde non può servir a V.A. in questo, S. Ecc.a ha accettato prontamente di aiutar in ciò il desiderio di V.A. per quanto potrà, ancor ch'ella reputa se ricerchi il porre la mano ove la pone V.A. alla quale S. Ecc.a bacia le mani. (1379)

6: Zibramonti a Guglielmo, 4 marzo 1581.

La sudetta Ser.ma sposa, dopo haver cantato molte villanelle in compagnia del Cimino fratello di quello che morì al servitio di V.A. et d'un gentilhuomo da Sinigaglia servitore de Sua Ecc.a, mi ha con molta instanza dimandato che nova havevo di V.A., domandandomi che sempre che n'intendo gliélo faccia saper subito; et poi distendendosi su l'obligo che ha a V.A. per tanti favori che lei le fa con parole tale ch'io stupisco ch'in così tenera età ella sappia tanto et sia così manerosa [...]. Io non m'intendo di musica, ma per quello che mi detta la natura, parmi che la voce non sia delle migliori et che habbia bisogno di maggior disciplina nel cantare. Le ho dimandato se S.A. disegni di seguir in imparar musica et nel componere; mi ha risposto che si, et che sa quanto V.A. se ne diletti et come siano celebrate le sue cose, volendo inferire che spera di imparare sotto la sua protettione. S. Ecc.a mi ha fatto rispondere intorno il castrato et il basso che ella non può fare senza li sudetti perché senza essi la musica è guasta, che nondimeno se le dimandavano licenza la darà loro, ch'in ogni caso se V.A. li vole in prestito glieli presterà finché V.A. sia provista de altri, et se pur essa li vorrà per sempre, li potrà ritenere perché S. Ecc.a intende che V.A. sia padrona delle cose sue; le quale parole, pur quello che tocca alli sudetti musici, sono date per creanza, essend'io sicuro che le spiacerebbe il vedersi guasto un così raro concerto de' voci come ha, quale accompagna alle volte con tromboni et altri instrumenti con intiero gusto di quelli che s'intendono di musica. (1379)

7: Cesare Cavriani a Guglielmo, 4 marzo 1581.

Questa sera la S.ora Principessa ha cantato, et di comissione del S.or Prencipe Serenissimo ci son stato presente. S. Al. canta allegramente tanto, per non pigliare tempo di guardare su'l libro, falla qualche volte. La voce potrebbe portare più giusta, ma veramente credo che venga per defetto naturale, et tanto maggiormente lo credo perché nel cantare che si faceva soggionse el S.or Duca di Parma Ecc.mo; et dopo l'essere incontrato dalla S.or Prencipessa Ser.ma et fatte le solite accoglienze, S. Ecc.a disse che invero fin nella voce ella mostrava molto bene di essere di casa Farnese, et infatto a me pare che la voce non sia molto buona et si può credere, conforme al detto del S.or Prencipe Ser.mo, ch'ella sia più atta al componire che al cantare. La si gode assai della musica et per quel ch'io posso comprendere, anco di stare allegremente [...] Mons.or d'Osmo dice che non è buono per il negotio di quella giovine, ma che proponerà (et già dice d'ispedire un messo domattina a V.A. Ser.ma) il meggio [mezzo] buono a questo fatto, et dice che è figliuola naturale di quel mons.re et non nipote. (1379)

8: Zibramonti a Guglielmo, 5 marzo 1581.

S. Ecc.a ha scritto all'Ill.mi S.i Card.li che sono in Bologna per disponer con la loro autorità Mons. Bovio a mandar sua nipote (chiamata dal vescovo d'Osmo figliuola) al servitio della S.ra sposa. (201, c. 28r-v)

9: Cavriani a Guglielmo, 5 marzo 1581.

Questa mattina la S.ora Prencipessa col S.or Prencipe Serenissimo è uscita col Frontale fuore di casa, et è andata a messa in San Sisto, chiesa de' Frati di San Benedetto di Mantova, ove mentre si diceva la messa, si è fatto un concerto di tromboni et cornetto nell'organo honestamente buono [...]. Discesi che giovedì prossimo a venire il S.or Duca partirà per Parma, et domattina la musica si ha da incaminare, nella quale ci sono duoi quali a me parono veramente molto rari; l'uno è un basso che già stava col S.or Duca d'Urbino di felice memoria, l'altro è Messer Horatio della Viola che a me par che faccia cose rarissime. (1379)

10: Guglielmo a Zibramonti, 6 marzo 1581.

Non havessimo ricercato d'havere il castrato et basso del sudetto S.r Duca se Antonio cantore che ce li propose non ci havesse detto ch'essi ci sariano venuti a servire voluntieri, però fate saper a S. Ecc.a la causa che ci ha mossi a riceverli, dicendole che non intendiamo di privarliela, ma che bene la haveremo obligo s'ella si contentarà di prestarcili per qualche giorni come ci ha offerto. (2953, lib. 383, cc. 114v-115r)

11: Zibramonti a Guglielmo, 7 marzo 1581.

Ella mi ha anco detto che prestarà a V.A. il suo castrato et il basso per quei giorni che a lei piacerà. (1379)

12: Zibramonti a Guglielmo, 9 marzo 1581.

Il sogetto della nipote di Mons. Bovio è tenuto qui per puoco atto al servitio della sudetta S.ora perché, oltre all'esser figliuola di un prete, la sua fama non è interamente buona; anzi pare che fosse porta in un monasterio per rimediar a qualche inconveniente. Così mi ha detto la S.ra Vittoria, figliuola della S.ora Girolama maritata nel Cav.re Casale in Bologna, la quale mostra di haverne cognitione. (1379)

13: Cardinal Paleotti al duca di Parma, 10 marzo 1581.

Ha mandato qua il S.r Duca di Mantova persone sue per informarsi bene delle qualità della giovene di che ancora m'ha scritto V. Ecc.a Ill.ma talmente che si è contentato Mons.r Bovio di lasciarli e vedere et ascoltare anco la giovene nelle cose di musica, et si è risoluto di voler prima intendere se il S.r Duca persisterà nel medesimo pensiero dopo ch'havrà havuta la relatione dai suoi; et crederò io che quando le SS.VV. Ill. desiderino che la cosa vada inanzi, che Mons.r suo zio non mancarà di servirle ancor che a me non ha dato già questa risolutione, ma non si mancarà di operare per redurla al fine se accaderà. (1161)

14: Cardinal Cesi al duca di Parma, 11 marzo 1581.

Ho havuta la lettera che V. Ecc.a mi ha scritta con quella del S.r Duca di Mantova per il desiderio che si ha della giovane per servitio della S.ra Principessa, et non sono mancato di far uffitio co'l Primicerio Bovio zio di detta giovane acciòché non solo accetti il partito ma rengratii Dio di questa così buona et honorata occasione. Esso ha messe inanzi diverse difficultà, ma al fine credo che se resolverà di accettare il partito, parendomi che si restringa che il S.r Duca di Mantova gli scriva in modo che esso et gli altri parenti della giovane possino dar sodisfattione a loro medesimi et agli altri di questa resolutione sopra che si è scritto distesamente il S.r Duca di Mantova, dal quale però si aspettarà quello che più le piacerà che si faccia, et io poi non mancarò di fare quanto occorrerà per compimento del tutto con quel desiderio che vive in me sempre di servir a V. Ecc.a. (1161)

15: Cardinal Cesi a Guglielmo, 11 marzo 1581.

Havendo visto quello che mi scrive V. Alt.a per la sua delle iii del presente, et inteso quanto mi ha esposto il mandato da lei che me l'ha resa, ho mandato a chiamare il Primicerio Bovio, zio della giovane che desidera V. Alt.a al servitio della S.ora Principessa sua nuora, et gli ho detto quanto mi è parso a proposito per mostrargli quanto gli deve esser cara questa occasione et quanto ne deve ringratiare Dio. Esso mi ha messo inanzi diverse difficultà: della inclinatione della giovane di essere monaca et del modo che si era trovato di sodisfarla in questo facilmente et con poco loro dispendio, et della tenerezza con ch'amano tutti li parenti questa giovane, et altre. Ma per quello ch'io gli ho replicato ha mostrato al fine di restare assai ben disposto di accetare questa buona fortuna, et mi pare che si restringa in sustantia che per favorire lui, la giovane, et la casa sua, esso Primicerio desideraria che V. Al.a si degnasse di scrivere a lui in modo che paresse che V. Al.a desidera veramente di havere la giovane per servitio della S.ora Principessa, et che quando si levarà di qua et mentre starà a tali servitii, et al tempo che occorerà a recognoscere la sua servitù si farà in modo che tutti haveranno causa di restar sodisfatti. (1161; riportato parzialmente in I. FENLON, *op. cit.*, I, doc. 71)

16: San Giorgio a Pendaso, 11 marzo 1581.

Ho dato a vedere al S.r mio Ser.mo la lettera di V.S. delli 7 del presente in materia di quella gentildonna che canta, alla cui Al.a è stato molto caro d'intendere la diligenza che V.S. usa e l'amorevolezza di cotesti Ill.mi SS.ri, ma perché questo negotio non si è potuto risolvere così subbito come l'Al.a S. desiderava, ha commandato ch'io scriva a V.S. che tenga la practica viva ma che non passi più oltre sin a nuovo ordine dell'Al.a S. (2952, lib. 381, c. 12v)

17: San Giorgio a Pendaso, 11 marzo 1581.

La lettera qui anessa è scritta in forma che V.S. la possi mostrare, ma con questa le dico in nome del Si.r nostro Ser.mo che l'Al. S. fa soprastare questo negotio perché V.S. habbi tempo d'informarsi bene della vitta et costumi di questa gentildonna, importando molto che in lei non solamente sia effetualmente alcuna machia ma ne anco sospetto. V.S. donque usi in ciò quella diligenza che l'Al.a desiderà et che V.S. stessa sa che conviene, trattandosi di dar detta gentildonna al servigio d'una prencipessa di tanta qualità et di così tenera età com'è la nostra; et vedda particularmente d'intendere quanto tempo ha vissuto fuore del monastero et per che causa poi vi sia stata posta. (2952, lib. 381, c. 12v-13r)

18: Zibramonti a Guglielmo, 12 marzo 1581.

Il Ser.mo S.or Prencipe vidde prima di me Antonio Ritio et però havendo S.A. inteso il riporto di M. Antonio sudetto intorno alla S.ora Bovia, ne diede conto alla Ser.ma S.ora sposa, alla quale piace quello che piace a V.A., presuponendo però sempre che V.A. debba esser informata se la giovane sia honesta, che così mi ha detta la prefatta Signora Girolama. (1379)

19: Zibramonti a Guglielmo, 12 marzo 1581.

Sua Ecc.a mi manda a mostrar dal Signore [illegibile] la lettera di Mon. Ill.mo Paleotto la quale contiene che Mons.r Bovio si è risoluto di voler prima che dia certa promessa intender prima se V.A. persisterà nel medesmo pensiero dopo che havrà havuto relatione delle qualità della giovane da chi V.A. ha mandato a Bologna per questo effetto, et che persistendo V.A. et S. Ecc.a in disiderio che la cosa vada inanzi, crede S. S.a Ill.ma che Mons.re Primocero zio della giovane (che così lo nomina) non mancarà di servirle. Un altra lettera mi mandò anco S. Ecc.a da vedere del S.or Card.le Cesis nel istesso soggetto, la quale contiene che S. S.a Ill.ma ha parlato al Primiciero Bovio zio della giovane acciò non solamente accetti il partito ma ringratii Dio di così buona et honorata occasione, et ch'egli le ha posto avanti diverse difficultà ma alla fine crede che accetterà il partito se V.A. gli scriverà in modo ch'esso et li altri parenti della giovane possano dar soddisfattione a loro. (1379)

20: Minuta, 13 marzo 1581.

Che le informatione che si sono havute sin hora della nipote di Mons.r Bovio S.A. ne fa pigliar di nuove ne se risolverà d'accetarla al servitio della Ser.ma S.ra sposa se ella non è sicura che la sudetta nipote di Mon.re sia non sol senza macula ma anco senza suspetta d'essa. (2211)

21: Pendaso a Zibramonti, 21 marzo 1581.

Ho fatto sapere al s.r segretario di Mons.r Ill.mo et R.mo legato la causa perché S.A. Ser.ma non ha riposto hor alla lettera di S. S.a Ill.ma et R.ma; ho ancho communicato seco le due conditioni che non sono di sodisfattione dell'A.S. aciòché possa riferire il tutto a Mons.r Ill.ma del che non tacerò a V.S. per informatione sua che se bene questa figliuola è naturale, nondimeno Mons.r Bovio, invaghito straordinariamente di lei, non vede, come si dice, per altri occhii che per li suoi, et son certo che, sicome aviene a molti che non possono udir nominare in se le diffetti che sanno di havere, così Mons.re con modestia udirà questa voce di naturale, attesa specialmente la natura sua di prezzare assai le sue cose, si persuederà ancho che le virtù della figliuola debbano supplire a questo difetto; questa sia detto con ogni riserva et riverenza et puramente per far venire in notitia di V.S. quanto scopro qui non per altro fine, essendo prontissimo ad esseguire con tutto il mio spirito quanto da S.A. Ser.ma sarà commandato. Quanto poi all'altra conditione, habbiamo discorso il s.r segretario et io che Mons.r Bovio fa veramente torto alla figliuola medesima, né doveria volere che le sue virtù la privassero di quel tanto ch'esso saria necessitato a spendere quando la volesse accommodare qui, ma più presto che lasciato questo fermo, le augmentassero tutto quello che dalla benignità et liberalità di S.A. Ser.ma le verrà donato, ma non so come la vorà intendere esso Mons.re; sono ben certissimo che Mons.r Ill.mo et R.mo legato spenderà ogni sua authorità per far riuscire quanto dall'A.S. sarà desiderato. (1161)

22: Pendaso a Zibramonti, 21 marzo 1581.

Dopo ch'io ho scritto la inclusa, mi è occorso parlare di nuovo col s.r segretario di Mons.r Ill.mo et R.mo legato, il quale mi ha detto assai rissolutamente che tiene per certo che quelle due conditioni escluderanno la prattica, essendo Mons.r Bovio da una parte altiero et dall'altra molto parco nel spendere. Io gli ho replicato che per il passato a simile serviggio sono state gentildonne et signore principalissimamente di famiglie illustrissime, et che non si è usato mai di pigliarle a maritare intieramente; esso mi ha risposto che lo tiene per certo nondimeno che in questo particolare non spera che sia per riuscire, et mi ha essortato ch'io come da me lo faccia sapere a V.S. Io son entrato in openione che questo raggionamento sia stato con particapatione di Mons.r Ill.mo et R.mo legato, la cui S.a Ill.ma et R.ma, come prudentissima ch'è, nel raggionare con esso Mons.r Bovio haverà scoperto tutto l'animo suo, et anch'io l'ho conosciuto per tale, ma il s.r segretario non mi ha già detto ciò essere d'intentione di S. S.a Ill.ma. Io tengo per certo che ella adoperarà ogni sua authorità perché S.A. Ser.ma conseguisca l'intento suo, sicome io come servitore humilissimo et fidelissimo non lascierò cosa da me imaginabile per ubidirla et servirla. Aspettarò donque ordine di quanto si haverà a fare. (1161)

23: Zibramonti a Guglielmo, 24 marzo 1581.

Non solamente S. Ecc.a non è per haver dispiacere che la giovane Bovia serva alla S.ora Prencipessa, ma le havrà caro, havendo S. Ecc.a informatione da quella città che la giovane figliuola è di valor grande et di bonissima vita. (1379)

24: Minuta per Pendaso, 25 marzo 1581.

S. Alt.a ha veduto quello che V.S. scrive al S.r Zibramonte con la sua dei 21 di questo intorno al particolare che ha trattato con lei il segretario di cotesto Mons.r Ill.mo legato, né si è risoluta ad altro per hora se non che V.S. tenghi la cosa in suspeso senza escluderla affatto. (2211)

25: Pendaso ad Aurelio Pompanazzi, 27 marzo 1581.

Io ubidirò al commandamento di S.A. Ser.ma in tenere questa prattica sospesa, né inovarò cosa alcuna senza ordine dell'A.S. La figliuola al presente è nelle monache di Santo Lorenzo, dove nelli ufficii di questa settimana santa è concorso molto populo per udirla a cantare et sonare. Mons.r Bovio, raggionando meco li giorni passati, mi disse che se bene si riputava a grandissima gratia che S.A. Ser.ma si fosse degnata di chiedere questa figliuola a serviggio tanto principale et honorato, nondimeno esso saria ancho restato molto consolato quando l'A.S. si fosse compiaciuta di lasciarla qui, et che in questa prattica esso principalmente desidera di fare acquisto della buona gratia dell'A.S. Ser.ma, alla quale vole essere sempre servitore humilissimo et fedelissimo, et resterà perpetuamente obligato con molte altre humile et affettuose parole, a tal che o escludasi o concludasi tal prattica, io spero che la cosa non potrà passare se non bene, massimamente s'io haverò come mi rendo certo quattro parole amorevoli verso la persona di esso Mons.r Bovio da potergli mostrare et far leggere. (1161; riportato parzialmente in I. FENLON, *op. cit.*, I, doc. 72)

26: Minuta, 31 marzo 1581.

Pare che sia stato dubitato intorno alla castità di Mons.r Bovio, però ordina S.A. che V.S. usi diligenza per intender se elle è senza colpa o senza sospetto di colpa, et poi ne avisi l'A.S., alla quale io ho dato conto di quello che V.S. mi scrive con la sua di 27 di questo. (2211)

27: Pendaso a Pompanazzi, 11 aprile 1581.

Et posto insieme quanto ho inteso, son venuto in chiarezza che la moltitudine et qualità de' musici chiamati da Mons.r Bovio per fare insegnare a questa figliuola et li mali modi di loro tenuti, aggiontavi ancho la troppa indulgenza et tenerezza di esso Mons.r, hanno causato qualche disordine et ronione de parole, ma che la figliuola è tenuta per da bene, et specialmente Mons.r Ill.mo Palleotto, la cui S.a Ill.ma, come diligentissima ch'è nel governo spirituale, procura di giustificarsi del vero, mi ha acertato di tenerla per honesta et buona, et io veramente nell'animo mio la tengo per tale. (1161)

28: Cavriani a Guglielmo, 20 aprile 1581.

La S.ra Prencipessa sta molto allegra perché s'avicina il tempo di venire a Mantova. Non si fa altro che cantare dopo la partita de' medici, né io resto di suonar il flauto seco in compagnia che così piacesi all'Altezza Sua. (201, c. 61)

29: Cavriani a Zibramonti, 20 aprile 1581.

Non restando di dirle che tanto ai musici quanto a le altre facende, il S.or Galvano è tanto lungo che non so quando veriranno. (1379)

30: Cavriani a Zibramonti, 21 aprile 1581.

Gli cantori mi sono stati a trovare, et promettono di essere all'ordine tanto a tempo che domenica che viene saranno costì. (1379)

XV

31: Cavriani a Zibramonti, 22 aprile 1581.

Ecco i musici che vengono allegramente. (1379)

32: Minuta per Ottavia Malvezzi, 2 giugno 1581.

Havendo il S.r mio Ser.mo veduto una lettera scritta da V.S. Ill.ma a M. Filippo suo musico in materia di quella giovane di Mezovillani che desidera venire a servire la S.ma S.ora Principessa nostra, poiché sa la servitù ch'io tengo col S.r Pirro, mi ha commandato ch'io pigli sicurtà con V. S.a Ill.ma di pregarla ad esser contenta d'assicurarsi bene dell'honestà de' costumi non solo della sodetta giovane ma anco della madre et sorelle s'ella ne ha, et confidando che V.S. Ill.ma la quale sa quanto questa importi avertir di prendere questa information con ogni diligenza et da persone non apassionate. Quanto alle virtù della giovine, già S.A. n'è informata talmente che ne rimani sodisfatta onde concordi anco la sodetta parte dell'honestà, questa giovine potrà venire subbito che serà accettata, et trattata come richiederà sue conditione et le virtù. (2211)

33: Minuta per Ottavia Malvezzi, 25 giugno 1581.

Ho per informatione veramente sinistra che s'havesse della giovine Mezzovillani ch'è venuta a servire la S.ma S. Prencipessa mia padrona, ma perché trattandosi di mettere persone al servigio di prencipesse simile all'Al. S. ne si deve, come V.S. sa molto ben giudicare, andar molto circonspecto et chiaro, mi messi a scrivere a lei di ordine del S. mio Ser.mo quant'ella vidde; ond'è poi stata molto cara la rellatione havuta non solo da lei propria colle sue lettere ma anco quelle che ha procurate di far fare dalla S.a Camilla Fantuzzi, però ringratiandone V.S. Ill.ma a nome dell'Al. Sua et restando quel servitore a lei che sono al S. Pirro suo consorte, le bacio le mani pregandola a commandarmi ovunque ella mi cognosca atto a poterla servire. (2211)

34: Minuta per Camilla Fantuzzi, 25 giugno 1581.

Se ben bastava la informatione che ha mandata la S.ra Ottavia Malvezzi intorno alla giovane Mezzovillani ch'è venuta a servire la S.ra Prencipessa mia padrona, è nondimeno stata anco cara quelle che V.S. ha datta colle sue. (2211)

35: Galvano Cantello a Zibramonti, 2 luglio 1581.

Il S.r Duca mio s.ore me ha comandato subito che io li ho datto conto di quanto V.S. mi scrive intorno alli musici per parte di S.A. che io li comandi che se ne vengano subito, como ho fatto in presentia di quello ha mandato qua V.S. per condurli. Però como V.S. intenderà da lui, me hanno pregato a voler darli tempo quatro giorni, come ho fatto che poi alhora li farò venire per servire a S.A. in quel modo che lui vorrà. È ben verro che non vogli lassare di metterli in consideratione che da quello essi hanno trattato con me mostrano di non volere partire di qua se non per pocho, dicendo che havendo essi qua altri guadagni oltra a quello lì da S.E., non lo vogliano perdere, et fra li altri il basso si faccia sino a otte boche da far le spese che se non guadagni assai molto più a imparar a molte persone como fa di quello lì da S.E. di provisione che sono ducati 22½ d'oro, lui non potrebbe viver la mettà del anno. Vi è poi Messer Gottifredo, quale è uno homo di sua testa et fiamengo, qual ha altra la provision di S.E. che son credo ducati 28 il messo, l'organo del domo che li ha ducati 5 il messo. Il castrato è il più sbrigato di tutto, però siano como si vogliono. S.E. haverà molto più a cor che servano a S.A. che a lui medesimo, et quando sarrano accordato con S.A., lui li darà voluntierissima licentia, però come ho detto a questo che V.S. ha mandato qua si mandarano che ad hora V.S. faccia trattar con lui, che dal canto di S.E. po molto bene S.A. essere sicura di dispore sempre di tutto quello sarrà in potere di S.E. (1379)

36: Cantello a Zibramonti, 4 luglio 1581.

Li musici verrano fra tre giorni per servire a Sua Alt.a. (1379)

37: Cavriani a San Giorgio, 21 novembre 1582.

La S.ora nostra Ser.ma, che non pensa in altro mai che nell'Altezza del S.or Prencipe suo marito, mi ha fatto fare il canto sopra la sottoscritto stanza dell'Ariosto ma riformata dal suo maestro di commissione dell'Altezza Sua, il che voglio scrivere a V.S. Ill.ma acciò per lei il S.or Duca nostro Ser.mo sappia questo suo buon volere.

> Mi parea su una lieta et verde riva
> D'odoriferi fior tutta depinta
> Mirar'il bell'avorio et la nativa
> Porpora che havea Amor di sua man tinta
> Et le due chiare stelle onde notriva
> Ne le reti d'Amor l'anima avinta
> Io parlo de begli occhi et del bel volto
> Che mi hanno il cor di mezzo il petto tolto. (201, c. 224)

38: Cavriani a Marcello Donati, 1 dicembre 1582.

Il latrocinio che havete fatto del sonetto è stato molto a gusto della S.ra Prencipessa nostra Ser.ma. L'Al. Sua l'ha letto riletto et tenuto ben stretto appresso di lei, et alfine l'ha riposto fra le più care cose che ella si habbia, et vi ringratia senza fine. Mi ha S.A. accennato di voler ch'io lo metta in canto; quando mi la comandarà lo farò purché volontieri et lo mandarò in mano di S.S. si come le mando ancora il madrigale che la mi comette da parte del S.r Prencipe Ser.mo nostro padrone ch'io mando, et è qui annesso. (1380)

39: Minuta per Piero Malvezzi, 11 luglio 1582.

Et che la Mezzovillana se ne sia partita parimente [...] et quanto alla Mezzovillana, non si crede che si possi lamentare che non sia stata ben trattata, et s'ella è partita è stata perché la Serenissima Signora Principessa per servitio dalla quale fu presa non s'è dilettata della musica come si credeva. (2213; riportato in forma più estesa in I. FENLON, *op. cit.*, I, doc. 73)

40: Cavriani a Guglielmo, 19 aprile 1583.

Questa S.ora in apparenza mostra desiderare il fine quanto prima di questo negotio, et già ha detto questa mattina alla S.ora Contessa Margarita ch'ella stia allegra perché presto andarà con tutti gl'altri a mangiare quelle gioncate a Mantova a che ha risposta di fare quanto le fia comandato, ma che ovunque ella sarà sarà sempre mai serva dell'Altezza Sua. Con tutto ciò ella si è immagrita tanto et impallidita che muove a gran compassione ogn'uno chi la vede. Et in cambio della stanza che soleva sempre mai o dire o cantare, la quale comincia: «Scarpello si vedrà di piombo e lima etc.» dice adesso spessime volte quella: «Deh per chi voglio anco di me dolermi», et quell'altra ancora: «Gravi pene in Amor' si provan molti, etc.», onde nell'intrinseco suo si scorge una grandissima passione, et tanto più che non ride se non per forza si può dire. (202, c. 219)

XVI

Gugliemo Gonzaga and the Castrati*

WHILE it is well known that castrati ruled the Italian operatic stage in the seventeenth and eighteenth centuries, very little scholarly work has been done on the first phase of their history. The little that can be gleaned from special studies, from general articles about musical life in the late sixteenth century, from various histories and biographies, and from two articles dealing specifically with the introduction of castrati into the papal chapel suggests that castrati entered Italy in the middle of the sixteenth century, and were needed to support (eventually supplant) boy sopranos and male falsettists employed by chapel and church choirs.[1] The present study takes a further look at the early days of the castrato, concentrating on the court of Guglielmo Gonzaga, third Duke of Mantua (r. 1550–1587), a man who was apparently extremely interested in this type of singer.

Guglielmo Gonzaga was certainly one of the major musical patrons of his time. No mean composer himself, he kept in his employ a number of famous musicians (Wert, Gastoldi, Pallavicino) and was in regular correspondence with others.[2] Nevertheless, his penuriousness

---

* This article is an expanded version of a paper read at the Forty-Fourth Meeting of the American Musicological Society, Minneapolis, Minnesota, October, 1978. Research was carried out partially with the help of a Summer Stipend from the National Endowment for the Humanities. I would also like to thank here Dr. Adele Bellù, Archivista of the Archivio di Stato, Mantua, and her staff for their extremely cordial and helpful assistance.

[1] Franz Haböck, *Die Kastraten und ihre Gesangskunst* (Stuttgart, 1927); Arthur Heriot, *The Castrati in Opera* (London, 1956); Carl Anthon, "Some Aspects of the Social Status of Italian Musicians During the 16th Century," *Musica Disciplina (Journal of Renaissance and Baroque Music)*, I (1946), 111–123, 222–239; August Wilhelm Ambros, *Geschichte der Musik*, vol. IV (Leipzig, 1909), 464–466; Wolfgang Boetticher, *Aus Orlando de Lassos Wirkungskreis* (Kassel, 1963), pp. 76ff.; Helmut Hucke, "Die Besetzung von Sopran und Alt in der Sixtinischen Kapelle," *Miscelánea en Homanaje a Monseñor Higinio Anglés* (Barcelona, 1958–61), I, 379–406; Anthony Milner, "The Sacred Capons," *The Musical Times*, 114, No. 1561 (March, 1973), 250–252.

[2] For general discussions of music during his reign, see Antonio Bertolotti, *Musici alla corte dei Gonzaga in Mantova dal sec. XV al XVIII* (Milan, 1890); Pietro Canal, "Della Musica in Mantova," *Memorie del Reale Istituto Veneto di Scienze lettere ed arti*,

seemed to have prevented Mantua from having the brilliant musical establishment so evident at the neighboring court of Ferrara. In fact, Guglielmo was openly scornful of one of the prime Ferrarese musical attractions, the *concerto delle donne* created in the 1580s to please Gonzaga'a daughter, Margherita, wife of Duke Alfonsi II. On May 15, 1581, Guglielmo attended a concert by the "three ladies," and his reaction to them was recorded by the Florentine ambassador:

> Having presented with great ceremony to His Excellency [Guglielmo] the music of these ladies, while he [Alfonso] was waiting for him to praise them to the skies [Guglielmo] interrupted, saying in a loud voice that could be heard by the ladies and the duchesses who were present, "Ladies are a big deal; actually I would rather be an ass than a lady," and with this he rose, and forced everyone else to rise so that the singing would come to an end.[3]

Actually, this negative response to what was to become one of the wonders of Italy is strange considering Guglielmo's great knowledge of music and that one of the singers was a Mantuan subject.[4] Perhaps personal reasons influenced his taste, for Guglielmo, as a hunchback married to one of the uglier of the Imperial Archduchesses, was not known to be comfortable in the presence of women.

But while Gonzaga disapproved of the three ladies, he did not object to soprano voices, and the Archivio Gonzaga contains a large number of letters from his reign concerned in whole or in part with attempts to hire castrati. Some of the most interesting of these letters were caught by the eagle eye of Stefano Davari, the nineteenth-century archivist who spent twenty years organizing the Mantuan archive,

---

21 (1879), 655–744; Carol MacClintock, *Giaches de Wert (1535-1596), Life and Works* (Rome, 1966). For Guglielmo as composer, see Claudio Gallico, "Guglielmo Gonzaga, Signore della Musica," *Mantova e i Gonzaga nella civiltà del rinascimento* (Mantua, 1977), pp. 277–283 (also in *Nuova Rivista Musicale Italiana*, 11 (1977), 321–334), and Richard Sherr, "The Publications of Guglielmo Gonzaga," *Journal of the American Musicological Society*, 31 (1978), 118–125.

[3] "... havendo con gran ceremonia fatto udire a questa ecc.za la musica di queste Dame, mentre aspettava ch'ella dovesse esultarle al cielo ella proruppe dicendo forte di mode che fu sentito dalle Dame e dalle Duchesse che erano presente, Gran cose son le Donne; in effetto io vorrei esser inanzi un asino che una Donna, e con questo si levò e fece levar ogn'altre perche se desse fine al cantare..." Taken from Anthony Newcomb, "The Musica Secreta of Ferrara in the 1580's," Ph.D. diss., Princeton, 1970, p. 404.

[4] Laura Peverara, see Newcomb, p. 40.

making notes and transcriptions of anything that might possibly be of interest to anybody.⁵ His information formed the basis of Pietro Canal's short discussion of castrati in his study "Della Musica in Mantova," and some further scattered notes were added in Antonio Bertolotti's error-laden and badly organized *Musici alla corte dei Gonzaga*. Appendices A and B present lists and selected transcriptions of over seventy letters, a larger set of documents which provide a context for those already known, and in some cases give more information about the business of providing castrati for the Mantuan court. ⁶

The earliest mention of castrati in Guglielmo's reign may be contained in a letter from Cardinal Ippolito II d'Este, one of the greatest patrons of the sixteenth century, dated November 9, 1555.⁷ In it, the cardinal says that he has heard that the duke has become interested in his "... cantoretti Francesi ...," and offers to send two of them so that the duke can choose one for himself. "Cantoretti" is not a term that is often used in this period. It means "little singers" and might be a reference to boy sopranos, except that the more usual terms in that case would have been "putti," "fanciulli," "figluoli," or possibly "cantorini." In fact, the use of "cantoretti" suggests to me that Ippolito did not exactly know what to call his French singers. It is possible then that he is talking about castrati, an idea reinforced by a letter of June 2, 1563, in which castrati are specifically offered to Guglielmo on precisely the same terms as were the "cantoretti." It would appear, then, that Gonzaga's interest in and acquisition of castrati began in the middle 1550s or early 1560s.

Documents from Mantua and Spain shed further light on castrati in Guglielmo's employ. A letter of August 15, 1565, to ducal officials mentions a pension to be paid to "... Guglielmo Fordos castrato Francese...,"⁸ and in the same year the ducal singer Giulio Bruschi wrote to the duke in Casale of a rare chance to acquire another castrato.

---

⁵ For an interesting discussion of Davari and his work, see Adele Bellù, "Il Davari e le sue ricerche nell'Archivio Gonzaga," *Mantova e i Gonzaga*, pp. 481–491.

⁶ I have indicated in Appendix A when a letter is quoted or paraphrased in either Canal or Bertolotti. In all cases, my own quotations and paraphrases are based on the original documents. Needless to say, this list does not pretend to contain all the letters on this subject that may exist in the Archivio Gonzaga.

⁷ This letter is transcribed in Appendix B.1.

⁸ Mantua, Archivio di Stato, Archivio Gonzaga (hereafter ASG), busta 2573. Bertolotti, p. 40, prints a list of the ducal chapel without date, but containing Fordos.

XVI

It happened that the chapel of the Cardinal of Augsburg (Otto Truchsess von Waldburg) had been disbanded, and Bruschi had managed to catch some of the singers as they were passing through Mantua, invited them to breakfast one morning and heard them sing. There were three castrati in the group, but Bruschi was particularly interested in a twenty-eight year old Spanish priest, whom he auditioned and managed to entice into the duke's service. In this letter are also given some indications of what the duke was looking for in these singers: one was the ability to sing high notes, the other, facility in improvised counterpoint or "contrapunto" (a skill required of almost all professional singers at the time). The castrato was hired, took his place in the cappella, and on June 27, 1565, Guglielmo received an enthusiastic report of his singing.

But while this was going on in Mantua, the duke's agent in Spain, Girolamo Negri, was keeping his eye out for castrati there. In a letter of May 12, 1565, Negri complained that it was very hard to find any castrati who were any good. One had been promised, but he had died, and the king's own *maestro di cappella* had told Negri that there were not more than six really excellent ones in the entire country, and they could command salaries of at least five hundred ducats a year. In desperation, Negri went so far as to suggest that, since it was so hard to get castrati from abroad, the duke might do well to get some boys and "make his own."[9] This actually was not such an impractical idea, for Gonzaga, who came from a family famous for congenital deformity and illness, was surrounded by learned doctors, all of whom could probably have performed the necessery operation. Furthermore, such a course of action would have saved money and would have allowed Gonzaga to control the boys' educations. But Gonzaga did not take this step, and instead instructed Negri to continue to look for castrati in Spain. The ducal letter, dated July 14, 1565, informed Negri that Gonzaga had at the moment three castrati to whom he gave the unprincely salary of three ducats a month and expenses. It was true that to one who had been in his service a long time he gave five ducats a month and sundry other gifts, but the new castrati should be content with three, and, if not, Negri was to forget about them.

---

[9] This is, at least, my reading of the passage ". . . ch'io crederei che fosse men male veder havergli figliuoli, et che havessero solumente habilità di farsi .. ." The letter is transcribed in Appendix B.2.

When Negri heard that, he became even more pessimistic. First of all, because of a famine, it was difficult to track anyone down, but Negri was convinced in any case that no castrato could be enticed to Italy by the sums the duke was offering. So while promising to continue his quest, he did not leave much hope, and no castrati ever arrived in Mantua directly from Spain.

These documents reinforce the opinion that interest in castrati in Italy dates from the 1550s; indeed, if my interpretation of Ippolito d'Este's first letter is correct, the very term may not have been current in 1555. By the middle of the 1560s, however, Gonzaga had managed to hire three castrati and was actively seeking more. It also is apparent that what was to become an exclusive Italian practice in the eighteenth century was in its origins a foreign import, the supply coming from France and Spain. And even at this early date, castrati who were good singers were demanding and getting very high salaries.

Castrati from France

In 1582-84, Gonzaga made a concerted effort to procure castrati from France. A certain Colonel Andreasi was sent to Paris in the summer of 1582 with a commission to find a pair of young castrati, and he duly wrote on July 16, 1582 that he had talked to the Queen Mother (Catherine de Medici), and that letters had been written to Normandy to procure a castrato from there. Nothing seems to have come of this, however, and Ferrante Ghisoni, the duke's agent in Paris, soon took the matter in hand, reporting on two castrati, one of whom was about fifteen, with a beautiful voice, who composed sacred music and lived in Orléans; the other of whom was Flemish, ". . . who generally seem to be better. . . ."[10] By March 12, 1583, Ghisoni was able to report that the Orléans castrato was ready to travel to Mantua, but that the Fleming had left Paris.

In response to the information sent by Ghisoni, the duke resolved to send another agent to Paris, and three letters of instruction were written to that agent on May 4, 1583. The first letter is the most detailed, giving a history of the negotiation, and stating that the duke wanted to hurry things along as summer was coming, and this was the season in which he enjoyed *musica da camera* the most. The agent was instructed to determine if there really was any hope of getting castrati

---

[10] Letter of December 31, 1582.

from France, for if not the duke was prepared to turn once again to Spain. The castrati were, if possible, to have the following qualifications:

> ... principally that they be good Catholics and modest youths so that we can hope for long and happy service from them. They should sing in a secure manner and have good voices. And if they know contrapunto and how to accompany themselves on the lute, they will be appreciated all the more....[11]

From this letter it can be seen that Guglielmo was now employing castrati for his own recreation rather than in his court chapel. He did not have enough castrati to satisfy his needs, and was pushed to special measures to see that he got some more. But in the matter of salary things had not progressed much beyond 1565, and the agent was told that five ducats a month was all the duke was prepared to give "... to people of that sort...." At the same time, a letter was written to Ghisoni telling him to continue in his efforts.

By May 14, 1583, problems had arisen concerning the castrato in Orléans (Ghisoni had long given up on the Flemish castrato). It appeared that the boy's uncle, a canon in the church of St. Croix in Orléans, was having second thoughts about his nephew's ability to travel, and had decided it was better to keep him in France, accordingly awarding the boy a benefice with an income of one hundred francs. Not knowing what else to do, Ghisoni was actually forced to call upon the Queen Mother herself, who obligingly had a letter written to the Bishop of Orléans asking him to pressure the uncle to accede to the duke's demands. Finally, Ghisoni resolved to go to Orléans himself to see if all the the trouble was worth it. When he got there, he found the uncle was raising further difficulties concerning money. But in any case, Ghisoni was not happy with the boy:

But in truth, the boy's voice did not please me, because it is weak and somewhat hoarse. When he sings, he has trouble with high notes, cannot sing softly, cannot ornament, and (like one accustomed to singing in a chorus) knows no songs by heart. So I would not have thought him appropriate for Your Highness, the more so because he is seventeen years old, as his uncle

---

[11] "... che prencipalmente siano buoni cattolici et gioveni quieti, si che si possa sperare longa et amorevole servitù da loro. Che siano sicuri nel cantare et habbiano buona voce Se havranno contrapunto, et sapranno sonare di leutto per cantarvi dentro saranno tanto piu cari...." Since this letter is only partially quoted in Canal, I give the whole text in Appendix B.3.

told me himself (even though he does not show it), so it is not to be hoped that he can work and improve....¹²

It is apparent from this that the boy was completely unsuited for *musica da camera*, and Ghisoni was probably relieved when the matter was taken out of his hands by the uncle, who definitely refused to give the boy to the Duke of Mantua.

But even while the negotiations in Orléans were alive, Ghisoni continued to look for castrati in Paris. On May 21, 1583, he reported that the royal singer Jacques Busserat, after stating that even the king was having great difficulty finding castrati, had offered to procure some for the duke, and to instruct them (Ghisoni implies that Busserat would have to be paid for this). On October 7, he wrote that François du Caurroy had discovered a castrato who was the son of a Parisian goldsmith, but it was felt that the boy needed more training in singing and playing the lute before he would be good enough for Mantua. Finally, on October 17, 1583, he was able to announce a promising new lead. A friend of his suggested a castrato from Picardy of about twenty years of age named Carbona (later Canibroan), who had been educated by the Queen Mother, had served the king, and had recently been lent to the Queen of Navarre. The friend had already sounded out the Queen Mother on the subject of the castrato, asking her if she might be willing to let him serve some foreign prince—she rather testily replied "I suppose you mean the Duke of Mantua, ... well go ask Corbona yourself and see what he thinks." The castrato said that he did not want to stay with the Queen of Navarre, even though he was getting four hundred ducats a year, and that he would serve the duke if he could be paid traveling expenses. This singer was apparently very famous, and Ghisoni assured the duke that he had one of the best soprano voices in France, although mainly used only to singing *in camera*, and for that reason it did not seem likely that he would come for less money than the Queen of Navarre was giving him. Ghisoni must have received the order to go ahead, for in November, 1583, he began serious negotiations.

¹² Ma veramente la voce del figliolo non m'è piaciuta, perche ella è debile, et alquanto rauca, et quando egli canta dava fatica in andar'alto, et non mette le voci quiete, et non ha dispositione di gorgi, et come quello ch'è avezzo à cantare in choro, non sà nissuna canzone a mente onde non lo havendo io giudicato al proposito di V. A., è tanto piu ch'essendo d'età di dicesette anni, come il zio proprio m'ha detto se bene non gli mostra, non è da sperare che lavore sia per migliorare...."

On December 6, 1583, Ghisoni was able to report that the castrato had agreed to go to Mantua, providing he was paid traveling expenses, the singer even offering not to discuss salary until the duke had heard him. In this letter the agent reiterated that the castrato had one of the best voices in France and could further accompany himself on the lute, and so had to be treated very well. The duke's answer to the castrato's proposal must not have been satisfactory, however, because the singer soon began stalling, saying first that he would only serve the duke for a year, and finally refusing outright.

But Ghisoni did not give up. When the king's brother, the Duke of Anjou, died (June 11, 1584), Ghisoni tried to find out if there had been any castrati in the late duke's service. There were none, but a number of "whole boys" ("figluoli entieri") were proposed. These were, however, rejected by the ducal singer Malgarino Dupre who had been sent (he said) to France only to find castrati. Finally in 1584, after two years of constant search and negotiations (so prolonged that in the Mantuan Chancery they began making special copies only of those sections of letters dealing with castrati), and after a final attempt to find castrati in Normandy, castrati drop out of Ghisoni's correspondence.

The essence of Guglielmo's negotiations in France seems to have been the attempt to hire young castrati (fifteen was apparently a good age) who could serve as chamber musicians; hence the emphasis on ornamentation and ability to play the lute. That there were a number of such singers in France at the time, some of them enjoying high-paying positions at court, shows that sixteenth-century France did not have the particularly Gallic horror of the singers so evident in the seventeenth and eighteenth centuries.[13] It is stranger still that the castrati came mostly from northern France or even Flanders, places where we would think the aversion to castrati to have been the strongest (if only because they were the farthest removed from Italy and "Mediterranean" attitudes). Of course, these were the very areas that had always produced the best singers for export.

---

[13] It should be mentioned that there are scattered references to French castrati in literature about music in sixteenth-century France; see, for example, François Lesure and D. P. Walker, introduction to Claude Le Jeune, *Airs* (Rome, 1951), vol. I, and Isabelle Cazeaux, *French Music in the Fifteenth and Sixteenth Centuries* (New York, 1975). Nevertheless, most people are very surprised, not to say shocked, to learn that there were any French castrati.

Castrati from Rome

Rome was, of course, one of the major musical centers of the late sixteenth century, offering employment not only in the papal chapel, but in innumerable churches and princely ecclesiastical houses. Guglielmo was generally kept informed of the possibility of getting musicians from Rome, and it is not surprising to see correspondence dealing with castrati from there. One set of letters dates from January to February, 1571.

On January 10, 1571, Gonazga's trusted advisor Aurelio Zibramonte reported from Rome certain difficulties he was having in inducing the Cardinal of Ferrara (Ippolito II d'Este) to fire a Spanish castrato. The reason the singer was to be fired was that he had "run away" from Mantua to Rome, and was using his employment with the cardinal, coupled with a wish to learn contrapunto, as an excuse not to return. Zibramonte decided that if the castrato did not have employment, he would have to return to Mantua, and so persuaded the cardinal as a personal favor to the duke to let the singer go. On January 27, Zibramonte stated that the cardinal had indeed fired the castrato, who nevertheless was still making up reasons for staying in Rome. As the letter stated, the singer may have thought he had a future in that city:

> This boy, as he wishes to be called, was considered a very worthy man when he first arrived here, it being known that he had been a singer of His Excellency [in Mantua], and it was to be only a short time before he entered the papal chapel; but then, in the opinion of many other Spanish castrati, he turned out not to be as good as they had thought, and the above mentioned cardinal accepted him into his service because he did not have any other castrati....[14]

This singer, then, was attempting to cash in on a reputation made simply because it was known that he had been in the employ of Guglielmo Gonzaga (an indication of the great respect in which Gonzaga's musical taste and discernment were held).

On February 10, Zibramonte had to relate that the castrato had

---

[14] Questo putto che cosi vole esser nominato fu tenuto un grande valent'huomo nel principio ch'egli arrivo qui sapendosi ch'era stato per cantore di s. e. costi, et puoco gli mancò se non entraste alla cappella di S. S.ta ma poi al parangone di molt'altri pur spagnuoli castrati è risuscito molto meno di quello che questi musici credevano, et il sudetto S.r Car.le l'accettò al suo servigio per non haver altri castrati...."

frustrated his plans by entering the employ of the Cardinal of Trent (Cristoforo Madruzzo), and he accordingly began with that cardinal the same maneuver that had worked with Ippolito d'Este. Madruzzo was amenable, except that he had just sent his own castrato to the Emperor, and wanted to hold on to this one for two months, promising that when he passed through Mantua he would simply fire the castrato, who would then have to stay in the city. Zibramonte informed the duke that this was the best course, since the castrato would not return of his own free will, adding that he would have long given up on this frustrating negotiation were it not that "... these creatures are found only rarely, and the few that are found are fickle like men of little sense, so it does not seem to me that I have any choice other than to see that [this one] comes."[15] The duke agreed to the proposal, feeling sure that the cardinal would drop the "creature" off, but I have been unable to find out if the castrato ever did return to Mantua. The reason for these Byzantine negotiations lay in the difficulty in finding castrati; even a great patron like Ippolito d'Este was forced to hire one who was not judged to be the best, simply because he was available, and Gonzaga clearly did not think it an easy task to hire another singer to replace the one he had lost.

Another series of letters from Rome dates from the year 1586, a year in which Gonzaga attempted to entice a number of very famous virtuosi from that city to Mantua. Chief among these was Luca Marenzio, but the duke was also interested in a famous instrumentalist, Giovanni Battista Giacomello (known as "del violino"), the well-known falsettist Giovanni Luca Conforto, and a castrato.[16]

With regard to Conforto, it is interesting to note that the duke was first advised by the Mantuan agent Capilupi to consider him because there did not seem to be any chance of hiring a castrato. Conforto was famous for his agile soprano voice and his ability to ornament (in fact, he later published a treatise on the subject of ornamentation).[17] The duke began serious negotiations to entice him to Mantua, and received

---

[15] "... perche non si ritrovando se non rarissime di quelli animali et essendo quelli puochi che si trovano tutti volubili come huomini di puoco senso non mi par di dover haver altra mezza che di far che venga...."

[16] I cannot go through all these negotiations here. Those for Marenzio are discussed fully in Steven Ledbetter, "Luca Marenzio: New Biographical Findings," Ph.D. diss., New York University, 1971.

[17] *Breve et facile maniera d'essercitarsi ... a far pasaggi* (Rome, 1593).

many reports on his singing. His chief informant in this matter was Scipione Gonzaga, Patriarch of Jerusalem, who did sent to Mantua a number of specific descriptions of Conforto's voice. On March 29, 1586, he wrote:

> I have never had M. Giovanni Luca in my house, and so cannot say how well he succeeds in private. In public, where he sings in a rather full voice (as in the Oratories) I have heard him a few times, and since I have heard him always praised by others, he seemed very good to me. However, his disposition pleased me more than his voice, not that I think it [the voice] bad, but that I think it could be better. He usually sings soprano, but when he was in the papal chapel he always sang, so I understand, contralto, perhaps to avoid joining his falsetto to the natural voices of the castrati....[18]

In a letter of April 5, Scipione reiterated his opinion that Conforto's voice was not the best he had ever heard, adding that the singer sang contralto "in full voice" ("voci piene") but sang soprano in camera and in the Oratories, using many *passaggi* in the Neapolitan manner.[19]

These letters are interesting because they show that there were castrati in the papal chapel several years before the first unequivocal notice of one,[20] and also because of the references to different styles of

---

[18] "Di M. Gio. Luca non ho havuto niente conoscenza domestica et però non posso dire, come egli riesca in privato in publico, cioè dove si canta à voci alquanto piene, come appunto in quelli oratori, l'ho sentito alcune poche volte, et come dagli altri l'ho udito sempre commendare, cosi à me n'è paruto molto bene, ma però mi è piaciuto assai pur la sua dispositione, che la voce, non che questa mi paia cattiva, ma crederei, che potesse esser migliore la sua parte ordinariamente è di soprano tuttavia nel tempo che egli stette in cappella di N. S.re cantò sempre, si come intendo, il contralto, forse per non accoppiar il suo falsetto alle voci naturali de'castrati."

[19] See Appendix B.4.

[20] The first reference to castrati in the papal chapel up to now has been a notice in the *Diarii Sinstini* for 1588, dated May 18 (*Diario* 14, fol. 76ᵛ), stating that a "Jacomo Spagnoletto eunoco" had been admitted to the chapel in place of Jacques Brunet; this is followed on June 7, 1588, by a note that a "... soprano castrato sopranumerario ... chiamato Martino ..." had been accepted (i.e., he would get the first vacant post; see Hucke). Further information is added by another document in the archives of the Cappella Sistina (Vatican City, Biblioteca Apostolica Vaticana, MS Cappella Sistina 625, fols. 1–2). Brunet was a soprano who was leaving the chapel to return to a benefice in France, and the Castrato (full name, Jacomo Vasquez) was hired to replace him. The castrato Martino's last name was Soto.

The first castrati in the chapel were apparently all Spanish, and in the seventeenth century, Pope Clement VIII dismissed all the Spanish falsettists to make room for castrati, thus beginning a tradition in the papal chapel that was to last until the

singing. Apparently when singing in chorus, full voice (if that is the true translation of "voci piene") was employed, while a different quality was desired for chamber and solo singing. Furthermore, the male falsetto voice did not blend well with that of the castrato, forcing Conforto to sing in a different range when singing in chorus with castrati. Finally, the highly ornamented style of singing for which Conforto was famous is labeled as "Neapolitan."

It proved impossible to entice Conforto away from Rome, however, and Scipione was soon reporting on a castrato who had been in the employ of Margaret of Austria, and who had a canonry in Aquila.[21] This singer had a reputation (he had already refused offers from the papal chapel and the Duke of Bavaria), and Scipione was not sanguine about his chances of convincing the castrato to go to Mantua. He did note one hopeful sign, however: the canonry was in litigation, and the singer on that account might be disposed to leave it. Accordingly, he began some five months of negotiations, these finally crowned with success.

Scipione proceeded with this castrato with his usual care, being sure to hear him in person and to collect the opinions of others. On June 14, 1586, he told the duke that he had heard the castrato, was pleased with the voice, and had been told that the singer had a strong voice

---

twentieth century. It was not until 1599, however, that an Italian castrato was allowed to join the chapel.

The presence of Italian castrati eventually caused certain problems related in a seventeenth-century document in the Cappella Sistina collection (VatS 679, fols. 1–2^v). The document contrasts the good old days when the castrati were all Spanish with the (middle?) seventeenth century when they were all Italian. The Spanish castrati, it seems, used their position in the chapel to acquire benefices in Spain on which to retire, and so would serve the chapel only as long as their voices lasted, then returning to Spain. The Italians, on the other hand, stayed on long after they had lost their voices, and were even forced to hire substitutes to sing for them on occasion. (This document, attributed to Antimo Liberati [a member of the chapel from 1661 to 1692], is mentioned in Andrea Adami, *Osservazioni per ben regolare il Coro della Cappella Pontificia* [Rome, 1711], pp. 190–191.)

In any case, Scipione's letter of 1586 states clearly that there were castrati before 1588; Conforto's service in the chapel is mentioned in the past tense. In fact, Conforto was in the chapel from December, 1581, to October, 1585, so castrati must have been in the chapel in force in the early 1580s.

[21] See Appendix B.5. The letter is given in its entirety because it was incorrectly paraphrased by Bertolotti.

and good contrapunto. The negotiations were then reduced to financial terms, and Scipione finally got the castrato to accept the duke's offer of seven ducats a month plus expenses and room for him and a servant. But the castrato, Jacomo Antonio Pales by name, kept putting off his journey to Mantua because of the litigation for his canonry in Aquila. He finally arrived in Mantua in November, 1586, but Scipione was surprised and distressed to learn that he had made a very bad impression (coming without money or clothes, "denari e veste"). In a letter of November 8, 1586, Scipione felt it necessary to defend his recommendation of the singer, saying that he could not have predicted this particular turn of events. Pales was apparently fired, because he does not appear in a roll of the court made in 1587, after Guglielmo's death.[22] It might also be noted that this castrato appears to have been Italian (at least it is constantly said that he comes from Aquila) although his name does have a Spanish ring. If Italian, he would be the first to be mentioned in these documents.

The preceding study has brought up several points about the introduction of castrati into Italy. First of all, they were not an Italian creation (indeed, there seemed to be resistance in Italy to performing the operation) but were imported from the very countries, France and Spain, that had been supplying singers to Italy for a century. That they were scarce and expensive at the time is understandable considering their novelty, and considering that all virtuoso musicians could command high salaries. Less understandable is Guglielmo Gonzaga's success in attracting castrati to his court while refusing to pay a great deal. Perhaps his success in the long run was due to his willingness to employ more castrati than would others; in 1565 he had three, and was trying to increase that number, while in 1571 Ippolito d'Este and Cristoforo Madruzzo were content with one. And there also may have been a belief among musicians in general that Gonzaga's patronage in itself was a thing worth having. There is some evidence for this in the castrato who, in 1571, found he had a good reputation because he had been in Gonzaga's employ; further evidence is supplied in a letter written from Rome in 1586 stating specifically that one of the enticements offered musicians was the chance to serve a prince who ap-

---

[22] In 1589, he joined the Cappella Giulia in Rome. See Giancarlo Rostirolla, "La Cappella Giulia in San Pietro negli anni palestriniani," *Atti del convegno di studi Palestriniani*, ed. Francesco Luisi (Palestrina, 1977), p. 227.

preciated and understood their art.²³ In some cases, apparently, these factors made up for the paltry salaries the duke was paying.

The Mantuan documents also suggest that although castrati may have first entered the scene as members of princely chapels, there was a change in their position at least by the 1580s. In these years, Guglielmo seems to be interested in them primarily as chamber musicians, and he actively seeks singers who can ornament and accompany themselves on the lute (attributes of soloists). It may not be coincidental that his is precisely the period when, according to the *Discorso sopra la Musica* of Vincenzo Giustiniani, a new florid type of solo singing was introduced from Naples into Rome.²⁴ It may have been that Guglielmo and others recognized the aptness of the castrato voice for such performance, and became more occupied with *musica da camera*. In fact, castrati may have entered the Church in force rather late; the earliest we can now find them in the papal chapel, for instance, is the 1580s.²⁵ It seems to me then that Guglielmo Gonzaga in his later constant search for castrati was in fact motivated by the same considerations that caused Alfonso d'Este to establish the "three ladies": a wish to be entertained by high virtuoso solo voices. His use of castrati can be seen finally not as an aspect of sacred music as much as a response to the changing style of secular music with its increased emphasis on the solo singer.

As to the question of who performed the first operations and introduced the singers to Europe, we may have to agree with Ambros that "Lichtscheu und heimlich liegen die Anfänge des Verbrechens in geheimnisvolle Nacht begraben."²⁶ The obvious answer is that the beginnings can be traced to Moorish influence or to that Moslem behemoth, the Ottoman Empire. Certainly, there were in the sixteenth century ample means of contacts with both peoples, and it must not be forgotten that from the 1530s on France was in undisguised alliance with the Sublime Porte. If castrati began appearing around 1550, then the operations must have been performed in the early '50s, late '40s, or even earlier, precisely at the time the Sultan's fleet was anchored at Marseilles.

---

²³ ASG, busta 943, letter from Capilupi dated April 12, 1586.

²⁴ Hercole Bottrigari, *Il Desiderio* and Vincenzo Giustiniani, *Discorso sopra la musica*, trans. Carol MacClintock (Rome, 1962), p. 69.

²⁵ The idea that castrati entered chapel choirs after having been employed at courts is also put forth by Anthon.

²⁶ Ambros, vol. IV, 464.

But there are problems with considering the Ottomans and Moors as the source of the castrato craze. First of all, although the Moors may have influenced Spain, it is hard to see how they could have influenced northern France, the source of French castrati. Also, as Ambros pointed out, the position of the eunuch in Ottoman society was entirely different from the one assigned to European castrati. Moslem eunuchs did not sing, but rather rose to powerful positions in the court and government. And since their primary duty was to guard the harem, the operation producing them was of necessity different from the one producing European castrati.[27] It might also be added that the Moslems got the idea of eunuchs from the Christian Byzantine Empire, and since castration was forbidden by Moslem law, the Turks had to import their eunuchs from Christian countries within their empire.[28]

Another problem with the Ottoman theory is that the castrato's port of entry into Europe would most logically have been Venice, the city with the closest economic and diplomatic ties with the Sultan, and there is no evidence that castrati were ever a part of Venetian trade. I would conjecture then that the beginnings of the castrato can be tied to Europe—to France and Spain—and that they flourished because they fit the needs of the coming style, one that would overtake the Renaissance and usher in the Baroque. Whether the castrato voice was discovered by accident or design, we will probably never know.

SMITH COLLEGE

---

[27] The operation producing castrati, as described by Charles d'Ancillon in his *Traité des eunuques* (Berlin?, 1707), did not involve the removal of anything. The operation producing the Moslem eunuch did.

[28] For a recent discussion of Ottoman history and society, see John Patrick Douglas Balfour, Baron Kinross, *The Ottoman Centuries: the Rise and Fall of the Turkish Empire* (London, 1977).

APPENDIX A

MANTUA, ARCHIVIO DI STATO, ARCHIVIO GONZAGA (ASG): LETTERS CONCERNING CASTRATI

LETTERS FROM FERRARA, MANTUA, SPAIN

1.	ASG, busta 1209	Ippolito II d'Este to the duke	November 9, 1555
**2.	ASG, 1211	Ippolito d'Este to the duke	June 2, 1563
*3.	ASG, 2573	Giulio Bruschi to the duke	June 15, 1565
*4.	ASG, 2573	Massimiliano Gonzaga del Borgo to the duke	June 27, 1565
5.	ASG, 593	Girolamo Negri to the duke	May 12, 1565
6.	ASG, 593	Girolamo Negri to the duke	June 18, 1565
*7.	ASG, 2950, lib. 368a	The duke to Negri	July 14, 1565
8.	ASG, 593	Girolamo Negri to the duke	August 3, 1565

*Mentioned or quoted in Pietro Canal, "Della Musica In Mantova," *Memorie del Reale Istituto Veneto di scienze lettere ed arti*, 21 (1879), 655–744.

**Mentioned or quoted in Antonio Bertolotti, *Musici alla corte dei Gonzaga in Mantova dal sec. XV al XVIII* (Milan, 1890).

LETTERS FROM PARIS

9.	ASG, 659	Ascanio Andreasi to the duke	July 16, 1582
10.	ASG, 660	Ferrante Ghisoni to the duke	December 31, 1582
11.	ASG, 660	Ferrante Ghisoni to Pietro Petrozanni	March 7, 1583
12.	ASG, 660	Ferrante Ghisoni to the duke	March 12, 1583
13.	ASG, 660	Ferrante Ghisoni to the duke	April 3, 1583
*14.	ASG, 2621	Teodoro di San Giorgio to an unnamed ambassador	May 4, 1583
15.	ASG, 2621	Teodoro di San Giorgio to an unnamed ambassador	May 4, 1583
16.	ASG, 2621	Teodoro di San Giorgio to an unnamed ambassador	May 4, 1583
17.	ASG, 2214	The duke to Ghisoni	May 4, 1583
18.	ASG, 660	Ferrante Ghisoni to the duke	May 14, 1583
19.	ASG, 660	Ferrante Ghisoni to the duke	May 21, 1583
20.	ASG, 660	Ferrante Ghisoni to the duke	June 3, 1583
*21.	ASG, 660	Ferrante Ghisoni to the duke	June 10, 1583
22.	ASG, 660	Ferrante Ghisoni to the duke	September 30, 1583
23.	ASG, 660	Ferrante Ghisoni to the duke	October 7, 1583
24.	ASG, 660	Ferrante Ghisoni to the duke	October 17, 1583
25.	ASG, 660	Ferrante Ghisoni to the duke	November 28, 1583
26.	ASG, 660	Ferrante Ghisoni to the duke	December 6, 1583
27.	ASG, 660	Ferrante Ghisoni to the duke	January 20, 1584
28.	ASG, 660	Ferrante Ghisoni to the duke	April 9, 1584
29.	ASG, 660	Ferrante Ghisoni to the duke	May 3, 1584
30.	ASG, 660	Ferrante Ghisoni to the duke	May 25, 1584

XVI

31.	ASG, 660	Ferrante Ghisoni to the duke	July 23, 1584
32.	ASG, 660	Ferrante Ghisoni to the duke	July 30, 1584
33.	ASG, 660	Ferrante Ghisoni to the duke	August 3, 1584
34.	ASG, 660	Ferrante Ghisoni to the duke	August 6, 1584
35.	ASG, 660	Ferrante Ghisoni to the duke	August 13, 1584
36.	ASG, 660	Ferrante Ghisoni to the duke	August 23, 1584
37.	ASG, 660	Ferrante Ghisoni to the duke	October 18, 1584
38.	ASG, 660	Ferrante Ghisoni to the duke	November 2, 1584

LETTERS FROM ROME

39.	ASG, 905	Aurelio Zibramonte to the Castellano of Mantua	January 6, 1571
40.	ASG, 905	Aurelio Zibramonte to the Castellano of Mantua	January 20, 1571
41.	ASG, 905	Aurelio Zibramonte to the Castellano of Mantua	January 27, 1571
42.	ASG, 2950, lib. 370	The Castellano to Zibramonte	February 6, 1571
*43.	ASG, 905	Aurelio Zibramonte to the Castellano of Mantua	February 10, 1571
44.	ASG, 2950, lib. 370	The Castellano to Zibramonte	February 20, 1571
45.	ASG, 943	Protonotary Capilupi to Federico Cataneo	January 18, 1586
*46.	ASG, 943	Protonotary Capilupi to Cataneo	March 22, 1586
47.	ASG, 941	Scipione Gonzaga to Cataneo	March 22, 1586
48.	ASG, 941	Scipione Gonzaga to Cataneo	April 5, 1586
49.	ASG, 943	Protonotary Capilupi to Cataneo	April 5, 1586

XVI

**50.	ASG, 941	Scipione Gonzaga to Cataneo	April 19, 1586
51.	ASG, 941	Scipione Gonzaga to Cataneo	May 3, 1586
52.	ASG, 941	Scipione Gonzaga to Cataneo	May 31, 1586
53.	ASG, 941	Scipione Gonzaga to Cataneo	June 14, 1586
54.	ASG, 941	Scipione Gonzaga to Cataneo	June 21, 1586
55.	ASG, 941	Scipione Gonzaga to Cataneo	June 28, 1586
56.	ASG, 941	Scipione Gonzaga to Cataneo	July 5, 1586
57.	ASG, 941	Scipione Gonzaga to Cataneo	July 12, 1586
58.	ASG, 941	Scipione Gonzaga to Cataneo	July 19, 1586
59.	ASG, 941	Scipione Gonzaga to Cataneo	July 26, 1586
60.	ASG, 941	Scipione Gonzaga to Cataneo	August 2, 1586
61.	ASG, 941	Scipione Gonzaga to Cataneo	August 9, 1586
**62.	ASG, 944	Giacomo Antonio Pales to Gonzaga	August 9, 1586
63.	ASG, 941	Scipione Gonzaga to Cataneo	August 16, 1586
64.	ASG, 941	Scipione Gonzaga to Cataneo	August 29, 1586
65.	ASG, 941	Scipione Gonzaga to Cataneo	August 30, 1586
66.	ASG, 941	Scipione Gonzaga to Cataneo	September 17, 1586
67.	ASG, 941	Scipione Gonzaga to Cataneo	October 4, 1586
68.	ASG, 941	Scipione Gonzaga to Cataneo	October 11, 1586
69.	ASG, 941	Scipione Gonzaga to Cataneo	October 18, 1586
70.	ASG, 941	Scipione Gonzaga to Cataneo	October 20, 1586
71.	ASG, 941	Scipione Gonzaga to Cataneo	October 21, 1586
72.	ASG, 941	Scipione Gonzaga to Cataneo	November 8, 1586

APPENDIX B

SELECTED DOCUMENTS IN TRANSCRIPTION

B.1

ASG, busta 1209
Ippolito II d'Este to the duke, November 9, 1555

Havendomi Ascanio Pera fatto intendere il disiderio, che V. Ecc.a haveva d'un di questi miei cantoretti Francesi le ne mando questi due, affinche possa eleggere qual d'essi ella riputerà più a proposito, et come mi piacerà, che cio sia con sua contentezza, cosi ha da rendersi certa l'ecc.a V. che mi sarà sempre cara ogni occ.ne che mi si presenti di poterle mostrar quanto io disideri di servirla, et di satisfarla in ogni cosa, che sia in poter mio, come anche le dirà piu largamente esso Ascanio, al qual rimettendomi alla ... [hole in the page] gia sua contutto l'animo mi raccomando, et le prego ogni felicità.

B.2

ASG, 593
Girolamo Negri to the duke, May 12, 1565

Ho fatta pratica per quei due eunichi, che il Fidele mi disse, che V. Ecc. commandava, che si ritrovassero infine è cosa piu difficile di quello, che io mi cresi in su'l principio esendossi cosi perso quà in questo particolare com'in molt'altri, di maniera che si conclude (et è vero, che lo sò molto bene) che nella capella del Re non è piu che uno di questi tali, che si possi dire esser buono, et quello, che fù hora il Mastro di capella di S. M.ta per esser morto quello ch'era mi offerto, mi giura la sua fede, ch'è poco che disse al medesimo Re, che in tutta Spagna non se ne trovavano de eccellenti più che sei et che ciascuni di loro stava molto ben'accommodato non havendo niente meno d'un cinquecento scudi di entrate, Io non lasciarò di farne altre diligenze, intanto che V. Ecc. mi commanderà ancho piu particolarmente quello, che sarà servita intorna à ciò non lasciando io di dirle quello che mi soviene cosi hora; et è, che quando V. Ecc.a resti per servita d'havere, ch'io crederei, che fosse men male veder di havergli figliuoli, et che havessero solumente habilità di farsi credendo io che la si farebbero meglio che quà. ...

B.3

ASG 2621
Teodoro di San Giorgio to an unnamed ambassador, May 4, 1583

Desiderando il s.r n.ro ser.mo di havere un paro di giovani castrati per cantare in camera, et in capella dedde carrico sino l'anno passato al s.r colonello Andreasi il quale l'Al. s. mandò in Francia di ricercarneli, et di procurare anco che li venessero sotto il nome della M.ta della Reina madre, a fine ch'essi havessero piu rispetto di non partirsi dal servitio et gli altri di solevarli. Ma se ben parve che le fosse dato intentione che si sarebbero trovati, et di poi anco il s.r Ferrante Ghisoni Agente dell'Alt.a sua in quella corte, habbi scritto che n'haverne alle mani due, non di meno non si sono sino a quest'hora puotuti havere, anci detto s.r Ghisone scrive ultimamente, che uno d'essi se n'era andato in modo ch'egli non ne sapeva nuova, et che l'altro anco era fuor di corte et che vedrebbe d'haverlo co'l mezo di M.re l'Abbate di S. Memino. Il che mostra che questo negotio debba andar molto in longo, e forse non risolversi mai, se l'Al. s. non le dà magiore calore. Venendo adonque il tempo de caldi ne quali l'Alt.a sua gode piu di questa ricreatione della musica in camera che in altra staggione ha risoluto di mandarvi con diligenza a Parigi, per chiarirsi a fatto se ne può havere di là, che altrimente si voltera alla volta di Spagna, ove M.re Cavriani che gionge di presente dalla Corte Cattolica assicura che se n'havranno facilmente. Andarete donque a Parigi, e facendo ricapito al sodetto s.r Ghisone, le direte la mente di S. Al. e trovandosi un paro di questi giovani ch'habbiano le qualità che saranno espresse qui a basso, ne condurete con voi uno ritornandovene per la posta, et l'altro lo lasciarete che sia condotto dal s.r Nuvolone m.ro di casa di s. m.ta Christ.ma il quale s'intende che non deve tardar molto a venire in Italia, dicendole che S. Alt.a le farà rimborsare la spesa, et perche essi vengano piu volontieri, le prometterete che gionti che saranno qui, se non le piacerà di fermarvisi l'Al. S. le darà il modo di ritornare a casa.
Le qualità che S. Al. ricerca in questi sono che prencilpalmente siano

buoni cattolici et giovani quieti, si che si possa sperare longa et amorevole servitù da loro. Che siano sicuri nel cantare et habbiano buona voce Se havranno contrapunto, et sapranno sonare di leutto per cantarvi dentro saranno tanto piu cari.

Il medesimo s.r Colonello Andreasi hebbe carrico di far fare a Parigi una credenzetta d'argento commoda per portare in volta, la quale essendo stata condotta, s' è trovato ch'è stata cosi mal fatta et lavorata che l'Al. S. n'è restata malissimamente sodisfatta ne sa altro che farne salvo che farla riffondere, caso che l'orefice che l'ha fatta il quale si chiama m.ro Tomasa Echialla al segno del Pomo rosso, non la ripigli. Pero vedrete co'l mezo del sig.r Nuvolone m.ro di casa di s. m.ta di rimediare a questo et perche un m. Antonino Colombo da Pontestura che dimora in casa dell'Ecc.moSr. Duca di Nevers fù quello ch'hebbe carrica di solecitarla, potrete anco valersi del suo mezo aparlar al detto mastro.

Di Revere a 4 di Maggio 1583

B.4

ASG, 941
Scipione Gonzaga to Federico Cataneo, April 5, 1586

... quanto alla voce piu tosto ho da aggiungere, che da scivare alla prima informatione essendomi riuscito molto buona, et tale vedendola stimate generalmente confirmo però anche in questo, che di megliori ne ho sentito à miei di. ma non v'e difetto, che la faccia in alcuna maniera, secundo il mio giudizio, rifiutabile egli a voci piene canta contralto, e cosi cantò in cappella di N. S.re in camera e in oratori canta soprano, et và alto asai, canta con molti passaggi per ordinarie et porta la voce con buona gratia, secundo l'uso però di quà, che tiene un poco del Napolitano, il quale non sò come convenga con quello di Lombardia. ...

B.5

ASG, 941
Scipione Gonzaga to Federico Cataneo, April 19, 1586

Ho preso informatione di tutti i musici che teneva Madama d'Austria[1] et trovo, che altre il m.o di cappella, il quale era chiamato M. Verius Vallone, ella haveva quattro soprani, tre putti, e un castrato il castrato è quello, del quale scrive Mons.re Capilupi, che ha un canonicato nell'Aquila et perche stà bene, verisimil cosa è ch'egli non partirebbe di la senza molto gagliardo partito, à i tre putti Madama ha lasciato danari, e commodità, perche se ne tornino in Fiandra, dove furno presi, e cosi hanno gia fatto appresso à questi haveva tre contralti, è uno spagnuolo, e come intendo, non molto buono, il quale se n'è ito à Napoli gli altri due Fiaminghi, i quali anch'essi gia se ne sono tornato alla patria i tenori erano medesemente tre, due pur fiaminghi che sono partiti, et un Italiano chiamato Gio. Paulo da Urbino, et questo è quello che per esserci stato altre volte, è stato di nuovo accettato qui in San Luigi, ma per quanto mi vien detto, non senza qualche difficoltà, non essendo cosa molta rara. finalmente i bassi erano due, l'uno Trombone, del quale non sò che sia avvenuto, l'altro chiamato Ugo, è quello che si è accomodato nella cappella di S. Giovanni Laterano, ma intendo non esser huomo di farvi gia fondamento sopra per haver una vena rotta nel petto. . . .[2]

APPENDIX C

A MARRIED CASTRATO

In December, 1586, Guglielmo Gonzaga made an attempt to hire some musicians from Parma, and on December 11, Ippolito Olivo reported

---

[1] Margaret of Austria, illegitimate daughter of Charles V and married to Ottavio Farnese, Duke of Parma.

[2] Bertolotti paraphrases this letter on p. 67 and makes several errors: the name of the castrato is not mentioned in the letter, Gio. Paulo da Urbino is a tenor not a contralto. Bertolotti also read Trombone as meaning a trombone player, but it seems from the context that he was a singer.

on the success of his attempt to get a bass and a castrato to enter Mantuan service. The bass needed a great deal of money to feed his large family, but the little castrato ("castratino") had a problem of an entirely different nature.

> I spoke immediately with the little castrato who told me that at present he cannot make any plans for himself because of a great trouble he has at the moment which is this: having taken a wife a few months ago, and having slept together for some time, having gotten permission to do so from a parish priest who is now in prison because of this and is being prosecuted by the pope (that is, the Congregation [of the Inquisition?])—and he also is being prosecuted, it being said that he could not take a wife, being a castrato—it appears that until this negotiation is finished, he cannot make any resolutions about himself or promise himself to anyone....

This letter presents an aspect of the lives of castrati which is generally overlooked. It seems that the operation did not always destroy the sexual impulse, and some castrati formed real romantic attachments to women. In fact, the problem of whether castrati could marry comes up again and again.[2] The theological judgment was that they could not because they were incapable of producing children, although in the eighteenth century, one or two singers did manage to marry. It must be mentioned, by the way, that Olivo's letter of December 11 was clearly too much for Davari, who transcribed all of it *except* the passage about the castratino, which is left out without so much as an ellipsis.[3] It was apparently more than the nineteenth century could bear to think about.

---

[1] ASG, busta 1381, "Ho parlato imedimament col castratino, il qual mi a deto che al presente non puo far detterminatione alcuna della persona sua per un travaglio grande che ha al presente il qual e questo che havendo preso moglie alcuno mesi sonno et essendo dormito lungo tempo seco, havendo havuto licentia da un prete parrochiano il qual per questo effetto e prigione et il papa lo travaglia cio è la congregatione, et anchor lui dicendo che per esser castrato non poteva pigliar moglie, si che fia che questo negotio non e finito non veder far rissolutione nissuna della persona ne prometter di certo a nissuno...."

[2] About half of d'Ancillon's book is devoted to the question.

[3] Mantua, Archivio di Stato, buste Davari 16. Canal simply prints Davari's transcription.

XVII

The Publications of Guglielmo Gonzaga

THERE CAN BE LITTLE DOUBT that Guglielmo Gonzaga, third Duke of Mantua (reigned 1550–87), was one of the most important and influential patrons of music in the late sixteenth century. The duke was an avid music lover in the best Gonzaga family tradition. He was constantly looking for singers and instrumentalists, employed two of the most famous composers of the day (Wert and Gastoldi), and even tried to entice greater men (Palestrina and Marenzio) into his service.[1] But more than this, the duke was a composer of recognized professional ability.[2] Respect for his talent can be discerned through the usual obsequious phrases of letters to him by composers, many of whom sent him pieces for study as well as enjoyment. Gonzaga would sometimes respond to these letters with remarkably civil notes. For instance, on November 21, 1581, Francisco Guerrero wrote from Rome that he had journeyed to Italy for two reasons: one to visit the pope, the other to visit the duke, whose fame as a musician was worldwide. With the letter he sent his *Missa La bataille* and a motet.[3] On January 13, 1582, the duke answered as follows:

Reverendo Signor Non m'e stata meno grata l'amorevole volunta che *Vostra Signoria* mostra colla sua dei 21 di No*ve*mbre tener verso di me di quello che mi siano piacciuti la messa et il moteto mandatomi da lei, pero et dell'uno et dell'altro la ringratio, assicurando V.S. che s'essa venira qui come la mi scrive nella sudetta sua, io la vedera volentieri, et saro pronto a farle piacere, fratanto mi raccoma*n*do a V.S.[4]	Reverendo Signore: I was as much pleased by the friendship your lordship has shown me with your letter of November 21 as I was with the Mass and the motet you sent me, and I thank you for them both, assuring your lordship that, if you come here as you write in your letter, I will gladly see you, and will be ready to make things agreeable for you; until then, I recommend myself to your lordship.

A similar letter was sent to Costanzo Porta in response to some music which Porta,

---

[1] For general discussions of music during his reign see A. Bertolotti, *Musici alla corte dei Gonzaga in Mantova dal sec. XV al XVIII* (Milan, 1890); Pietro Canal, "Della Musica in Mantova," *Memorie del Reale Istituto Veneto di scienze, lettere ed arti* XXI (1879), pp. 655–774; and Carol MacClintock, *Giaches de Wert (1535–1596), Life and Works* (Rome, 1966).
[2] For the most recent discussion of his compositions, see Claudio Gallico, "Guglielmo Gonzaga, Signore della Musica," *Convegno "Mantova e i Gonzaga nella civilta del Rinascimento"* 1974 (forthcoming).
[3] Mantua, Archivio di Stato, Archivio Gonzaga (hereafter, ASG), busta 929.
[4] ASG, busta 2954, lib. 386.

© 1978 by the American Musicological Society. All rights reserved.

clearly expecting the duke to look at it as a composer, not simply as a patron, had been careful to score for easy study.[5]

Certainly the most famous of Gonzaga's musical connections was Palestrina. The record of the twenty-year correspondence among the composer, the duke, and ducal counselors has been amply studied elsewhere, and testifies to the esteem in which the duke's opinions were held.[6] Palestrina went so far as to say that he would adopt the duke's new version of Gregorian chant (prepared for the chapel of Santa Barbara) in his own revision of it, and at one point specifically asks for instructions on the writing of a polyphonic mass, asking whether it should be long or short, and whether the words should be understandable or not.[7] And we have at least one ducal instruction stating that the music should be "constantly imitative and on a cantus firmus."[8]

Contemporary documents further show that Gonzaga was the author of one printed set of madrigals, one of motets, and one of magnificats.[9] There are no publications attributed directly to Gonzaga, but Alfred Einstein suggested that the madrigal print be identified with an anonymous print brought out by Angelo Gardane in 1583;[10] this has been substantiated by Claudio Gallico, who points out that the print contains a text referring to three Margheritas (mother, daughter, and daughter-to-be)[11] which could only have been written for or by Gonzaga. Furthermore, the first madrigal in the print, "Padre del ciel," is another version of a madrigal by the same title attributed to the duke in Giaches de Wert's fourth book of madrigals (published Venice, 1567). It seems reasonable to assume also that the motets are contained in an anonymous book of five-part motets printed (again by Gardane) in 1583, now in the Santa Barbara collection in Milan with "Di Sua Altezza Serenissima" on the flyleaf; the motets are duplicated in an anonymous manuscript in the collection.[12] The magnificats have not yet been found.[13]

---

[5] Porta's letter, dated January 19, 1585, is quoted in A. Bertolotti, *Artisti in relazione coi Gonzaga duchi di Mantova nei secoli XVI e XVII* (Bologna, n.d.), pp. 115–16, and is to be found in ASG, busta 940. The duke's reply is in ASG, busta 2954, lib. 389, and is dated January 25, 1585. It is couched in much the same terms as the letter to Guerrero.

[6] See in particular Knud Jeppesen, "Pierluigi da Palestrina, Herzog Guglielmo Gonzaga und die neugefundenen Mantovaner-Messen Palestrinas, ein ergänzender Bericht," *Acta Musicologica* XXV (1953), pp. 132–79, and Oliver Strunk, "Guglielmo Gonzaga and Palestrina's *Missa Dominicalis*," *The Musical Quarterly* XXXIII (1947), pp. 228–39, reprinted in Strunk, *Essays on Music in the Western World* (New York, 1974), pp. 94–107. Two of Palestrina's letters to the duke are translated by Lewis Lockwood in his edition of Palestrina's Pope Marcellus Mass, *Norton Critical Scores* (New York, 1975), pp. 24–5.

[7] Lockwood, p. 24.

[8] "Fugate continouamente e sopra soggetto." Jeppesen, p. 162.

[9] The dedication in Ludovico Agostini's *Le Lagrime del peccatore* (Venice, 1586) mentions a book of madrigals, and the dedication in Benedetto Pallavicino's *Il primo libro de madrigali a sei voci* (Venice, 1587) mentions motets and magnificats. See Emil Vogel, *Bibliothek der gedruckten weltlichen Vocalmusik Italiens. Aus den Jahren 1500–1700*, 2 vols. (Hildesheim, 1962). Published catalogues of works printed by Gardane mention a madrigal print, a motet print, and two books of magnificats: see Geneviève Thibault, "Deux catalogues de libraires musicaux: Vicenti et Gardane (Venise, 1591)," *Revue de musicologie* XI (1930), pp. 10, 11, 15.

[10] Einstein, *The Italian Madrigal* (Princeton, 1969), II, p. 518.

[11] Margherita Paleologa, Margherita Gonzaga, and Margherita Farnese. See Gallico.

[12] Milan, Biblioteca del conservatorio, "Giuseppe Verdi," fondo Santa Barbara 6 (print)

From documents in the Archivio Gonzaga something can be learned of the history of these publications, their reception, and the problems the duke had with them. The first mention of the madrigals came in a letter sent to him on July 23, 1583, by Ludovico Agostini, a member of the Ferrarese court chapel and a frequent correspondent.

Poiche Vostra Altezza Serenissima m'ha fatto gratia che'l Signore Ercole Ricciardo m'habbia datto i libri delli suoi non mai abastanza lodati Madregali, non so con qual più debito mio di riverenza interiore, et esteriore laudare, et riferire gratie immortali a V.A.S. di cotanta benignità, e buona gratia sua, perchè quanto più proporei dire men potrei. Godrò dunque questa sua felicissima Musica, come cosa à me più cara.[14]	As your serene highness has done me the honor of giving me through Signor Ercole Ricciardo, the books [i.e., partbooks] of your madrigals which can never be enough praised, I do not know in what manner to show my internal and external reverence and to extol and give undying thanks to your serene highness for so much goodness and grace, because the more I wish to say, the less I am able to express. I will thus treasure your most happy music as something most dear to me.

It is clear from this that the madrigals were published by July 1583. In fact, four days after Agostini wrote his letter, Guglielmo sent Muzio Gonzaga to the Archduke Karl in Graz with instructions to present to him "a copy of the books of music composed by his highness and recently printed" (detailing in the instructions the type of binding these were to have), including the remark that Muzio was to tell the archduke that Guglielmo had not had his works printed out of ambition, but merely so that he could keep a record of his compositions, some of which had apparently been lost.[15] The madrigal print then seems to have been a collection of madrigals written over a long period of time.

On July 30, 1583, the faithful Agostini reported again, this time on the reception of the madrigals in Ferrara.

Ho cantati con assai buona compagnia i Madrigali di quella che di gran lunga hanno avanzati la grandissima speranza che di quelli si haveva, tal che hanno colmati di meraviglia, chi gli hà cantati et uditi, et non solo d'ammirationi, ma d'imitatione ancora sono stati reputati degni.[16]	I have sung the madrigals in good company, and they have justified greatly the grand hopes we had for them, so much so that all who sang and heard them marveled, and they were considered worthy not only of admiration, but of imitation.

and 8 (manuscript—the manuscript contains one motet not included in the print). It should be mentioned that the Santa Barbara collection contains manuscripts with other pieces (masses and a Te Deum) ascribed to "Serenissima" and presumably by Guglielmo Gonzaga. See *Conservatorio di musica "Giuseppe Verdi" Milano, Catologo della biblioteca diretta di Guglielmo Barblan, Fondi speciali 1: Musiche della cappella di S. Barbara in Mantova*, Biblioteca di bibliografia italiana LXVII (Florence, 1972). See Gallico for a complete catalogue of Gonzaga's works.

[13] Nor have they been sought after: See discussion below.

[14] ASG, busta 1256. All of Agostini's letters have been transcribed by Adriano Cavicchi. See his "Lettere di musicisti ferraresi: Lodovico Agostini (1534–90)," *Ferrara viva* Anno IV, n. 11–12 (Dec. 1962), pp. 185–210.

[15] ASG, busta 2215. The letter is mentioned in Canal and Strunk.

[16] ASG, busta 1256.

XVII

The last part of the letter is particularly interesting, because it was not long before "imitations" of the duke's madrigals began to be published (in collections dedicated to him). Agostini himself brought out his *Lagrime del peccatore* in 1586, making explicit reference to Gonzaga's madrigals in his dedication, and including two madrigals "sopra padre del ciel del Sereniss. Duca di Mantova," and one ("Tu vedi ben") "ad imitatione del Serenissima & Invitiss. S. duca di Mantova" at the beginning of the publication. The first two pieces are parodies of the first madrigal in the anonymous print of 1583, employing phrases drawn from the beginning and end of that work (see Examples 1 and 2) and providing more evidence that the madrigal print was indeed

Example 1

[Gonzaga], 1583, Madrigal 1

Example 2

Agostini, 1586, Madrigal 1

by the duke. I have not been able to locate, however, the source for "Tu vedi ben." Quotations from madrigals in the print of 1583 are also to be found in the second edition of Girolomo Belli d'Argenta's *Furti amorosi* (Venice, 1587), pieces constructed of quotes from other famous works. The edition is dedicated to Gonzaga and Belli insinuates that he has taken pains to use the duke's own music.[17]

But 1583 saw more than the publication of madrigals. On October 15 of that year, Agostini writes again:

Hieri mattina fummi dato a nome di V.A.S. i libri delli Mottetti dell'A.V.S. i quali legai e la sera gli presentai al Sere*nissi*mo Signor Duca in presenza del Sig*no*re Giaches. L'Al*tezza* S.S. gli accettò lietamente, et ne fece cantare ben che fosse l'hora tarda, e se ne compiacque assai. Poi comandò, che fossero portati alle Casette che là gli udirebbe tutti. Io cantando udì tanta arte, et inventione, che non sò se ardiro piu di pigliare penna per mottetti, perche confesso ne miei studi passati non havere posto quella cura, che dovevo.[18]	Yesterday morning I was given in your highness's name the books of your serene highness's motets, which I had bound and presented to the serene lord duke [of Ferrara] in the evening in the presence of Signor Giaches [de Wert]. His serene highness accepted them gladly and had them sung, even though it was late, and he was generally pleased with them. Then he commanded that they be taken to the Casette [a country villa of the dukes of Ferrara], so that everybody could hear them. As I was singing, I heard so much art and invention that I do not know if I will have the courage again to write motets, because I must confess that in my past studies I have not worked at writing them as much as I should have.

These motets, apparently published a little later than the madrigals, may not have been part of the gift to Archduke Karl, but they and the madrigals were probably the "books of music" sent by Vincenzo Gonzaga to the Duke of Bavaria in February 1586.[19] Agostini's fulsome praise is similar to comments made by Palestrina on a ducal motet, although Palestrina was bold enough to offer suggestions for improvements.[20] Also interesting is Agostini's remark that he would no longer have the courage to write motets, implying that he, the professional composer, did not have half the training and knowledge of Guglielmo Gonzaga.

Although the duke had told Archduke Karl that he had not published his music out of ambition, he was nonetheless interested in its sales. This is known from a famous letter sent by Angelo Gardane to Giaches de Wert on July 12, 1586, and printed in full by Bertolotti.[21] It deserves to be given again, however, not only because of the details it provides about the music trade in the 1580s, but because Bertolotti's transcription, besides being generally faulty, contains one major mistake.

---

[17] Girolomo Belli d'Argenti, *I Furti amorosi a sei voci/con nova gionta ristampati, & Coretti* (Venice, 1587); see Vogel, and Einstein, II, p. 756. For example, Belli's Madrigal I contains musical and textual quotes from Gonzaga's Madrigals VI and XI, and Belli's Madrigal II contains a quote from Gonzaga's Madrigal VI.
[18] ASG, busta 1256.
[19] ASG, busta 2955, lib. 394.
[20] See Jeppesen, Lockwood, Strunk.
[21] *Musici*, pp. 45–6.

XVII

Molto magni*fi*co sig*nor* mio Ho dalla sua inteso quanto ella mi scrive in materia delle compositioni di S.A. al che rispondo et dico, che senza alcun dubio, se sula stampa di esse opere vi fosse stato il suo nome, se ne saria dato via assai magior quantità di quello, che si è fatto, ma poi che è piaciuto à S.A. che non vi sia, non importa niente che il stampator da Bressa li habbia scritto di haverne venduto da 60 copie, et che se piu ne havesse havuto ne havrebbe venduto ancora, io crederò, che costui habbia scritto tal cosa poi che V.S. me lo dice, ma dirò bene, che egli hà scritto una bugia tanto grande, che quasi mi ha fatto ridere, poi che *per* dirlo à V.S. non credo, che tra tutte quelle, che sono uscite dalla mia bottega arrivano al numero di 60, si che ella veda se è possibile, che lui solo ne habbia venduto quel numero, che pur bisognaria, che prima fossero state compre da me, se però egli non le havesse ristampate in Bressa, il che anco non credo, non essendo possibile, che ne havesse stampato cosi picol numero, poi che egli dice, che se ne havesse havuto ancora ne havria venduto, et mi credo, che se egli ne volesse ne mandaria a pigliare, si come fanno li altri librari di Bressa, che quasi ogni settimana se li mandi fagotti di libri di musica si che V.S. consideri se questa è cosa, che possi haver luoco di credenza. Quanto poi alli Mag*nifica*t io veramente desidero di fare ogni sorte di servitio che io possa *per* S.A. ma non mi vien concesso dal tempo, sendo che mi trovo tanto obligato, et carico di promesse, che non so, come potrò fare à satisfare à tutti, si che credo, che sarà meglio, che S.A. li facci stampare in Bressa poi, che ella mi scrive, che quel stampatore si è offerto di stamparli, perche io veramente non posso. li Madrigali di V.S. fra quindici giorni si cominciarà, che si finirà un'opera dell'Ingegnieri, la qual era cominciata due giorni avanti, che io havesse quelli di V.S.[22]

Molto magni*fi*co sig*nor* mio: I've understood from your last letter the things you write to me concerning his highness's compositions, to which I respond and say that without any doubt, if his name had appeared on the print, then a larger number of them would have been sold than was the case. But because it pleased his highness that his name should not be on them, it matters little that the printer from Brescia wrote him and said that he had sold about 60 copies, and would have sold more if he had had them. I will believe that he wrote this because your lordship tells me so, but I will say that he has written such an enormous lie that it nearly made me laugh. Because, to tell your lordship the facts, I don't believe that all the prints [of these compositions] that have left my shop equal the number 60, and you can judge if it is possible for him by himself to have sold such a number, since it was necessary for him to buy them first from me. Except, of course, if he had them reprinted in Brescia, which I don't believe either, it not being possible that he had printed such a small number, especially since he said he would have sold more if he had had them. And I believe, if he had wanted them, he would have sent for them here, as do all the other booksellers in Brescia to whom we send piles of music books every week. So I will let your lordship decide if this story is to be believed. As to the magnificats, truly I desire to do any services I can for his highness, but I don't have the time, seeing that I have made promises to so many people that I don't know how I will satisfy them all, so I think it would be better if his highness had them printed in Brescia since you write me that this printer has offered to print them, because I really cannot. Your lordship's madrigals will begin to be printed in 15 days, as soon as the work by Ingegnieri is finished which began two days before I had your lordship's [music].

Gardane's letter is the first indication that Gonzaga was thinking of composing and publishing magnificats, but there are other indications that composition was under way in the summer of 1586. On August 14, Giaches de Wert wrote a letter to a ducal counselor asking leave to go to Ferrara, adding that it was extremely necessary for him to go, for otherwise he would not be so indiscreet as to leave Mantua while the duke was in the midst of composing ("sul comporre"), implying that Wert expected to

---

[22] ASG, busta 1517. Bertolotti transcribed "alli Magt" as "alla magnificat," sending scholars in search of a single magnificat by Gonzaga when it was really a question of a set of them.

be called in for advice and correction.[23] Wert apparently did not get to Ferrara, having caught a fever, and the letter transmitting that news also mentions that a score of a magnificat by Gonzaga was being prepared.[24]

After these testimonies came the information that Gardane had actually published the magnificats. On October 25, 1586, Benedetto Pallavicino wrote from Venice that he had seen the publication and was to act as proofreader.

Molto Illustrissimo Signor mio osservandissimo Vostra Signoria restera servita di dire a S.A. Serenissima che ho trovato dal Gardano che gl'herrori che si sono trovati nelli Magnificat stampati, parte ne sono per le coppie scritte à mano, et parte herrori scorsi, pero il Gardano non manchera di accomodar tutti quelli che si potranno per dar sotisfatione a S.A. Ser.ma è ben vero che ve ne sono de quelli di poco importanza et che à lui pare non sia neccesario accomodarli poi che non si vedrebbe altro che boletini, massimamente gl'herrori de parole, Io andero minutamente vedendo et accozzando insieme le coppie, cioe le stampate et scritte à mano, et non manchero di far che si accomodino tutti quelli herrori importanti che si troveranno altro non diro a V.S. salvo che lui me dice che non mi petra spedire cosi presto come desidero poi che gli vol del tempo, et piu presto vorrebe quasi restamparli che repessarli, si che non mi vol promettere per tutta questa settimana che viene di spedirmi V.S. mi fara gratia di dire a S.A. Ser.ma quello che hò a fare et se non fusse spedito alla posta che viene se io me ne ho da ritornare col il Corriero, et con questo bascio le mani a V.S. Illustrissimi.[25]	Molto Illustrissimo Signor mio osservandissimo: Your lordship may tell his serene highness that I have been to Gardane, and have seen that, of the errors that were found in the printed magnificats, some were caused by the manuscript copies, and some were typographical; however, Gardane will not fail to do everything to give his serene highness satisfaction. It is true that there are a number of unimportant errors, and he believes that it will not be necessary to correct them other than with *boletini*, especially the errors in the words. I will go over the manuscript and printed copies minutely, and will not fail to correct all the important errors. I have no more to say to your lordship except that he [Gardane] tells me that he can't send [the corrected prints] to me as quickly as I want because it takes time, you could almost reprint them in the time it takes to correct them, so that he doesn't want to promise to send them next week [?]. Your lordship will do me a favor by telling his serene highness what I am doing, and if it is not sent through the mails, I will return with the courier; and with this I kiss your hands.

So, four months after his original refusal, Angelo Gardane printed the duke's magnificats; from his catalogue we learn further that he published two books of them. The duke had heard of errors in the print, and wanted them corrected, which Gardane was willing to do, although he resisted having to reprint the entire work, suggesting the use of *boletini*, probably errata slips. By November 1, 1586, the correction process had not yet been completed, as another letter from Pallavicino demonstrates.

---

[23] ASG, busta 2634. See also MacClintock, pp. 39-40. On August 9, Giuseppe Vicintini, known as il Vicentino, at one time copyist for the church of Santa Barbara, sent a letter to a ducal counselor stating that he was sending 12 folios of lined *carta reale*, six of which were to be used "to begin the final copy to be sent to the press" ("hor de questi 12 foglii sei ve ne sono da poter dar principio al ultima copia per mandar alla stampa." ASG, busta 2634). This may also refer to the magnificats.
[24] ASG, busta 2635. This letter is also mentioned in Carol MacClintock, p. 40, n.91.
[25] ASG, busta 1517.

Subito ricevuta la sua lettera insieme con il signor Moro andassimo dal Gardano et li facessimo sapere come l'intentione di S.A. Ser.ma hera che non mancasse di far che tutti gli herrori trovati che si accomodassino, si ne le parole come dele notte, et che non cura S.A. che si adopere bolettini piu presto che restar mal coretta l'opera il Gardano ha risposto che le desideroso servir S. A. Serenissima et che tutto quello che si potra accomodare che non manchera et che per tutta questa settimana che viene dara fine a l'opera.²⁶	As soon as I received your letter, Signor Moro and I went together to Gardane and let him know that it was his highness's will that all the errors be corrected, both in the words and in the music, and his highness does not care if *boletini* are used as long as the work does not remain with the mistakes. Gardane responded that he desired to serve his serene highness, and that he will do everything he can, and will not fail him, and that he will finish the work this week.

The magnificats were the last of Gonzaga's publications; he died on August 14, 1587. The actual print has not been located, but it should be mentioned that the Santa Barbara collection contains two manuscript sets of anonymous magnificats which may reproduce the print.²⁷

Research for this paper was carried out with the help of a travel grant from Smith College.

²⁶ ASG, busta 1517; partially quoted in Bertolotti, *Musici*, p. 62.
²⁷ Fondo Santa Barbara, MSS 9, 30.

XVIII

LORENZO DE' MEDICI, DUKE OF URBINO, AS A PATRON OF MUSIC

Although Lorenzo de' Medici, Duke of Urbino and grandson of the Magnificent Lorenzo, is generally considered to have been an undistinguished ruler, he is of some importance to the history of the arts. He was directly involved with at least two of Raphael's paintings (his portrait, now lost, and the famous group portrait with Leo X),[1] and he has long been identified as the major recipient of the lavish manuscript of polyphony known as the Medici Codex.[2] In view of his connection with this manuscript, however, it is surprising how little is known of Lorenzo as a patron of music. He was, after all, the ruler of Florence after the Medici restoration (although he was clearly taking his orders from Rome), and later he ruled in his own right as Duke of Urbino. One might expect him to have shown some interest in musical matters as did such contemporaries as the Gonzaga of Mantua and the Este of Ferrara. Yet, of the chief documents hitherto associated with his musical patronage, one has nothing to do with him, and the other has been taken out of context and so has lost its true meaning.[3]

The first of these documents is Guasti's transcription from the *Carte Strozziane* of undated payments interpreted as monthly stipends paid by the Bini bank in Rome "... per conto del duca Lorenzo de' Medici."[4] The list includes a payment (No. 7) to "Giriberto, Gran Gian e Girardino sonatori," and led Edward Lowinsky to conclude that Lorenzo had a modest musical establishment, fit mostly for secular music (as only three instrumentalists are mentioned).[5] However, it is unlikely that this document refers to Lorenzo because of a payment (No. 6) to "Giannicholò guardarobba," who in 1515 belonged to the household of Giuliano de' Medici, Duke of Nemours (Lorenzo's uncle).[6] Therefore the three instrumentalists cited in the *Carte Strozziane* document must be taken away from Lorenzo and given to Giuliano.

© Copyright 1985 by Giunti Barbèra – Florence

Another document, inaccurately transcribed, published in Pieraccini suggests that Florentines then were stingy in musical matters and that Lorenzo had little interest in music.[7] However, the context permits another interpretation.

The context is as follows. On February 18, 1514, Lorenzo wrote to Cardinal Giulio de' Medici in Rome, asking him to intercede with the pope to persuade Cesena to release two *pifferi* (players of shawms, sometimes doubling on trombone) in the town's employ for service in Florence,[8] stating further that the Florentine Signoria had already written to their ambassador in Rome about the same matter.[9] This apparently straightforward request to strengthen the Florentine corps of *pifferi* and *tromboni* (almost all cities in Europe had such a corps),[10] received an unexpectedly rather harsh reply criticizing both the city and Lorenzo.[11]

For Cardinal Giulio, the quality of a musical establishment was related to how much was spent on it. In acquiescing to the Signoria's wishes to spend as little as possible, Lorenzo was not acting like a true Medici. The only explanation offered by Cardinal Giulio is that Lorenzo did not like music, and therefore did not share the tastes of the family's two most important members: Leo X and Cardinal Giulio himself. Lorenzo's resentment is expressed in his reply to Cardinal Giulio's letter (dated February 24, 1514), where he argued that although the *pifferi* were inexpensive, this did not compromise the quality of Florentine music and therefore did not demean his patronage, adding that he was well aware of his duty as a Medici in these matters.[12]

Although Cardinal Giulio had promised to help, it appears that by March 14 nothing had yet been done, because the Signoria again requested action from the ambassador in Rome.[13] On March 18 Cardinal Giulio reported that letters about the *pifferi* had been sent.[14] Documents in the Vatican name one of those involved: Johannes Jacobus from Cesena, musician of the Florentine Signoria, is granted land in Cervia by the pope.[15] Later, in December 1514 the Signoria wrote to Cervia to help "Gian Jacomo piffero" collect rent on his land.[16] During the same month, Gian Jacomo wrote to Lorenzo defending himself from accusations of financial mismanagement.[17] Interesting here is that this *piffero* officially in the Signoria's employ, nonetheless refers to himself as Lorenzo's faithful servant. This is reiterated in the last known document concerning him: a note in the accounts of Leo X states that he entered papal service after Lorenzo's death.[18] The second *piffero*'s name can be deduced from a letter to Lorenzo by Giovanni Como *piffero*, recommending his brother for a

DUKE OF URBINO AS A PATRON OF MUSIC

place in the guards, stating that the brother, who was also a musician, had replaced him in Cesena.[19]

Lorenzo's predilection for *pifferi* is confirmed by his numerous payments to them [20] and by the letters negotiating for their employ. Besides the example already cited, another reveals the members of an instrumental ensemble in the employ of Cardinal Luigi d'Aragona, renowed for his love of music. On January 21 1519, three days after the cardinal's death, Goro Gheri wrote from Florence to Benedetto Buondelmonti telling him to engage all the *pifferi* and *tromboni* in the late cardinal's employ.[21] Shortly afterwards, Lorenzo decided that he needed only two of the group both of whom were called Bartholo, and again the ambassador was urged to make haste.[22] The need for urgency was justified in the ambassador's letter of January 27, 1519: the pope had already hired all the *pifferi* and *tromboni* for himself.[23] However, according to the ambassador, they had been paid more than they were worth; furthermore, he doubted that it would be possible to hire only two of the entire ensemble. And indeed, a pair of Bartolos, clearly those formerly in the Cardinal Aragon's employ and sought after by the Duke of Urbino, appear in the papal accounts for February 1519 among payments to five *pifferi*.[24]

This was not the only time that Leo X competed with his nephew for musicians. When Ariosto's comedy *I Suppositi* was to be presented with elaborate musical *intermedii* in Rome during Carnival of 1519, it was found that there were not enough musicians in Leo's employ for the occasion. An urgent letter was sent to Florence on February 17 requesting the needed players from the Signoria.[25]

The post between Rome and Florence then was swift, and two days later, on February 19, the Florentine authorities replied saying that since a list of the required musicians had not been included, they did not know whom to send. Finally, the list arrived.[26] But suddenly there was a change of plan because the Duke of Urbino was unwilling to deprive himself of the pleasure of their music.[27] In the end, though Florence yielded to papal pressure and the musicians were released to Rome, for Leo X wanted elaborate music for Ariosto's comedy, and was determined to obtain it.[28] Indeed, the musical interludes provoked much comment, although it is unknown which of the instrumentalists came from Florence or what their instruments were.[29]

That the musicians were to come from the "Palazzo" of Florence says something of Lorenzo's patronage of musicians, and explains why, for all his interest in *pifferi*, none seem to have been in his personal employ. Clearly, he had at his disposal the Signoria's *pifferi* because "Palazzo" in the documents certainly means the "Palazzo della Signoria." There is confirmation of this in his early intervention with Cardinal Giulio on the city's behalf (which was accompanied by the promise to concern himself more with musical matters), as well as in a letter from Gheri to Lorenzo of March 18, 1518.[30] Here, Lorenzo's explicit permission is needed before the city could even use a player who was willing to work for nothing; his wishes must also have been respected in all matters of civic music. Furthermore, as we have seen, the Duke had free access to the Signoria's musicians. This should be borne in mind when considering his private musical establishment as defined by his financial accounts.[31] The known records (at least for 1515-17) include two private singers, Giovanbattista d'Arezzo and Ser Virgilio, who probably were employed for religious functions. Instead of a salary from the Duke, they were compensated as members of the Baptistry choir and by benefices procured for them.[32] Although Ser Virgilio may not have lived in Lorenzo's palace, Giovanbattista was certainly a regular member of Lorenzo's household as he served not only as a musician but also as Master of the Pages.[33] There were also four salaried musicians. The first, Tadeo, to judge from his appellation as *musico* and his relatively high wage, may also have been a singer. The other three are specifically designated as instrumentalists, which probably meant lutes and viols because otherwise they would have been called *pifferi*, and paid about one quarter of Tadeo's salary.[34] That these three all entered Lorenzo's employ after August, 1516, may not be coincidence. In June of that year, Lorenzo had been proclaimed Duke of Urbino and in August had been officially invested with the title. As the first Medici to be made a reigning duke, he now was entitled to a "court" including musicians; in fact, it is likely that he was familiar with the handbook for courtiers at Urbino (prepared around 1502) which specified that there should be three resident instrumentalists at court.[35] Indeed, the three musicians Lorenzo employed in Florence may even have come from the disbanded court of the former Duke of Urbino, Francesco Maria della Rovere.

Lorenzo's musical establishment therefore was not large, and does not seem to have included enough singers to perform elaborate polyphony. But it should not be forgotten that Medici patronage of polyphony operated through the existing chapels of the Baptistry and cathedral, chapels nominally under the control of certain guilds; Lorenzo was apparently satisfied with this arrangement, and made no effort to form a private chapel of polyphonic singers. For such music, as well as the *pifferi*, he used the resources of civic institutions. And although he made some effort to increase the singers in the chapels, there is nothing to indicate that he took a great interest in

DUKE OF URBINO AS A PATRON OF MUSIC 631

them. Furthermore unlike Lorenzo the Magnificent and Cardinal Giulio, who patronized Isaac and Verdelot, Lorenzo made no attempt to bring composers of repute to Florence. From this evidence, then, it appears that the Duke of Urbino preferred secular music and compared to other Medici his patronage of music was of a minor nature.[36]

A Note on the Medici Codex

Musicologists have been interested in Lorenzo II de' Medici because he is associated with the famous collection of motets, designated by Lowinsky as "The Medici Codex."[37] Not only does Lorenzo's name appear in an acrostic formed by many titles in the manuscript, but several Latin inscriptions apparently refer directly to him. Furthermore, fol. 1v displays his coat of arms with those of Cardinal Giulio de' Medici and Pope Leo X.[38] However, the coat of arms on 2r, shows the Medici arms impaled with those of the house of de la Tour d'Auvergne, surmounted by a ducal coronet. Lowinsky remarked that these arms represent the joining of two noble houses and therefore "... symbolize the wedding of two persons of noble origin."[39] This interpretation is logical and persuasive, and has been accepted as part of the evidence that the manuscript has something to do with the marriage of Lorenzo and Madeleine de la Tour d'Auvergne. But in general, coats of arms do not symbolize events, rather they represent individuals or families, and if three separate people are represented by the arms on folio 1v, then it might be that an individual rather than an event is represented on fol. 2r. In fact, there are reasons to believe that this was the case, and that this person was none other than Madeleine de la Tour d'Auvergne. It was conventional for a wife's arms to incorporate those of her husband (and not necessarily the other way around),[40] and letters in the Florentine Archives prove that Madeleine's arms were supposed to incorporate the Medici *stemma*—a decision made by Leo X himself—while Lorenzo was to continue to use his own arms.

Soon after the marriage contract was signed, Goro Gheri wrote to Baldassare Turini in Rome noting that the arms of Madeleine and Lorenzo shared a common feature: red *palle*.[41] This also struck the pope and Cardinal Giulio who saw this heraldic correspondence as a sign of destiny;[42] furthermore, such an armorial connection with the noble house of de la Tour d'Auvergne enhanced Medicean pretensions, for although Lorenzo was a duke, it was obvious to everyone that he had not inherited noble rank. Then, the two arms were put together in order to form a new *stemma*.

Among the two versions proposed in Rome and sent to Florence, it is fairly certain that one showed impaled the husband's coat of arms on the left and the wife's on the right, as in the Medici Codex, an arrangement that Turini said was to be used only for Madeleine while Lorenzo should continue to use the Medici arms.[43] This is confirmed by Lorenzo's seal on a letter in the Archivio Gonzaga, written after his marriage to Madeleine which displays only the Medici *stemma*.[44] The other version "which can serve for the children" can be deduced from the arms of the child of Lorenzo's marriage, Catherine de' Medici, later Queen of France; her arms, once she married, show the usual split (the three fleurs de lys of France on the left) with quartered Medici and de la Tour d'Auvergne arms on the right.[45]

But if the arms on the right are simply Madeleine's, then they do not by themselves imply that the codex had anything to do with the actual celebration of her marriage, as they merely indicate that it was owned by Madeleine at some point after her betrothal (when she would have adopted the arms in question). There was, however, another occasion when the codex might have been presented, an occasion suggested by the curious relationship the manuscript has with Raphael's portrait of Leo X with cardinals de' Medici and Rossi, now in the Uffizi.

Raphael's portrait has always been dated between 1517 and 1519, but it is now possible to show that it was already finished by September, 1518, and that it was sent in haste from Rome to Florence on September 2, 1518 for the festivities celebrating Lorenzo's and Madeleine's formal entry into the city and the celebration of their "seconde nozze." The painting arrived in time and was displayed above a banqueting table.[46] In the portrait, Leo is shown looking at a book. This volume is a bible opened to the pages with: "In principio erat verbum et verbum erat a[pud] deum," the words at the beginning of the Gospel according to St. John. This choice was hardly casual. Leo's real name was Giovanni, and the beginning of John's Gospel contains the phrase: "Fuit homo missus a Deo cui nomen erat Johannes," referring to the Baptist, the patron saint of Florence, as well as to the Medici pope.

Now, it has long been noticed that the first folios containing music in the Medici Codex, as well as the coats of arms, belong to a separate bifolium and that the gatherings of the manuscript proper begin with what is now the second piece.[47] The first section also has the kinds of indentations at the beginnings of the voice parts that usually appear at the openings of manuscripts which also include heraldic information about the owner. Here, the heraldry is lacking and large fanciful initials are used instead. However, the intended owner is strongly suggested by the words set by this motet: "In principio erat verbum," the very words that Raphael had in late summer or early fall of 1518 associated with Leo X. This implies that the Medici Codex was not originally conceived for the wedding of Lorenzo and Madeleine but was intended for Leo X whose musical tastes it in fact represents. This hypothesis is supported by Joshua Rifkin's painstaking reconstruction of the manuscript's genesis which shows that only at a late stage in its compilation was the manuscript brought into association with the newly-married couple.[48] With the decision to change owners, apparently came the idea to represent the whole Medici family in the manuscript: not only Lorenzo and Madeleine, but also Cardinal Giulio de' Medici and Pope Leo X, all of whom are identified by the coats of arms on folios 1v-2r. Even a younger generation is present, for the motet on these folios is a prayer to St. Margaret, patron saint of childbirth.[49] Thus, it may be that Raphael's portrait was not the only object rushed to Florence for the "seconde nozze," and the Medici Codex could celebrate the union of Lorenzo and Madeleine (but not the wedding itself).

Nevertheless, the true function of the Medici Codex remains unclear. Leo could have used it in his private chapel, but it is hard to see what Lorenzo and Madeleine could have done with it. Lorenzo did not have enough singers to perform the pieces in the codex, and although the Baptistry and cathedral choirs did, this would have required transport every time something was sung from it. I would like to suggest something else. Could it be that since Lorenzo and Madeleine were the first Medici couple to have a bona fide secular court, Leo felt that they also should have a private chapel of some magnificence? In this case, the Medici Codex could have served a purpose not unlike that of a government grant given to start people off on a certain project (in this case building a chapel repertory) and to provide the basis for expansion. By sending them a manuscript full of "his" music, Leo could then be sure that his musical tastes would be actively cultivated by the young couple. Unfortunately, the early deaths of Lorenzo and Madeleine frustrated all his designs, both political and cultural, leaving only the manuscript as a testimony of what might have been.

NOTES

[1] See R. Sherr, "A New Document Concerning Raphael's Portrait of Leo X," *Burlington Magazine*, cxxv (January, 1983), pp. 31-32. On Lorenzo, see H. Reinhard, *Lorenzo von Medici, Herzog von Urbino*, Freiburg, 1935; A. Giorgetti, "Lorenzo de' Medici, Capitano Generale della Repubblica Fiorentina," *Archivio Storico Italiano*, ser. 4, xi (1883), pp. 194-215; A. Verdi, *Gli ultimi anni di Lorenzo de' Medici Duca d'Urbino*, Este, 1888; R. D. Jones, *Francesco Vettori, Florentine Citizen and Medici Servant*, London, 1972; E. E. Lowinsky, *The Medici Codex of 1518*, Chicago, 1968.

[2] Florence, Biblioteca Medicea-Laurenziana, *Acquisti e doni*, 666. See Lowinski, 1968.

[3] See A. Cummings, "Medici Musical Patronage in the Early Sixteenth Century: New Perspectives," *Studi Musicali*, x (1982), pp. 197-216.

[4] C. Guasti, *Le carte Strozziane del R. Archivio di Stato in Firenze, Inventario*, Serie I, I, Florence, 1884, p. 51. The list comes from Florence, Archivio di Stato (ASF), *Carte Strozziane*, Serie I, X, f. 160.

[5] Lowinsky, 1968, p. 32, n. 23.

[6] There are other reasons to connect this list with Giuliano. The first stipend, to be paid to the "Ill.ma consorte," cannot be connected with Lorenzo's wife, because she never visited Rome and would not have needed money there from a Roman bank. On the other hand, Giuliano's wife was often in Rome. The payment to Leonardo da Vinci suggested to Lowinsky a relationship between the artist and the Duke of Urbino. This is unlikely because in 1518-19 (the only possible period in which Lorenzo could have been involved) Leonardo was in France. However, the artist was in Giuliano's employ in 1514-16.

[7] G. Pieraccini, *La stirpe de' Medici di Cafaggiolo*, I, Florence, 1924, p. 260. Cf. Lowinsky, 1968, p. 33.

[8] ASF, *Carte strozziane*, Serie I, 3 (Minutario di Lorenzo de' Medici), f. 44. "Questi excelsi signori, per havere una musica di pifferi et tromboni qual si conviene a questa città sanza entrare in altra spesa extraordinaria, havea condocto dua che servivono alla comunità di Cesena, la quale, havendolo inteso, fa di molte dificultà ad eo che impedisce tal la venuta loro, et per questo li prefati excelsi signori ne scrivono costì allo ambasciatore, commettendoli ne parli con N. S. et vegha di trarne breve alla prefatta dicta comunità che lasci venire a servire etc.; in che la S. V. R. per essere questa cosa honorevole alla città et ad noi, si degnerà insieme col prefato ambasciatore operare che ne siamo compiaciuti sanza preiudicio de' prefati sonatori apresso la loro comunità, perché ne farà universalmente piacere a tucta questa città et in specie ad me."

[9] ASF, *Archivi della repubblica (AR)*, Signori-Carteggi, Missive I Cancelleria, 57 (1510-14), f. 173: to Francesco Vettori in Rome, 17 February, 1514.

[10] See K. Polk, "Ensemble Instrumental Music in Flander 1450-1550," *Journal of Band Research*, xi (1975), pp. 12-27; and W. Prizer, "Bernardino Piffaro e i pifferi e tromboni di Mantova: strumenti a fiato in una corte italiana," *Rivista Italiana di Musicologia*, xvi (1981), pp. 151-84.

[11] ASF, *Archivio medicee avanti il principato (MAP)*, filza 113, letter 15: Cardinal Giulio to Lorenzo, 20 February, 1514. "Avanti hieri scripsi a la M. V., et questa sera ho due sue de 18, et ho inteso el desiderio che quella ha di havere e pifferi et tromboni di Cesena di che se ne userà la diligentia; e perché non credo vi sia cosa excellente, judico che costì si chiami buona musica quella che costa poco, et parmi che la M. V. non se ne dilecti come fa el papa." Cf. Pieraccini's account, I, 1924, p. 260.

¹² ASF, *MAP*, filza 141, f. 1: Lorenzo to Cardinal Giulio, 24 February, 1514. "La S. V. R. mi farà piacere se la farà opera alchuna per conto di quelli tromboni, perché haviamo relatione da chi ne ha iuditio che sono buoni, et spendendosi quel medesimo che nelli altri si debbe cerchare di havere e migliori; et però quella sarà contenta farci quella opera che li potrà, anchora che la sia in opinione che io non me ne dilecti; et se fino ad hora non ho dato opera a tal cosa, non è stato che io non sia disceso di loro ['d'huomo' crossed out] da non me ne dovere dilectare, ma ne è stato causa lo havere havuto a pensare ad altro, come sa la S. V. R."

¹³ ASF, *AR*, Signori-Carteggi, Missive I Cancelleria, 57, f. 175: to Francesco Vettori in Rome, 14 March, 1514.

¹⁴ ASF, *MAP*, filza 108, letter 21: Cardinal Giulio to Lorenzo. "Al Vescovo di Pistoia si scripsi per conto de' pifferi et tromboni per cotesta signoria, ma la sua indispositione harà impedito la expeditione."

¹⁵ Vatican City, Archivio Segreto Vaticano (VAS), *Arm.*, 39, vol. 30, f.344v. Papal breve dated May, 1514 to "Jo. Jacobo Caesenaten, Senatus Florentin. Musico Instrumentario."

¹⁶ ASF, *AR*, Signori-Carteggi, Missive I Cancelleria, 57, f. 193-193v: To the podestà of Cervia, 2 December, 1514.

¹⁷ ASF, *MAP*, filza 116, letter 557: Joannes Jacobus piffero to Lorenzo, 3 December, 1514. "Ill. ac Ex.me D.ne D. Sing.me post humilem commendationem. Cum singolarissimo dispiacere ho inteso io essere inculpato a V. Ex.ma S. che io sono stato causa de fare partire li danari come forno partiti, del che, essendo io innocentissimo, ne ho preso quello affano che ad uno fidel servitore si conviene. Il che, per mostrare a quella esser così, Vostra prefacta Ill.ma lo pol intendere da la S.ta di N. S. ho [o] da frate Mariano et dal conte Hercule Rangone, che furun quelli che me fecino tacere. Et a questo, V. Ex.tia cognoscerà io non essere in dolo, il che chiarito et satisfacto quella, serò più contento che io potesse essere d'ogn'altra cosa che mi potesse fare V. Ill.ma et Ex.ma S., alla grazia de la quale humiliter et genibus flexis me recommando. Florentie, die iii decembris mdxiii. E. V. I. D. Servitore, Joannes Jacobus piffero."

¹⁸ H.-W. Frey, "Regesten zur päpstlichen Kapelle unter Leo X und zu seiner Privatkapelle," *Die Musikforschung*, ix (1956), p. 57. Payments in August, 1519 to "Io. Iacomo piffero che fu de la bo. me. del Duca di Urbino."

¹⁹ ASF, *MAP*, filza 116, letter 646: Giovanni Como to Lorenzo, 23 January 1515. "Ill.me D.ne et D.ne mi singularissime post humilem comendationem premisam etc. Sapia V. Ill.ma S. como ali giorni pasato è statto qui quel mio fratello, il qual disi a V. S. esendo a Montofiascona con la San.tà de N. S. ora esendo venuto qui da me, pregandomi che io gli voglia fare aver qualche partito. Conosendo io eser lui disposto ne l'arme oltra il sonare bene, andai a trovare el iutio comesario et el capitano de la guardia, pregandogli che lo volessero racetare in la guardia, e le sue signori mi risposteve che, avendo huna minima parolina da V. Ill.ma S., lo recetteriano molto volontiera, masime parendoglie el ditto mio fratello disposto atiò. E per tanto priego V. S. genifleso che l'abia per ricomandato atiò, che'l povero giovano non piglia qualche vita, masime per mio amore, perché lui dice aver preso el loco de Cesena, cioè del sonar per mi, como la Ill.ma S. V. è informatta e così potrà sapere la verità da Pierino pifaro. Per tanto, Ill.mo S. mio, lo ricomando ala Ill.ma S.ria V., ala qual per humilisime volte genifleso me ricomando. Florentie, die 23 ienuarii mdxiiii [sic-according to the Florentine calendar?]. De la Il.ma S. V.ra S.vitor, Giovanni Como pifaro."

²⁰ ASF, *MAP*, filza 132. Payments for 1515-17. *Pifferi* are mentioned on ff. 30-32v, 33v, 35, 43.

²¹ ASF, *Fondo Goro Gheri (GG)* 3, f. 333v to Benedetto Buondelmonti, 24 January, 1519. "La Ex.a del Duca dice con quelli pifferi e tromboni che haveva Mons. R.mo d'Aragona et li intrattiniate così qualche dì, cioè con parole tanto che S. Ex.a vi advisirà, chi vorrà che voi ricerchiate che venga a stare con seco; perché et quanto sarà fra dua o 3 di, però usate diligentia in questa come ho decto."

²² ASF, GG 3, f. 334v: to Buondelmonti, 26 January 1519. "Hiar sera vi scrissi che voi dovessi intractiniare quelli musici che stavano col el R.mo Car.le Ragona; la Ex.a del Duca questa sera me ha commesso che io vi scriva che voi vigiate di intratinare dua et in questo usiate diligentia che l'uno et l'altro hanno nome Bartholo. Et li altri non bisogna altrimenti intrattenarli ma questi dua S. Ex. harà piacere haverli a sua servitù."

²³ ASF, *MAP*, filza 143, letter 35: Buondelmonti to Gheri, 27 January, 1519. "De' musici del Car.le d'Aragona N. S. questa mactina mi ha decto che gli ha tolti per se, ma che se S. Ex.a gli vorrà, tutti gliene darà, anchora che a S. S.tà pare che Aragona gli habbi male avezi per dare loro più di quello che era conveniente. Circa l'havere que' due, che ioni del Car.le de' Rossi che non crede che si voglino rompere dalli altri, però V. S. farà tutto intendere alla S. Ex.tia."

²⁴ Frey, 1956, p. 57. Payment to 5 *pifferi* beginning in February, 1519: Bartholo Fiammingo, Bartholo da Milano, Domenico et Antonio da Cesena, Giorgio Greco.

²⁵ ASF, *MAP*, filza 143, letter 56: Buondelmonti to Gheri, 17 February, 1519. "Perché questo carnevale si fa certa comedia al cospecto di N. S., però accadendonsi diversi sorti di musica, Mons. R.mo Cibò mi dice che vorrieno alchuni dei sonatori di palazo con li strumenti loro, de' quali vi mando una nota in questa; però fate intendere alla Ex.a del Duca il che, contendandosi che venghino, fate che subito si mectino a camino perché assai sono desiderati."

²⁶ ASF, *MAP*, filza 143, letter 59: Buondelmonti to Gheri, 21 February, 1519. "Mandovi la nota de' sonatori, però quanto più presto si può, fate che venghino."

²⁷ ASF, GG 3, f. 358v: To Buondelmonti, 23 February, 1519. "E sonatori non vi si mandono perché el Duca a questi giorni ha preso gran piacere alli volte udirli sonar et perché ci bisogna pensare a tutte quelle cose che li possono dare piacere e li haverle preparate. Però preghate Mons. R.mo Cibò che ci admetta la scusa se non si mandano, che son certo che se S. S. R.ma havesse de sua còstà, li manderia qua perché S. Ex.a ne potesse pigliare piacere."

²⁸ ASF, GG 3, f. 361: Gheri to Buondelmonti, 26 February, 1519. "E sonatori non havevo mandati per il rispecto che ve ne advisai, però vedendo che N. S. li disidera, domani li farò partire."

²⁹ See N. Pirrotta, *Li Due Orfei*, Turin, 1969, p. 56.

³⁰ ASF, GG, 2, f. 86v: Gheri to Lorenzo, 18 March, 1517. "Pierin piffero mi dice che ha un fratello a Bologna che è bon sonatore et vorrebbe che tornassi a Firenze et che potesse andare a sonar in palazo sanza far spesa alchuna al comune e solo star a speranza che quanto vacasse qualche luogo de haverlo. Benché el servire sanza spesa si possa acceptar facilmente, pure non sapendo la intentione della Ex.a V. circa questa musicha, non ne ho voluto far niente insino che da quella non intende la sua voluntà, benché non ci essendo cosa che io non intenda, mi pare che si possa fare facilmente."

³¹ ASF, *MAP*, filza 132.

³² See F. d'Accone, "The Musical Chapels at the Florentine Cathedral and Baptistry During the First Half of the 16th Century," *Journal of the American Musicological Society*, xxiv (1971), pp. 15-16; and "Some Neglected Composers in the Florentine Chapels, ca. 1475-1525," *Viator: Medieval and Renaissance Studies*, i (1970), pp. 281-84.

33 ASF, *MAP*, filza 132. Many payments to "Giovannibattista" sometimes called master of the pages, sometimes *musico*. I identify him with Giovanbattista d'Arezzo discovered by d'Accone, 1971, because it seems logical and because Lorenzo tried to get Giovanbattista benefices in Arezzo. See ASF, GG 3, f. 194.

34 ASF, *MAP*, filza 132, f. 93v. The payments are as follows (covering the period from 1 July, 1515 to 30 June, 1517): "Tadeo musicho a ragione di ducati 200 d'oro larghi per anno e per mesi xiiii che venne al princypio di maggio 1515. 166.13 (= salary for 10 months-August 1516 to June 1517). Girolamo da Melia sonatore a ragione di ducati 4 per mese e per mesi x che venne al princypio di settembre 1516. 40. Urbano sonatore a ragione di ducati iiii d'oro per mese e per mesi x che venne al principio di settembre 1516. 40. Giamandrea da Brescya sonatore a ragione di ducati iiii d'oro per mese e per mesi v come disse Tadeo. 20."

35 Vatican City, Biblioteca Apostolica Vaticana, *Urb. lat.*, 1248, chapter 45. See B. Ligi, "La Cappella Musicale del Duomo di Urbino," *Note d'Archivio*, ii (1925), p. 4, n. 3; and C. H. Clough, "Cardinal Bessarion and Greek at the Court of Urbino," *Manuscripta*, viii (1964), p. 168, n. 9.

36 This is also confirmed by his relations with the composer "Zoppino," who sent him a setting of an Italian text, and with Elzéar Genet (Carpentras), master of the papal chapel, who sent him a setting of some words that Lorenzo had left with him (certainly Italian words). See Cummings, 1981, pp. 207-08, and ASF, *MAP*, filza 144, letter 12: Baldassare Turini to Goro Gheri, 1 February, 1518. "Con questa vi mando l'alligata alla ex. del Duca, la quale è del maestro di cappella di N. S.re, et dice che li mandò il canto che ha fatto sopra quelle parole che s. ex. gli lasciò."

37 Lowinsky, 1968.
38 *Ibid.*, pp. 3-16.
39 *Ibid.*, p. 15.

40 There is much evidence that this kind of split arms generally represented only the wife of a noble or royal marriage. See C. Csapodi and K. Csapodi-Gardonyi, *Biblioteca Corviniana*, Budapest, 1969, p. 17 and T. de Marinis, *La Biblioteca Napoletana dei Re d'Aragona*, II, Milan, 1952, p. 137. Also in Mantua, Archivio di Stato, *Archivio Gonzaga* (ASG), buste 1073-1075, there are many letters with original seals from the dukes and duchesses of Urbino. The personal arms of the duchesses (except the widowed Elisabetta Gonzaga who signed herself de Montefeltro), are all split, with the Montefeltro arms on the left and the arms of the woman's family on the right, while the arms of the dukes never are.

41 ASF, GC 4, f. 114-114v: Gheri to Baldassare Turini, 17 February, 1518. "Con questa vi mando l'arme della consorte della Ex.a del Duca, et notate che quelle tre palle dice [sic?] che sono l'arme della contea di Bologna [Boulogne]; lo dico perché l'intendiate che sono naturalmente l'arme sua, et è una cosa considerabile che l'arme sua sia le palle con e medesimi colori de le nostre."

42 ASF, *MAP*, filza 144, letter 31: Turini to Gheri, 19 February, 1518. "Io ho ricevuto l'arme della S.ra Duchessa, et N. S.re et Mons. R.mo ne hanno preso piacere grande, parendoli la conformità delle tre palle con l'arme di casa loro cosa che meriti consideratione et admiratione non piccola, et quando ad modo li pare uno miraculo Dio sia quello che faccia che li animi correspondino a la conformità del arme."

43 ASF, *MAP*, filza 144, letter 33: Turini to Gheri, 22 February, 1518. "Io ho facto fare per commandamento di Mons. R.mo l'arme dela sposa insieme con quella della Ex. del Duca per vedere come la torna bene, et quella che è segnata de una A è quella che satisfa più a N. S.re a Mons. R.mo et a tutti quelli che l'hanno vista; et dicano che a questo modo ha ad stare quella della sposa, così anchora mi dicano

questi Franzesi che sono venuti qui. Et Mons. R.mo dice che la Ex. del Duca lassi usare questa a la sposa et che S. Ex. usi la sua. Quella che è segnata B è bella come vederete, ma non conveniente secondo che dicano da la moglie et marito. N. S.re dice che la potrà servire per e figluoli di S. Ex. M. Goro, scrivete a Francesco Victori che vi advisi quale è l'arme vera anticha della casa di Bologna [Boulogne] et da quanto tempo in qua quelle tre palle quella casa ha usato, et se è possibilie ritrovarne l'origine, che N. S.re et Mons. R.mo haveranno charo intenderlo." See also ASF, GG 4, f. 129: Gheri to Torini, 25 February, 1518. "Ho ricevuto le arme della Ex.a del Duca con quelle della sposa. Si seguirà quanto advisate essere el parere di N. S. et Mons. R.mo."

[44] ASG, busta 1070, letter of 28 April, 1519.

[45] I. Cloulas, *Cathérine de Médicis*, Paris, 1979, illustration 12 (Catherine's personal seal).

[46] Sherr, 1983. On Sept. 8, 1518, Alfonsina Orsini, Lorenzo's mother, wrote to Giovanni Lapucci da Poppi that the painting had been displayed above the banqueting table where Madeleine and others sat. In fact, it became customary to display the portrait at Medici weddings thereafter. See J. Cox-Rearick, *Dynasty and Destiny in Medici Art: Pontormo, Leo X, and the two Cosimos*, Princeton, 1984, pp. 240-48.

[47] Lowinsky, 1968, p. 5.

[48] J. Rifkin, "The Creation of the Medici Codex," paper read at the 49th Annual Meeting of the American Musicological Society, Louisville, Kentucky, October 27-30, 1983. While he believes that the manuscript was at some early point intended for Leo, Rifkin also entertains the possibility that, in its very first conception, the codex could have been intended for someone other than the pope.

[49] Suggested by Rifkin, 1983. Indeed, if knowledge of Madeleine's pregnancy circulated in Rome as early as June of 1518 (cf. Cloulas, 1979, p. 32) this may have inspired the opening folio and the gift of the manuscript to the new couple.

XIX

Verdelot in Florence, Coppini in Rome, and the Singer "La Fiore"*

RESEARCHERS IN ARCHIVES often come across individual letters and documents not easily fit into a large study but still of interest to other scholars. This essay presents a few such documents culled from the Archivio di Stato in Florence. They concern two composers, Philippe Verdelot and Alessandro Coppini, and the popularity of a female singer and her accompanying vocal ensemble.

I. VERDELOT IN FLORENCE: AN EARLY DOCUMENT

Verdelot seems to have arrived in Italy long before any known document clearly establishes his presence there. If we are to believe Vasari in the 1568 edition of the *Lives*—and after Colin Slim's analysis of the question there seems to be no reason not to—then Verdelot was in Venice at least by 1511, perhaps as *maestro di cappella* of some Venetian church.[1] But we first hear of the composer unequivocally after he moved to Florence. Until now, the earliest archival reference to him has been from April, 1523, at which time he was *maestro di cappella* of the Baptistry; but Slim has shown, through analysis of a passage in one of the dialogues of Antonfrancesco Doni's *I marmi* (a dialogue in which Verdelot is a participant), that the composer must have been in Florence before the closing of the Rucellai gardens in June, 1522.[2] I am happy to report here a new document supporting Slim's conclusions as well as a suggestion made by Nino Pirrotta about the relationship of the early madrigal composers to the court of Cardinal Giulio de' Medici (later Pope Clement VII).

The document is a letter from Niccolò de Pictis [Pitti], a man who, from what the little surviving evidence about him shows, must have been very

---

* I am grateful to the Leopold Schepp Foundation and the Villa I Tatti (The Harvard University Center for Italian Renaissance Studies) for support during the research and writing of this article.

[1] H. Colin Slim, *A Gift of Madrigals and Motets*, 2 vols. (Chicago, 1972), I, 45–48.

[2] *Ibid.*, I, 50–52. The reliability of Doni's testimony has been questioned by James Haar in his article "The Early Madrigal: A Re-Appraisal of Its Sources and Its Character," *Music in Medieval and Early Modern Europe: Patronage, Sources and Texts*, ed. Iain Fenlon (Cambridge, 1981), p. 191, n. 70.

© 1984 by the American Musicological Society. All rights reserved.

important to the workings of Medici patronage of music. De Pictis is first seen as a singer in the papal chapel of Julius II in a list of March, 1506, a list that is part of a blanket grant of expectatives to all members of the chapel.[3] A document of six years later relates that de Pictis had been granted, in 1506, a canonry and prebend in the cathedral of Florence with expectatives in the diocese of Fiesole. The later bull extends this to include a canonry and prebend in the cathedral of Calahorra along with expectatives in that diocese, while excusing de Pictis from the requirement that he know the language of the diocese, since he was "de natione Itallus."[4] In fact, the researches of Haberl and Frey have shown that he was a Florentine and that he was closely connected with the Medici family.[5]

De Pictis must have been a particularly esteemed and trusted member of the Medici entourage. As soon as Leo X became pope, he created a new position for de Pictis, making him Prior of the papal chapel with a salary increase of four ducats and the duties of looking after the chapel books and seeing that the singers behaved properly during the Divine Service. (He was given the right to assign fines if they did not.) Later the pope conferred on him the provostship of Saint Catherine in the house of the Order of the Humilites in Cremona.[6]

It was in his position as Prior of the papal chapel that de Pictis wrote formally to Lorenzo de' Medici (later Duke of Urbino) in 1514, on behalf of the pope, asking for a pension to be granted to the aging Heinrich Isaac. Another letter, dated November 30, 1528, shows, in its respectfully friendly tone, the kind of relationship de Pictis must have had with Clement VII, and it provides the information that the singer was also a composer, although all of his works seem to have been lost.[7] The newly found letter, written to the future Clement VII, Cardinal Giulio de' Medici when he was papal legate in

---

[3] Vatican City, Archivio Segreto Vaticano, Registri delle Suppliche (RS) 1221, fols. 63^r–64^v. The document itself is not dated; instead, it is indicated that all the separate bulls to be drawn up from the document (one had to be written for each person mentioned in the list) were to be dated March 1, 1506. The document itself was registered at the end of March, 1506, the scribe noting on fol. 43^r that he had begun work copying this fascicle on March 28. As this list has never been published, I append it as Appendix, no. 1.

[4] Vatican City, Archivio Segreto Vaticano, Registri Vaticani 982, fols. 186^r–87^r, a copy of a bull dated July 12, 1512.

[5] Franz Xaver Haberl, *Die römische "schola cantorum" und die päpstlichen Kapellsänger bis zur Mitte des 16. Jahrhundert*, Bausteine für Musikgeschichte, 3 (Leipzig, 1888), p. 66; Hermann-Walther Frey, "Klemens VII. und der Prior der päpstlichen Kapelle Nicholo de Pitti," *Die Musikforschung*, IV (1951), 175–84; Frey, "Regesten zur päpstlichen Kapelle unter Leo X. und zu seiner Privatkapelle," *Die Musikforschung*, VIII (1955), 190–91.

[6] See Frey, "Regesten."

[7] The letter of 1514 is transcribed in Martin Staehelin, *Die Messen Heinrich Isaacs*, 3 vols., Publikationen der Schweizerischen Musikforschenden Gesellschaft, ser. 2, 28 (Bern, 1977), II, 76–77; the letter of 1528 is transcribed in Frey, "Klemens VII," pp. 180–81.

Florence, is couched in the same respectful yet familiar language, and for the first time it shows de Pictis actively involved in recruiting a musician for the cardinal. That musician was Philippe Verdelot.[8]

> Most Reverend Cardinal and Lord. Several days ago I wrote to you concerning Verdelot, again recommending him to you. It was with confidence that I had him come, considering that a person of his qualities would be welcome and satisfactory first to you and then to everybody else, with the honest salary that it seemed to me he merited. Wherefore, since he is personally there [Florence], and if you think he merits that for which he has come, I recommend him to you, believing that you will be well served by him. And I hope (God willing), after the Feast of St. Peter, to come there and stay a few days to enjoy myself with you and our friends, to whom I continually recommend myself, praying God that He keep you in a healthy and happy state. That is all, farewell. Rome, May 25, 1521.
> From Your Servant,
>
> > Nicolaus, Prior, Papal Chaplain, and Provost of St. Catherine in Cremona.

The letter states specifically that Verdelot was in Florence in May, 1521, much earlier than anyone has yet supposed. Furthermore it suggests that the composer had just arrived in the city and that his purpose in going there was to enter the service of Cardinal Giulio de' Medici. It seems also that de Pictis himself persuaded Verdelot to make the move, apparently assuring him that he would find employment at a good wage. Whether this means that the composer had actually been in Rome to meet de Pictis or whether this was done by letter is not clear. The concern for a decent salary, suitable for a man of quality, may also testify to a reputation already established, confirming the suggestion that Verdelot was well known some time before his pieces began appearing in manuscripts and prints. Finally, the letter documents a relationship between Verdelot and Cardinal Giulio, whom he probably served for two years before moving to the Baptistry, and it confirms Pirrotta's supposition that the madrigal, so important a part of Verdelot's oeuvre, grew up in the Roman and Florentine circles around that cardinal.[9]

II. New Letters about Alessandro Coppini

The new information about Coppini, although not as striking as that about Verdelot, does add something to our knowledge of the composer's life and his relationships.[10] It is contained in a series of three letters, all on the same topic, sent from Rome to Lorenzo de' Medici in May, 1515. The

---

[8] Florence, Archivio di Stato, Archivio Mediceo avanti il Principato (MAP), filza 67, letter 43, transcribed as Appendix, no. 2

[9] Pirrotta makes the suggestion in his article "Rom," *MGG*, XI, 706.

[10] The most detailed biography of Coppini is in Frank A. D'Accone, "Alessandro Coppini and Bartolomeo degli Organi: Two Florentine Composers of the Renaissance," *Analecta musicologica*, IV (1967), 38–76.

writers were Cardinal Giulio de' Medici, Cardinal Antonio del Monte, and Giuliano de' Medici, but the true instigators were Alessandro Coppini and Pope Leo X.[11] Cardinal de' Medici wrote as follows:

> Magnificent and beloved Brother. Maestro Alessandro Coppini of the Servites, good friend and servant of our house, desires to be elected this year Provincial of the province of Tuscany, and has asked that I write to you in his behalf because, if not elected, it seems to him that it will result in dishonor, considering that (according to what he says) it is usual, and furthermore in the regulations of the Order, that he who had been the Provincial Vicar in the past year should be elected and none other; and he has been in the office [of Vicar] for this year and will continue to be until there is a chapter meeting. Now, considering this, his excellent qualities, and the friendship he has always had for our house, I recommend him most highly. And I ask you to help him in any way necessary with the General or with others, and even more so because I know that His Holiness wants Maestro Alessandro to be contented in this matter; and I hope that he will exercise the office reasonably and with prudence. Farewell. Rome, in the Apostolic Palace, May 16, 1515.
> Your brother, Julianus Cardinal de' Medici.

Cardinal del Monte's letter, sent on the same day, is couched in a slightly different tone:

> Illustrious Lord and beloved Brother, greetings. Even though we were inclined to see that the Prior of the Annunziata was elected this year as Provincial of Tuscany according to Your Lordship's wishes and request, and had already done some things in that direction, it has now become necessary that we write in recommendation of Maestro Alessandro Coppini, singer of His Holiness, by commission of His Holiness, who has commissioned us to write to Your Lordship that he looks favorably on Maestro Alessandro, that he would be pleased if this year his singer were elected, and that you [should] write recommending him to the Reverend General. This is what we ask you to do, being persuaded that Maestro Alessandro, being a person well liked by His Holiness, is also acceptable and suitable for you. Farewell. Rome, May 16, 1515.
> Your Illustrious Lordship's Servant,
>
> Antonius, Cardinal of
Sancta Praxedis.

And on May 17, Giuliano sent a similar letter of recommendation.[12]

Two new facts about Coppini emerge from these letters. The first is that Cardinal Giulio (and also Giuliano) considered him an old friend and servant of the Medici family, something that might have bearing on his probable whereabouts during the years 1494–97 and something that has not been suggested by previously known documentation. The second is that Coppini was a papal singer in 1515, possibly as early as 1514, and was in Rome for

---

[11] MAP, filza 117, letters 22 and 24; filza 123, letter 57, transcribed as Appendix, nos. 3–5.

[12] See Appendix, no. 4.

that reason during May, 1515.¹³ Using his position, he tried to bring pressure on the Servite Order to elect him as Provincial, because he thought that not being elected would reflect on his honor. Clearly Cardinal del Monte and Lorenzo had other ideas about this post, and it was only under orders and entirely without enthusiasm that the Cardinal wrote his letter. In fact, the attempt to have Coppini elected Provincial failed; the *Entrata et Uscita* of the Santissima Annunziata record in July, 1515, a payment to "Maestro Aurelio Provinciale," undoubtedly the same Maestro Aurelio who was Prior of the Annunziata in May, 1515.¹⁴ Either Lorenzo did not do what the pope asked, or opposition to Coppini within the Order was too strong to be swayed even by papal will. In 1517 Coppini disappears from Florentine records. Given the new information about him, it seems likely that he went to Rome to take up permanent residence as a papal singer; he is found as a member of the papal chapel in 1522.¹⁵

III. A Scandal Caused by a Female Musician

On January 14, 1517, Goro Gheri, secretary of Lorenzo de' Medici, Duke of Urbino, wrote to the duke's mother, Alfonsina Orsini, a letter providing a glimpse into the role music could play in Renaissance society and the tensions that could spring up around musicians.¹⁶ Gheri begins with some news about what were probably troop movements, but since the duke had already been informed of this, there did not seem to be any reason to repeat the information. Instead, he tells Alfonsina of a small scandal involving members of Florence's most important families, caused by the desire to be entertained by a female singer:

> Most Illustrious Lady and [my] only patroness. I am writing to His Excellency about what is happening on account of the Spaniards who will depart from Verona, and, because I have written at length to His Excellency, I will not say

---

¹³ It is not clear, however, whether he was a member of the regular papal chapel or the *cappella segreta*. In MAP, filza 105, letter 77, dated April 19, 1514, Cardinal del Monte wrote to Lorenzo de' Medici in Florence that he was sending "Maestro Alexandro Florentino, familiare di Sua Bea.ne et servitore della prefata magnifica casa" to Florence on some business concerning the Servite Order. This almost certainly is a reference to Coppini. That he is also present in the records of the Santissima Annunziata and Santa Maria Nuova during this time does not pose a real contradiction, as he could have traveled back and forth between Florence and Rome, or had somebody else pick up his salary.

¹⁴ Florence, Archivio di Stato, Corporazioni Religiose Soppresse 119, Vol. 705 (Entrata et Uscita della Santissima Annunziata, 1512–1516), fol. 167ᵛ (July, 1515): "Maestro Aurelio Provinciale a dì detto, lire venti una sono per sua tassa; portò Maestro Valerio contanti." In June, 1515, Aurelio ceased being the Prior, his place taken by Maestro Jachopo da Firenze (fol. 166ʳ).

¹⁵ Haberl, *Die römische*, p. 71.

¹⁶ Florence, Archivio di Stato, Fondo Goro Gheri 1, fols. 307ᵛ–308ʳ, transcribed as Appendix, no. 6

XIX

407

more (as he will understand everything from his own letter) in order not to keep the courier waiting. I remind His Excellency to let me know what to do and what his wishes and those of His Holiness are, and they can rest assured that everything will be taken care of. I will tell Your Ladyship something that occurred so that you can tell His Excellency the duke about it. It happened that about six nights ago, there being twelve or fourteen gentlemen having dinner in a house where there was [also] La Fiore who sings, Madonna Clarice [Medici-Strozzi] sent to find out whether La Fiore would be willing to go to her house, because there were certain ladies having dinner with her who wished to hear her sing. And they [the gentlemen] did not want to send her; and, putting it off to another time, they did not send her. And she [Clarice] and Filippo [Strozzi] were told that, besides not wanting to send her, they used several impolite expressions, so that Filippo [was] angered by this (and perhaps the person who told him about it put more fuel on the fire than was necessary). As a result, two nights ago, these same young men being together at dinner and having the said Fiore [with them], he went to where they were together at dinner and reminded them first of their manner and of the intemperate words they had used, and he complained about it. And he turned to Averardo [Salviati], said some insulting words to him, and declared to have received this displeasure more from him than from the others. And he took La Fiore by the hand and led her away with him. When he had left, the four singers who sing with La Fiore came to the young men, and [the young men] sent them to Filippo, saying that La Fiore's singing without these singers did not satisfy as well, on account of which [the young men] sent them. [Filippo] then sent La Fiore and the singers back to them. Having heard of the incident I was displeased, especially as I perceived that it occurred among friends and relations, since these young men are Averardo Salviati, Giovanni Seristori, Giovanni della Stufa, Giovanni Bandini, Averardo's brother-in-law, and many other fine gentlemen. Yesterday, I sent for Matteo Strozzi because I was told that this continuing [ill] feeling was getting worse. I advised him to go see Averardo and the others himself and to demonstrate that these actions were not fitting either in the first place or the second, [demonstrating] with such a rebuke that it would be more honorable if everybody forgot about the incident. Yesterday Matteo talked to Averardo, and the incident has been resolved well. And it has been discussed here, and they will come to see me (that is, Averardo [will]) to explain themselves and apologize. This seemed better to me and more suitable than my having to rebuke them or having to give the job to Filippo. When I have time, in three or four days, I will invite Filippo and Averardo to dinner in order that they may become friends again and to extinguish entirely (or as much as possible) this [ill] feeling and contempt that has grown up between them. I would have done it this evening, but it was more important to see to the matter of the Spaniards. However, I will put it off for [only] two or three days more. Your Ladyship should tell His Excellency the duke about this so that he knows everything, because I think that all of these young men or Filippo will send him messages about it.

Gheri described this incident in great detail, not, of course, because he was much interested in music or the female singer, but because it signified to him an incipient feud between Filippo Strozzi and Averardo Salviati. Nonetheless, it does say something about the place of music in domestic situations. La Fiore, like the singer La Zinzera who jokes with Verdelot in *I marmi*, was part of the regular entertainment at a meeting of young men. But her musical reputation extended beyond these circles, as she was requested by Clarice Medici-Strozzi on the part of what certainly were respectable ladies. It was the young men's refusal to let her depart (one can imagine what the "impolite expressions" were) that sparked the argument and caused Filippo Strozzi (Clarice's husband) to remove La Fiore physically the next time they all met. This letter, therefore, contains an early, although not unique, reference to the place of a professional female singer in Renaissance life.[17]

It is difficult to guess the kind of music La Fiore and her four accompanying male singers would have performed. True five-part Italian secular music seems out of the question. There were very few, if any, five-part *frottole* or *canti carnascialeschi*, and 1517 is a little early for five-part madrigals. Five-part French chansons are a possibility, but why would they have been performed at an Italian bachelor dinner party? Perhaps La Fiore did not participate in five-part music at all but merely doubled one of the lines in a three- or four-part piece, or perhaps the four singers did not all sing in every piece. And what did La Fiore sing without the men? Did she accompany herself on an instrument? The answers to these questions are not in Gheri's letter but may yet be found in the Florentine Archives.

APPENDIX

1. List of the papal chapel appended to Archivio Segreto Vaticano, Registri delle Suppliche 1221, fols. 63^r–64^v (March, 1506)

Franciscus Episcopus Sessanus [Suessanus] dicte capelle magister
Nicolaus Archiepiscopus Daracenus [Duracenus] capelle sacriste
Remigius de Maistani [Mastaing]
Berthrandus Vaqueras
Gaspar Werdbec [Weerbecke]
Christophorus Rocsau [Rousseau]
Philippus de Primis
Johannus de Lyanes [Hillanis]
Chrispinus de Stappen
Jacobus Wordpot [Walpot]
Paulus de Trottis
Bonus Raydulphi
Johannes Grutter
Alphonsus Fryas
Garsias Salinas

---

[17] See the description of a similar employment of a female singer in Howard Mayer Brown, "A Cook's Tour of Ferrara in 1529," *Rivista italiana di musicologia*, X (1975), 216–41.

XIX

409

Thomas Jacobi
Johannes Pauchetoy [Pocquetoy]
Johannes Scribanus
Johannes Palomaras
Michael Touppe
Macteus Elzate [Alzate]
Nicolaus de Pitis
Felix de Nola
Johannes Radulphi
<u>Capellani Missarum</u>
Antonius de Riocys Piperno
Alphonsus de Troia
<u>Clerici Ceremoniarum</u>
R. D. Johannes Brochardi [Burkhard]
Paris de Grassis
Michael Sanderii
<u>Clerici Campanarum</u>
Herasmus Nicolay
Ferricus Jacobi

2. Florence, Archivio di Stato, Archivio Mediceo avanti il Principato, filza 67, letter 43: Niccolò de Pictis to Cardinal Giulio de' Medici, May 25, 1521

R.me d.ne Kar.lis Sal. d.ne mi osservandissime. Più dì fa, vi scrissi di Verdellotto sempre racomandendovelo. Lo feci venire a sicurtà, stimando uno huomo di quella qualità dovere essere grato e satisfaciente prima a voi e poi a ciascheduno, con quella provisione onesta che mi pareva dovessi meritare; dove, essendo lui personalmente costà, e secondo che vi pare lui meriti per quello che lui è venuto, io ve lo racomando, stimandomi ne sarete bene servito, et spero (deo dante) fatto San Piero, venire a starmi qualche g[i]orno costà a piacere e recrearmi con voi e con li amici nostri, al qual di continuo mi racomando, pregando iddio vi conservi sano e in felice stato. Nec plura, bene valete. Rome, 25 mai 1521.

   per lo vostro servitore

Nicolaus, prior capellanus pape et
prepositus S. Caterine Cremonensis

3. Florence, Archivio di Stato, Archivio Mediceo avanti il Principato, filza 117, letter 22: Cardinal Giulio de' Medici to Lorenzo in Florence, May 16, 1515

Mag.ce frater amantissime. Maestro Alexandro Coppino de' Servi, bono amico et servitore di casa nostra, desidera essere electo questo anno provinciale della provincia di Thoscana, et ne ha ricerco che io vi scriva in sua comendatione perché, non essendo electo, parebbe gle ne resultassi disonore, attento che, secondo che lui dice, è di consuetudine ut plurimu in li capitoli loro eleggiere quello che è stato vicario passato et non altro, in lo quale ufitio è stato questo anno, et è, fino si farà capitolo. Onde, considerato tal cosa, la suffitientia et bona qualità sua, et la amicitia che ha sempre tenuta con la casa nostra, sumamente ve lo rachomando; et vi prego in omni loco dove occorrà adpresso el Generale o altri, li prestiate adiuto et favore, et tanto più che io so che la S.tà di N. S. desidera che ditto Maestro Alexandro in questa cosa sia consolato; et spero che tale uffitio sarà da lui ragionevolmente et con prudentia administrato. Et bene valete. Rome, ex Palatio Apostolico, XVI Maii, MDXV.

   Fr. Ju. Car.lis de Medicis

4. Filza 117, Letter 24: Giuliano de' Medici to Lorenzo, May 17, 1515

Mag.ce D.ne etc. La S. V. ha notitia delle virtù et bone qualità di Maestro Alexandro frate de l'ordine dei Servi et quanto e[gli] sia fidel servitore di casa nostra, et per tal cosa sarò breve in rachomandarlo a quella; solum li dirò che delle lettere di favore et d'ogni altra cosa che epsa li concederà per aiutarlo et honorarlo apresso al Generale et in ogni altro loco, io ne harò piacere et obligo con V. S., alaquale mi rachomando etc. Que bene valeat. Rome, die XVII Maii, MDXV.
 V.r Julianus Medices, S. R. E. Capitanus Generalis

5. Filza 123, letter 57: Cardinal Antonio del Monte to Lorenzo, May 16, 1515

Ill. D.ne tanquam frater amantissime salutem. Benché noi fussimo inclinati procurare che el Priore de la Annunciata fusse designato questo anno provinciale di Toscana a complacentia e requisitione de V. S. et già facto qualche opera, de poi stato necessario scriviamo in recomandatione de Magistro Alexandro de Cuppinis, cantore de N. S.re, de comissione de Sua S.tà, quale ci ha comesso scriviamo a la S. V. esserli grati de Magistro Alexandro et che li serà piacere questo anno sia deputato questo suo cantore, et che quella voglia scrivere in comendatione sua al R.do Generale; cusì la exhortamo, persuadendone, per essere Magistro Alexandro persona grata a N. S.re, sia anche accepto et a proposito de quella. Que bene valeat. Rome, XVI Maii, 1515.
 E. Ill. D. V. Servitor,
       A. Car. S. Prax.

6. Florence, Archivio di Stato, Fondo Goro Gheri 1, fols. 307^v–308^r*

Ill.me d.ne Alphonsine, die xiiii januarij [1517].
Ill.ma D.na et patrona unica. Io scrivo alla Ex.a del Duca quanto occurre per conto delli Spagniuoli che partiranno da Verona, et perché alla S. Ex.a ho scripto allungo, però non dirò altro perché per la sua intenderà tutto, per non perdere più tempo a spacciare la staffetta. Ricordo bene alla Sua Ex.a a risolvermi di quanto adviso della sua voluntà et di N. S., et poi stieno di bono voglia che a tutto si provederà in bono modo. Io adviserò un caso occurso alla S. V. perché lei lo intenda alla Ex.a del Duca. Sono circa vi sere che, essendo xii o xiiii giovani da bene in una casa a cena dove era la Fiore che canta, M.a Clarice mandò a ricercarla che decta Fiore volesse andare insino a casa sua, perché vi era certe donne a cena seco che desideravano udirla cantare; et loro non ve la volseno mandare, et rimandando un' altra volta in somma anco non la mandonno, et alle[i] et a Philippo fu referito che, ultra non la havere voluto mandare, usorono qualche parola poco conveniente, in modo che Philippo, sdegniato di questa cosa (et chi la referiva forse accendeva più fuocho che non bisogniava) in modo che, dua sere fa, Philippo, essendo questi medesimi giovani accena insieme, et havendo dicta Fiore, andò dove erano tutti insieme et havevano accenare, et replicò prima loro e modi che havevano tenuti et parole poco ragionevoli che havevano usate, et se ne dolse, et si voltò ad Averardo et li dixe qualche parola inguriosa et mostrò havere ricevuto questa dispiacere più dallui che da altri; et prese la Fiore per mano et la menò seco. Et quando fu partito, venneno a quelli giovani quattro cantori che cantano con dicta Fiore, et loro li mandorono a Philippo, dicendoli che la Fiore sanza e cantori non satisfaceva così bene al cantare, però li si mandavano; et lui allora rimandò loro et e

---

* I would like to thank Professor Gino Corti for checking my transcriptions of this letter and no. 5, as well as some readings in Appendix, no. 6.

XIX

411

cantori et la Fiore. Intendendo io el caso, ne ho hauto dispiacere, et maximamente parendomi che sia fra parenti et amici; che quelli giovani sono Averardo Salviati, Giovanni Seristori, Giovanni della Stufa, Giovanni Bandini, cogniato d'Averardo, et molti altri huomini da bene. Io hieri mandai per Macte[o] Strozzi, perché mi fu decta che questa cosa et humore continuo multiplicava, et io lo confortai che come dasse trovasse Averardo et li altri, et mostrasse che questi modi non stanno bene ne' primi ne' secondi, et col modo del reprehendere che è più honorevole la cosa si extinguisse; et così Macteo hieri con Averardo ha facto l'uffitio dicto, et la cosa è resoluta bene, et qui è t[r]atata et mi verrano (cio è Averardo) a trovare per iustificarsi et excusarsi, che così mi è parso meglio et più approposito che havere io ho [o] a reprenderli o caricare Philippo. Come harò tempo, fra 3 o 4 dì, li chiamerò Philippo et Averardo una sera a cena per ridomesticarli insieme et extinguere in tutto, o el più che si può, questa humore et sdegnio che è suto fra loro, che lo harei facta questa sera, ma egl'importa più attendere alle provisioni per questa cosa delli spagniuoli, però, diferirò dua o 3 dì più. La S. V. lo può fare intendere alla Ex.a del Duca, acciò intenda tutto, perché penso tutti quelli giovani o Filippo ne daranno notitia a S. Ex.a.

XX

The Membership of the Chapels of Louis XII and Anne de Bretagne in the Years Preceding their Deaths

The French court has always been recognized as one of the major musical centers of the early sixteenth century, but study of it is difficult; there seem to be no extant court records that throw much light on the workings of the royal musical establishment, and very few extant musical sources can be claimed as originating in the court of the French king. However, enough can be surmised to show that composers active in court circles were influential (perhaps even more influential than is at present believed) in creating and spreading a new style of polyphony based on points of imitation, that quickly became part of all sacred and secular genres as the sixteenth century progressed. Because of this, the lack of specific information about the membership in the French royal chapel becomes all the more frustrating. In an attempt to shed some light on this subject, the following documents are offered. They originated, not in the French court, but in the papal curia in Rome (or wherever the pope happened to be—some of the documents cited below were signed in Bologna and other places on papal itineraries), and are drawn from the vast series of documents known as the *Registers of Supplications*.[1]

Anyone who wished a benefice or favor from the pope, had to submit a legal document, a supplication, to the pontiff who personally approved or disapproved it.[2] If approved by the pope or his surrogate,

[1] Vatican City, Archivio Segreto Vaticano, Registra Supplicationum [hereafter, RS].
[2] For a quick summary of the procedure, see Richard Sherr, "The Papal Chapel ca.

the supplication was dated and registered before becoming the basis for the various bulls that were to be drawn up. Although it was sometimes efficacious to come to Rome in person to look after requests (and many people traveled to Rome for that purpose), it was not absolutely necessary; those who had the right connections in Rome did not have to make the journey. Supplications, then, do not prove that the applicant was in Rome at the time of the request, but they are usually quite specific about other matters concerning the applicant, often specifying his home diocese, the exact nature of the benefices or favors he wished to have from the pope, and the nature of his employment by important patrons.

Sometimes the study of supplications leads to unexpected results. The information presented here, drawn from the *Registers of Supplications* for the reign of Julius II (1503–13) and the first year of the reign of Leo X (1513–14), concerns the French royal chapels during a period for which we have previously had no information. While isolated supplications from French singers can be found occasionally in the Registers, in 1510, a large number of requests for dispensations and minor benefices from members of the French court and other French clerics appear grouped together in certain of the Registers; these and other supplications from singers allow a partial reconstruction of the membership of the chapels of Louis XII and Anne de Bretagne in 1510–14, thus providing the only information about the membership in those organizations before 1515 (the year of Louis's death; Anne had died on 9 January, 1514).[3] These chapel members are listed below.

Chapel of Louis XII[4]

Hilaire Bernoneau, Master of the Chapel

That there was a musician named Hilaire in the influential position of Master of the king's chapel in the years 1510–12 is important for two minor but interesting problems of renaissance musi-

---

1492–1513 and its Polyphonic Sources," (Ph.D. dissertation, Princeton University, 1975).

[3] For a summary of what little is known about royal musicians at that time, see Stephen Bonime, "Anne de Bretagne (1477–1514) and Music: An Archival Study," (Ph.D. dissertation, Bryn Mawr College, 1975). The distinction between king and queen was made clear, by the way, by the use of formulas like "cantor capellanus capelle Christianissimi francorum regis" and "cantor capellanus capelle Anne francorum regine." I have chosen to present detailed summaries of the documents in order to give an idea of the nature of the requests, the people involved, and the actual places where the benefices were located. Names of singers are always given in the nominative case in the Notes.

[4] An asterisk indicates that the singer appears in the list of singers who attended the funeral of Louis XII in January, 1515. See Ernest Thoinan, *Les Origines de la Chapelle-Musique des Souverains de France* (Paris, 1864), pp. 91–92.

cology.⁵ The first problem concerns the career of Johannes Prioris. From documents of 1503 and 1507, we know that Prioris was the Master of the king's chapel in those years (and presumably in the intervening ones); and it has been further assumed, because Prioris is called "notre maistre et bon père" in Crétin's lament on the death of Lourdault (who really did die in January, 1512—see below), that the composer was the Master of the chapel at least until 1512.⁶ But the documents presented below clearly contradict the last assertion, for Hilaire Bernoneau is unequivocally referred to as "magister capelle Christianissimi francorum regis" in all but one of them, and they cover the years 1510–12. And as a poet may be allowed poetic license while the preparer of a legal document is not, I think we must accept the priority of the Vatican documents over the somewhat ambiguous statement in Crétin's lament. Prioris had ceased being Master of the king's chapel by the beginning of 1510. Whether this means that he had died by then is not so clear, but it is certainly a possibility.⁷

The second problem concerns composers/singers with the name Hilaire. As Sidney Charles pointed out, there are a number of pieces in manuscripts and prints of the first two decades of the sixteenth century ascribed to "Hilaire." Reasoning that the composer Hilaire Penet was too young to have written these works (in 1514, Penet was a boy in the employ of Pope Leo X), she suggested that the Hilaire of these pieces was Hilaire Turleron, a well-known singer of the chapels of the Duke of Ferrara, Marquis of Mantua, and Pope Leo X.⁸ This suggestion, perfectly congruent with the then-available evidence, has been generally adopted, and Turleron has been credited with works ascribed to "Hilaire."⁹ But the knowledge that there was an important musician named

---

⁵ The king's chapel seems to have had two Masters, one of whom (Cardinal René du Frie, d. 1519) must have been an ecclesiastical administrator. Other people designated as Master of the Chapel (Prioris, Conrad Renuger) were singers.

⁶ See Richard Wexler, "The Complete Works of Johannes Prioris," (Ph.D. dissertation, New York University, 1974).

⁷ Bernoneau's position as Master of the Chapel in 1511 explains his presence on 17 January, 1511, as an authenticator of a copy of documents relating to the maîtrise of the Sainte-Chapelle. As Wexler has pointed out, the Master of the royal chapel had an interest in the maîtrise of the Sainte-Chapelle, and in fact had interfered with it so much, that Louis XII was forced to issue a document declaring that the true authority rested not with the master of his chapel, but with the Treasurer of the Sainte-Chapelle. This might explain why Bernoneau was called to witness a copy of some of the documents that relate to that dispute. See Michel Brenet [Marie Bobillier], *Les musiciens de la Sainte-Chapelle du Palais* (Paris, 1910), pp. 51–54.

⁸ Sidney R. Charles, "Hillary-Hyllayre: How Many Composers?" *Music and Letters* LV (1974), 61–69. Turleron was a member of the Ferrarese chapel from 1504–1511, moving then to the chapel of the Marquis of Mantua, and to the papal chapel in 1513. See Lewis Lockwood. "Jean Mouton and Jean Michel: French Music and Musicians in Italy 1505–1520," *Journal of the American Musicological Society* XXXII (1979), 208–09.

⁹ See Joshua Rifkin's article "Hilaire [Hylaire] Daleo [Turleron]" in *The New Grove*.

62

Hilaire actually in the French royal chapel precisely in the period during which these works were produced changes things radically. Since it seems certain that the composer Hilaire must have been connected in some way with the French chapel,[10] and since there is no documentary evidence linking Turleron with the French court—even the assumption that he was a composer depends on his being the only Hilaire who fits the chronology of works ascribed to Hilaire—I think we may now consider seriously whether or not he is the wrong choice for authorship of those works. A better candidate is clearly Hilaire Bernoneau, who may now join the list of minor composers of the Renaissance. In fact, Bernoneau, as Dean of the cathedral of Poitiers (see below) might have had some hand in advancing the career of his younger namesake, Hilaire Penet (who came from the diocese of Poitiers and was sent as a boy to Leo X by Louis XII).[11] As Bernoneau does not appear in the chapel list of 1515, and the position of Master of the Chapel is given to someone else (Conrad Renuger), he may have died by then.

RS 1337, fols. 137v–138r: supplication dated 7 February, 1510. Bernoneau, described as Master of the king's chapel,[12] has resigned the parish church of St-Julien de Masuillo Patrini in the diocese of Bayeux in favor of Gabriel Hunet, described as a priest of "N" diocese, and is granted a pension of 30 livres tournois "monete in regno francie."

RS 1339, fol. 104r: supplication dated 21 February, 1510. Bernoneau, described as rector of the parish church of St-Denis in Amboise in the diocese of Tours and as Master of the king's chapel,[13] asks for permission to keep the parish church of St-Denis in Amboise for another two years without having to become a priest.

---

[10] When the name Hilaire appears in poetic lists of singers, it is always in the company of members of the chapel, and his works generally appear in sources preserving music from the French court. See the lists in a poem by Jean le Maire de Belges quoted in Charles, and also the list in Moulu's "Mater floreat florescat." His chansons are found in Cambridge, Magdalene College, Pepys Library MS 1760 and London British Library Reference Division, Department of Manuscripts, MS Harley 5242, both chansonniers emanating from the French court in the first decades of the sixteenth century—see Louise Litterick, "The Manuscript Royal 20.A.XVI of the British Library," (Ph.D. dissertation, New York University, 1976); his one motet, "Ascendens Christus in altum" appears first in the *Motetti de la Corona*, vol. I (Fossombrone, 1514), a print that is made up mostly of motets by French court composers; his Mass appears in Vatican City, Biblioteca Apostolica Vaticana, Fondo Cappella Sistina MS 16, a Roman source copied during the reign of Leo X containing music by other French court composers (Févin and Mouton). Rifkin points out these relationships in *The New Grove*.

[11] Hermann-Walther Frey, "Regesten zur päpstlichen Kapelle unter Leo X. und zu seiner Privatkapelle," *Die Musikforschung* VIII (1955), 178.

[12] "Hilarius Bernoneau, magister capelle Christianissimi francorum regis."

[13] "Hilarius Bernoneau rector parrochialis ecclesie Sancti Dionisii de Ambasia Turonensis diocesis . . . capelle Christianissimi domini Ludovici francorum regis magister."

RS 1341, fol. 36r: supplication dated *14 March, 1510. Adrianus Goffier resigns the position of dean of the cathedral of Poitiers to Bernoneau, who is described as being a canon and the treasurer of the collegiate church of St-Sauveur in Blois in the diocese of Chartres and Master of the king's chapel.*[14] *The income was said not to exceed 24 ducats.*

RS 1356, fol. 201r: supplication dated *9 October, 1510. Bernoneau, described as dean of the cathedral of Poitiers and Master of the king's chapel,*[15] *asks for a dispensation allowing him to hold as many as four incompatible benefices.*

RS 1359, fol. 302r: supplication dated *2 January, 1511. Bernoneau, described as Treasurer of the church of St-Sauveur in Blois in the diocese of Chartres [and not as a member of any royal chapel],*[16] *asks for a dispensation allowing him to hold as many as four incompatible benefices.*

RS 1381, fol. 85r: supplication dated *21 February, 1512. Bernoneau, described as dean of the cathedral of Poitiers and Master of the king's chapel,*[17] *asks for a dispensation to allow him to hold the parish church of St-Denis in Amboise for two more years without becoming a priest.*

Michel Allart*

RS 1368, fol. 175v: supplication dated *1 September, 1511. Allart, described as a priest of Paris and singer in the king's chapel,*[18] *asks for the parish church of Notre Dame de Moner in the diocese of Coutances that had been granted to Ludovicus Herbert. The income was not expected to exceed 24 ducats.*

Arnulphe Boutin

RS 1346, fol. 136v: supplication dated *17 May, 1510. Boutin, called a priest and canon of the church of St-Florentin in Amboise in the diocese of Tours and as a singer in the king's chapel,*[19] *has resigned the priory of St-Saulve of the Augustinian Order in the diocese of Poitiers in favor of Johannes Piguet [after a*

---

[14] "Hilarius Bernoneau, canonicus et thesaurarius ecclesie Sancti Salvatoris castri Blesensis Carnotensis diocesis ac capelle Christianissimi francorum regis magister."
[15] "Hilarius Bernoneau, decanus ecclesie Pictavensis ac capelle Christianissimi francorum regis magister."
[16] "Hilarius Bernoneau, thesaurarius ecclesie Sancti Salvatoris castri seu oppidi Blesiensis Carnotensis diocesis."
[17] "Hilarius Bernoneau rector parrochialis ecclesie Sancti Dionisii de Ambasia Turonensis diocesis . . . ac magister capelle L. Christianissimi francorum regis."
[18] "Michael Allart, presbiter Parisiensis et capelle Christianissimi francorum regis Ludovici moderni cantor capellanus."
[19] "Arnulphus Boutin, presbiter, canonicus ecclesie Sancti Florentini de Ambasia Turonensis diocesis devoti vestri ac Sancte Romane Ecclesie Ludovici francorum regis Christianissimi cantor capellanus."

lawsuit], and asks for a pension of 60 livres tournois "monete in regno francie" or about 30 ducats to be paid from the fruits of the priory.

RS 1346, fols. 189r–189v: supplication dated 17 May, 1510. Boutin [not described as a singer in any royal chapel],[20] has resigned the above priory to Johannes Piguet priest and Augustinian canon. The income was said not to exceed 24 ducats. A later clause mentions that Boutin has perhaps died outside of Rome.[21]

RS 1422, fols. 75v–76r: supplication dated 24 August, 1513. Boutin, described as the rector of the parish church of St-Georges sur Charon and St-Martin de Coselles in the dioceses of Tours and Sens and as a chaplain in the king's chapel and doctor of canon and civil law,[22] asks for a dispensation to hold as many as four incompatible benefices.

Jean Braconnier alias Lourdault

Very little is known about the life of Lourdault. The documents presented here add some more information, and substantiate his death date (sometime shortly before 22 January, 1512).

RS 1348, fol. 135r: supplication dated 3 June, 1510. Johannes Hurault[23] had resigned the commenda of the priory of Notre-Dame-des-Champs outside the walls of Paris into the hands of Cardinal d'Amboise who had given it to Braconnier, described as canon and provost of the provostship of Valeria in the collegiate church of St-Martin of Tours and as a singer in the king's chapel;[24] Braconnier, asks for a new provision to the benefice. The income was said not to exceed 24 ducats.

RS 1361, fols. 14r–14v: supplication dated 19 March, 1511. Braconnier, described as canon and provost of the church of St-Martin in Tours, rector of the parish church of Aialliate [Aylly] in the diocese of Evreux, and as a singer in the

---

[20] "Arnulphus Boutin, presbiter."
[21] NB. This is not mentioned in the other document.
[22] "Arnulphus Boutin, rector parrochialis ecclesie Sanctorum Georgii super Charon et Martini de Corselles Turronensis et Senonensis diocesis . . . christianissimi francorum regis capellanus ordinarius et in utroque vel altero jure doctor vel licentiatus."
[23] Hurault may be identical to Johannes Hurtault, who was a singer in the church of St-Louis des Français in Rome in 1519. See Rome Archivio di Stato, Archivio del Tribunale del Vicariato, busta 335 [Liber Ordinationum], no foliation. Hurtault is identified as a cleric of the diocese of Paris, and is promoted to the rank of subdeacon. Possibly he was a member of the French royal chapel as well.
[24] "Johannes Braconnier, canonicus et prepositus prepositure de Valeria in ecclesia Beatissimi Martini Turonensis ad Romanam curiam nullo medio pertinente ac Christianissimi francorum regis cantor capellanus."

king's chapel,²⁵ has also been granted a priory and canonry of the church of Notre-Dame-des-Champs of the Benedictine Order near Paris. He asks for a dispensation allowing him to hold these three incompatible benefices.

RS 1381, fol. 24v: supplication dated 10 February, 1512. The priory of Notre-Dame-des-Champs of the Benedictine or Augustinian Order in the diocese of Paris had become vacant on the death of Braconnier. Johannes Morelli, cleric of the diocese of Rennes and in the household of Antonius de Sancto Severino [an apostolic abbreviator], asks for the benefice. The income was not expected to exceed 24 ducats.

RS 1388, fol. 298v: supplication dated 22 January, 1512. Egide Charpentier, described as a priest of the diocese of Amiens [and not as a singer in any royal chapel—see Charpentier below] asks for a canonry and prebend in the cathedral of Evreux and the parish church of Alleriate alias de Aylly in the diocese of Evreux, vacant on the death of Braconnier outside of Rome. The income as not expected to exceed 24 ducats.

RS 1380, fol. 229v: supplication dated 13 February, 1512. Egide Charpentier, described as a priest of the diocese of Amiens [and not as a singer in any royal chapel—see Charpentier below], asks again for the above benefices, and adds the priory of Notre-Dame-des-Champs of the Benedictine Order in Paris, vacant on the death of Braconnier outside of Rome. The income was not expected to exceed 24 ducats.

Guillaume Cousin*

Cousin was one of a number of singers of the chapel of François I to receive benefices and favors from Leo X.²⁶

RS 1368, fol. 177v: supplication dated 3 September, 1511. Cousin, described as a singer in the King's chapel, has resigned the parish church of Cauches in the diocese of Lisieux to Henricus Clurtin, a papal notary. Cousin is to get a pension of 30 livres tournois.

RS 1389, fol. 224r: supplication dated 25 June, 1512. Cousin, described as rector of the parish church of Cuy and Sermonest in the diocese of Soissons [and not as a singer in any royal chapel],²⁷ asks for a dispensation to allow him to hold two incompatible benefices.

---

²⁵ "Johannes Braconnier alias Lourdault, canonicus et prepositus Beatissimi Martini Turonensis . . . ac rector parrochialis ecclesie de Alliate Ebroicensis diocesis . . . capelle Christianissimi francorum regis cantor capellanus."

²⁶ RV 1206, fols. 470r–471v: bull dated 30 January, 1516. Cousin is granted a dispensation allowing him to hold incompatible benefices.

²⁷ "Guillermus Cousin, parrochialis ecclesie teneri de Cuy et Sermonest Suessionensis diocesis rector."

Antoine de Feripy

RS 1351, fol. 266v: supplication dated 11 July, 1510. Feripy, described as a cleric of "N" diocese, of noble birth, and as a singer in the king's chapel,[28] asks for a canonry and prebend in the cathedral of Rouen, vacant by the death of Johannes Garin outside of Rome. The income was said not exceed 24 ducats.

Elzéar Genet alias Carpentras

Carpentras can be connected with the chapel of Louis XII not through documents, but through his own admission; in the dedication to Cardinal Ippolito de' Medici of the print of his *Liber Hymnorum* (1532), he stated that he had been recalled to Rome from the French court by Leo X at the beginning of his pontificate. It is now possible to give an idea of the dates of his service to the king. Genet had been a member of the papal chapel at least since 1508, but on 21 May, 1512, he announced his intention of leaving Rome and asked permission to keep the privileges of the papal singers while he was away; presumably, he joined the French royal chapel soon after.[29] Nor was he recalled immediately to Rome on the accession of Leo X. The radical idea of making a composer (Genet) the Master of the papal chapel did not occur immediately to the pope, who on 6 April, 1513, gave the position to the Archbishop of Durazzo, the former sacristan of the chapel.[30] Genet was in Rome soon after, however, and was made Master of the papal chapel on 5 November, 1513.[31]

Antoine de Longueval

Longueval had moved from Ferrara to the royal chapel around 1507.[32] He was one of a number of singers in the chapel of François I granted benefices and favors by Leo X.[33]

RS 1340, fol. 67r: supplication dated 2 March, 1510. Longueval, described as a canon of the Ste-Chapelle of Bourges, of noble birth, and as a singer in the king's chapel,[34] asks for a dispensation allowing him to hold three incompatible benefices.

---

[28] "Antonius de Feripy, clericus N diocesis seu civitatis de nobili genere ex utroque parente procreatus devoti vestri et Sancte Romane Ecclesie filii Ludovicii francorum regis Christianissimi cantor capellanus."

[29] RS 1386, fols. 120r–120v.

[30] RS 1406, fol. 105v.

[31] RS 1433, fols. 2r–2v.

[32] See Lewis Lockwood, *Music in Renaissance Ferrara 1400–1505* (Cambridge, MA, 1984).

[33] See RV 1206, fols. 466r–466v: bull dated 17 December, 1515. Longueval is made an apostolic notary. Also RV 1206, fols. 476v–479r: bull dated 30 January, 1516. Longueval is granted a dispensation allowing him to hold incompatible benefices.

[34] "Anthonius de Longueval, canonicus ecclesie Sancte Capelle Bituricensis de nobili

RS 1341, fol. 243r: supplication dated 20 March, 1510. Longueval, described as a canon of the Ste-Chapelle of Bourges, of noble birth, and as a royal chamberlain [and not as a singer in any royal chapel],[35] had obtained the parish church of Aqueteville in the diocese of Coutances or Rouen ["ecclesia de Aqueteville Constantiensis diocesis perinde Rothomagensis"] and asks for a dispensation allowing him to continue to hold the benefice for three more years without becoming a priest.

RS 1439, fols. 113r–113v: supplication dated 23 December, 1513. Longueval, described as a canon of the Ste-Chapelle of Bourges, of noble birth, and as the king's chamberlain,[36] had been given a dispensation to hold two incompatible benefices by the papal legate Cardinal Georges d'Amboise, and had been granted the parish churches of Aqueteville in the diocese of Coutances and Esquenernaville in the diocese of Lisieux. He now asks for a dispensation to allow him to hold as many as four incompatible benefices.

Nicholas Marescal

RS 1302, fol. 206v: supplication dated 8 September 1508. Marescal, described as rector of the parish church of St-Martin de Caudemuche in the diocese of Lisieux and as a singer in the king's chapel,[37] asks for a dispensation allowing to hold as many as three incompatible benefices.

Jean de Montul

RS 1317, fol. 39r: supplication dated 6 May, 1509. Montul, described as a priest and singer in the king's chapel,[38] had engaged in a permutation of benefices with Antonius de la Baude whereby Montul had resigned the parish church of Castillon in the diocese of Chartres and La Baude had resigned the parish church of Boilleto in the same diocese; and this permutation had been accepted by the papal legate Cardinal d'Amboise. Now, because the income from the church of Castillon was more than the income from the church of Boilleto, Montul asks for a pension of 10 livres tournois "monete in regno francie" from the fruits of the church of Castillon to be paid to him by La Baude.

---

genere ex utroque parente procreatus ac Christianissimi francorum regis cantor capellanus."

[35] "Antonius de Longueval, canonicus ecclesie sancte capelle Bituricensis . . . de nobili genere ex utroque parente procreatus ac Christianissimi francorum regis cubicularius."

[36] "Antonius de Longueval canonicus ecclesie Sancte Capelle Bituricensis de nobili genere ex utroque parente procreatus . . . illustrissimi christianissimi francorum regis camerarius."

[37] "Nicolaus Marescall, rector parrochialis ecclesie Sancti Martini de Caudemuche Lexoviensis diocesis cantor capellanus Christianissimi domini francorum regis."

[38] "Johannes de Montul, presbiter, capelle Christianissimi regis francorum cantor capellanus."

XX

Guillaume Porci*

RS 1337, fols. 136r–136v: supplication dated 5 February, 1510. Porci, described as the rector of the parish church of St. Viexius de Ruvere in the diocese of Bayeux, Master of Arts, and as a singer in the king's chapel,[39] asks for a dispensation allowing him to hold two incompatible benefices.

Georges Reverdi*

RS 1431, fols. 84r–84v: supplication dated 2 November, 1513. Reverdi, described as a priest of an unnamed diocese and singer in the king's chapel,[40] had engaged in a lawsuit with Guillaume Muscuvyer concerning the parish church of Fressemeville in the diocese of Amiens. Reverdi has ceded the benefice and asks for a pension of 12 livres "monete in regno francie" to be paid from the fruits.

RS 1437, fols. 37r–37v: supplication dated 13 January, 1514. Reverdi, described as priest of an unidentifiable diocese, and of the parish church of St-Egide de Crotot in the diocese of Rouen, and singer in the king's chapel,[41] asks for a dispensation allowing him to hold as many as three incompatible benefices.

Conrad Renuger*

Although Renuger was in the king's chapel in 1510, he apparently had moved to the queen's chapel by 1513. He is the Master of the Chapel in the 1515 list.

RS 1346, fol. 142r: supplication dated 14 May, 1510. Renuger, described as the archpriest "insule Bourgardi" in the cathedral of Tours and as a singer in the king's chapel,[42] asks for a dispensation allowing him to hold three incompatible benefices.

RS 1433, fols. 271v–272v: supplication dated 30 October, 1513. Renuger, described as a priest of an unidentifiable diocese and singer in the queen's chapel,[43] had been given four benefices: a canonry and prebend in the church of

---

[39] "Guillermus Porci, rector parrochialis ecclesie Sancti Viexiis de Ruvere Baiocensis diocesis, magister in artibus, ac capelle Christianissimi francorum regis cantor capellanus."

[40] "Georgius Reverdi presbiter N . . . christianissimi francorum regis capelle ordinarius cantor."

[41] "Georgius Reverdi presbiter Monsconensis [?] diocesis parrochialis ecclesie Beati Egidii de Crotot Rothmagensis diocesis, capelle christianissimi regis cantor."

[42] "Conradus Renuger, archipresbiter insule Bougardi in ecclesia Turonensis ad Romanam ecclesiam nullo medio pertinente ac Christianissimi francorum regis cantor capellanus."

[43] "Conradus Renuger, presbiter Astatensis (?) diocesis . . . qui in capella devotissime et Sancte Romanae Ecclesie Anne francorum regine et Britanie duxisse illustrissime cantor capellanus existit."

St-Sauveur in Blois, the archpriestship "insule Bouchard" in the cathedral of Tours, the parish church of St-Gervais de Mantellam in the diocese of Tours, and the priory of St-Médard de Ylla in the diocese of Tours. He has the necessary dispensation, and asks for a new provision to the benefices. The income of each of the benefices was not expected to exceed 24 ducats.

Nicasius de Villin

RS 1337, fol. 136r: supplication dated 5 February, 1510. Villin, described as a canon of the church of Notre Dame de Cleriaco "nullius diocesis," and as a singer in the king's chapel,[44] asks for a dispensation extending permission to hold incompatible benefices to three.

Chapel of Anne de Bretagne

Antoine Divitis, Master of the Chapel*

That Divitis was the Master of Anne's chapel in 1510 is perhaps the most interesting information provided by these documents, but it causes problems. For in the very month that he is so named in the document cited below, Jean Mouton is also called Master of the Queen's chapel in a chapter act of St-André of Grenoble.[45] Perhaps the Vatican document is mistaken or Mouton and Divitis shared the position of Master. In any case, Divitis probably moved to Anne's employ shortly after the disbanding of the chapel of Philip the Fair in 1506.

RS 1345, fols. 21r–21v: supplication dated 2 May, 1510. Robert Challand [Britto, Guibé], Cardinal of Nantes, [also known by his titular church of St. Anastasia], had obtained in commendam the priory of St-Jacques de Premul of the Benedictine Order, outside the walls of Nantes, but now asks to cede it to Divitis, described as cleric of Liège and singer and Master of the queen's chapel.[46] The income was said not to exceed 200 ducats and the cardinal is given the right of regression.

RS 1357, fols. 11r–11v: supplication dated 15 October, 1510. Divitis, described as cleric of the diocese of Liège and singer in the queen's chapel, cedes the priory de Sensibus of the Augustinian Order in the diocese of Rennes, to Petrus

---

[44] "Nicasius de Villin, canonicus ecclesie Beate Marie de Cleriaco nullius diocesis ad Romanam ecclesiam nullo medio pertinente, capelle Christianissimi francorum regis cantor capellanus."

[45] See Josephine Shine, "The Motets of Jean Mouton," (Ph.D. dissertation, New York University, 1953), p. 18; document dated 10 May, 1510.

[46] "Antonius de Riche, clericus Leodiensis diocesis qui capelle carissime in Christo filie et Sancte Romane Ecclesie filie vestre Anne francorum regine et ducisse Britannie magister et cantor existit."

Jouault, *described as a priest of the diocese of Rennes and singer in the queen's chapel. The income was not expected to exceed 100 ducats.*

RS 1444, fols. 57r–57v: supplication dated 29 January, 1514. Divitis [not described as a singer in any royal chapel][47] *has ceded the priory of Premul of the Benedictine Order in the diocese of Nantes. Bernardus Clerici, canon of the diocese of St-Malo and apostolic scriptor, asks for the benefice. The income was not expected to exceed 150 petits livres tournois.*

Jean de Hollewigue alias Mouton, Master of the Chapel*

Mouton is named as a singer in Anne's chapel on 22 April, 1509, and is called Master of the Chapel in a document of 1510 (see Divitis above), but it is likely that he joined Anne's chapel around 1501–02.[48] He was also one of a number of singers in the chapel of François I granted benefices and favors by Leo X.[49]

RS 1312, fol. 210r: supplication dated 14 February, 1509. Mouton, described as a cleric of the diocese of Thérouanne [and not as a singer in any royal chapel], asks for a new provision to the parish church of Tolay, vacant on the death of Egide de Quibriac and given to Mouton by Cardinal Robert Challand. The benefice had originally been resigned by Divitis. The income was not expected to exceed 24 ducats.

RS 1333, fol. 118r: supplication dated 28 November, 1509. Mouton, described as a cleric of the diocese of Thérouanne [and not as a singer in any royal chapel],[50] *asks for a dispensation to allow him to hold three incompatible benefices.*

RS 1359, fol. 302v: supplication dated 2 January, 1511. François le Vigoreux and Mouton ask to be allowed to make a permutation of benefices whereby le Vigoreux [not described as a singer in any royal chapel or as the cleric of any diocese] will resign a canonry and prebend in the cathedral of Tours and Mouton [not described as a singer in any royal chapel or as the cleric of any diocese] will resign the parish church of St. Elnodus "alias de Sancte Dolien" in the diocese of Nantes (and Cardinal Robert Challand who held this benefice in commendam will cede it). The income of the canonry was not expected to exceed 24 ducats and the income from the parish church was not expected to exceed 140 ducats.[51]

---

[47] "Antonius Divitis alias de la Riche."
[48] Bonime, "Anne de Bretagne," pp. 67–68.
[49] RV 1206, fols. 473r–473v: bull dated 17 December, 1515. Mouton is made a papal notary.
[50] "Johannes de Hollewigue alias Mouton, clericus Morinensis diocesis."
[51] The document is not totally clear on this point.

XX

Egide Charpentier

Most of Charpentier's career was spent as a singer in the papal chapel; he first appears in a chapel list of June 1508.⁵² In February of 1510, he announced his intention of leaving Rome and was granted permission to keep the privileges of a singer in the chapel.⁵³ He returned to the papal chapel in August, 1514.⁵⁴ The relatively large number of documents presented here may be the result of the experience he gained as a hunter of benefices while a papal singer. And at least one of them contains a subterfuge related to his former employment. In January, 1514, Charpentier made a permutation of benefices with the papal singer Johannes Radulphi, and the original supplication (presented below) and the actual bull listed by Frey (along with many others of 1513) state that Charpentier was also a member of the papal chapel, thus suggesting that he returned to Rome in 1513.⁵⁵ Yet this seems to be contradicted by a *motu proprio* which states that Charpentier actually rejoined the chapel in August, 1514.⁵⁶ The conflict is resolved by a supplication dated 24 February, 1514, in which Charpentier specifically asks to be considered as a papal singer in the bull of 30 January, 1514 (and therefore as a recipient of their special privileges), even though he was not in fact in Rome or a member of the chapel when the bull was promulgated (see below); this legal subterfuge probably applies to the bulls of 1513 as well. He most likely remained in the queen's chapel until her death in January, 1514, and then made his way back to Rome.

*RS 1388, fol. 298v: supplication dated 22 January, 1512. Charpentier, described as a priest of the diocese of Amiens [and not as a singer in any royal chapel],*⁵⁷ *asks for benefices vacant on the death of Jean Braconnier alias Lourdault. See Braconnier above.*

RS 1380, fol. 229v: supplication dated 13 February, 1512. Charpentier, described as a priest of the diocese of Amiens [and not as a singer in any royal chapel], asks for benefices vacant on the death of Braconnier. See Braconnier above.

RS 1397, fols. 219v–220r: supplication dated 10 November, 1512. Franciscus [Hamon], Bishop-elect of Nantes, has resigned the parish church of Oratorius Boterelli in the diocese of Nantes. Charpentier, described as a cleric of Amiens

---

⁵² See Rome, Archivio di Stato, Misc. Corvisieri busta 1, fasc, 12.
⁵³ See RS 1339, fol. 225v: supplication dated 21 February, 1510.
⁵⁴ Rome Archivio di Stato, Camerale I, 859A, fol. 108r. See also Frey; *MF* VIII (1955), 61–62.
⁵⁵ See Frey *MF* VIII (1955), 66–67.
⁵⁶ See Rome, Archivio di Stato, Camerale I 859A, fol. 108r.
⁵⁷ "Egidius Charpentier, presbiter Ambianensis diocesis."

XX

[and not as a singer in any royal chapel],[58] *asks for the benefice. The church was united to the parish church of St-Hilaire de Cugno [Organo?]. The income was not expected to exceed 100 ducats.*

RS 1399, fols. 157–158r: supplication dated 10 November, 1512. Franciscus, Bishop-elect of Nantes, nephew of Cardinal Robert Challand, resigns [and the cardinal cedes his right of regression] to the above and other benefices in favor of Guido Lorens, cleric of Nantes, François Rubeis, cleric of Tréguier and Doctor of Laws [these two do not seem to have been musicians], Charpentier, cleric of the diocese of Amiens, Jean Nolin, cleric of the diocese of Chartres, Jean Richafort, cleric of the diocese of Liège, and Balduin Lupi, cleric of the diocese of Thérouanne.[59]

RS 1423, fol. 152v: supplication dated 6 September, 1513. Charpentier, described as a canon of the cathedral of Beauvais [and not as a singer in any royal chapel],[60] *asks for an unnamed archpriestship in an unnamed church, vacant on the death of Johannes de Halestant outside of Rome, and a dispensation allowing him to retain the parish church of Oratorio Boterelli in the diocese of Nantes. The income was not expected to exceed 24 ducats.*

RS 1426, fol. 208r: supplication dated 12 September, 1513. Basically a repeat of the previous supplication.

RS 1426, rol. 213r: supplication dated 24 September, 1513. Charpentier, described as a canon of Beauvais and a singer in the queen's chapel,[61] *had engaged in a lawsuit with Jean de Lyons concerning the parish church of St-Médard des Poult in the diocese of Soissons. Charpentier resigns the benefice and asks for a pension of 20 ducats to be paid to him from the fruits of the benefice.*

RS 1427, fols. 111–112r: supplication dated 5 October, 1513. Charpentier, described as a priest and rector of the parish church of St-Médard des Paux in the diocese of Soissons has resigned the benefice. Jean de Lyons asked to be granted it. The income was not expected to exceed 24 ducats.

RS 1440, fols. 69v–70r: supplication dated 30 January, 1514. Charpen-

---

[58] "Egidius Charpentier, clericus Ambianensis diocesis."

[59] The benefices were: canonries and prebends in the cathedrals of Nantes and Rennes and the parish churches of Nort, des Touches, Albaretz, St. Hilarius de Cugno/ Oratorius Boterelli. These were requested by: "Guido Lorens et Franciscus Rubeis . . . , ac Johannes Nolin necnon Johannes Richafort et Balduinus Lupi ac Egidius Carpentier clerici Nannetensis et Trecoriensis ac Carnotensis necnon Leodiensis et Morinensis ac Ambianensis." See under the respective names.

[60] "Egidius Charpentier, canonicus ecclesie Belvacensis."

[61] "Egidius le Carpentier, canonicus Belvacensis diocesis ac cantor capellanus illustrissime domine francorum regine."

tier and Johannes Radulphi, both described as singers in the papal chapel, have made a permutation of benefices whereby Charpentier has resigned the parish church of Oratorio Boterelli in the diocese of Nantes and Radulphi has resigned the parish church of Seguelnan in the diocese of Vannes. The incomes of these benefices were not expected to exceed 100 ducats.

RS 1445, fols. 96v–97r: supplication dated 24 February, 1514. In the bull allowing the above permutation, Charpentier had been described as a papal singer even though he was not in fact in Rome or a member of the papal household.[62] Because he is worried that this fact may cause him legal problems with the permutation, he asks for an indult whereby the bull will be read as if he really were a member of the chapel at that time.

Jean de Fresne

RS 1411, fol. 141v: supplication dated 9 May, 1513 (reign of Leo X). Fresne, described as a cleric of the diocese of Cambrai and as a singer in the queen's chapel,[63] asks for a dispensation allowing him to hold two incompatible benefices.

Noel Galoys

Galoys was one of the singers of the chapel of François I receiving benefices and favors from Leo X in 1515.[64]

RS 1436, fols. 154v–155r: supplication dated 21 December, 1513. Galoys and Robert Presel, both identified as singers in the queen's chapel,[65] have engaged in a lawsuit concerning a canonry and prebend in the church of St-Gervais de Viromanda in the diocese of Noyon. They have come to an agreement whereby Presel cedes his rights to Jean Le Myre, Galoys cedes the benefice to Le Myre, and Le Myre pays a pension of 40 livres tournois "monete currente in francia" to Galoys.

Pierre Jouault alias Brule

Brule joined the papal chapel shortly after the Queen's death.[66] Although in the present documents, he is described as

---

[62] "Dictus orator pro eoque tempore dicti literarum huiusmodi absens a curia erat prout adhuc existit, nec e Sanctitatis Vestri continuus comensalis pro presenti existit."

[63] "Johannes de Fresne, clericus Cameracensis diocesis, capellanus et cantor cappelle devote vestre francorum regine."

[64] RV 1206, fols. 474r–475v: bull dated 30 January, 1515. Galoys is granted a dispensation allowing him to hold incompatible benefices.

[65] "Robertus Pressel . . . et Natales Galoys cantores capelle illustrissime domine regine francie."

[66] He entered the papal chapel in August, 1514 (Anne died on January 9, 1514). See Rome, Archivio di Stato, Camerale I 859A, fol. 108r. See also Hermann-Walther Frey,

a cleric of Breton dioceses, in a supplication he submitted on 4 May, 1507 (in which he is not described as a singer in any royal chapel), he is called a cleric of the diocese or city of Liège.[67]

RS 1325, fol. 296v: supplication dated 17 September, 1509. Jean Corbin, prior of the priory of St-Julien de Cancelles of the Benedictine Order in the diocese of Nantes, dependent on the monastery of St-Florent de Salmuro in the diocese of Angers, has resigned the benefice, and Brule, described as a cleric of the diocese of Angers and as a singer in the queen's chapel,[68] asks to be granted the benefice. The income was said not to exceed 24 ducats.

RS 1357, fols. 11r–11v: supplication dated 15 October, 1510. Antoine Divitis, cedes a priory to Brule, described as a priest of the diocese of Rennes and singer in the queen's chapel. See Divitis above.

RS 1359, fol. 259v: supplication dated 30 October, 1510. Brule [not described as a member of any royal chapel] requests an addition to a supplication dated 15 October, 1510, stating that Cardinal Robert Challand had the right of regression to the priory [not identified further] and has ceded it.

RS 1417, fols. 131r–131v: supplication dated 29 June, 1513. The parish church of St-Eloi de Montauban in the diocese of St-Malo,[69] vacant on the death of Charles Hautbois, bishop of Tournai, had been given to Brule, described as a cleric of the diocese of Rennes and as a singer in the queen's chapel.[70] Brule asks for a new provision to the benefice. The income was not expected to exceed 24 ducats.

Balduin Lupi (?)

Although Lupi is not identified in any other documents as a singer, his placement in the list of people in the first document below (between Richafort and Charpentier) suggests strongly that he was a singer, probably in the chapel of Anne de Bretagne.

"Regesten der papstlichen Kapelle unter Papst Leo X und zu seiner Privatkapelle," *Die Musikforschung* VIII (1955), 71.

[67] See RS 1253, fols. 215r–215v: supplication dated 4 May, 1507. Brule, described as a cleric of Liège "vel alterius diocesis" or of the city of Liège, had made a permutation of benefices with Johannes Douchet, whereby Brule had resigned a canonry and prebend in the church of St. Albanus in the town of Nauburien [Namur?] in the diocese of Liège and Douchet had resigned the parish church of Carabosco and the chaplainry at the altar of St. Nicholas in the church of St. Johannes in the diocese and city of Liège. Because the income of the canonry/prebend was more than the income of the other benefices, Brule asks for a pension of 24 rhenish florins to be paid by Douchet.

[68] "Petrus Jouault alias Brule, clericus Andegavanensis diocesis cappelle Illustrissime Anne francorum regine et Britannie ducisse cantor."

[69] "Parrochialis ecclesia Sancti Eligii de Monte Aubano Macloviensis diocesis."

[70] "Petrus Jouault alias Brule clericus Redonensis diocesis capelle illustrissime francorum regine cantor ordinarius."

RS 1399, fols. 157v–158r: supplication dated 10 November, 1512. Franciscus [Hamon], Bishop-elect of Nantes has resigned many benefices to many people [see Charpentier, above], among them the parish church of Albaretz in the diocese of Nantes. Lupi, described as a cleric of Thérouanne [and not as a singer in any royal chapel], asks for the benefice. The income was not expected to exceed 80 ducats.

RS 1418, fol. 142v: supplication dated 15 July, 1513. Lupi, described as the rector of the parish church of Abaratz in the diocese of Nantes [and not described as a singer in any royal chapel],[71] has resigned the benefice. Franciscus [Hamon], Bishop-elect of Nantes asks for the benefice. The income was not expected to exceed 100 ducats.

Jean Maupin*

Maupin had previously been in the king's chapel and was a member of the chapel of the Duke of Ferrara in 1506 and 1508.[72]

RS 1347, fol. 27v: supplication dated 6 June, 1510. Maupin, described as rector of the parish church of Novonico in the diocese of Autun and a singer in the queen's chapel,[73] asks for a dispensation to allow him to hold three incompatible benefices.

RS 1379, fol. 106v: supplication dated 27 January, 1512. Maupin, described as the rector of the parish church of Durat in the diocese of Meaux [and not as a singer in any royal chapel], deacon, and in his 23rd year,[74] asks permission to be ordained a priest.

Pierre Mouton*

Pierre Mouton, the Queen's organist in 1509,[75] is closely connected with the cathedral of Notre Dame; it was as a canon of the cathedral that he died on 11 May, 1534.[76]

RS 1337, fols. 129v–130r: supplication dated 29 January, 1510. Mouton, described as a priest of the diocese of Paris and a Master of Arts [and not as a

---

[71] "Balduinus Luppi, rector parrochialis ecclesie d'Abaratz Nannetensis diocesis."

[72] See Lewis Lockwood, "Jean Mouton and Jean Michel: French Music and Musicians in Italy 1505–1520," *Journal of the American Musicological Society* XXXII (1979), 210.

[73] "Johannes Maupin, rector parrochialis ecclesie de Novonico Eduensis diocesis, capelle devote vestre Anne francorum regine illustrissime cantor capellanus."

[74] Johannes Maupin, rector parrochialis ecclesie loci de Durat Meldensis vel alterius diocesis, in diaconatu ordine et vicesimo tertio vel circa sue etatis anno constitutus."

[75] He is so designated in a chapter record of St-André in Grenoble in which he witnessed the conferral of a benefice on Jean Mouton on 22 April, 1509. See Josephine Shine "The Motets of Jean Mouton," p. 16; and Bonime, "Anne de Bretagne," chapter 5.

[76] Information supplied by Craig Wright.

singer in any royal chapel],⁷⁷ asks for a new provision to the canonry and prebend in the cathedral of Notre Dame de Paris, vacant on the death of Guillaume le Condurier. The income was not expected to exceed 24 ducats.

RS 1347, fols. 275r–275v: supplication dated 6 June, 1510. Mouton, described as a canon of the cathedral of Notre Dame, Master of Arts, and rector of the parish church of St-Denis de Bourdenfer in the diocese of Paris [and not as a singer in any royal chapel],⁷⁸ asks for a dispensation allowing him to hold three incompatible benefices.

Jean Nolin*⁷⁹

RS 1347, fol. 274r: supplication dated 6 June, 1510. Nolin, described as rector of the parish church of St-Remy de Ponchon in the diocese of Beauvais and as a singer in the queen's chapel,⁸⁰ asks for a dispensation to allow him to hold three incompatible benefices.

RS 1397, fols. 219r–219v: supplication dated 10 November, 1512. Franciscus, Bishop-elect of Nantes, has resigned the parish church of Nort in the diocese of Nantes. Nolin, described as a cleric of the diocese of Chartres [and not as a singer in any royal chapel],⁸¹ asks for the benefices. Franciscus was in the household of Cardinal Robert Challand. The income was not expected to exceed 90 ducats.

RS 1399, fols. 157r–157v: supplication dated 10 November, 1512. Another document concerning the same benefice, and others claimed by Jean Richafort, Egide Charpentier, and Balduin Lupi. See Charpentier above.

Robert Presel

See Galoys above.

Conrad Renuger

See king's chapel list above.

Jean Richafort

Although none of the documents mentioned here specifically states that Richafort was a member of any royal chapel, it

---

⁷⁷ "Petrus Mouton, presbiter Parisiensis, in artibus magister."
⁷⁸ "Petrus Mouton, canonicus ecclesie Parisiensis, ac rector parrochialis ecclesie Sancti Dionisii de Bourdenfer Parisiensis diocesis, magister in artibus."
⁷⁹ He may be the "Noly" in the 1515 list.
⁸⁰ "Johannes Nolin, rector parrochialis ecclesie Sancti Remigii de Ponchon Belvacensis diocesis, capelle devote vestre Anne francorum regine illustrissime cantor capellanus."
⁸¹ "Johannes Nolin, clericus Carnotensis."

seems almost certain that he belonged to Anne's chapel because the benefice he received was in Brittany. These are the earliest documents connecting him with the French court.[82] He was also one of the singers of the chapel of François I to receive benefices and favors from Leo X.[83]

RS 1397, fol. 219v: supplication dated 10 November, 1512. Franciscus, Bishop-elect of Nantes has resigned the parish church of Touches in the diocese of Nantes. Richafort, described as a cleric of Liège [and not as a singer in any royal chapel],[84] asks for the benefice. The income was not expected to exceed 100 ducats.

RS 1399, fols. 157r–157v: supplication dated 10 November, 1512. Another document concerning the same benefice, and others claimed by Egide Charpentier, Jean Nolin, and Balduin Lupi. See Charpentier above.

Claudin de Sermizy*

The earliest document about Sermizy places him in the Sainte-Chapelle in July, 1508. The documents presented below fill out part of a gap in his biography, and suggest that he was one of the musicians whom the queen enticed away from the Sainte-Chapelle in late 1508.[85] He is also one of the singers of the chapel of François I who received benefices and favors from Leo X.[86]

RS 1339, fols. 65v–66r: supplication dated 4 February, 1510. Sermizy, described as a cleric of "N" diocese and as a singer in the queen's chapel,[87] asks to be granted in commendam the priory of St-Jean de Bouguennes of the Augustinian Order in the diocese of Nantes, vacant on the death of Gohin, Abbot of the monastery of Ste-Marie Magdalène de Genestonio in the diocese of Nantes. The income was said not to exceed 100 ducats.

RS 1348, fol. 129r: supplication dated 8 June, 1510. Sermizy, described as a cleric of the diocese of Noyon, prior of the priory of St-Jean de Bouguennes [see above] in the diocese of Nantes, and as a singer in the queen's chapel,[88] asks for a dispensation to allow him to hold three incompatible benefices.

---

[82] See Lawrence Bernstein, *La Couronne et Fleur des Chansons à Troys*, Part 2: Commentary; Masters and Monuments of the Renaissance, vol. 3 (New York, 1984) for a summary of Richafort's biography.
[83] RV 1206, fols. 468r–469v: bull dated 30 January, 1516. Richafort is given a dispensation allowing him to hold incompatible benefices. He is also described as rector of the parish church of Touches in the diocese of Nantes (see document above).
[84] "Johannes Richafort, clericus Leodiensis."
[85] Bonime, "Anne de Bretagne," pp. 36–37.
[86] RV 1206, fols. 466v–468r: bull dated 30 January, 1516. Sermizy is given a dispensation allowing him to hold incompatible benefices.
[87] "Claudius de Sermisi, clericus N diocesis, dilecte in Christo et Sancte Romane Ecclesie filie vestre Anne Francorum regine et Britannie ducisse Christianissime cantor."
[88] "Claudius de Sermissy, clericus Noviomensis diocesis, prioratus commendatorius

Jean de Vasse

RS 1347, fol. 275v: supplication dated 6 June, 1510. De Vasse, described as a cleric of Le Mans and as a singer in the queen's chapel,[89] asks for a dispensation to allow him to hold three incompatible benefices.

RS 1347, fol. 277v: 11 June, 1510. De Vasse, described as a cleric of Le Mans [and not as a singer in any royal chapel][90] asks for a new provision to a canonry and prebend in the cathedral of Le Mans vacant on the death of Marius Guerrande. The income was said not to exceed 24 ducats.

François Le Vigoreux*

Le Vigoreux is not identified in this document as a singer in either royal chapel, but I am assuming that he was a member of Anne's chapel because the benefice involved was in the diocese of Nantes.

RS 1359, fol. 302v: supplication dated 2 January, 1511. See entry under Mouton.

The most interesting information presented here concerns the extent and quality of the chapel of Anne de Bretagne (although of course it is a question as to how separate the chapels of the king and queen really were). While it has long been known that she had a private chapel, and that Mouton was one of her singers,[91] it had not been known (as these supplications show) that the Queen employed others of the rising generation of French composers; in fact she employed almost all of them (Mouton, Divitis, Richafort, and Sermizy), or that she had such a large chapel (16 people can be identified as her chapel singers in the years 1510–14; in 1515, the king's chapel numbered 22, and this presumably represented a merger of the two royal chapels). Anne's chapel might have been formed as an expression of her special devotion to religion and love of music; more likely she maintained one more as part of her dignity as the reigning Duchess of Brittany than as Queen of France. Indeed, her personal patronage of her musicians is distinguished by the number of benefices located in her hereditary lands (similarly, the king's singers received benefices in the places like Tours, Blois, and Amboise), and that the Breton cardinal Robert Challand was

---

prioratus Sancti Johannis de Bouguenes ordinis Sancti Augustini Nannetensis diocesis, capelle devote vestre Anne francorum regine illustrissime cantor capellanus."

[89] "Johannes de Vasse, clericus Cenomanensis diocesis, capelle devote vestre Anne francorum regine illustrissime cantor capellanus."

[90] "Johannes de Vasse, clericus dicte diocesis."

[91] Bonime, "Anne de Bretagne."

involved in a number of them. Her liberality (as opposed to the king's) may also be measured by the general high worth of the benefices: Richafort, Divitis, and Sermizy, for instance all received benefices worth at least 100 ducats. That these composers were so rewarded may also point to Anne's position as a lover and patron of the new imitative style they cultivated, and may place her closer to the development of the new style than heretofore realized.

It should also be mentioned that the years in which most of the supplications were submitted to Rome (1510–12) were a time when the political relations between Julius II and Louis XII came to a decisive break, culminating in the pope's adherence to the Holy League against France and the French king's calling of a Council to depose the pope.[92] These would not seem auspicious times to request favors from Julius II, yet the documents show that French court officials were not inhibited by the state of war existing between their master and the pope, and that the pope, for his part, was perfectly willing to grant their requests. Nonetheless, the large number of supplications submitted in 1510 might have been caused by the anticipation of difficulties with Rome, French clerics trying to get all they could in the way of minor benefices and dispensations (on which the pope would not have wasted much time anyway) before the break with the papacy became irrevocable.[93] Furthermore, the death of Cardinal Georges d'Amboise, who had been Legate with wide powers, in May of 1510, may have made some feel that the legality of their situations had become tenuous.[94] In any case (luckily for us), war, schism, and an eventual Interdict did not totally cut off the Roman traffic in minor benefices and favors so necessary to the careers of singers and composers of sacred music in the sixteenth century.

---

[92] The schismatic Council of Pisa, called by Louis XII, opened on September 1, 1511. The pope joined the Holy League against France in October, 1511, but the strained relations began in 1510.

[93] Most of the supplications from members of the French court in the RS for 1510 appear together in the same fascicles of the Registers indicating that they had been acted on as a group.

[94] In fact, many supplications are dated after the cardinal's death.

APPENDIX

Other Unpublished Documents Concerning French Musicians

Pietrequin Bonnel

A composer who worked for a time in Florence, Pietrequin was a member of Anne's chapel in the late 1490s.[95] The document cited below shows that Bonnel was still alive in 1518.

RS 1604, fol. 16v: supplication dated 11 April, 1518. Pierre Bonnel, described as priest of the parish church of St-Martin de Ortego in the diocese of Paris [and not as a singer in any royal chapel] has resigned the benefice.[96] Pierre Fouquet, described as a priest of the diocese of Rouen "vel alterius diocesis" and Master of Arts, asks for the benefice. The income was not expected to exceed 24 ducats.

Mathieu Gascongne

To my knowledge, this is the only document yet uncovered linking Gascongne with the French royal chapel.

RS 1635, fol. 58r: supplication dated 17 December, 1518. Gascongne, described as a priest of the diocese of Meaux, as chaplain of the chaplainry of Ste-Marie-Magdalène in the cathedral of Tours, and as a singer in the king's chapel,[97] asks for a dispensation allowing him to hold three incompatible benefices.

Pierre Moulu (?)

The following documents concern a "Petrus Moulu" who is not further identified as a singer or musician. However, the general date and the name allow for the possibility that these are the only documents yet found about the composer.[98]

---

[95] See Joshua Rifkin, "Pietrequin Bonnel and Ms. 1794 of the Biblioteca Riccardiana," *Journal of the American Musicological Society* XXIX (1976), 284–96; and Stephen Bonime, "Anne de Bretagne," p. 8.

[96] "Petrus Bonnel presbiter," resigns "parrochialem ecclesiam Sancti Martini de Ortego Parisiensis diocesis."

[97] "Matheus Gascogne, presbiter Meldensis diocesis, capellanus perpetuus capellanie Beate Marie Magdalenes in ecclesia Turronensis necnon cantor capellanus ordinarius Christianissimi francorum regis."

[98] However, the last document, which appears to show him resident in Meaux in 1513, a period when he should have been connected with the French court, may speak against the identification.

XX

RS 1213, fol. 52r: supplication dated *30 August, 1505.* Moulu, described as a cleric of the diocese of Meaux and in his *21st year,*[99] asks for an indult to allow him to take possession of one of the major chaplainries of the cathedral of Meaux. He states that he has fulfilled the obligation that possessors of such chaplainries be educated at the cathedral *("in prefata ecclesia nutritus et divinis officiis instructus"),* and he asks permission to be able to fulfil the other condition that he be ordained a priest.

RS 1214, fols. 22r–22v: supplication dated *18 September, 1505.* Moulu, described as a cleric of the diocese of Meaux and in his *21st year*[100] asks for a new provision to the chaplainry of St-Eloi in the cathedral of Meaux. The income was not expected to exceed *24 florins.*

RS 1422, fols. 226r–227v: supplication dated *10 September, 1513.* Moulu has resigned the chaplainry at the altar of St-Eloi in the cathedral of Meaux, but asks to continue to be allowed to live in the house in the cathedral close reserved for the person who held this chaplainry.

---

[99] "Petrus Moulu, clericus Meldensis diocesis in vicesimoprimo sue etatis anno constitutus."

[100] "Petrus Moulu, clericus Meldensis diocesis in vicesimoprimo sue etatis anno constitutus."

XXI

A Canon, A Choirboy, and Homosexuality in Late Sixteenth-Century Italy: A Case Study

Research concerning the history of homosexuality has, in recent years, given rise to a number of articles and books dealing with homosexuals and the reactions to them from Classical Times to the Renaissance.[1] These studies have generally dealt with large periods of time and have been restricted to specific places, in an attempt to give an overview of the changing attitudes toward homosexuality. What is presented in this article is not such a study, but rather a discussion of a single case, one preserved in enough detail to allow a reconstruction of the actions, not only of the principals (accused and accuser), but also of the judges. Furthermore, it is not drawn from the records of secular authority (the source of most of the

The author is particularly grateful to many colleagues for suggestions and encouragement during the writing of this study.

© 1991 by The Haworth Press, Inc. All rights reserved.

2

evidence published so far), but presents the actions of an ecclesiastical court.² This is the story of a crisis that came to a head in the spring and fall of 1570 in the town of Loreto, and involved a canon of the church of Our Lady of Loreto, singers in the church choir, townsmen, the Governor of Loreto, a cardinal, as well as other authorities. As will be seen, the time and place of the crisis were essential to the method of its resolution. The time (1570) was just a few years after the Council of Trent had set the Counter Reformation in full swing, and falls within the reign of Pius V, one of the greatest of the reforming popes. And the place (Loreto) was Italy's holiest shrine, sheltering in its church the Santa Casa, believed to be the house in which Mary was born and received the Annunciation, miraculously transported to Italy and deposited in a wood ("lauretum"). Long a center of pilgrimage, Loreto was, in 1570, governed by its non-resident Cardinal Protector, Giulio Feltro della Rovere, grandnephew of Pope Julius II (one of Loreto's important benefactors) and brother of Duke Guidobaldo II of the neighboring duchy of Urbino, Protector since 1566.

Although he was not an important political figure, Cardinal Giulio took his duties as Protector of Loreto very seriously, and his correspondence (now in Florence, Archivio di Stato. Archivio di Urbino, Cl.I.Div.E) is filled with reports sent to him by his resident governors detailing all aspects of life in the town, concentrating, of course, on ecclesiastical matters, and on subjects of special interest to him, one of which happened to be music.³ Indeed, the cardinal seemed to be particularly concerned about the state of music in the places under his control, and one of his first actions as new Protector of Loreto was to strengthen the choir of the church (he personally approved the hiring of all the new singers, and even sent prospective singers to Loreto from Rome). Thus it was, that on April 21, 1569, Cardinal Giulio was informed of the wish of the *maestro di cappella* (Jean Pionnier) to take into the chapel choir an orphaned son of Luca dalla Balla, recently deceased, who sang very well and could take the place of a [boy] soprano the *maestro* was going to dismiss. This boy was Luigi dalla Balla, a major actor in the crisis of 1570; the cardinal approved the *maestro*'s suggestion, and dalla Balla appears in the chapel list of 1569 as a soprano.⁴ His actual age at this time is not exactly known; in some of the documents of the case that follows he is described as being an "adolescent," that is, older than 14 and younger than 25. Given that his voice had not changed (and that this change may have come to people later in the 16th century than today), I would guess that he was about 15 or 16. In any case, he is generally referred to as a "putto."

In the same year, Cardinal Giulio must also have approved the appointment of Luigi Fontino from the neighboring town of Corinaldo to one of the vacant Lauretan canonries (Fontino later testified that he had taken possession of the benefice in June and had begun residence in July, 1569). In the fall of that year, the cardinal was also informed of problems that had arisen concerning one of the boy sopranos in the choir (who through other evidence can be seen to have been Luigi dalla Balla), problems that contained a premonition of what was to come. On November 10, 1569, the cardinal's appointed Governor of Loreto, Roberto Sassatello, wrote that he had learned that the choirboy who had been sent to live with a monk (a certain Frate Simone) had become ill, apparently with a venereal disease (the boy was found to be "marcato et consumato alle parti di sotto"). The boy declared that this had been the result of ill treatment he received outside of Loreto, but Sassatello frankly did not believe him. The obvious suspect was Frate Simone, and the crime sodomy, but Sassatello, displaying a trait we shall see much of later on, decided to do nothing; first because such things were difficult to prove, second to avoid scandal. He merely sent the monk back to his monastery and removed the boy into the house of the *maestro di cappella*. Several months later, however, an incident occurred that Sassatello could not ignore, and the crisis began.

On March 29, 1570, Sassatello wrote a disturbing letter to Cardinal Giulio. A terrible thing had happened, a thing of such "enormous ugliness" that he had not had the heart to tell the cardinal about it until Easter week was over. It seems that some gentlemen from Venice had come and stayed in a certain inn in Loreto, bringing with them a musician and composer called Il Primavera, who must be Giovanni Leonardo Primavera, a well-known composer of madrigals and *villanelle alla napolitana*, graced with at least a column of biography in *The New Grove Dictionary of Music and Musicians* (to which a few sentences can now be added). To make a long story short, Luigi dalla Balla had gone with other singers to

4

visit with Primavera, and then had slept in the same bed as Primavera "and also did worse." Informed by the innkeeper of the incident, Sassatello had interrogated the boy, who not only admitted to having committed a homosexual act with Primavera, but went on to incriminate other members of the community, in particular an artisan of the town and another singer. Then, things became more serious, for Sassatello was told that dalla Balla was constantly in the rooms of the canon Luigi Fontino, and although the boy denied heatedly that anything unseemly had occurred, stating that he was only in the canon's rooms because he often slept in the same bed as Fontino's servant, and that he had slept once in Fontino's bed, but only because he had a fever and needed warmth, Sassatello's suspicions were aroused. Nonetheless, his advice to the cardinal was basically to cover up the incident by removing it from Loreto. (He says that he would send the boy by night and secretly to one of the other of the cardinal's dominions where he could be interrogated; the other perpetrators could then also be sent out of Loreto secretly, tried, and "burned" in another place, thereby saving Loreto from all hint of scandal.) For it was imperative in his view that nothing be allowed to stain the reputation of "this holy place." The cardinal, however, did not agree to this plan, and ordered Sassatello to rearrest the boy and to find out the whole story; and from the transcript of the interrogation of dalla Balla, which took place on April 20, 1570, it becomes clear that the major object of concern was the possible involvement of the canon, Luigi Fontino, in homosexual acts, and the growing conviction in the minds of Sassatello and the judges that there was too much smoke evident in his case for there not to be some fire.

At first, dalla Balla tried to assert that he had lied when he had claimed to have had relations with Primavera. He declared that he had discussed this with his confessor, and the confessor had told him to exculpate the composer, and that he would not be able to take communion until he had done so. But the interrogators would have none of this, and broke down the story easily. Dalla Balla was asked if he had received absolution from the confessor, and he said that he had. Then, how could his confessor forbid him to take communion considering that he had just absolved him of his sins? At that point, dalla Balla asked: "What do you want me to say?" and abandoned his story. Then, the questioners wormed out of him the details of his night with Primavera. He had gone to the inn along with other singers, because Primavera had come from Venice (as had dalla Balla's father), and he had wanted to get some information about his relatives there. Then, after the others had left, he and Primavera had slept in the same bed, and Primavera had sodomized him while he was asleep.

He then admitted to having slept with a townsman who had given him money, and with another singer in the chapel choir. Then, for the first time he admitted what he had denied before, and added Luigi Fontino to the list of his relationships. According to him, Fontino had tried to seduce him, saying that it would be a one-time affair; dalla Balla had first refused, but then had been won over by constant pleadings and promises of paying for music lessons. They had had sexual relations many times during the day, and once at night. The next day, dalla Balla reconfirmed what he had confessed, gave new details, and refused to change his story when challenged. Finally, his complete testimony was read to him and he approved it and signed a document of confession and accusation.

Now Sassatello's worst suspicions and fears had been confirmed: a canon, one of the people charged with guarding Italy's holiest shrine, had been explicitly accused of having committed the worst sexual crime imaginable in a religious community not once, but many times, and there was no way to avoid taking further action. Dalla Balla did not help matters any by escaping from his place of confinement (he was being kept in one of the basement rooms of the governor's palace) on April 23, motivated, as Sassatello suggested, by fear for his own life considering what he had confessed. The escape further annoyed Sassatello as it was now going to be harder to keep the matter secret. Dalla Balla was recaptured on April 27 and placed under greater security (although not in the prison). He later described how he had broken out of his rooms and had gone to a relative (Leonardo Furlano), eventually making his way to Fermo, where Sassatello's emissary had caught up with him. Furlano was also questioned, and he gave the interesting information that Fontino had tried to use him to contact dalla Balla to get him to return secretly to Loreto and to stay in Fontino's rooms, but that dalla Balla had been recaptured before the message could be relayed to

6

him. On May 8, Luigi Fontino was arrested, placed in prison, and was interrogated a week later (May 15).

Fontino was first asked what was probably a standard question: "Did he know why he was in prison?" And he gave what was probably the standard answer that he hadn't the slightest idea. When pressed a bit further, he suggested that malicious rumors were the cause of his imprisonment, but denied that he knew what the rumors were. At this point, his interrogators let the subject drop, and began asking him questions of general information: how long he had been a canon at Loreto, where his rooms were, and (significantly) whether he often had visitors, whether there were many, whether they were clerics or not. To this he responded that many people used his rooms (claiming also that he himself was almost never there), and volunteered the names of some clerics. But when asked what laymen frequented his rooms, he mentioned four singers: Lorenzo Fabriano [Fabriano, by the way, was the singer accused by dalla Balla of having had relations with him], Luigi dalla Balla, and two other choirboys. The implications of this list of people can hardly have been lost on the interrogators, and were not lost on Fontino either, for next, unbidden, he offered a lengthy statement explaining that his relationship with Luigi dalla Balla was entirely paternal, and that the boy had not been in his rooms very often.

This outburst showed immediately that Fontino was not used to interrogations, and that he was not a practiced liar; we can imagine the grim smiles on the faces of the judges as they asked the next question, which was: "Why had he talked so much about Luigi the singer, considering that he not been asked about him?" After that, Fontino could not keep up his pretense of ignorance, and eventually had to admit that he knew that he was in prison because he was suspected of having had homosexual relations with the boy. He also finally admitted that dalla Balla had come very frequently to his rooms, but insisted that the boy had come to sleep in the servant's bed because his own mattress was infested with lice. Only once had the boy slept in his (Fontino's) bed, but that was only because he had a fever, and the servant's bed was not warm enough, not having bed curtains, and in any case the boy had slept at the foot of the bed [Dalla Balla had already declared this story to be a lie]. At this point the interrogation ended, Fontino still maintaining his innocence, declaring that his interest in dalla Balla was fatherly, motivated by respect for his musical talents.

On May 16 (the next day), Fontino was interrogated for a second time. He claimed repeatedly that he was attracted to dalla Balla solely because the boy had the best voice in the choir, and that he had resolved because of this and because he enjoyed listening to music to become the boy's patron and to further his musical education. To that end he had bought a clavichord ("monocordo"), and had arranged for dalla Balla to have singing and organ lessons; he was hoping to be repaid by filial devotion, even more fitting as he and the boy had the same first name. He was then asked if the boy would corroborate his statements: he answered that he would because it was the truth, but if he did not, he (Fontino) should be believed because he was old, a gentleman, and a priest, and the boy could have been corrupted. When asked what he meant by corruption, he suggested that dalla Balla's testimony could have been suborned by torture or imprisonment. This clear accusation of having manipulated a witness angered the judges, and they ordered that dalla Balla's testimony be read to Fontino. Recovering as best he could from what must have been a great shock, Fontino declared that it was all untrue, and that he was shocked by the revelation of the boy's true evil character. At the same time, he said that the boy's musical gifts were so great that it almost made up for any defects of character. Fontino found it impossible to deny absolutely that he was strongly attracted to dalla Balla, but he blamed it all on the charms of music; and indeed it may have been true that the first thing he had noticed about the boy was his voice. Needless to say, the judges were not convinced by these protestations, and they resolved to interrogate dalla Balla one last time.

Three days later (May 19), that interrogation took place. It was now imperative that the judges be absolutely certain (or at least be able to assert) that dalla Balla had been telling the truth, and in their minds, the only way to be certain was to see if he stuck to his story under torture. First, dalla Balla repeated his accusations. He was then led to the torture chamber, shown the torture apparatus (called "la corda" because it worked by attaching ropes to arms bound behind the back and raising the body by the arms) and finally at-

8

tached to it and tortured. At each step, he continued to assert that he had told the truth. Dalla Balla was then released and asked once again if he confirmed his statement, which (not surprisingly) he did. There was now no more doubt in anyone's mind that he had been telling the truth and that Fontino was guilty.

But for the judges to be convinced of Fontino's guilt was not enough. The cardinal wanted to proceed to the ultimate punishment of the law for the offense of sodomy. That punishment was death (with burning usually involved either before or after), and this placed the authorities in a delicate position. As an ecclesiastical court could not pronounce the sentence of death, it would be necessary to degrade Fontino of his ecclesiastical dignities and turn him over to the secular arm. But apparently a confession from Fontino was needed before this could happen. By June 15 (a month after dalla Balla's final interrogation), Fontino was still maintaining his innocence, and Sassatello wrote to the cardinal in a discouraged mood. The only way he could see of getting a confession was through torture, but the torture apparatus was broken ("essendo rotto non se gli può dar corda"), the doctors would not permit the torture of fire because of Fontino's age, and Sassatello was afraid that the lighter tortures "would not serve the cause of justice" (". . . et gli altri tormenti come leggieri mi fanno dubbio che la giustizia non venghi delusa"). So, ever looking for a way out, Sassatello suggested that they declare Fontino guilty without waiting for a confession, renounce the hope of an execution, and instead consign him to prison for whatever length of time the cardinal deemed fit. But the cardinal was inflexible, and he must have ordered Sassatello to get the confession even if that meant fixing the torture machine. Sassatello obeyed and did three things: he arranged for a direct confrontation between Fontino and dalla Balla, he threatened Fontino with torture, and he suggested that if Fontino confessed, he might be treated with leniency. These tactics worked, for the next document in the case is Fontino's letter of confession, dated July 11, 1570, and addressed to the cardinal. In the letter, the unfortunate canon states that when told he would be tortured, he realized that he would confess, and so was writing the letter of his own volition, in order to beg for mercy. The boy's accusations were true but slightly inaccurate: he had "done it" to him only 8 times (dalla Balla had said 20), but he had slept with him 4 times (dalla Balla had said once); in all cases, he had abstained from celebrating Mass after the incident. The letter ends with a plea for mercy. It was met with silence as the cardinal decided how to proceed.

He resolved finally to send back to Loreto Andrea Gentilioni da Macerata, who had presided over Fontino's interrogations, armed with Fontino's letter, to make sure that he had written it and that he still subscribed to its contents; this was done in the month of August. Gentilioni wrote to the cardinal that Fontino had recognized the letter as his own and did not deny its contents, but that he said that he had confessed only because Sassatello had promised him leniency. But it was Gentilioni's advice to the cardinal that no leniency be granted because of the enormity of the crime. Fontino was, however, allowed to languish in prison for two months, where, as he wrote in a pathetic letter, he was abandoned by all, including his family, and furthermore subjected to the painful inconvenience of leg irons which seriously impeded his movements. He was by this time, however, resolved to accept his fate, and it caught up with him on October 14, 1570, when he was defrocked, consigned to the secular arm, and executed by decapitation. Luigi dalla Balla was whipped and banned from the Papal States.

So ended the story of Luigi Fontino. Dalla Balla was more fortunate; not only was his life spared, but he was set free. And I can report that he put the musical training provided by Fontino to good use, for two collections of *canzonette* of 1584 and 1587 published in Venice contain pieces ascribed to "Luigi dalla Balla."[5] It is even likely that research in Venice will uncover him as a member of some church choir or other musical establishment.

The year after Fontino's tragedy, the cardinal was once again involved with a case of homosexuality, this time in the seminary of his archiepiscopal see of Ravenna. The cardinal's correspondence contains letters from three of the students in the seminary, complaining in explicit terms about homosexual advances made on them by the rector of the seminary, Pierlazzaro Guasconi (who was one of Cardinal Giulio's frequent correspondents). They claimed that he had touched them and kissed them and had made verbal advances, further claiming that if they told anyone, no one would believe them and boasting of the high esteem in which he was held

10

by the cardinal. But apparently, he miscalculated, for on November 5, 1571, the suffragan of Ravenna informed Cardinal Giulio that the rector had had part of his tongue bitten off by a boy he was attempting to kiss, and had admitted everything. This was extremely ugly and action had to be taken, but it is clear that the desire here was to be as lenient as possible. Luckily, there was a way to avoid the extreme punishment, for the suffragan reported that the rector's advances had been limited to touching and kissing and that he had not engaged in sexual intercourse with anyone. This allowed the cardinal to decree that the rector should be sent to prison (apparently for life), and special measures were taken to see that he had some degree of comfort. Similarly, in 1576 in Loreto itself, another choirboy made accusations similar to dalla Balla's against priests and a townsman. But all that happened to the priests was that they were defrocked and their goods were confiscated, while the townsman successfully appealed his case to the pope, and received a commutation of his death sentence.

Unfortunately for Luigi Fontino, he did not have a personal relationship with the cardinal, and further had admitted to many acts of sexual intercourse. Even more unfortunately, he was caught not in 1576 but in 1570, and not in Ravenna but in Loreto, for it is very likely that a combination of the stern reforming climate of 1570 led by Pius V (in 1576 Gregory XIII was pope) and the religious importance and position of Loreto convinced Cardinal Giulio that he could not be lenient even if he had wanted to be. In 1570, the Council of Trent had been over for only five years, and in 1566 and 1568 Pius V himself had promulgated bulls requiring the punishment of clerical sodomites.[6] If it ever came out that the cardinal had ignored the problem or had attempted to cover it up, he could be accused of laxity in carrying out the moral reform of the clergy required by the Council, and of avoiding his responsibilities as protector of Loreto by not investigating the evil and stamping it out in the place where it occurred. The cardinal really could not afford to risk anything, and therefore ordered Sassatello to find out the whole story. And when dalla Balla made specific accusations against Fontino, the case had to move forward.

And in fact, the whole focus of the case was on the one priest involved. There were other people accused, but I cannot find out what happened to them (except to report that the other singer, Lorenzo Fabriano, disappears from the chapel pay records from 1571 on); their interrogations (if there were any) are not preserved and their fates not recorded. But they were laymen, and this might have meant either that greater leniency could be shown them or that they were not important enough for the cardinal to have to follow their proceedings. Indeed, in a letter written to Fontino after his confession by someone calling himself his "brother" (whether spiritual or fraternal I do not know) it is specifically stated that if Fontino had not been "in the business" (del mestiere) he might have been pardoned.

But he was "in the business"; furthermore there was ample evidence of a long period of homosexual activity (this was certainly significant), probably more evidence than is preserved in the documents. Given that, the cardinal really did not have any choice except to carry the case to its ultimate bloody conclusion. And in this he was seconded by the highest authority of the Church, for at least by August, 1570, Pius V had been informed of the affair and had approved the cardinal's handling of it. Mercy could not be granted, a cover up could not be allowed, and Fontino found that his fate was sealed; he was a victim of time and place, as well as of his own passions.

NOTES

1. See for instance John Boswell, *Christianity, Social Tolerance and Homosexuality* (Chicago, 1980); Guido Ruggiero, *The Boundaries of Eros: Sex Crime and Sexuality in Renaissance Venice* (Oxford, 1985), Chapter VI; Patricia H. Labalme, "Sodomy and Venetian Justice in the Renaissance," *Tijdschrift voor Rechtsgeschiedenis/Revue d'Histoire du Droit/The Legal History Review* 52 (1984):217-53.

2. Another ecclesiastical case is reported in Judith Brown, *Immodest Acts: the Life of a Lesbian Nun in Renaissance Italy* (New York, 1986).

3. The documents on which this essay is based can be found in *filze* 62, 77, 79, 80, 81, 82, 88 of the *fondo*. I know of no studies of this cardinal, although one could certainly be written using the information in this *fondo*. His actions as a patron of music in Loreto and Ravenna have not gone unnoticed, however. See E. Alfieri, *La cappella musicale di Loreto dalle origini a Costanzo Porta (1507-1574)* (Bologna, 1970); R. Casadio, "La cappella musicale di Ravenna nel sec. XVI," *Note d'archivio* 16 (1939):140-54; Richard Sherr, "A Letter from Paolo

Animuccia: A Composer's Response to the Council of Trent," *Early Music* (1984):75-78.
 4. Alfieri, *op. cit.*
 5. *Répertoire Internationale des Sources Musicales* ser. B. vol. I, 1584/4, 1587/7.
 6. Pietro Agostino d'Avack, "L'Omosessualità nel diritto canonico," *Ulisse* 7 (1953):691. The constitution *Horrendum illud scelus* of 1568 required guilty clerics to be turned over to the secular arm for punishment.

APPENDIX I

CHRONOLOGY OF THE CASE OF LUIGI FONTINO

ca. March 17, 1570	Meeting of Giovanni Leonardo Primavera and Luigi dalla Balla; dalla Balla is arrested and interrogated.
March 29, 1570	Sassatello's first report to Cardinal Giulio della Rovere.
April 20 and 21	First official interrogation of dalla Balla after his second arrest.
April 27, 1570	Dalla Balla escapes.
April 30, 1570	Dalla Balla is recaptured.
May 8, 1570	Luigi Fontino is arrested.
May 15, 1570	Fontino is interrogated.
May 16, 1570	Interrogation of dalla Balla; second interrogation of Fontino.
May 19, 1570	Further interrogation of dalla Balla.
July 11, 1570	Fontino writes a letter of confession.
August 15, 1570	Fontino confirms that he wrote the letter.

October 14, 1570

Fontino is defrocked and executed; dalla Balla is whipped and banned from the Papal States.

APPENDIX II

FOUR LETTERS CONCERNING THE CASE

The following transcriptions and translations are offered simply as an example of the documents on which this article is based. The letters have not been transcribed with the rigor demanded by literary texts. I have expanded abbreviations (except in titles), have added punctuation and accent marks, and have regularized obvious inconsistent spelling, while keeping certain other vagaries of spelling.

1. Florence, Archivio di Stato, Archivio di Urbino, Cl.I.Div.E [hereafter, AU.E], *filza* 80, fols. 922r-923r. Roberto Sassatello to Cardinal Giulio della Rovere, 29 March, 1570.

Ill.mo et R.mo S.r P.ron Coll.mo. Accade un caso inanzi la settimana di Passione tanto enorme che per la brutezza sua non ho havuto animo di scriverne a V. S. Ill.ma se non fatto li giorni santi, et perché ha bisogno di presto rimedio, dopo che con questa mia le havrò detto il mio parere, mi fermarò senz'altro fare sino a suo aviso, del quale la supplico con ogni maggior celerità.

Il fatto è questo. Capitorono qui la settimana ch'io mi ordinai, alcuni gentilhuomini (credo genovesi) et venirano con uno loro barca armata da Venetia; allogiorono al'Hosteria di Micuccio Hoste, et con essi era un musico compositore detto il Primavera. La sera, andorono alcuni di questi nostri cantori, et seco havevano quel putto che altra volta le scrissi esser stato molto mal trattato. Dopo l'essersi trattenuti buon pezzo, partirono tutti, et restò il putto alla detta hosteria, dove dormi col prefato Primavera et anco fece peggio. La mattina al'alba, partirono i forastieri. La sera, l'hoste venne a raccontarmi questo fatto; faccio prendere il putto, et alla presenza del maestro di capella, del arciprete, archidiacono, et maestro di casa, lo feci dare da un sbirro cento staffillate, et poi lo mandai priggione di notte, mostrando a tutti che il castigo se gli dava solo per esser senza licenza del suo maestro di capella andato al'hosteria.

La sera seguente, lo feci condurre nanti a me, lo interrogai del fatto del

XXI

14

hosteria. Mi racontò cose che prometto a V. S. Ill.ma che se il detto Primavera fosse andato per terra et non per mare, gli mandavo dietro et lo facevo ritenere in qualunque luogo, acciò se gli fosse dato il castigo che merita un simil ribaldo; ma non andarà impunito. Interrogato anco detto putto se con altri era caduto in simil errore, mi confessò di due persone: un artigiano del borgo et un cantore detto il Fabriano che fa contralto; et avertendomi il maestro di casa che il detto putto stava quasi del continuo nelle stanze di M. Luigi canonico et forse anco haveva dormito seco, lo interrogai similmente sopra questo particolare, et il putto mi respose arditamente esser la verità che haveva molti giorni continuato di retirarsi a dormire col servitore di M. Luigi, et che questo lo faceva perché il detto M. Luigi si pigliava più cura di lui che non faceva il maestro di capella, in casa del quale pativa di dormire; et che lo haveva fatto medicare et curare essendosegli scoperto un crudel malfrancese che ben se gli conosce. Dello haver mai dormito con lui, mi disse una sera sola esserli accaduto che haveva la febbre, et non essendo fatto il letto del servitore, si mise in quello del padrone et ivi dormi. Lo feci stare otto giorni priggione, et sopravenendo la settimana santa, lo feci liberare, commandandoli che non riferisse ad alcuno cosa che havesse detta a me, havendo finto con tutti che egli non ha incolpato persona alcuna.

Stando dunque le sopradette cose tanto brutte, mi è parso prima che metterai mano per la gelosia di questo santo luogo avisarne V. S. Ill.ma, la quale si come son certo non vorà che simili sceleragini vadino impunite, cosi anco mi rendo sicuro vorà si vadi con molta consideratione per il scandolo universale che ne soprasta. Essendo io dunque in fatto, mi pare di volerli dire per mio parer il modo ch'io iudico ispediente a voler conoscere causa tali. Potrà eleger V. S. Ill.ma uno de' suoi luoghi, o Mondolfo, o San Lorenzo, comettendo detta causa a persona che a lei pare che possi esser atta di quei suoi giudici ordinarii, che di qui il gli mandarò il putto di notte, con modi che alcuno non lo saprà, et di mano in mano, secundo che il putto scoprirà, il comissario lo farà sapere a me ch'io farò prendere delinquenti, et gli rimetterò a lui con tanta secretezza et bel modo che son certo non se ne accorgerà persona. Et quelli che si trovaranno in colpa, se ne facci là quanto vuole la giustizia, et là si abruccino, che questo non è luogo da far fuoghi; et a questo modo si placarà Dio benedetto et non si vituperarà il ministerio nostro. Et perché quando feci metter priggione il putto si cominciò a mormorare nel luogo, mi risolsi, liberandolo senz'altre pene, et così se ne sta lui e alcuno non è mosso.

Questo è tutto quello che mi occorre dirli, et se bene mi persuado debba apportar a V. S. Ill.ma dispiacere, provandolo io grandissimo, tuta volta non mi è parso tacerlo acciò con la sua predenza ordini il remedio che si ha da usare, al quale la prego di solicitudine, non potento io più tolerare queste puzze. Dio N. S. la conservi felicissimo.

* * *

Something happened before Easter Week of such enormous ugliness that I have not had the heart to write to Your Illustrious Lordship about it until the Holy Days had passed; and because it has need of a quick solution, after I have given you my opinion with this letter, I will hold off and not take any action until I receive your instructions which I ask you to send as soon as possible.

What happened was this. The week I was ordained [mi ordinai] there came here some gentlemen (Genovese I believe) in their armed vessel from Venice. They stayed at Micuccio's Inn, and with them was a musician and composer called Il Primavera. In the evening, some of our singers visited them and they had with them the boy about whose bad treatment I wrote to you on another occasion [Luigi dalla Balla]. After having been together for quite a while, everybody left, [but] the boy stayed at the inn where he slept [in the same bed as] Primavera and also did worse. At dawn the next morning, the foreigners left; that evening, the innkeeper came and told me what had happened. I had the boy arrested, and in the presence of the maestro di cappella, of the archpriest, archdeacon, and maestro di casa, I had an officer give him a hundred blows, and then I sent him to prison for the night, giving everybody to understand that the punishment had been given only because he had gone to the inn without the permission of his maestro di cappella.

The next evening I had him brought before me. I interrogated him about the incident at the inn, and he told me such things that I promise Your Illustrious Lordship that if that Primavera had left by land and not by sea, I would have sent people after him and had him detained in some place so that he could be given the punishment that such a scoundrel merits; but he will not go unpunished. When the boy was asked if he had fallen into similar errors with others, he confessed to two people, an artisan of the town and a singer called Fabriano who sings contralto. And the maestro di casa having told me that the boy was almost continuously in the rooms of the canon Messer Luigi [Fontino] and perhaps had slept with him, I interrogated him also about this point. The boy responded heatedly that it was true that he had for many days gone to sleep with Messer Luigi's servant and that he did this because Messer Luigi cared more about him than the

16

maestro di cappella in whose house he usually slept, and that he had had him treated when it had been discovered that he had a bad case of syphilis [malfrancese] as everybody knows [che ben se gli conosce]. On the subject of having slept with him, he said that one evening only when he had a fever and the servant's bed was not made up he slept in the master's bed. I kept him in prison for eight days, and after Holy Week was over I had him set free ordering him not to tell anyone what he had told me, I having pretended with everybody that he had not accused anybody.

The aforementioned incidents being so ugly, I thought that before I do anything, in consideration of this holy place I should tell Your Illustrious Lordship about it for, although I am sure that you will not want such crimes to go unpunished, I am also positive that you will want to proceed with much caution considering the enormous scandal that they entail. Knowing the facts of the case, I would like to give my opinion as to the best way to deal with these matters. Your Illustrious Lordship could choose one of your dominions, Mondolfo or San Lorenzo, putting the matter into the hands of those of your ordinary judges that you deem best able to handle it. I will send them the boy from here by night in such a way that no one will know, and as the boy makes them known, the commissioner can tell me so I can arrest the criminals. And I will send them in such secrecy that I am sure that no one will notice. And those who are found guilty can be treated according to the law and they can be burned there for this is not a place to have burnings; and in this way we will placate God and will not poison our ministry. And because when I put the boy in prison people began to talk here, I have decided to let him go free without further punishment, and so he is here and nothing else has happened.

That is all I have to tell you, and even though I am sure that it must displease Your Illustrious Lordship, being very displeased myself, nonetheless it did not seem right not to tell you so that you could in all prudence order the remedy to be used. And I ask you to send the remedy quickly as I cannot tolerate such filth.

* * *

2. AU.E, *filza* 62, fols. 241v-242r. Copy of Luigi Fontino's letter of confession to Cardinal Giulio della Rovere, dated 11 July, 1570.

Intus vero se il peccatore per molte volte caduto ricorre alla maestà d'Iddio con pentimento de'suoi errori trova sempre aperte le braccia della misericordia, ogni creatura, et maggiormente li principi ecclesiastici, inmitando quello da cui ricognoscono quanto di bene hanno, debbano raccogliere ogn'uno che con grandissimo pentimento chiede perdono et gratia di suoi commessi errori; et tanto più debbano ciò prontamente fare quanto che il supplicante si trova havere meritato assai per longha et fedele servitù sua et de moltri altri dell'istesso parentato. Questo tale son io, quale mi vedo caduto in peccato grandissimo et enorme lo confesso tale. Et trovandomi carcerato sonno hoggi 65 giorni, et contro me trovandosi infiniti inditii, et essendo venuto ordine de Roma che si passi a rigoroso esamine, et vendendo che per la forza di tormenti harrei detto il peccato mio et chiusomi la porta della misericordia, perciò ho pensato con il mezzo di questa mia farlo noto a V. S. Ill.ma, sperando di non trovare secco l'istesso fonte della misericordia.

Le dirrò donque come è vero non già quanto dice il putto del suo esamine, ma si bene in buona parte, perché non tante volte quante dice lui l'ho conosciuto, ma solo da otto volte et non con quelle circunstantie et prieghi come racconta lui. L'havere dormito seco è stato quattro volte, che è più che dice lui. Tutto ciò è seguito non prima che dopo le feste di Natale, nel qual tempo io mi guardai dal celebrare. Per manco male, questa è la verità di tutto questo fatto.

Sta hora nelle mani di V. S. Ill.ma la vita et l'honore mio, et non sol mio, ma de tutta casa mia, et si come lei ne fu sempre padrona, così hora più che mai ne è, et sarrà sempre. Et io in particulare tutto quello che me ne verrà dell'uno et dell'altra, lo ricognoscerò per riceuto dall clemenza et infinita bontà di V. S. Ill.ma, et misericordias domini in eternum cantabo. Delle pregioni di Loreto, il xi di luglio del 70.

* * *

In truth, if the sinner who has erred many times, and appeals to God's Majesty in the true repentance of his errors, finds the arms of Mercy always open, every being and especially ecclesiastical princes, imitating Him from whom they acknowledge what good things they have, should receive everyone who with great repentance asks pardon and grace for errors he has committed, and even more, they should do this expeditiously when the supplicant is found to have merited much through his long and faithful service and that of many others of his family. I am such a person, who, finding that I have fallen into great and enormous sin, confess it for what it is. And finding myself in prison for 65 days as of today, and finding against me infinite evidence, and the order having come from Rome to pass to rigorous examination, and seeing that under torture I

18

would have confessed my sin and closed the door of mercy, for that reason I have thought through this letter to make it known to Your Illustrious Lordship, hoping not to find the same fountain of mercy dry.

I will tell you, therefore, that not all of what the boy said in his testimony was true, but much of it was, because I did not know him as many times as he said, but only eight times, and not in the circumstances and with the entreaties that he related. I slept with him four times, which is more than he said. All this took place not earlier than after the Feast of Christmas, during which time I refrained from celebrating [mass]. For what it is worth, this is the truth of the whole matter. My life and honor, not only mine but of my whole house, rest now in Your Illustrious Lordship's hands, and as you were always my patron, so you are now, and will be always. And in particular, I will recognize everything that will come to me concerning the one and the other as having been received through the clemency and infinite goodness of Your Illustrious Lordship, "et misericordias domini in eternum cantabo." From the prisons of Loreto, 11 July, '70.

* * *

3. AU.E, *filza* 62, fols, 196r-196v: Luigi Fontino to an unnamed recipient, no date [but probably after 21 August, 1570].

R.do fratello. Io potrò dire con il profeta: super dolorem vulnerum meorum addiderunt. Non basta che io sia stato in una prigione forte come questa, oscura et puzzulente in questa stagione, et io di questa stata[?] passano quatro mesi che mi l'ànno messo nelle ghambe un paro di ferri. Et domandendo io perché mi si facesse questo, mi responde il podestà che si dubbita che i miei parenti non ritenghano a levarmi di prigione. Oymi, che di novo potrò dire con il salmo: extranius factus sunt fratribus meis et peregrinus filiis matris meae. Et non si vede l'effetto che tutti mi hanno abandonato, che sono passati tanti giorni che non è stato pur un cane di loro a vedermi, che dopo che hanno visto che cusı vilmente habbia confessato forse più di quel che ho fatto, vergognandosi d'havere un parente infame et vile, non che se metessero a fare un tale insolentia con perdere il bene et restare banditi de la vita, non mi reconstituiriano[?] per uno quatrino, come M. Viviano me chiarisce nella sua lettera che voi havete vista, quale mando per acciò la potiate mostrare a Mon.re Governatore, che vedutola, credo se asecurarà di questo suspetto.

Se i ferri mi sono stati messi che io non fugha, e, come posso sugerire, se dubitano che quando verranno fare di me la crudele essequtione che già la

19

vedo, io non facci qualche pazzia, non si comezzi, di gratia, a darmi più afflitioni che potrano in quel hora che me anuntiaranno l'antifona Mette omili, se pure vorranno. Io per non essere stropiato ne i tormenti, ho confessato, e mo un paro di ferri mi stropiaranno. Sapete pur voi che io ho male alle gambe, sapete che io dormo pochissimo, sapete anco che io spassegio volontiere si per fare essercitio come anco per levarmi qualche pensiero dalla testa; et mo bisogna che io stia di continuo a sedere. Il sonno è fugito in tutto, et se sto cusì quatro dì, haverò guaste tutte le gambe, oltre che le pulci me mangiaranno vivo perché non mi posso cavar le calze. Et però, miseremini mei, miseremini mei, saltim vos amici mei, honorato fratello, non so in che possa havere più fede che in voi; non conosco che più volontiere se adoperi in mio benefitio et che conpatisca con me che voi. Et per questo, di gratia, operate con Mons.r R.mo Governatore che mi si cavino questi ferri, che la prigione è talmente forte che non ha [a] dubitare di cosa alcuna; et poi se si ha a venire contro di me a essequtione altrove, eccomi qua. Dirò bene; si posset fieri que transiret a me calix iste, che io ne rengratiarei Iddio et haveria obligo a i mezzi.

Ho lassato fare qui di scrivere questo, che questo matina, smontando del letto per pigliare il mio giopone, che era in un banchetto un poco discosto, ne inghavinai ne i ferri, et carchai alla suppina, et detti la cotozza nelle tavole del letto; et mi ho fatto male alla testa oltre che stetti un quarto d'hora che non me potti relevare, si che sentite quanti incommodi ho di questi benedetti ferri. Io desidero parlarne, anzi, ne ho più che necessità; però di gratia quando sia con bona licenza di Mon.re R.mo Governatore, venite più presto che potete. Et raccommandome a S. S. R.ma et a voi, fo fine.

Male aventurato Luigi

* * *

Most Reverend Brother. I could say with the Prophet: "Super dolorem vulnerum meorum addiderunt." It is not enough that I am in a strong prison like this one, dark and stinking in this season, and after having been in this state for four months, they have put a pair of leg irons on me. And when I asked why they did this, the Podestà responded that there was fear that my relatives might be planning to rescue me from prison. Alas, again I could say with the Psalm: "extranius factus sunt fratribus meis et peregrinus filiis matris meae." And they do not see that all have abandoned me, that many days have passed since any of them came to see me, that after having seen that I so cowardly confessed perhaps more than I actually did, being ashamed of having a notorious and vile relative, not only they would not plan to do such an insolent deed [risking] the punishment of losing their goods and being banned for life, they would not give a penny for me, as M. Viviano makes clear in his letter that you have seen, which I send you so that you can show it to Mons.gr the Governor who, having seen it, I believe will be reassured about this suspicion.

If the irons have been placed so that I do not escape, and, as I might suggest, because they are afraid that I might do something crazy when they come to carry out the cruel execution that I already see in the future, they should not commit themselves[?], for pity's sake, to give me now more afflictions than they will be able to in the hour when they announce the antiphon "Mette omili," if they will wish to. In order not to be crippled with torture, I have confessed, and now a pair of irons cripple me. You know further that my legs hurt, you know that I sleep little, you know also that I like to walk around for exercise and also to drive certain thoughts from my head, and now I must continuously remain seated. Sleep has completely gone, and if I remain like this for four days, I will have completely ruined both my legs, and further the fleas will have eaten me alive because I cannot remove my stockings. And yet, "miseremini mei, miseremini mei, saltim vos amici mei" honored brother, I do not know in whom I can have more faith than in you; I do not know anyone who might so willingly act in my behalf and would feel for me as you. And for this reason, please intervene with Monsignore the Governor so that they take off these irons, because the prison is so strong that they have nothing to fear, and then, if they come to execute me in another place, here I will be. I will gladly say "si posset fieri que transiret a me calix iste," that I would thank God and would be grateful to the messengers.

I have this left to write; that this morning, getting up from the bed to get my tunic which was on a bench not far away, I was immobilized by the irons and fell on my back, and gave the back of my head to the boards of the bed, and I hurt my head so badly that I could not get up for a quarter of an hour, so you can see what problems I have with these blessed irons. I desire to talk to you, rather, it is more than necessary that I do so, therefore please, with the license of Monsignore the Governor, come as quickly as you can. And recommending myself to His Reverend Lordship and to you, I end.

Unfortunate Luigi

* * *

4. AU.E, *filza* 81, fols. 984r-984v: Roberto Sassatello to Cardinal Giulio della Rovere, 14 October, 1570.

Vener mattina, con universal dispiacere, et particularmente mio et di Mons. Vescovo di Racanati, fu degradito l'infelice canonico M. Luigi Fontino; et ciò fu a bonissima hora nella sagretia vecchia con l'assistentia delle due dignità, li due primi canonici, il vicaro di detto mons.r vescovo, e mia, in difetto dei più vescovi che si ricercano a simile attioni come ordina il cap. III nella sessione XIII del Sacro Concilio di Trento, osservandosi compiutamente ogni ceremonia come nel pontificale. Non fu alcuno che non piangesse dirrotamente, et io per me provai dolore inestimabile.

Finita la degredatione, fu consegnato all corte secolare, facendo il vescovo la solita racommandtione, e così fu rimenato all prigione dove era. La sera, circa le 22 hore, secondo ho inteso, la corte secolare lo sentitiò a morte, quale gli fu mandata ad intimare per li padri ministro provenzale e rettore di giesuiti, e alle 4 hore lo trasportorono dalle prigioni della rocca a quelle del ponte, e nel far del giorno il sabbato mattino, hanno esseguito la sentenza, facendoli tagliare il capo. E subbito fu levato il corpo da quattro di questo della Compagnia della Misericordia, e portato nel cimiterio sotto la chiesa. Sopra il sangue rimasto al luogo della giustitia fecero gettare del fuogo e molto cenere, et nell'istess'hora fecero anco frustare il putto et lo bandirono da tutto lo stato ecclesiastico.

Questo è tutto la tragedia del povero sfortunato, seguita con quel minor scandalo che imaginar si possi. Il meschino ha mostro tanto pentimento et ha soportato questa morte con tanta patienza, che si può sperare ogni bene dal anima sua, come più amplamente intenderà il tutto per lettera del sodetto padre ministro, quale con tre altre compagni suoi con molta carità non l'abandonaro mai sin al fine di sua vita. Sopra ciò non le dirò donque altro.

* * *

Friday morning to universal regret and particularly my own and the Bishop of Recanati's, the unfortunate canon Luigi Fontino was degraded, and this happened at an early hour in the old sacristy in the presence of the two dignities, the two first canons, the vicar of the said bishop and me, in the absence of the greater number of bishops that similar actions require according to Chapter III of Session XIII of the Holy Council of Trent, scrupulously observing every ceremony as in the Pontifical. There was no one who did not openly weep, and as for me, I felt extremely sad. After

XXI

22

the degradation, he was consigned to the secular arm, the bishop making the usual recommendation, and he was returned to the prison where he had been kept. In the evening around the 22nd hour, according to what I have heard, the secular court sentenced him to death, and the Father Minister Provincial and the rector of the Jesuits were sent to inform him, and at the 4th hour he was taken from the prisons of the Rocca to the prisons of the Ponte, and at dawn on Saturday they carried out the sentence by cutting off his head. And the body was immediately taken away by four members of the Compagnia della Misericordia, and carried to the cemetery under the church. Fire and much ash were strewn over the blood remaining at the place of execution, and at the same time the boy was whipped and banned from the Papal States.

This is the end of the poor man's tragedy, which was played out with the least scandal possible. The wretch showed so much repentance and went to his death with such patience, that we can hope that all is well with his soul, as you will learn more fully through the letter of the said Father Minister, who with three other companions, with much charity stayed with him until his death. On this subject, I will say no more.

ADDENDA AND CORRIGENDA

I. Notes on Some Papal Documents in Paris

pp. 6–8: An exhaustive study of the papal chapels during the Great Schism is presently being undertaken by Giuliano Di Bacco and John Nádas. See most recently Giuliano Di Bacco and John Nádas, 'The Papal Chapels and Italian Sources of Polyphony during the Great Schism', in Richard Sherr (ed.), *Papal Music and Musicians in Late Medieval and Renaissance Rome* (Oxford, 1998), 44–92.

p. 9: societatis for societate; annata for annate; proximos for proximi

p. 11: Mutinel Sermentis must be a misreading of Michael Clementis [de Lucca]

II. A Note on the Biography of Juan del Encina

Since the publication of this article, I have discovered further documents concerning Encina's beneficial career in Rome. They imply that he left the city almost immediately after the death of his patron Cardinal Loriz in July 1506, and that he returned in 1512, entered the service of Cardinal Jaime Serra and the papal household, and began his attempts to become a priest (which came to fruition only much later).

I. An early supplication

1. RS 1170, fols. 206r–206v: supplication dated 15 October 1503
Encina, described as a cleric of the diocese of Salamanca, has been in litigation in Rome concerning the parish church of Lendreval & Villadelecho in the diocese of Salamanca, vacant on the death of Fernandus Roderici de Vena outside of Rome and claimed by Encina by virtue of an expectative granted by Pope Alexander VI. Encina asks to be given the benefice whose income was not expected to exceed 80 ducats (see IV.5 below).

II. Entries in Vatican City, Archivio Segreto Vaticano, Libri Resignationum [LR] 10 showing Encina either resigning benefices or as a witness, therefore testifying to his presence in Rome:

1. 143r: entry dated 13 November 1505

2. 140v: entry dated 15 November 1505

3. 163v: entry dated 14 March 1506

4. 174r: entry dated 23 April 1506

III. Entries in LR 10 in which Encina uses a procurator, implying that he was not in Rome.

1. 204r: entry dated 26 July 1506 [Cardinal Loriz had died on 22 July 1506.]
2. 217r: entry dated 4 December 1509

IV. Supplications and other documents after Encina returned to Rome in 1512 regarding his attempts to become a priest and his service in the papal household and in the household of Cardinal Jaime Serra.

1. RS 1389, fol. 210v: supplication dated 2 July 1512
Encina, described as archdeacon in the cathedral of Málaga, asks for a dispensation from the requirement of residence since he is now in Rome.

2. RS 1390, fol. 182r: supplication dated 8 July 1512
Encina, described as archdeacon in the cathedral of Málaga, asks for permission to be ordained a priest in Rome.

3. RS 1399, fol. 207r: supplication dated 26 September 1512
Encina, described as archdeacon in the cathedral of Málaga, asks for a dispensation for two years from the requirement of becoming a priest.

4. Rome, Archivio di Stato, Archivio del Tribunale del Vicariato, busta 335, Liber Ordinationum, no folio number: entry dated December 1512
Encina is promoted to the rank of deacon and pays the fee.

5. RS 1407, fol. 64v: supplication dated 3 April 1513
Encina, described as a cleric of the diocese of Salamanca and a member of the papal household and in the service of Cardinal Jaime Serra, has been in litigation in Rome with a number of people concerning the parish church of Lendreval & Villadelecho in the diocese of Salamanca, vacant on the death of Fernandus Roderici de Vena outside of Rome. Encina asks to be granted the benefice whose income was not expected to exceed 80 ducats (I.1. above).

6. RS 1431, fol. 46v: supplication dated 7 November 1513
Encina, described as a cleric of the diocese of Salamanca and a member of the papal household at the insistence of Cardinal Jaime Serra, asks for a new provision to the parish church in Sanctus Perlayo in the diocese of Salamanca, vacant through the resignation of Diego de Villoslada. The income was not expected to exceed 24 ducats.

7. RS 1405, fol. 143r: supplication dated 4 December 1513.
Encina, described as archdeacon of the cathedral of Málaga and as a member of the papal household and in the service of Cardinal Jaime Serra, asks for a dispensation from the requirement of residence.

8. RS 1544, fols. 253r–253v: supplication dated 25 November 1516
Encina, described as a cleric of the diocese of Salamanca, has been engaged in litigation in Rome with Alfonsus Moreno about a canonry and prebend in the united churches of St. Martinus de Alnelda and St. Maria Rotunde de lo Granno in the diocese of Calahorra. Encina asks to be granted the benefice, whose income was not expected to exceed 24 ducats. See Document 16.

This material is also summarised in Richard Sherr, 'The 'Spanish Nation' in the Papal Chapel 1492–1521', *Early Music* 20 (1992), 601–608.

ADDENDA AND CORRIGENDA

III. New Archival Data Concerning the Chapel of Clement VII

p. 472: Xaver for Xavier.

p. 472, Note 3. *sacrista* for *sacriste*. The material upside down on fol. 75 actually contains biographical information about a number of the maestri di cappella: Scaliono, Gabrielli (first the sacristan, then sacristan and maestro, 1529–1533), Bartolomeo Croto (maestro, 1535–1540), Ludovico Magnasco (maestro, 1540–1550), Girolamo Maccabei (maestro, 1550–1562 and 1564), Giovanni Amato (maestro, 1564–1566), Egidio Valenti (maestro, 1566), Tolomeo Galli (maestro, 1562–1563).

p. 473: *mundator* for *mundatori*.

p. 476: Misonne for Missionne

p. 477/ line 17: should probably read: Silvestro preerio or[dinis] pre[dicatorum].

p. 477/line 19: qu[od] for q[ui].

p. 477/line 21: morbiolus for morbiotus.

p. 477/line 25: petrus for pet[rus].

p. 477/line 6 from bottom: Comparison of the handwriting suggests that this was not written by Festa, but by Felicis a bit too high.

p. 478/line 2: vien for vieni.

p. 478/line 12: preeryo for preerys.

p. 478/line 15: morbiolus for morbiotus.

p. 478/line 18: martini for martinii in both instances.

IV. From the Diary of a 16th-Century Papal Singer

The entire diary has been published (with improved transcriptions) as Richard Sherr, ed. 'The Diary of the Papal Singer Giovanni Antonio Merlo', *Analecta Musicologica* 23 (1985), 75–128.

p. 83: The date of death is incorrect. Merlo died in the duchy of Mantua in September or October 1590. He had been sent there along with the singer Christian Ameiden to look after a benefice, the Abbey of Fellonica, that had been granted to the College of Singers in 1586 by Pope Sixtus V.

p. 89: The papal choir was reduced by thirteen singers, not ten, as a result of the cardinal's commission of 1565.

pp. 91–93. Jeffrey Dean offers another transcription, translation, and interpretation of the repertory list in his dissertation, 'The Scribes of the Sistine Chapel 1501–1527' (Ph.D. diss., University of Chicago, 1984), 207–216, where he dubs the list 'The Merlo Memorandum'. He suggests that "basso" which I had translated as "softly" actually means "low" as in low pitch, and indeed he may be correct about that. He identifies the motet *Illumina* with Mouton's *Illuminare Illuminare Jerusalem* when I had associated it with de Silva's *Illumina oculos meos*, because the Mouton motet is appropriate for Epiphany and the de Silva motet is not. He also chides me with being too cautious in suggesting that this list may not reflect the actual repertory of the papal singers in 1568, and he is probably right about that too. See also Jeffrey Dean, 'The Evolution of a Canon at the Papal Chapel: The Importance of Old Music in the Fifteenth and Sixteenth Centuries', in Richard Sherr (ed.), *Papal Music and Musicians in Medieval and Renaissance Rome* (Oxford, 1998), 138–166, at 152–154.

p. 94: My description of Giovanni Antonio's brother Alessandro Merlo as a composer arose from the mistaken conflation of Alessandro Merlo with the composer called Alessandro Romano, first perpetrated by Baini and then taken up by other scholars. It can now be shown that these were two different people. Alessandro Merlo was indeed a famous bass, however, said to have a range of three octaves. He died in Rome on 22 April 1601.

VI. Notes on the Biography and Music of Bertrandus Vaqueras (ca. 1450–1507)

p.113: When I wrote that Faugues used canon to create 'four out of two voices' and that Vaqueras used canon to create 'five out of two voices', I of course meant that Faugues used canon to create a four-voice texture out of three written voices and Vaqueras uses canon to create a five-voice texture out of four written voices.

VIII. '*Illibata dei virgo nutrix* and Josquin's Roman Style'

There have been two substantial reactions the article, both of which offer interesting observations on the work and dispute my suggested dating. Both critiques take as their basic assumption that Josquin spent a long time in Milan in the 1460s and 1470s and was intimately connected with the establishment of the 'Milanese' style reflected in the motetti missales of Compère, Weerbecke, and other members of the chapel of Galeazzo Maria Sforza (I used this argument as well, but not to establish chronology). Thomas Brothers ('Vestiges of the Isorhythmic Tradition in Mass and Motet,' *Journal of the American Musicological Society*, 44 (1991), 1–56) discusses the motet at the end of a long article. He argues that its stylistic model was Busnoys and not Regis (I had argued the same thing), specifically Busnoys's motet *In hydraulis*, and that the change of style in the second part reflects the "varietas" he sees in the mottetti missales. He rejects my idea that Josquin used these styles on purpose precisely in order to differentiate himself from his colleagues in Rome, who were following the Regis model. He concludes that the motet was written in the 1470s in Milan. Patrick Macey ('Some Thoughts on Josquin's *Illibata dei virgo nutrix* and Galeazzo Maria Sforza', in Albert Clement and Eric Jas (eds.), *From Ciconia to Sweelinck, donum natalicum Willem Elders* (Chloe Beihefte zum Daphis 21: Amsterdam, 1994), 111–124) argues that the ostinato 'la mi la' for Maria is intended to represent the middle name of Galeazzo Maria Sforza and therefore places the motet in Milan in the 1470s.

The recent discovery that Josquin was not in Milan in the 1470s and had no relationship with Galeazzo Maria Sforza or the development of the motetti missales (see Lora Matthews and Paul Merkeley, 'Iudochus de Picardia and Jossequin Lebloitte dit Desprez: The Names of the Singer(s)', *The Journal of Musicology*, 16 (1998), 200–226) renders the specific chronological arguments of these articles moot. However, as it can be shown that Josquin was in Milan at some point in the 1480s (1484, and 1489 just before moving to the papal chapel). I suppose that it still could be claimed that the style of the motet reflects a stay in Milan, and since Maria was a favorite middle name of all the Sforzas, that motet had something to do with Ludovico Maria Sforza (who succeeded Galeazzo) or Cardinal Ascanio Maria Sforza, to whose familia Josquin belonged in 1484–85. So it turns out that my original dating of the late 1480s is now much more probable. I stick to my hypothesis that the motet represents Josquin's reaction to his Roman milieu.

p. 441, Example 3b: Matrix for genitrix

p. 446: A transcription of Weerbecke's motet has been published by Jeremy Noble. See Jerremy Noble, 'Weerbecke's Motet for the Temple of Peace', in Jessie Anne Owens and Anthony M. Cummings, eds, *Music in Renaissance Cities and Courts: Studies in Honor of Lewis Lockwood* (Detroit Monographs in Musicology/Studies in Music, No 18: Warren, MI, 1996), 227–240

IX. The Medici Coat of Arms in a Motet for Leo X

Jean Lionnet has pointed to another work that reproduces the Medici arms in music; a canon by Giovanni Maria Nanino referring to Pope Leo XI (Alessandro de'Medici). See Jean Lionnet, 'Another Musical Medici Coat of Arms', *Early Music* 15 (1987), 520–21.

XI. The Singers of the Papal Chapel and Liturgical Ceremonies in the Early Sixteenth Century: Some Documentary Evidence

p. 256: As Anthony Cummings has shown, the usual place for the performance of motets during Mass was after the Offertory, so the singers did know when to sing the pieces. See Anthony M. Cummings, 'Toward an Interpretation of the Sixteenth-Century Motet,' *Journal of the American Musicological Society* 34 (1981), 43–59. In Essay VIII, Appendix, I discuss one type of motet that may have indeed been sung in place of the liturgical text its sets.

p. 260/Note 15: Marc Dykmans S.I., *L'Oeuvre de Patrizi Piccolomini ou le Cérérémonial Papal de la Première Renaissance*, 2 vols. (Studi e Testi 293: Vatican City, 1980, 1982) should be added to the list of works on the papal ceremonial in the Renaissance.

XIII. Performance Practice in the Papal Chapel during the 16th Century

p. 433: the 'illegible word' is 'occurrerentis'
p. 455, p. 457, p. 461/Notes 20, 27: Improperia for Improprerii

XIV. Competence and Incompetence in the Papal Choir in the Age of Palestrina

p. 626, Appendix 3: This document had been published previously by Jose Llorens. See Jose Maria Llorens Cistero, 'Los Maestros de la Capilla Apostolica hasta el Pontificado de Sixto V (1585–1590)', *Anuario Musical* 43 (1988), 35–65, at 54.

XVI. Guglielmo Gonazaga and the Castrati

p. 34: Alfonso II for Alfonsi II
p. 43/Note 20: Spanish castrati entered the papal chapel much earlier than 1588. Hernando Bustamante, who entered in 1558 may have been a castrato and Francisco de Soto, who entered in 1562 almost certainly was a castrato. Martino Soto was undoubtedly a relative.

XVII. The Publications of Guglielmo Gonzaga

Gonzaga's madrigals are transcribed in Jessie Ann Owens and Megumi Nagaoka (eds.), *Guglielmo Gonzaga: Madrigali a cinque voci (Venice, 1583)* (Sixteenth-Century Madrigal, vol. 14: New York, 1995); his motets are transcribed in Richard Sherr (ed.), *Guglielmo Gonzaga: Sacrae cantiones quinque vocum (Venice, 1583)* (Sixteenth Century Motet, vol. 28: New York, 1990). Gonzaga is probably also the composer of the *Villotte mantovane* published by Gardane in 1583. See Claudio Gallico, *Damon pastor gentil: Idilli cortesi e voci popolari nelle 'Villotte mantovane' (1583)* (Mantova, 1980).

p. 125: The print of the magnificats has been located by James Armstrong: *Cantici Beatiss. Mariae Virginis quod magnificat inscribitur per universo octo tonos modulati ad usum*

Ecclesiae Sanctae Barbarae, prima pars [odd verses], *secunda pars* [even verses] (Venice: Angelo Gardane, 1586). See Owens, *Guglielmo Gonzaga: Madrigali a cinque voci (Venice, 1583)*, Introduction, xi. The Santa Barbara mansucripts do not reproduce this print.

XVIII. Lorenzo de'Medici, Duke of Urbino, as a Patron of Music

p. 633: In connection with the Medici Codex, I report a payment recorded in the private accounts of Leo X, Rome, Archivio di Stato, Camerale I, 1489, fol. 85r: entry dated 8 November 1518: *La S.tà di N.o S.re de dar duc. dieci d'oro di camera dati a Jo. Maria Borsetto palafrenero di N. S. per andar a firenze a presentar un libro al ex.ia del Duca.*

His Holiness is to pay ten gold cameral ducats given to Giovanni Maria Borsetto, papal courier, to go to Florence in order to present a book to His Excellency, the Duke.

The type of book is not mentioned, but only a special kind of book would have been sent all by itself by special messenger, and the Medici Codex was certainly a special kind of book.

XIX. Vedelot in Florence, Coppini in Rome, and the Singer 'La Fiore'

p.409: Campanarii for Campanarum

XX. The Membership of the Chapels of Louis XII and Anne de Bretagne in the Years Preceding their Deaths

For more on the French Royal chapel in the late 15th and early 16th centuries, see John T. Brobeck, 'The Motet at the Court of Francis I', Ph.D. dissertation, University of Pennsylvania, 1991, and Brobeck, 'Musical Patronage in the Royal Chapel of France under Francis I (1515–1547)', *Journal of the American Musicological Society*, 48 (1995), 187–239.

p. 62/Note 3: Prie for Frie.
p. 70: Nicaise for Nicasius.
p. 72: Gilles for Egide.

INDEX OF NAMES AND WORKS

This index includes names and works from the text and notes, but excludes tables and authors of references. First names are given in vernacular when known.

Abbate, Giovanni: XIII 462 n. 42; XIV 615
Adami, Andrea: XII 113, 115
Adrian VI [Florisz Boeyens], pope: III 472
Agostini, Ludovico: XVII 119 n. 9, 120, 121, 122
Alcala, Saint Diego: XIII 462 n. 51
Alexander VI [Rodrigo Borgia], pope: XI 251, 257; II 159, 160, 161, 164; VIII 445; X 397
Allart, Michel: XX 64
Alma redemptoris [*mater*] (Festa): IV 92
Alzate, Matteo de: XI 250
Amanditis, Virgilio: XIII 462 n. 42; XIV 615
Amatis, Emilia de: IV 86
Amatis, Madonna Antonia de: IV 86
Amboise, Cardinal Georges d': XX 68, 80
Ambros, Wilhelm: XVI 46, 47
Ameiden [Ameyden], Christian: III 472 n. 5; IV 96 n. 11; XIV 615, 616, 621, 628 n. 23
Andreasi, Colonel: XVI 37, Appendix B.3
Anjou, Duke Henri d': XVI 40
Anne dAnimuccia, Giovanni: IV 98 n. 42; V 75
Animuccia, Paolo: V *passim*e Bretagne, queen of France: XX *passim*
Antignano, Agnello: XIV 616
Antonio da Cesena: XVIII 636 n.24
Antonowycz, Myroslaw: VIII 436, 440
Aquila, Antonius de: I 7
Aquila, Jacobus de: I 7
Arcadelt, Jacques: IV 91 *passim*; VIII 455
Archadio, Benedetto: XIV 620
Arezzo, Giovanbattista: XVIII 630

Argentil, Charles d': XIV 628 n. 12, 629 n. 31
Ariosto, Ludovico: XVIII 629
Aragona, Cardinal Luigi da: XVIII 629
Atlas, Allan: IX 32
Aurelio, Maestro Provinciale: XIX 406
Ave Maria (Compère): IV 92, 93
Ave regina coelorum (Vaqueras): VI 118–120
Aversa, Paulus de: I 7
Azzolino, Cardinal Dezio: IV 90

Baini, Giuseppe: XIV 629 n. 33
Baldini, Signore: XIII 455
Bandini, Giovanni: XIX 407
Barrone, Niccolo: IV 86; XIV 628 n. 12
Bartholo da Milano: XVIII 636 n.24
Bartholo Fiammingo: XVIII 636 n.24
Bartholo piffero: XVIII 629
Bartoli, Bartholomeo: V 77; XIV 615
Bartholomeus, bishop of Segovia: VI 120
Bartolomuccio, Pietro: XIII 461 n. 37; XIV 616
Basiron, Philippe: VIII 443 n. 9
Baverîa, duke of: XVI 44
Baxandall, Michael: XIII 461
Baylluy, Johannes: I 11 n. 24
Beata gens (chant): IV 91
Beck, Aaron: X 402
Beethoven, Ludwig van: X 402
Belli d'Argenta, Girolamo: XVII 122
Bellonci, Maria: XV 3
Bellucius, Cesare: XIII 457
Benedicamus domino (Mouton): IV 91, 93
Benigni, Tomasso: XIII 461 n. 4, 36
Bent, Margaret: VII 266

Bergomotis [Bergomozzo], Lorenzo de: I 11, 16
Bernoneau, Hilaire: XX 61 64
Bertolotti, Antonio: XVII 122; XVI 35
Betti[ni] [Fornarino], Stefano: XIV 615, 621
Biancho, Paolo: IV 88
Bianco, Mattia: XIV 615, 618
Binnerandi, Johannes: II Document 11
Blackburn, Bonnie J.: VIII 453 n. 17
Blasio da Cesena: III 474 n. 6
Bobadilla, Francisco de, bishop of Salamanca: II Document 17
Boccapaduli, Antonio: IV 90
Boniface IX [Pietro Tomacelli], pope: I 6
Bonitatem fecisti (Carpentras): XII 103 *passim*
Bonnel, Pietrequin: XX 81
Bonnevin [Beausseron], Jean: III 476
Bonot/Barre, Leonardo: XIV 621, 628 n. 12
Boorman, Stanley: VII 269; XII 108
Borgia, Cesare: II 160, Document 3
Borgia, Juan: II 161
Borromeo, Cardinal Carlo: IV 89; V 75; XIII 462 n. 51; XIV 611
Boutin, Arnulphe: XX 64 65
Bovio, Laura: XV 5 6
Bovio, Monsignor: XV 5 6
Bracconier, Jean alias Lourdault: XX 62, 65, 66, 72
Bramo, Alonso: II Document 6
Briçonet, Cardinal Guillaume: XI 252
Bruhier, Antoine: I 12 13
Brumel, Antoine: X 392
Brunet [Gallus] Jacques: XIII 461 n. 37; XIV 620; XVI 43 n. 20
Bruschi, Giulio: XVI 35 36
Bultheti, Genesius: XIII 462 n. 42
Burkhard, Johannes: XI 251 *passim*; VIII 461; XIV 622, 623; X 398 n. 29
Bursano, Paolo: XIII 462 n. 42
Busnois, Antoine: VIII 439 442, 452, 454; VI 113, 114
Busserat, Jacques: XVI 39
Bustamante, Ferdinando [Hernando]: IV 89
Bustamante, Francisco: IV 89
Buti, Leonardo: X 391 n. 2

Calamaro, Baldessare: IV 85
Calasanz [Calasans], Antonio: XIII 453, 456, 462 n. 42; XIV 615; XII 109
Canal, Pietro: XVI 35
Canibroa *see* Carbona
Cantello, Galvano: XV 4
Capilupi, Protonotary: XVI 42, Appendix B.5
Cappello, Annibale: XV 5
Caraffa, Cardinal Carlo: IV 89; XIV 628 n. 12
Carbona [Canibroan]: XVI 39
Cardano, Girolamo: X 399, 400
Carniglia, Monsignor: IV 87
Caroiati, Egidius: VI Appendix 5
Cataneo, Federico: XVI Appendix B.4, B.5
Caurroy, François du: XVI 39
Cavriani, Cesare: XV 4, 7
Cavriani, Monsignor: XVI Appendix B.3
Cesi, Cardinal: XV 5, 6
Challand, Cardinal Robert: XX 70, 71, 73, 75, 79
Chardini, Don Leonardo de: IV 89
Charles, Sydney: XX 62
Charpentier, Egide [Gilles]: XX 66, 72, 74, 77
Christino, Barnabas: VI 112
Church, Michael: X 400
Cicchus: I 7
Clangat plebs flores (Regis): VIII 435, n. 3, 443, n. 9, 444
Clement VII [Giulio de' Medici], pope: III 472; XI 250; XIV 609, 627 n. 9; X 398, 399, 402; XIX 402, 404, 405; XVIII 628, 630, 631
Clerici, Bernardus: XX 71
Clinca, Nicolo: IV 89, XIV 628 n. 12
Clurtin, Henricus: XX 66
Confitebimur (Mouton) IV 91, 93
Confitemini Domino (Mouton): IV 93
Como, Giovanni: XVIII 628
Compère, Loyset: IV 91 *passim*; VIII 443 n. 9, 451 n. 14
Conforti [Conforto], Giovanni Luca: XIII 461 n. 4; XIV 620; XVI 42, 44

Conseil, Jean du: III 476
Contino, Giovanni: X 403 n. 53
Coppini, Alessandro: XIX 404, 406
Corbin, Jean: XX 75
Corona aurea (Arcadelt): IV 91, 93
Cortesi [Cortese], Paolo: XI 255;
    X 391
Cossee, Innocent: I 16
Cousin, Guillaumes: XX 66
Crawford, David: I 12
Credo de tous biens plainne
    (Josquin): XII 107–109
Credo in falsobordone: XII 107
Credo, performance of in the the
    papal chapel: XII 113 *passim*
Crescenzi, Leonardo: XIII 462 n. 38
Crescenzi, Orazio: XIII 461 n. 37
Crétin, Jean: XX 62
Croll, Gerhard: VIII 444, 450
Da pacem (de Orto): VIII 444
Dalla Balla, Luigi: XXI *passim*
Danckerts, Ghiselin: XIV 621; X 403
Davari, Stefano: XVI 34, 56
Dean, Jeffrey: XI 260 n. 13; VII 268
de la Baude Antonius: XX 68
de la Tour d'Auvergne, Madeleine:
    XVIII 631 632
Della Rovere, Cardinal Giulio: V 75
    passim; XXI *passim*
Della Rovere, Guidobaldo II, duke of
    Urbino: V 75: XXI 2
Della Rovere, Francesco Maria, duke
    of Urbino: XVIII 630
Della Stufa, Giovanni: XIX 407
Della Viola, Orazio: XV 4
Dentice, Fabrizio: XV Appendix 1
Divitis, Antoine: XX 70 71, 75, 79
Domenico da Cesena: XVIII 636 n.24
Domine non secundum peccata
    (Josquin): VIII 451
Domine non secundum peccata
    (Vaqueras): VIII 451
Domine non secundum peccata,
    settings of: VIII Appendix
Donatello: XIII 459
Doni, Antonfrancesco: XIX 402
Douchet, Johannes: XX 75 n. 67
Druda, Francesco: V 77; XIII 458
Dufay [Du Fay], Guillaume:
    VIII 434 n. 1, 435, 436 n. 4;
    VI 114, 115, 118
Dulcis amica dei (Weerbecke):

VIII 444 *passim*
Dunning, Alfred: VIII 444
Dupre, Malgorino: XVI 40
Dutry, Gerardus: VI Appendix 10

Ecclesiae militantes (Du Fay):
    VIII 435
Einstein, Alfred: XVII 119
Encina, Juan del: II *passim*
Episcopis, Giovanni Luigi de:
    XIV 615, 616, 628 n. 12
Este, Cardinal Ippolito II d': XVI 35,
    37, 41, 45, Appendix B.1
Este, duke Alfonso II d': XVI 34, 46
Este, Isabella d': XII 103
Eugene IV [Gabriele Condulmer],
    pope: XIV 623
Eustachio cantore: III 476
Eustachio Romano: III 476 n. 11
Extoris, Ludovicus: VI Appendix 11

Fabriano, Lorenzo: XXI 6, 11
Facchonio, Paolo: XII 117
Factum est cum baptizaretur
    (Prioris): IV 93
Fallows, David: XIV 623
Farnese, Ottavio, duke of Parma:
    XV 3, 5

Farnese, Cardinal Alessandro: IV 83
Farnese, Margherita: XVII 119 n. 10;
    XV *passim*
Fazanis, Tomasso de: I 11;
    VI Appendix 9
Felicis, Giovanni Francesco:
    III 474 n. 6
Feripy, Antoine de: XX 67
Ferrabosco, Domenico Maria:
    III 472 n. 5, XIV 621, 628 n. 12
Ferreri, Cardinal Antonio:
    VI Appendix 3
Ferruci, Ercole: XIII 462 n. 38
Festa, Costanzo: III 476; IV 93;
    I 11 14; VIII 455; X 392, 402,
    403
Févin, Antoine de: X 392
Févin, Robert de: IV 92 *passim*
Figueroa, Juan: IV 97 n. 22
Finscher, Ludwig: VIII 436
Fioran [Floranus], Matteo:
    XIII 462 n. 42
Flaminio, Antonius: VI 112

Fontino, Luigi: XXI *passim*
Fordos, Guglielmo: XVI 35
Fornari, Matteo: XIII 454, 456, 461 n. 4
Fortuna, Simone: V 75
Fouquet, Pierre: XX 81
François I, king of France: XIII 459; XX 67, 78
Fresne, Jean de: XX 74
Frey, Herman-Walther: I 10 11, 13
Frosolona, Paulus de: I 7, 8
Furlano, Leonardo: XXI 5

Gabrielli [Anconitano], Antonio, archbishop of Durazzo: III 472 n. 3; X 392 n. 6
Gagliardi, Signore: XIII 454, 455, 456
Galen: X 400, 401
Gallico, Claudio: XVII 119
Galoys, Noel: XX 74
Gamboccio, Ippolito: IV 87, 88, 97 n. 27; XIII 461 n. 37; XIV 618
Gardane [Gardano] Angelo: XVII 119, 122, 123, 124, 125
Garin, Johannes: XX 67
Gascogne, Mathieu: XX 81
Gastoldi, Giovanni Giacomo: XVI 33
Gatta, Johannes Andree de 9
Gaude felix Florentia (de Silva): IX *passim*
Gellandi, Claudius: I 11; X 393 n. 15
Gemelli, Ottaviano: XIII 462 n. 42
Genet, Elzéar [Carpentras]: IV 91; I 11; XII 103, 104, 106; X *passim*; XVIII 637 n. 36; XX 67
Gentilioni da Macerata, Andrea: XXI 9
Gheri, Goro: XIX 406 408; XVIII 629, 631
Ghisoni, Ferrante: XVI 37 40, Appendix B.3
Giacomello [Jacomelli], Giovanni Battista: XVI 42
Giamandrea da Brescya: XVIII 637 n. 34
Gian Giacomo piffero: XVIII 628
Giannicholò guardarobba: XVIII 627
Giorgi, Marino: X 391 n. 1
Girardino sonatore: XVIII 627
Giriberto sonatore: XVIII 627
Girolamo da Melia: XVIII 637 n. 34

Giusti, Martino: I 5
Giustiniani, Vincenzo: XVI 46
Glarean, Heinrich: VIII 451, 453; XII 104,105
Goffier, Adrianus: XX 64
Göllner, Marie Louise Martinez: XI 263 n. 40
Gomez, Thomas: IV 87, 97 n. 27
Gonzaga, Elizabetta, duchess of Urbino: XVIII 637 n. 40
Gonzaga, Gulgielmo, duke of Mantua: XVII *passim*; XVI *passim*
Gonzaga, Margherita: XVII 119 n.10; XVI 34
Gonzaga, Muzio: XVII 120
Gonzaga, Scipione: XVI 43 45, Appendix B.4, B.5
Gonzaga, Vincenzo: XVII 121; XV *passim*
Gran Gian sonatore: XVIII 627
Grandis, Johannes: VI Appendix 2
Grassis, Ippolito de: XII 111
Grassis, Paris de: XI *passim*; II 162; I 11; XIII 458 459; VIII 458; XII103, 107, 110, 111, 114; X 391, 396, 397, 398
Greco, Giorgio: XVIII 636 n.24
Gregory XIII [Ugo Buoncompagni], pope: XIV 621; XXI 10
Grundisalvi, Bartholomeus: II Document 9
Gruter, Johannes: VI Appendix 7
Gualfreducci, Onofrio: XIII 461 n. 37
Guasconi, Pierlazzaro: XXI 9
Guastaferro, Francesco, bishop of Sessa Aurunca: XIII 458; VI Appendix 6, 7, 8, 9, 12, 13
Guasti, C.: XVIII 627
Guerrande, Marius: XX 79
Guerrero, Francisco: XVII 118
Guillelmus [Ebreo]: VI 114
Gutteri, Bernardinus: II 161, Document 5

Haberl, Franz Xaver: III 472; I 6
Halestant, Johannes: XX 73
Hall, Thomas: VII 270 n. 6
Hamon, François, bishop elect of Nantes: XX 72, 73, 76, 77, 78
Hanguemar, Jean: I 11
Hapsburg, Archduke Karl von: XVII 120, 122

Hautbois, Charles, bishop of Tournai:
　　XX 75
Henry VIII, king of England:
　　XII 104 n. 4
Herbert, Ludovicus: XX 64
Hilaire: XX 62
Hippocrates: X 400, 401
Holy, Petrus de: VI Appendix 1
Hunet, Gabriel: XX 63
Hurault, Johannes: XX 65
Hurtault, Johannes: XX 65 n. 23

Illibata dei virgo nutrix (Josquin):
　　VIII *passim*
Illumina [oculos meos] (de Silva?):
　　IV 91, 93
Improperia (Palestrina): XIII 455
In hydraulis (Busnois): VIII 439
In illo tempore cum battizaretur:
　　IV 93
Intemerata dei mater (Ockeghem):
　　VIII 435, n. 3
Ingegnieri, Marco: XVII 123
Innocent VIII [Gian Battista Cibo],
　　pope: VIII 444; XIV 622
Inviolata integra et casta (Basiron):
　　VIII 443, n. 9
Isaac, Heinrich: IX 32; X 392;
　　XIX 403; XVIII 631

Jachopo da Firenze: XIX 406 n. 14
Jacquet [Collebault] of Mantua:
　　X 392, 402
Jean de Lyons: XX 73
Johannellus: I 7
Josquin des Prez: IV 93; XI 256;
　　I 8 9; VIII *passim*; VII
　　passim; XIV 623; XII 104 108,
　　116 n. 28; VI 113, 114, 118,
　　120; X 392, 395
Jouault, Pierre alias Brule: XX 71,
　　74, 75
Julius II [Giuliano Della Rovere],
　　pope: XI 250, 251, 252, 254;
　　II 160, 163; XIII 458; VII 268;
　　XIV 622, 628 n. 24; XII 111,
　　116; X 391, 392; XIX 403, 61;
　　XX 80; XXI 2
Julius III [Giovanni Maria Ciocchi del
　　Monte], pope: XIV 609, 611,
　　615
Justus ut palma: IX 33

La Fiore: XIX 407 408
La Zinzera: XIX 407
Lagisio [Algisius], Federigo:
　　XIII 462 n. 42
Lambert, Pierre: III 472 n. 5
Lamentations of Jeremiah
　　(Carpentras): X 396 *passim*
Latino, Giovanni Antonio: IV 86;
　　XIV 615, 628 n. 12
Le Condurier, Guillaume: XX 77
Le Conte, Bartholomé: XIV 615
Le Conte, Jean: XIII 462 n. 42
Le Myre, Jean: XX 74
Le Vigoreux, François: XX 71, 79
Lebel, Firmin: XIV 615, 621
Leo X [Giovanni de' Medici], pope:
　　III 472; XI 250, 252, 256,
　　262 n. 33, 263 n. 41; II 166 n.
　　10; I 10; IX *passim*;
　　XIII 458 459, 460; VIII 443 n.
　　9; VII 268; XII 107, 109 n. 14,
　　110, 111, 112, 116; X 391, 392,
　　395, 397, 398, 402; XIX 403;
　　XVIII 627, 628, 629, 632 633;
　　XX 61, 63, 67
Liberati, Antonio: XVI 44 n. 20
Lionnet, Jean: XIII 453, 456;
　　XIV 623; XII 117 n. 29
Litterick, Louise: VIII 435
Lockwood, Lewis: V 75
Longueval, Antoine de: XX 67
Lorens, Guido: XX 73
Loriz, Cardinal Franciscus de: II 161
　　passim, Documents 8, 9, 13, 14, 15
Louis XI, king of France: IX 32
Louis XII, king of France: XII 104;
　　X 392; XX *passim*
Lourdault: *see* Bracconier
Lowinsky, Edward E.: I 12; XVIII
　　627
Loyal, Antoine: XIII 462 n. 42
Lupi, Balduin: XX 73, 75 76, 77
Lupi, Marino: IV 83 84, 96 n. 9, 11;
　　XIII 457

Machaut, Guillaume de: VII 267
Madruzzo, Cardinal Cristoforo:
　　XVI 45
Magistris, Paolo de: XIII 457
Magnasco, Ludovico: XIV 609, 615
Manni, Antonio: XIII 462 n. 38
Marenzio, Luca: XVII 118; XVI 42

Marescal, Nicholas: XX 68
Margaret [Farnese] of Austria:
    XVI 44
Mariano, Frate: XVIII 635 n. 17
Marmad, Petrus: VI Appendix 13
Martin, Gregory: XIV 607, 616, 618
Martin-Chabot, Eugène: I 5
Martini, Agostino: XIII 461 n. 7;
    XIV 618, 621
Martini, Giovanni Baptista: XIII 457
Martini, Johannes: X 392
Martini, Lambertus: I 16
Mastaing, Remigius: VI Appendix 6,
    10, 12
Maupin, Jean: XX 76
Medici, Cardinal Giovanni de': *see*
    Leo X
Medici, Cardinal Giulio de': *see*
    Clement VII
Medici, Catherine de, queen of
    France: XVI 37, 38, 39,
    Appendix B.3; XVIII 632
Medici, Giuliano de', duke of
    Nemours: XIX 405; XVIII 627
Medici, Cardinal Ippolito de': X 395
Medici, Lorenzo de', duke of Urbino:
    XIX 403, 404: XVIII *passim*
Medici Strozzi, Clarice: XIX 407
Memmo, Dionisio: XII 104 n. 4
Memor esto verbi tui (Josquin):
    XII 104 *passim*
Merlo, Alessandro: IV 94; XIV 620
Merlo, Giovanni Antonio: IV *passim*;
    XIV 628 n. 12
Mezzoni, Signore: XIII 454
Mezzovillani, Ippolita: XV 6 7, 8
Michelangelo: XII 110, 118
Miller, Clement A.: X 399
Miserere mei deus in falsobordone:
    X 397; XI 256; XII 107
Misonne, Vincent: III 476, 476 n. 11;
    I 11
Missa Ad Fugam (Josquin): VII 269
Missa Alma redemptoris (Mouton):
    IV 92, 93
Missa Ave Maria (Robert de Févin):
    IV 93
Missa de Beata Virgine (Josquin),
    Gloria: VII *passim*
Missae de Beata Virgine in Vatican
    manuscripts: XII 110
Missa Du bon du coeur (Vaqueras):
    VI 117–118
Missa D'Ung aultre amer (Josquin):
    VIII 443
Missa Faysans regretz (Josquin):
    VII 269
Missa Gaudeamus (Josquin):
    VII 267
Missa Hercules dux Ferrariae
    (Josquin): VIII 436, 440
Missa La bataille (Guerrero):
    XVII 118
Missa La Chastagnia: IV 92, 93
Missa La sol fa re mi (Josquin):
    VIII 436
Missa L'Homme armé (Busnois):
    VIII 439 *passim*
Missa L'Homme armé (Compère):
    IV 93
Missa L'Homme armé (Pipelare):
    IV 92, 93, 94
Missa L'Homme armé (Vaqueras):
    VI 112 *passim*
*Missa L'Homme armé super voces
    musicales* (Josquin): VIII 436
Missa Le villain jaloux (Robert de Févin):
    IV 93
Missa Malheur me bat (Josquin): VII 267
Missa Papae Marcelli (Palestrina): V 77
Missa paris vocibus (Pellegrini):
    XIII 455
Missus est (Josquin, Mouton): IV 92,
    93
Monte Cupiobo, Julianus
    Christophorus de: II Document
    10
Monte Regalis, Eustachius de: III 476:
    I 12 13
Monte, Cardinal del : IV 85
Monte, Cardinal Antonio del: XIX 405
Monteaguto, Martin de: I 11
Montoya, Pedro: XIII 462 n. 38
Montul, Jean de: XX 68
Morelli, Johannes: XX 66
Morone, Cardinal: IV 87 *passim*
Moulu, Pierre: VIII 451 n. 14; XX 81 82
Mouton [de Hollewigue], Jean: IV 91
    passim; VII 267; X 392;
    XX 71, 79
Mouton, Pierre: XX 76 77
Mucantius, Franciscus: VIII 461
Musato, Vincenzo: XIII 461 n. 37
Muscuyver, Guillaume: XX 69

Nanino, Giovanni Maria: XIII 461
   n. 37
Napoleon: I 5
Navarre, queen of: XVI 39
Negri, Girolamo: XVI 36, 37,
   Appendix B.2
Nicolas V [Tommaso Parentucelli]:
   XIV 623
Nicolo cantore: III 476 n. 11
Noble, Jeremy: I 9; VIII 436
Nolin, Jean: XX 73
Nolin, Jean: XX 77
Nuñez, Blas: XIII 462 n. 42

O beata infancia (Piéton): IV 92, 93
Obrecht, Jacob: VI 118; X 392
Occon, Johannes: III 474 n. 6, 476
Ockeghem, Johannes: VIII 434 n. 1,
   435 n. 3, 450, 455; VI 112, 118
Olivo, Ippolito: XVI 55, 56
Optime pastor (Isaac): IX 35, n. 9
Orceau, Jean: VII 267, 268
Ordóñez, Pedro: XIII 462 n. 42
Ormaneto [Romanetto], Monsignor:
   IV 83 84
Orsini, Alfonsina: XIII 459; XIX 406
Ortega, Diego de: II Document 17
Ortega, Johannes: I 7, 8
Orto, Marbrianus de: I 16; VIII 444,
   445 n. 11, 447, 450, 451, 455
Osthoff, Wolfgang: VIII 436

Padre del ciel (Guglielmo Gonzaga):
   XVII 121
Padre del ciel (Agostini): XVII 121
Paleologa, Margerita: XVII 119 n. 10
Paleotti, Cardinal: XV 5
Pales, Jacomo Antonio: XVI 45
Palestrina, Giovanni Pierluigi da:
   III 472 n. 5; IV 93, 97 n. 37;
   V 77; XIII 455, 457; VIII 462;
   XIV 611, 621, 628 n. 12, 629 n.
   31, 34; X 402; XVII 118, 119
Pallavicino, Benedetto: XVII 124;
   XVI 33
Palle, palle (Isaac): IX 32
Palmartz, Gottifredo: XV 5
Pamfili, Giuseppe: IV 87
Pantasilea: IV 95
The Passion, polyphony in:
   XI, 256–257
Paul IV [Gian Pietro Caraffa], pope:
   IV 89; XIV 611, 621, 628 n. 12
Paul V [Camillo Borghese], pope:
   XII 116
Pauli [Pisano], Bernardo: I 11;
   XIII 462 n. 42
Paz, Francisco de: II Documents 3, 8
Pellegrini, Vincenzo: XIII 455
Pendaso, Federigo: XV 5, 6
Penet, Hilaire: XX 62, 63
Pera, Ascanio: XVI Appendix B.2
Perez, Juan: II 162, Documents 14, 15
Perez, Pedro: I 11
Perusinus [Bartolini], Simone:
   XIII 462 n. 42
Petrarch, Francesco: X 392 n. 11
Petrucci, Ottaviano: VIII 437 n. 5,
   444, 450; VII *passim*; XII 104,
   107; X 397
Peverara, Laura: XVI 33 n. 4
Pictis [Pitti], Niccolò de: III 473, 475;
   XIX 402 404
Pierin piffero: XVIII 636 n. 30
Piéton, Loyset: IV 92 93
Piguet, Johannes: XX 64, 65
Pintelli, Johannes: VI Appendix 5
Pionnier, Jean: XXI 2
Pipelare, Matheus: IV 92 *passim*
Piperno, Antonius: III 473 n. 6
Pirrotta, Nino: IX 35; XIX 402
Pius II [Aeneas Sylvius Piccolomini],
   pope: XIV 623
Pius III [Francesco Todeschini
   Piccolomini], pope: XI 250;
   II 160
Pius IV [Giovannangelo Medici],
   pope: XIV 611, 616
Pius V [Antonio Michele Ghislieri],
   pope: IV 88; V 75; XIV 616;
   XXI 10, 11
Porci, Guillaume: XX 69
Porta, Costanzo: V 77; XVII 118
Poyatos, Pedro: II Documents 3, 8
Precacesa [Aspra], Giovanni Battista:
   XIV 615
Presel, Robert: XX 74
Prez: *see* Josquin des Prez
Prie, Cardinale René du: XX 62 n. 3
Primavera, Giovanni Leonardo:
   XXI 34, Appendix II.1
Primis, Philippus de: VI Appendix 4,
   12
Priors, Johannes: IV 93; XX 62

Quem dicunt homines (Richafort): IV 91, 93
Qui velatus fuisti (Josquin): VIII 443
Quis numerare queat (Compère): VIII 443, n. 9

Radulphi, Johannes: XX 72, 74
Rangone, Hercole: XVIII 635 n. 17
Raphael: XIII 460; X 391; XVIII 627, 632, 633
Reate, Antonius de: I 7
Reed, G. F. : X 400
Reese, Gustave: VIII 436
Regis, Johannes: VIII 435; 443 n. 9, 444, 452
Renuger, Conrad: XX 63, 69 70
Reverdi, Georges: XX 69
Rex fallax miraculum (Vaqueras): VIII 444
Reynolds, Christopher: XIV 607
Richafort, Jean: IV 93; XX 77 78, 79
Rifkin, Joshua: VIII 436, 443, 450; XII 109, 110 n. 16; XVIII 633
Romana, Saint Francesca: XIII 462 n. 51
Romanetto: *see* Ormaneto
Roth, Adalbert: I 9 n. 14, 10 n. 16
Rubeis, François: XX 73
Ruffo, Vincenzo: V 75

Salinas, Garsias de: I 16
Salve regina (Carpentras): X 393–395
Salve regis mater (de Orto): VIII 444 *passim*
Salviati, Averardo: XIX 407
San Giorgio, Teodoro di: XVI Appendix B.3
Sancta Severina, Francesco Adriano da: IV 87, 97 n. 27
Sancti dei omnes (Mouton): VII 267
Santos, Giovanni: XIII 456
Sassatello, Roberto: XXI 3 *passim*
Savello, Cardinal: IV 86
Scaliono, Antonio, bishop of Aversa: III 472 n. 3, 475
Schuler, Manfred: XI 257
Scribano [Escribano], Juan: XI 250; II 166 n. 9
Segovia, Bartholomeus, bishop of: *see* Bartholomeus, bishop of Segovia
Seristori, Giovanni: XIX 407
Sermentis, Mutinel [Clementis, Michele]: I 11
Sermizy, Claudin de: XX 78, 79
Sermoneta, Cardinal Niccolò Caetani da: IV 83
Sessa Aurunca, Franciscus, bishop of: *see* Guastaferro, Francesco
Sforza, Cardinal Ascanio: XI 262 n.29
Sherwood, Gayle: X 399 n. 33
Silva, Andreas de: IV 93; IX *passim*; X 396 n. 20
Sinnibaldi, Franciscus: II 166 n. 8
Siraisi, Nancy G.: X 400 n. 40
Sixtus IV [Francesco Della Rovere], pope: XI 250; XIV 623; XII 111
Sixtus V [Felice Peretti], pope: IV 90, 91
Slim, H. Colin: XIX 402
Soto, Francisco: IV 90
Soto, Martino: XVI 43 n. 20
Spagnoletto [Vasquez], Jacomo eunoco: XVI 43 n. 20
Spinola, Scipione: IV 85
Stabat mater (Weerbecke): VIII 443, n. 9
Stephan, Wolfgang: VIII 435
Strozzi, Filippo: XIX 407 408
Strozzi, Matteo: XIX 407

Tadeo musico: XVIII 630
Talavera, Francisco: XIV 615
Taruskin, Richard: VIII 439, 442; VI 114
Teramo, Antonio Zacharia da: I 7
Tinctoris, Johannes: I 9 10; VIII 443 n. 9; VI 115, 118; X 393
Toro, Stefano de: XIII 462 n. 42
Torres, Cristóbal de: II Document 2
Touppe, Michel: VI Appendix 11
Troche, Francisco: II Documents 1, 3, 4, 5, 7, 8
Trombone: XVI Appendix B.5
Trottis, Paolo de: I 11; XIV 628 n. 30; VI Appendix 7
Truchsess von Waldberg, Cardinal Otto: XVI 36
Turini, Baldassare: I 13; XVIII 631 632
Turleron, Hilaire: XX 62

Ugo: XVI Appendix B.5
Urbano sonatore: XVIII 637 n. 34

INDEX

Urbino, Giovanni Paulo da: XVI

Vallone, Verius: XVI Appendix B.5
Vaqueras, Bertrand: I 16; VIII 444, 447, 450, 451, 455; VI *passim*
Vasari, Giorgio: XIX 402
Vassadel: *see* Vaqueras
Vassadelli de Vaqueratio, Johannes: VI Appendix 12
Vassadelli, Ludovicus: VI 111 n. 2
Vasse, Jean de: XX 79
Vatasso, Marco: VI 112
Veni domine (Festa): IV 92
Veni sancte spiritus: IV 91, 93
Verdelot, Philippe: XIX 404, 407; XVIII 631
Vicintini, Giuseppe: XVII 124 n. 23
Victoria, Tomas Luis de: VIII 462
Vien, Petrus de: I 11
Villadiego, Antonio: XIV 615
Villin, Nicasius [Nicaise] de: XX 70

Villoslada, Diego de: II Document 16
Virgilio cantore: XVIII 630
Vitelli, Cardinal: XIV 611
Vitelozzi, Cardinal: V 75
Vultm tuum deprecabuntur (Josquin): VIII 443

Walpot, Johannes: VI Appendix 8, 13
Weerbecke, Gaspar van: XI 250; VIII 443 n. 9, 444, 447, 450; X 392
Wert, Giaches de: XVII 118, 123; XVI 33
Wettere, Michael: I 7, 8
Willaert, Adrian: X 392, 402

Zamboni, Vincenzo: XIII 461 n. 37
Zibramonte, Aurelio: XVI 41 42; XV 4 *passim*
Ziino, Agostino: I 7
Zoilo, Annibale: XIV 618
Zoppino: XVIII 637 n. 36

INDEX OF MUSIC MANUSCRIPTS

This index lists music manuscripts mentioned in the text, it does not include the ones mentioned in tables and appendices.

Budapest, National Széchényi Library, MS Bartfa 20 (a–b): VII 268

Kassel, Murhard'sche Bibliothek der Stadt Kassel und Landesbibliothek MSS 4° Mus.24/1–4: XII 104 n. 3

Milan, Biblioteca del conservatorio 'Giuseppe Verdi', fondo Santa Barbara 8: XVII 119 n. 12, 9: XVII 125 n. 27, 30: XVII 125 n. 27

Milan, Opera del Duomo Gaffurius Codices: VIII 442, 443, 450, 453

Munich, Bayrische Staatsbibliothek, Handschriften-Inkunabelabteilung Musica MS C: VII 268

Naples, Biblioteca Nazionale 40: VI 113

Saint Gall, Stiftsbibliothek MS 463: XII 104 n. 3

Vatican City, Biblioteca Apostolica Vaticana, fondo Cappella Sistina 01865/ 76 11 10
- 14: VIII 441, 442; XII 110, 112 n. 22; VI 113; XII 110
- 15: IV 93, 98 n. 40; VIII 444
- 16: XII 106, 112 n. 22; XX 63 n. 10
- 19: IV 93
- 23: IV 93, 98 n. 39; X 267, 268, 269
- 24: IV 93
- 26: IV 93, 98 n. 39; XII 112 n. 22
- 35: IV 93, 98 n. 40; VIII 444; XII 110, 112 n. 22; XII 110
- 38: IV 93, 98 n. 39
- 41: IV 93; XII 108, 116 n. 28; XII 108
- 42: IV 93; VII 267; X 393
- 45: VII 268, 270 n. 12; XII 112 n. 22
- 46: IV 93
- 49: VII 269; VI 112
- 55: IV 93, XII 112 n. 22
- 63: VIII 444
- 76: VII 267, 270 n. 7
- 163: X 398

Vatican City, Biblioteca Apostolica Vaticana, fondo Chigi C VIII 234 ('Chigi Codex'): VIII 442